The Vampire in Contemporary Popular Literature

Prominent examples from contemporary vampire literature expose a desire to re-evaluate and re-work the long-standing, folkloristic interpretation of the vampire as the immortal undead. This book offers a critical analysis of vampires in contemporary popular literature, and demonstrates how they engage with essential cultural preoccupations, anxieties, and desires. Piatti-Farnell explores how, in reworking the formulaic elements of the vampiric tradition, authors such as J.R. Ward, Christopher Farnsworth, Stephenie Meyer, Charlaine Harris, and Lara Adrian have allowed vampires to be moulded into enigmatic figures who sustain a vivid conceptual debt to contemporary consumer and popular culture. Drawing from cultural materialism, anthropology, psychoanalysis, literary criticism, gender studies, and postmodern thought, Piatti-Farnell's study re-frames the concept of the vampire in relation to a distinctly twenty-first century brand of Gothic imagination, highlighting important aesthetic, conceptual, and cultural changes that have affected literary sub-genres in the post-2000 era.

Lorna Piatti-Farnell is Senior Lecturer in Communication Studies at Auckland University of Technology. Her research interests focus mainly on twentieth and twenty-first century popular culture, Gothic studies, cultural history, and food studies. She has published widely in these areas. Her publications to date have included a large number of academic articles and book chapters, and two monographs: *Food and Culture in Contemporary American Fiction with Routledge* (2011), and *Beef: A Global History* (2013).

Routledge Studies in Contemporary Literature

1 **Literature After 9/11**
Edited by Ann Keniston and
Jeanne Follansbee Quinn

2 **Reading Chuck Palahniuk**
American Monsters and Literary
Mayhem
Edited by Cynthia Kuhn and
Lance Rubin

3 **Beyond Cyberpunk**
New Critical Perspectives
Edited by Graham J. Murphy and
Sherryl Vint

4 **Criticism, Crisis, and**
Contemporary Narrative
Textual Horizons in an Age of
Global Risk
Edited by Paul Crosthwaite

5 **Food and Culture in**
Contemporary American Fiction
Lorna Piatti-Farnell

6 **Intertextual and**
Interdisciplinary Approaches to
Cormac McCarthy
Borders and Crossing
Edited by Nicholas Monk with a
Foreword by Rick Wallach

7 **Global Issues in Contemporary**
Hispanic Women's Writing
Shaping Gender, the Environment,
and Politics
Edited by María Cibreiro and
Francisca López

8 **Trauma and Romance**
in Contemporary British
Literature
Edited by Jean-Michel Ganteau
and Susana Onega

9 **Spatial Politics in Contemporary**
London Literature
Writing Architecture and the Body
Laura Colombino

10 **Diseases and Disorders in**
Contemporary Fiction
The Syndrome Syndrome
Edited by T.J. Lustig and
James Peacock

11 **Identity and Form in**
Contemporary Literature
Edited by Ana María
Sánchez-Arce

12 **The Vampire in Contemporary**
Popular Literature
Lorna Piatti-Farnell

The Vampire in Contemporary Popular Literature

Lorna Piatti-Farnell

Routledge
Taylor & Francis Group
NEW YORK   LONDON

First published 2014
by Routledge
711 Third Avenue, New York, NY 10017

Simultaneously published in the UK
by Routledge
2 Park Square, Milton Park, Abingdon, Oxon OX14 4RN

*Routledge is an imprint of the Taylor & Francis Group,
an informa business*

© 2014 Taylor & Francis

The right of Lorna Piatti-Farnell to be identified as author of this work
has been asserted by her in accordance with sections 77 and 78 of the
Copyright, Designs and Patents Act 1988.

Trademark Notice: Product or corporate names may be trademarks or
registered trademarks, and are used only for identification and explanation
without intent to infringe.

Library of Congress Cataloging-in-Publication Data
Piatti-Farnell, Lorna, 1980–
    The vampire in contemporary popular literature / by Lorna Piatti-
Farnell.
        pages cm. — (Routledge Studies in Contemporary Literature ; 12)
    Includes bibliographical references and index.
    1.   Vampires in literature.   I. Title.
    PN56.V3P53 2014
    809'.93375—dc23
    2013022800

ISBN13: 978-0-415-82301-2 (hbk)
ISBN13: 978-0-203-50157-3 (ebk)

Typeset in Sabon
by IBT Global.

SUSTAINABLE
FORESTRY
INITIATIVE
SFI label applies to the text stock
Certified Sourcing
www.sfiprogram.org
SFI-01234

Printed and bound in the United States of America
by IBT Global.

**For Rob,
and for my parents,
with thanks.**

Contents

Acknowledgments   ix

Introduction   1

1   The Vampire Make-Up   15

2   Vampire Bodies   54

3   The Vampire's Influence   95

4   Vampire Rituals and Customs   125

5   Vampire Spaces   165

Conclusion   193

Notes   199
Bibliography   221
Index   231

Acknowledgements

This was a difficult project to bring to a close. There was always a new and relevant book to read, and a different angle that deserved more attention. Needless to say, I did not cover everything I wanted to. But I guess that's what future projects are for. My affair with the literary vampire will continue to demand attention, no doubt.

I would not have accomplished all that I have without the help and support of those around me. I wish to thank Liz Levine, my editor at Routledge, for accepting the project for publication, and for her constant enthusiasm about the book throughout. Thanks also go to all the members of my 'Gothic network'—especially from the Gothic Association of New Zealand and Australia—who share with me the academic love for all things uncanny.

I am grateful to the School of Communication Studies at Auckland University of Technology (AUT) for giving me some time to work on the project in its early stages. Thanks go to my colleagues and students in the School, who always show an interest in my research, and ask me questions about 'the Gothic'. Special thanks go to Angelique Nairn, for introducing me to a certain popular fiction series that changed things forever.

There are hardly words to describe the support I received from my friends and family during the writing of this book. Thanks go particularly to Colette and Richard Wood, Cat and Rob Orr, Tracy Fahey, James Murdoch, Marjory and David Farnell, Catherine Spooner, Alessandra Mastrogiacomo, Kimberley McMahon-Coleman, Emily M. Gray, and the wonderful Maria Beville. Very special thanks go to Donna Lee Brien, to whom I am forever indebted for her helpful suggestions and constant encouragement.

A very heartfelt and sincere 'thank you' goes to my parents, Elena e Giorgio, who first introduced me to vampire fiction when I was eight, and never tire of 'talking vampires' with me.

And finally, my greatest gratitude goes to Rob, my darling and long-suffering husband, who spends his life patiently listening to my ramblings about fangs, blood, death, and 'six foot seven vampires'. Thank you, my love.

Introduction

Vampires are everywhere. Vampires are the latest trend. Vampires are the ultimate incarnation of the sexy, the desirable, the coveted. They are in cinemas, fronting the scenes of the most recent teenage blockbuster. They are on television, captained by hordes of sensual characters that inflame the hearts of millions as they indulge both their violent and erotic sides. They appear in the most popular animation series, and they have conquered advertising and marketing campaigns. And vampires, above all, rule supreme in the literary world. Hundreds of popular series and successful individual novels that are centred on vampires—or have at least a number of vampire characters—populate the bookshelves of shops around the Western world. And through imaginative mystification, simulation and subterfuge, these new examples of twenty-first century Gothic are no longer just about 'alienation and transformation', as Jean Baudrillard put it, but hold the key to unravelling the 'fascination' and 'transparency' of the contemporary world.[1]

The recent explosion of vampires in the media needs to be accounted for. This is an important part of the cultural framework of the twenty-first century that encourages the proliferation of pleasurable images within both the Gothic framework and the wider consumer context. Historically, vampires have found a prolific connection to sexual fantasies, so much that the creatures have become almost synonymous with forbidden desire and illicit experiences. The' sexiness of vampires', as Justin Edwards and Agnieszka Soltysik Monnet have pointed out, has existed 'throughout the history of the Gothic mode', thus furthering the humanisation of the monster into our contemporary moment.[2] The over-exposure of the vampire in contemporary media plays testament to the hyper-medicated nature of contemporary consumer culture, indulging in the fantasy of the forbidden, while, simultaneously, establishing its presence through the heteronormalised context of the everyday. In this sense, the vampire is the archetypal figure of want and yearning, the lateral representation of latent desires made manifest through the framework of consumerism that is intrinsic to the mediated contexts of popular literature, television, and film.

Taking the popularised state of the vampire as a point of departure, this book offers a critical analysis of vampires in contemporary popular literature. Drawing legions of fans to a distinctly twenty-first century brand of Gothic imagination, prominent examples from contemporary vampire literature have exposed a desire to re-evaluate and re-work the long-standing, folkloristic interpretation of the vampire as the immortal undead. As the fanged creature of myth finds popular status in different, and at times discordant, contemporary manifestations, it is necessary to unravel the inescapable shifts in imagery within vampire literature and, as a result, take into account how the genre engages with implications of a cultural nature. Joan Gordon and Michelle Hollinger have claimed that, by the late twentieth century, the vampire had already 'undergone a variety of fascinating transformations' in response to on-going changes 'in the broader cultural and political mise-en-scène'.[3] Continuing a line of enquiry within this critical framework, this study offers an analysis of the social, political, and conceptual implications of the twenty-first century vampire as an ambiguously coded figure and a literary trope. Paying particular attention to the changes—conceptual, political, and aesthetic— that these representations have undergone in the past decade, *The Vampire in Contemporary Popular Literature* explores how the metaphorical use of the 'new vampires' pluralises existing traditional understandings of the vampiric trope, and establishes an imagistic connection to culturally specific concerns such as genetics, corporeality, technology, consumerism, and urban landscapes. If it true, as Fred Botting suggests, that vampires have the ability to chart 'epochal shifts', then the post-9/11 context, with its political horror, cultural interrogations, and medical preoccupations, aids the critical uncovering of growing politics of anxiety, conflict, long-ing, and contested identities that have become fundamental to the literary vampire in the still nascent century.[4]

As the wider context of the vampire is brought into sharp focus, the question of 'why literature?' provides an important starting point. This interest in fiction generates firstly and foremost from the recognition of this medium as providing the original venue for vampiric representation, at least for what concerns the wider Western context. It is through the fictional framework of literature that the vampire reached its popularity as a Gothic creature, so much that the impact, effects, and legacy of texts such as John William Polidori's 'The Vampyre' (1819), Joseph Sheridan Le Fanu's 'Carmilla' (1872), and, of course, Bram Stoker's *Dracula* (1897), cannot be denied even in our multifaceted and multi-media contemporary context. And, even in our twenty-first century context, it is in literature that the vampire finds its most prolific creative territory. The sheer amount of vampire literature produced and circulated is astounding, accounting thousands of texts on the market, ranging in sub-genre from paranormal romance to urban fantasy, thriller and historical fictions. The vampire truly is a literary monster, even if in this case, monstrosity is now more connected to high-level sales than blood-thirsty endeavours. Furthermore, literature remains profoundly entangled with the production of other media products, such as films and television series. The majority of visual media centred of vampires in the post-2000 context has been adapted from long-standing literary series, with *The Vampire Diaries*, *True Blood* and, of course, the cinematic version of the *Twilight* saga functioning as apt examples here. This interlaced relationship plays testament to the vampire's ability, as Botting claims, to infuse the simulations of society 'with the grandeur of new myth'.[5] The impact and importance of literature in this discussion, therefore, cannot be neither underestimated nor ignored, even when other media are concerned. As the popularity of the vampire—and what that popularity signifies in the wider context—is fundamentally connected to literary fictions, literature itself provides an appropriate focus for analysis to uncover the representational parameters that have shaped, and are shaping, the role of the vampire in twenty-first century Western cultures.

The Vampire in Contemporary Popular Literature is particularly interested in exploring the relationship between literature, culture, and popular opinions and trends. In order for this to be achieved, an interdisciplinary framework is necessary. This is intrinsically connected to the subject of the study itself; in its various incarnations and conceptual contexts, the vampire refuses to be tied down to one specific aspects of life—or even death. If it is true, as Nina Auerbach contends, that vampires are 'personifications of their age' who 'are always changing', then it would be limiting and counterproductive to reduce perspectives on those changes to one methodological framework.[6] The variations of the vampire literary canon have pointed both to a heterogeneity and homogeneity of metaphor that can only be adequately considered through a metacritical awareness of the multidimensional cultural milieu in which the texts operate. In response to the vampire's multifaceted nature, my analysis synthesises perspectives from a number of critical frameworks, including cultural materialism, anthropology, postmodern thought, psychoanalysis, sociology, and evolutionary theory. Whilst bearing an awareness of possible frictions between methodologies and lines of thought, my interdisciplinary stance draws strength from the perspectives that can be found at the intersection between approaches.

In my analysis, I am interested in highlighting differences as much as I am in finding similarities. The large body of vampire fiction produced does not allow for every text to be surveyed and discussed in detail; a fully comprehensive analysis of contemporary vampire literature is virtually impossible in one volume. Choices, therefore, need to be made, and the texts I discuss in this book are taken to be evocative representations of particular incarnations of the vampire, and not the only or definitive list. In the greater scope of the vampire imagination, similarities uncover thematic patterns that are often representative of overarching cultural frameworks and the popularisation of icons, symbols, and conceptualisations. Even though they operate on a different structure, differences point to specific contextualised preoccupations within the fiction that are symptomatic of a particular moment in time, a particular setting, and a particular audience. In embracing both similarities and differences within the fiction as significant elements of representation, I pursue the cultural understanding of both vampire minorities and majorities. In this stance, I echo Aurbach's contention that, as one delves into the represented peculiarities of vampires within categories of literature, the 'differences among them' can be 'more telling than the surface similarities'.[7]

Following a thematic organisation that is attuned to the various 'aspects' of the vampire in contemporary popular literature, the core of this book is divided into five chapters. In charting the different manifestation of the vampire and vampirism, this study identifies specific social, cultural, and techno-political anxieties that are seen as proper to the vampire genre in the post-2000 era. Chapter 1, 'The Vampire Make-Up', focuses on genetic threading and its relationship to cultural identity. The analysis investigates two particular and seemingly contrasting aspects of the vampire experience: the idea of being born a vampire, on the one hand, and the concept of becoming a vampire, on the other. Through an analysis of mortality, immortality, and disease, the chapter aims to show that, in an era dominated by scientific experimentation and technological advances, categories of vampires emerge, and unveil underlying concerns about the state of humanity – in conceptual, political, and physical terms.

Chapter 2, 'Vampire Bodies', focuses on corporeality and physicality as an essential part of representing the vampire in contemporary literature. Vampires are now often depicted as physically superior, gifted with superhuman strength, fighting abilities, and heightened senses. In addition, most examples of vampires appear to be 'beautiful' and highly sexualised specimens that prove irresistible to humans and vampires alike. As the vampire physique is thrown into sharp relief, I discuss how, in its idealised working perfection, the newly defined vampire form compensates for seemingly unavoidable failures in the human world. Ultimately, the chapter aims to show that, through the varying representations of vampire physicality, the 'Gothic body' emerges as a mutated and ever-changing concept; as a result, a new definition of vampire monstrosity must be pursued, one that can encapsulate a shift in imagery, concept, and politics. Chapters 1 and 2 must be perceived as a continuation of each other and they are, in a way, indivisible in both their focus and analysis. As issues of genetics, embodiment, and corporeality are difficult to separate, the two chapters are intentionally connected and dependent upon each other. And while occasional overlapping may seem superfluous, the interlacing of preoccupations between the two areas shows the extension of a conceptual and cultural dialogue that puts the body of the vampire—and how it is 'made'—at the centre of socio-political and even ethical discourses over the re-elaboration of the human subject in contemporary literature.

Chapter 3, 'The Vampire's Influence', on the other hand, unravels how the vampire's mind is presented, paying particular attention to some seemingly fundamental characteristics of vampiric cognitive and extra-cognitive abilities—such as telepathy. Considering elements of 'influence' and 'control' that are often associated with the vampire, and reaching into the multiple aspects of the vampire's psychic abilities, the chapter also pursues the association between vampires and technology, with a focus on the digitisation of identity. My analysis uncovers metaphorical connections between digital forces and the vampire's mind in contemporary literature, offering a politicised reading of 'vampire technologies' as a twenty-first century incarnation of the uncanny.

Chapter 4, 'Vampire Rituals and Customs', uncovers the importance of ritualised activities and familiar connections in contemporary vampire literature. The concept of ritual within vampire civilisations is unravelled in relation to issues of spiritual belief and cultural affiliation. Particular emphasis is placed on rituals of death, commemoration, and mating ceremonies. Eating customs are also surveyed. My analysis draws attention to how vampire habits and traditions work in connection to an extended notion of vampire collective unconscious, a recognisable thread that binds individuals within the species, physically and psychologically. My analysis also draws attention to the problematic issue of 'blood ties' and incorporates discussion of vampire families within literary cultures. In this framework, post-9/11 preoccupations emerge as important in the construction of rituality and bonding, especially when the American context is concerned.

Finally, Chapter 5 pursues an analysis of the spaces inhabited by the vampire. These are understood not only in geographical terms—ranging in focus from city dwelling to the vampire's house and places of rest—but also in conceptual terms. Topically entitled 'Vampire Spaces', this chapter surveys the relationship between geography and culture, and discusses, on the one hand, 'conflict areas' that are mediated through the figure of the vampire, and the idea of commodified existence on the other, where possession is connected to the idealisation of self and identity, and vampires themselves function as agents of both ephemerality and materiality in the 'branded space' of popular literature.

Although the book is divided into themed sections, there are some important preoccupations, tropes, and motifs that emerge as irrevocably entangled with different aspects of the vampire experience. Blood, consumerism, death, and humanity are recurrent presences throughout my study, and arbitrate the conceptualisation of the vampire as a figure connected to social, cultural, and political structures in the post-2000 context of Anglo-American narratives. The vampire's refusal to be confined to clear-cut thematic organisation is in keeping with what is perceived, as Milly Williamson puts it, as the vampire's 'troubled ontology', a conflicted sense of self that, in the literary framework, resonates with the anxieties and aspirations of contemporary Western (post)modernity.[8]

VAMPIRE STUDIES

Studying literary vampires is not, in itself, new. Countless monographs, edited collections, and scholarly articles have focused on analysing vampires and how they are represented. In the past twenty years, important texts such as Auerbach's *Our Vampires, Ourselves* ((1995), Ken Gelder's *Reading the Vampire* (1994), and Williamson's *The Lure of the Vampire* (2005) have been instrumental in establishing the growing field of 'Vampire Studies' in the wider literary framework of the Gothic. These texts, among others, have uncovered the contextual importance of representing the vampire in fiction, and its connections to various and changing texts and situations. Scholarship has also been focused on highlighting the transformation of the vampire into a 'sympathetic creature', and how in the late twentieth century the creature made a definitive shift in personality and became entangled, as Jules Zanger puts it, with the 'depiction of emotional states and the marked experience of interior conflicts.[9] Overall, the critical literature of the vampire has been successful in unearthing how the creature—from Dracula and Carmilla to Miriam Blaylock and Lestat de Lioncourt—still occupies a privileged role as an image of emulation, glamour, and otherness.

Vampires, however, have also occupied an important position in the wider Gothic framework, and this important connection has not been ignored by academic scholarship. Even when not being presented as the main focus of interest, vampires have held a rightful place in research that has surveyed the wider spectrum of the Gothic in both literature and other examples from popular media and culture. Important studies such as David Skal's *Hollywood Gothic: The Tangled Web of Dracula from Novel to Stage to Screen* (2004), Jerrold Hogel's *Cambridge Companion to Gothic Fiction* (2002), Danel Olson and K.A Laity's *21st-Century Gothic* (2001), and, even more recently, Edwards and Monnet's *The Gothic in Contemporary Literature and Popular Culture* (2012), have been instrumental in re-evaluating the part played by the vampire in cementing the parameters of the Gothic mode in contemporary times, and the popular appeal that these 'creatures of the night' exercise in our current multi-media context.

In recent years, and undoubtedly in relation to the unavoidable impact of the *Twilight* saga as the latest vampire mainstream phenomenon, scholarship has focused on addressing the relationship between vampires, racial identities, ethics, and morality, contextual concerns that are strictly connected to a peculiarly twenty-first century re-envisioning of the vampire self. Works such as Rebecca Housel and Jeremy Wisnewski's *Twilight and Philosophy* (2009), Beth Felker Jones' *Touched by a Vampire* (2009), and Nancy Reagin's *Twilight and History* (2010) have provided a critical framework for the role of vampirism in adolescent literature. What these texts also testify to is that the vampire—once a dark creature of the night, whose instincts lay somewhere in between murder and eroticism—have been conquered by the mainstream market, and transformed into icons of change and conflict that are perfectly matched to the preoccupations of young adults and teenagers. The place of vampires in teenage fiction shapes them into creatures possessing, as Housel and Wisnewski argue, heaps of 'undead wisdom', able to make sense of matters of 'love and death', and providing the partially sanitised dangerous image of perfection that 'we all desire to love'.[10]

In focusing on contemporary popular literature, my interest falls primary on fiction aimed at adults, leaving the adolescent and young adult market for another occasion. The decision to concentrate on adult literature is inspired not only by the great quantities of fiction available, which provides a large pool of primary material, but also by a critical desire to focus on issues and problematics that, although clearly present and highly developed in teenage fiction as well, find their most fascinating incarnations in literary narratives aimed at adults. In considering how popular literary vampires engage with the cultural context, my study makes an exception by largely including Stephenie Meyer's *Twilight* saga at various points in the analysis. This inclusion is in view of the sheer impact of the literary series—and its cinematic adaptation—on the wider popular imagination, an influence that goes beyond the bound of readership and categorisation. One also needs to bear in mind, of course, the development of crossover markets, and how the wide-reaching promotion of examples from teenage fiction such as Meyer's *Twilight* and L.J. Smith's *The Vampire Diaries* has had a significant impact on the way literary works are perceived and circulated.

In these terms, this study focuses on literatures pertaining to the Anglo-American context; this choice is not only a practical one, but also bears an essential critical awareness of the role vampire literature plays in the popular imaginations of these geographical and cultural frameworks, especially when America is concerned. Maintaining an awareness of the far-reaching boundaries of the genre-mixing literary category of 'vampire literature', I am constantly reminded of Botting's persuasive contention that 'vampires are mirrors of contemporary identity', providing 'the normative image' of the twenty-first century consumer, with all the anxieties and preoccupations that image entails.[11] In pursuing this Anglo-American, adult-orientated focus on popular vampire fiction, I recognise the impact that Gothic has had on the wider popular culture scope, and its connection to issues of consumer identity and identification that are most prominently developed in the metaphorical exchanges of the broader literary market.

In approaching the contemporary literary vampire I am less interested in discussions of gender and sexuality than I am in discovering the conceptual relation the vampire holds with important contextual issues such as genetics, hybridisation, corporeality, digital technology, scientific experimentation, luxury living, and branding. Williamson has aptly pointed out that, in their literary interpretations, vampires always address issues that 'resonate' with 'today's experience of the self'.[12] Williamson's contention draws attention to the vampire's highly contextual nature, and its ability to uncover concerns and fixations that are proper to a given time and place. The twenty-first century, therefore, has its own set of preoccupations, which have generated a different focus in the fiction. This is not to say that gender and sexuality have disappeared from the literary framework, or that contemporary scholarship should not be attuned to these issuess. Indeed, gender and sexuality have always been an important part of studying vampires and their fictional portrayals, and the core of several important studies of the literary vampire, including Auerbach's and Gelder's. Texts such as these have looked at the sexualisation of vampires—including their recent connections to perversion, blood and disease, and the place they occupy within queer theory and psychoanalytical frameworks—and they have done it well. My intention, therefore, is to concentrate on different aspects of the vampire experience that, while still bearing an invaluable association to the historical literary framework, establishes a distinctive connection to cultural concerns that are proper to the twenty-first century.[13]

VAMPIRES AS 'NEO-GOTHIC'

It is a claim of a number of scholars—notably S.T. Joshi in *Twenty-first Century Gothic*—that twenty-first century vampire fiction is part of a freshly developed form of 'neo-Gothic'. This seemingly new incarnation of the mode, while still dealing with the realm of 'fear, terror, wonder, awe and the supernatural', also owes to a number of tendencies and trends which are partly historically, partly culturally developed forms. The neo-Gothic, therefore, is 'neo' in that it encompasses preoccupations that are salient to our contemporary moment, yet manages to recall those elements of the Gothic tradition which outline the 'literature of terror'.[14]

Within this range of thinking, vampires can be introduced as enigmatic figures that, while owing dramatically to centuries of artistic tradition, are also deeply connected with the cultural framework of the twenty-first century, constructing connections of a social and political nature which are almost indistinguishable from the historical context in which they are placed. Several, if not all, writers of twenty-first century vampire fiction bear a conceptual debt to the Gothic tradition, and its incarnations in contemporary times. These writers draw upon a long and established heritage of Gothic artistry, incorporating—often unconsciously—popular tropes, motifs, and iconographies. The newly formed Gothic, despite taking on different undertones and a fresh, new, contemporary outfit of subterfuge, still takes readers back to the traditionally haunting themes of fear, displacement, and disembodiment, simultaneously merged with a touch of historically significant romance. In spite of this debt, however, every era remains distinctly original in its 'manipulation of character and incident'.[15] That originality is connected not only to the concept of 'the vampire' itself, but also to how that concept is remoulded in view of wide-spread preoccupation, anxieties, and desires which are proper to any specific moment in time. Simply speaking, this would be a matter of both comparison and divergence: within their respective narrative trajectories, Count Dracula and Edward Cullen are both vampires, however very few would claim that they are 'the same'.

So the vampire—who Danel Olson humorously labels the 'uberfig-ure of the Gothic'—is putting on a fresh masquerade.[16] In spite of their alleged nature, however, both the vampire and the literature of terror are not formed in the land of the extraordinary. This particular group—in its stylistic, thematic and conceptual formations—has often been said to exist as such only when it has achieved independence 'from religion, myth and folklore'.[17] And yet, these latter forms of belief function as rich store pool of ideas on which the literature draws upon and to which it maintains a strong representational connection. The very term 'supernatural' necessar-ily implies the presence of something that is known as 'natural', common, accepted, and everyday. Or, to put it simply, 'normal'. Any literary incarna-tions of the supernatural can only be viewed as sustainable and unsegre-gated when there exists a relatively clear and graspable sense of the natural. The accepted natural, however, is inseparable from the cultural context in which it is generated, and it is therefore contextual, mutable, and liable to change by definition.

The knowledge and conception of normality—and its natural occur-rences—is perhaps the most inescapable basis on which the literature of ter-ror operates, and therefore an important feature of vampire fiction within its Gothic framework. Botting suggests that in our 'real' twenty-first cen-tury life, just as it is in the neo-Gothic fictional lives, one can identify equal amounts of opportunity and unease: 'anxiety floats freely, reflecting and thus ghosting the high-speed circulation of information and commodi-ties'.[18] This play with normality and differentiation allows the vampire to work its way into a number of literary—and more broadly cultural—forms. Working with culturally prescribed definitions, vampires unearth what we perceive and normal and natural by functioning as the opposite of that very concept. Floating in the margins of the remotely comprehensible, vampires are part of the literature of terror because they show the parameters of the 'normal' through their difference from it.

There is a tendency in contemporary scholarship to assume that vampires have completely changed, abandoning their blood-thirsty, murderous ways, and embracing love-sick performances that have very little to do with killing and fear, instead. Olson, for instance, claims that vampires have changed from the 'articulate and merciless count, one obsessed with hierarchy and battle' to a 'softheaded and mumbling boy less more a friend than a fiend'.[19] Disdain for the soppy vampire is almost palpable in Olson's claim. And in his sentiment, he is indeed not alone. Judyth McLeod echoes Joshi by claiming that, while in previous centuries vampires were either respectable undead corpses carrying pestilence, or sophisticated, almost aristocratic creatures enjoying a 'place in high society', twenty-first-century vampires have become 'teenagers with good hearts'.[20] The list of studies where vampires are thought of in these terms is long and detailed. The vampires who echo older tra-ditions—as evil, violent, blood-sucking monsters—are often marginalised, simply accepting to take their position as 'bad guys', without questioning the implications that such a dichotomy entails. This is particularly true of vampires inhabiting the bounds of the paranormal romance genre. The vampire is often just perceived as a sanitised version of the Gothic, a creature of mixed feelings and images who, while remotely recalling the evil of the old days, has now been transformed into a safe partner, one who is a source of reassurance for the fortunate lover—formerly 'the victim'. McLeod simply labels this understanding of the vampire as 'yet another generational shape change' which, as she puts it, 'has the traditional attractions of the bad boy with the reassurance of the good boy at heart'.[21] It seems that, conceptually speaking, a large number of scholars like to think of 'good guy vampires' as the preferred norm in the larger scope of the literature, allowing a few known examples of popular fiction to rule the conception of the motif with sparkly, romantic undertones.

It is the intention of this book to show that vampires have not lost their bloody, lethal appeal. Nor have they abandoned their forays into slaying and cruelty. This is regardless of whether they are portrayed as 'good' or 'bad' guys. The opposition, when it is established, simply draws attention to conflicts and preoccupations in both the fiction and the culture that generates it. Although it is undeniable that some incarnations of the contemporary vampire have settled on love-stricken creatures more interested in amorousness than blood, this is not an overarching occurrence. While the argument for seeing love-stricken vampires as a conservative re-elaboration of the sexual ideal—as suggested, among others, by McLeod—is persuasive in some contexts, this cannot be taken to be the main preoccupation of the fiction. And, as I intend to show, it certainly does not define twenty-first-century vampires at a classificatory level. I do join McLeod, however, in claiming that 'we can read the changing culture of Europe, and more recently, of America through the infinitely mutable archetype of the vampire'.[22]

THE VAMPIRE GENRE

Twenty-first century vampire literature has undoubtedly developed as a distinctly genre-bending category. The vampire has, overall, undergone what Tim Kane terms 'evolutionary changes' in genre that are visible not only in literary terms, but in the wider popular culture scope as well.[23] Refusing to be relegated to one area of popular fiction, vampires have now claimed a variety of categories. From thriller to comedy, from fantasy to paranormal romance, vampires do it all. When it comes to contemporary fiction, the colonisation of multiple genres is 'the order of the day'.[24] This blurring of categories within vampire fiction is undoubtedly connected to the conceptual understanding of the vampire. A creature that in itself incorporates so many different features—of the natural, the supernatural, the familiar, and the grotesque—is ideally suited to constant re-elaboration even in genre terms. And although the propensity for the idea of 'the vampire' to merge with disparate sub-genres often results in critical differences and difficulties with literary classification, it is also an undeniable part of the successful relationship between the creature and the text, providing some of the most intriguing frameworks that neo-Gothic has to offer.

It is not uncommon to hear of 'vampire fiction' being considered a genre in its own right. And while this approach may be generally more popular than academic, its impact cannot be ignored. Yet, to think of 'vampire fiction' as a univocal form of writing would be unadvisable. This framework does not allow for the significant differences between incarnations of vampires, which change from text to text, even when maintaining similar, base-line characteristics. Or, even if the differences are taken into consideration, it does recognise their importance in terms of thematic organisation and its place within the wider literary framework. The physically attractive, swooning, overemotional vampires of J.R. Ward's *Black Dagger Brotherhood* novels are not the same as David Wellington's monstrous, murderous, multiply fanged creatures in the *Laura Caxton Vampire* series. Differences among vampires abound. While it might be tempting to see them as simple creative variances within the literature, those differences need to be perceived as not the starting point, but the result of genre identification. The categorisation of vampires in terms of genre thus proves useful in approaching the conceptual differences surrounding the creature in the fiction, not only for its physical conception, but for the place it plays in relation to the human being.

In approaching the multiple categories of the 'vampire genre', one must be attuned to the representational tools provided by the literature that both aid and challenge definitions within the wider literary scope. John Frow has pointedly claimed that genre organises 'verbal and non-verbal discourse', and contributes to the 'social structuring of meaning'.[25] In these terms, and far from simply being a categorising term for the conventional, genre comprises of a list of symbolic interactions that 'create effects of reality and truth, plausibility and truth' within a given storytelling context.[26] This symbolically orientated approach to the genre sub-categories of the vampire's literary framework is important, if not essential, in delineating the way in which vampires themselves are portrayed, and to what aim, within their own narrative structures.

The categories of paranormal romance, urban fantasy, and thriller have proven to be very prolific literary territories for the vampire to colonise in the post-2000 context. An inexperienced eye may struggle to differentiate between the first two categories, as they do indeed share a number of characteristics. The general claim—a somewhat curious one—is that 'paranormal romance' fiction tends to be narrated in the third person, while 'urban fantasy' story usually present a first person narrator. This narrative approach to generic differentiation is disappointingly oversimplified. Indeed, both paranormal romance and urban fantasy are known to have

elements of the 'love story' included in the plot. In the same vein, both categories often deal with political intrigue, mystery and conflict in both social
and cultural terms. One might be tempted to assume that differentiating
between the two is virtually impossible. This stance, however, is not only
based on a distorted understanding of these sub-categories—and, perhaps,
the concept of genre overall—but also un-attuned to the representational
differences that paranormal romance and urban fantasy propose. As far as
vampires are concerned, genre differentiation also forms the basis for that
representation, and it is therefore an important part of metaphorical identification across the thematic board, and its place in the context of Gothic
writing. In this sense, genre identification helps us in identifying how, as
Amy Devitt suggests, text-based analysis is intrinsically connected to the
dynamic interaction of 'writers, readers, past texts, and context'.[27]

While elements are shared by sub-categories such as paranormal romance
and urban fantasy—and, indeed, the thriller—the centre on which the narrative axis pivots is what provides the most important clue to unravelling
the ways in which vampires are depicted (both physically and psychologically). If the love story is the centre of the narrative axis, and the fiction is
categorisable as 'paranormal romance', both the physicality and psychology
of the vampire will be moulded towards attractiveness so to be appealing to
a romance-attuned readership and the tradition in which the fiction places
itself. In examples from this category, one can see how both the physical
characteristics and psychology of the vampire are, Botting would put it,
'increasingly humanised', and therefore made 'alluring' to readers of this
'textual transformation of the Gothic'.[28] To see the vampire portrayed as
a strangely human 'romantic animal' is not an uncommon feature of paranormal romance. A similar approach can be taken to vampire fiction of the
urban fantasy category; while love stories appear here and there—as one
can find in apt examples such as Charlaine Harris' *Sookie Stackhouse: The
Southern Vampire Mysteries*, Ilona Andrews' *Kate Daniels* series, and Jim
Butcher's *The Dresden Files*—they are not the centre of the narrative, and
not the 'selling point' of the fiction itself. The vampires in these sub-categories, as a result, are not presented as the ultimate embodiment of eroticism
and sensuality. And while they are known to have these characteristics at
times, they are not part of their definitive characterisation. The importance
of the love story, one might venture to say, will be one of the most important aspects of delineating the vampire. This, of course, is always done
in connection to human—Western—understandings of heteronormativity
that, in terms of interpersonal and sexual relationships, guides the categorisation of 'attractive' and 'desirable' for both male and female specimens.
The wider popular culture context has a big part to play in constructing
'acceptable' visions of the vampire within each literary genre sub-category,
as the impact of actors, models and musical stars on the visualisation of
heroes and villains in the popular imagination cannot be ignored.

Genre categorisation, therefore, is an essential part of any analysis of vampires in contemporary popular literature. I am not suggesting that the vampire is a creature of convention; rather, it is important to evaluate how, in being moulding around genre-specific categories, literary vampires are able to reconfigure the ordinary by proposing 'their own complicated genealogies' and 'their own horizons of significance' within the meaning-making boundaries of the Gothic framework.[29] Although, in the popular culture context, the blending and melding of elements is not only to be expected, but also unavoidable, genre and readership construct incarnations of the vampire for what they are in different literary contexts. When it comes to recognising the differences and relevance of the vampire in its multiple manifestations, a framework based on genre differences will highlight overlapping and intersecting pre-conceptions that—while allowing themselves to be broken—also 'invoke and reinforce' the 'rhetorical structures' that permit thematic content to project specific Gothic 'worlds'.[30] Social settings and situations, in a literary sense, are fundamentally connected to genre, as are (the still flexible) understandings of characterisation and narratives structures. While it might not be difficult to imagine and fantasise over sexual encounters with the hunky, body-building male vampires of Lara Adrian's *Midnight Breed* paranormal romance series, it might be difficult to develop thoughts of an interpersonal nature in relation to the shark-like, bald, black-nailed vampiric creatures of Wellington's *Thirteen Bullets* and the whole *Laura Caxton Vampire* series. The lack of sexualisation for the vampire in the latter example is in keeping with the aims of the genre subcategory to which the texts belong, and the readership demands they are attempting to meet. The influence of genre on the definition of vampire characteristics is, it would seem, relational and structural both in symbolic and practical terms.

VAMPIRE TERRITORIES

The focus on the formation of a vampriric landscape—as one may refer to it—demands an examination of settings, depictions, and perceptions with an aim to decipher the multiples parts that generate meaning in their symbolic systems of organisation. To cast a light on this approach to the literary vampire intertext, it is perhaps necessary to extend its understanding and consider it, as several scholars have done in relation to several socio-cultural constructs, in relation to the concept of 'territory'. The understanding of the term that is being applied here derives in part from the work of Gilles Deleuze and Félix Guattari, focusing on describing features within multiple sites of knowledge.[31] Within these 'spaces', the attention shifts to the numerous and variable interactions between human and non-human participants.

This sense of inhumanity is often connected to the presence of objects and the physical definitions of the location itself. That is to say, upon entering a room, any individual must form an abstract connection not only with other people in the room, but also to the objects that populate it by extension. Every entity in the room, whether animate or inanimate, inhabits its own 'space', connected to specific elements—colours, shape, movement, and even language when it comes to people—that need to be dissected, interpreted and catalogued in order to make sense of it. The collection of these spaces forms a territory; entities, whether embodied or disembodied, are 'conquered' through these spatial relations of relationship and interaction. The individual spaces act in order to territorialise the human individual, and shape perception in certain ways that influence how we 'look, behave and feel, both consciously and unconsciously.[32]

This understanding of territorialisation can be applied to analysis when entering each individual vampire's representational intertext. Each space focuses on one aspect of the vampire experience—the body, the senses, the mind, the feeding, the technology—and attention to how vampires 'inhabit' these spaces will inevitably uncover understandings of those that interact with them—the human subjects in their social, cultural and political contexts. 'Vampires territories', as such, will be considered in their connections to several preoccupations within contemporary Western societies, starting with the deliberate foundation that the area inhabited by the vampires is an area of controversy, in view of the subject's inevitable connection with humanity. The overall vampire landscape, therefore, provides an aimed critique of the representational conflicts and paradoxes of the human world, while simultaneously attempting to make sense of them. By employing the concept of territory here, I aim to interrogate not only on the domination of the physical body, but also the psychic territorialisation mobilised by the vampire metaphor. By entering the vampiric territory, the human is colonised in turn by the features of that which is being experienced through the fiction: from the technologies to the abstract touch, the demeanours, the appearance, and the fantasies.

1 The Vampire Make-Up

There are several elements in contemporary vampire literature that point to genetics being an important concern. How vampires are made, and what they are made of, is a question that runs through virtually all examples from the fiction, from Harris' *Sookie Stackhouse* to D.B. Reynolds' *Vampires in America*, Ward's *Black Dagger Brotherhood*, and Christine Feehan's *Carpathians* series. When it comes to discourses regarding both the ontology and the epistemology of the vampire, this focus on 'genetic material' does not come as a surprise. Genes are an important part of biological discourse, and it is virtually impossible to talk about the biological structures of an organism without discussing, in one way or another, its genetic make-up. Genes, to put it very simply, determine what an individual looks like, from hair and eye colour, to the propensity to expand fat tissue. Genes also affect whether a person, as Thomas Parmalee reminds us, 'will develop some diseases', and how strong and efficient their immune system will be.[1] This important function alone draws attention to the fact that, when thinking about producing a resilient and well-functioning organism, the presence of 'good genes' will be essential. It also places an emphasis on how genetic discourses offer an important channel for unravelling the workings of the vampire's body not only at its innermost biological level, but also for telling us what anxieties about the human body those workings actually communicate. Indeed, I would like to suggest that the focus on the 'vampire's make-up' in contemporary literature can be viewed as an intricate re-elaboration of human genetic discourses, especially those revolving around engineering, culture, and disease.

THE TURNING AND THE CHANGE

The vampire clearly differs from the human being both genetically and biologically. Writers of vampire fiction are reluctant to include details of the physical transformation down to the scientific level. This is understandable, as a veritable—although inherently fictional—account of a genetic change could be potentially very difficult to narrate, without losing the entertaining effect of the description. Nonetheless, it is necessary to enquire into the nature of the change, and how the shift from human to vampire must necessarily involve a deep and radical restructuring of the genetic material of the creature, which will then dictate the biological changes to the individual body. In this framework, two types of vampires emerge as prominent in the fiction, at least in terms of their genetic make-up: the vampires who are, traditionally, 'turned', on the one hand, and those who are—more experimentally—born into their vampiric state, on the other.

In the case of vampires who are born as such, this genetic and biological discourse of difference naturally applies, but instead of being the result of a quick, quasi-supernatural altering, it is the outcome of generations of breeding and development. The most salient examples from this category are Laura Adrian's *Midnight Breed*, John F. Merz's *Lawson Vampire* series, and J.R. Ward's *Black Dagger Brotherhood*. These vampires are born, not resurrected; they are, in fact, an already existing different genetic group. The focus on 'change', however, is not lost and even in these narratives—when vampires reproduce in the old-fashioned, human-like way—their genetics demand a form of bodily transition, from weakly individuals to strong and biologically superior creatures. Merz humorously considers the changes to the vampire's body in terms of 'teething', when they hit 'puberty and the fangs come on out'.[2] The fangs 'coming out' here is intended as a physical representation of the vampire's nature: as the biological functions of the body and its genetic framework order the fangs to 'grow', the vampire's tendency for aggression and bloodlust also surfaces.

Ward's *Black Dagger Brotherhood* is also a relevant example in highlighting how vampire bodies, although inherently differently from human ones, operate by a similar system of change and bodily shifts, which are dependent on the structure of vampire genetics. In Ward's narrative, vampires are born as such, but they do not display the defining characteristics of the species straight away. They will reach their final physical state after going through what is known as 'the transition'. Although genetically 'vampire'—and therefore a separate species—young vampires seem rather human, especially to human eyes. They can withstand sunlight and, most importantly, they do not have fangs, so they can only consume everyday food and drink. Their bodies appear thin and emaciated, and are unable to be sexually aroused in any way, as we are told in relation to the pre-transition vampire Tehrror: 'At age twenty-three, he was five feet, six inches tall, 120 pounds. He didn't need to shave. Had no hair on his body. Had never had an erection. Unmanly. Weak.'[3] This *pretrans* state lasts roughly until the age of twenty-five, when the transition hits. The transition itself is a brutal process, when the seemingly human body transforms into its full vampiric incarnation. While both sexes go through the change, the transition is particularly severe for the males of the species, whose bodies grow to be extremely large, tall, and muscular within the space of a few hours. The change is a physically painful process, as the shape and size of the vampire's body is completely altered. The movement of the newly formed vampire body is also difficult to handle, as the sheer size of it makes it an almost alien presence: '[Wrath] felt his joints popping out of shape. His muscles had strained and then split open [. .] [Afterwards] his body hadn't acted at all like his own'.[4]

After the transition is complete, both males and females are considered 'full vampires', in that they will be unable to withstand sunlight and, of course, they will have to consume blood in order to live and thrive. In addition, they will finally be able to achieve sexual arousal—a state undoubtedly exploited by the males of the species—and will therefore be able to procreate. One can see here how the changes that affect the members of the vampire species in Ward's series are dictated both genetically and biologically. The genetic material preordains that the vampire body will go through the change, and present itself in a certain way. It is not possible to predict exactly when the transition will begin, but genetics set up the structure so that, at some point, the 'biology' of the body will shift to make the change possible. The body's 'hormones kick in' and it just 'happens'.[5]

The fact that post-transition vampires evolve into their full physical selves, and are able to engage sexually, makes it possible to think of the transition as a form of vampire puberty, a reflection of how the genetic structure of the vampire is given full resonance in the biology of the transformed body. The similarities between the vampire's transition into adulthood and the idea of human puberty highlight the possible nature of the genetically-based bodily changes in the fiction as a possible critique of the difficulty of adolescence. This, of course, applies to vampires across narratives, as any discourse of bodily change—in both its biological and social incarnations—seems to naturally recall the mutations that the human body experiences in its teenage years. Inge Wise argues that adolescence is 'a time for much disturbance and change'. The adolescent, Wise goes on to say, 'is confronted with a body that stretches, changes and grows in all directions'.[6] In this framework, the painful nature of the change in Ward's *Black Dagger Brotherhood* can be interpreted laterally as the metaphorical representation of what human teenagers experience during puberty, when issues of 'identity' and 'self' become virtually indistinguishable from the bodily dimension of being.[7]

But not all vampires are 'born'. And, as a result, not all vampires got through the 'transitional' stage. As the majority of contemporary narratives still maintain the mythology of the undead creature, 'turning' is a very important part of the process of becoming a vampire. It is the most obvious answer to how vampires come into being, and one that has been used and reinforced by vampire lore—not only folkloristically, but also in terms of literature, film, and television—for centuries. The idea of turning, Barb Karg, Arjean Spaite and Rick Sutherland point out, definitely answers the question of 'how vampires are created', by openly showing that to 'become a member of the undead' one need to be bitten by a vampire.[8] In conceptual terms, the notion of turning seems simple enough. A human is bitten by a vampire; this is, on several occasions, followed by the human being 'fed' the blood of the vampire—although this is a particular part of the ritual to which the vampires in the *Twilight* saga, as well as Scott Mariani's *Vampire Federation* series, do not subscribe. In spite of minute differences, however, the act of turning is actually usually described as some form of exchange. In Mariani's *Vampire Federation*, the bite of the vampire begins a give-and-take process that, while not being described in scientifically sophisticated terms, clearly leaves no doubt about the fact that the turning process relies on exchange, of the vampire taking blood and giving 'life'. This connection is openly acknowledged when the vampire Alex turns her lover Joel in order to save him from death: 'as he breathed his long, last sighing breath, she opened her mouth and bit deep into his neck. She drank and drank from him. Tasted his blood as it mingled with her vampire saliva and the tears running down her face. Felt his dying energy draining into her veins—and her own powers flowing into him'.[9]

After the bite, a transformation takes place; the humans experience 'death', in that their bodies cease to be human and 'become' vampire. In most cases, a period of 'being dead' actually takes place. In Harris' *Sookie Stackhouse* series, new vampires appear dead for 'three days', after which they are said to 'rise' into their new vampire existence.[10] The use of Christian mythology here is undeniable, as vampiric transformation is strangely and inevitably reminiscent of the Resurrection as described in the New Testament. It is curious to think that contemporary vampires like to defeat death by emulating a Christian process of redemption and spiritual engagement. Nonetheless, the main point remains that, through the process of 'turning', humans forfeit their ability to age, progress, and change, and accept to become something else, something 'other': the vampire.

Although the conceptualisation of the process of 'turning' appears straightforward, the practical reality of the act—still the quickest and most efficient way to become vampire in contemporary literature—is not quite as clear. Karg, Spaite and Sutherland point out that, while the simplicity of the process of turning rings true in conceptual terms, 'a vampire's making is infinitely more complicated than that'.[11] The complicated nature of vampiric change dynamics draws attention to an oddly unanswerable question regarding the notion of turning: what truly happens in the process, how one really 'becomes' vampire—genetically, physically, spiritually, psychologically—is not really addressed. The fiction makes several allusions to the noticeable changes that have taken place after the process is finished (the increased agility, the strength, the beauty, the hunger), but the practicalities of turning remain obscure. In Kristen Painter's *House of Comarré* series, the process happens quickly. When the vampire Tatiana turns her lover Octavian, the only certain information about the procedure is the she must drink his blood until his body 'dies'. In order to become a vampire himself, Octavian must have the strength, even in death, to swallow drops of Tatiana's blood:

She fell on him, thrusting her fangs into his tender neck [. . .] There was pain now, she knew that, but worse, he would feel the press of death's shadow upon his soul [. . .] he went utterly still as the last of his sweet, life filled blood drained down her throat. She took one last draw to be sure. The mouthful tasted of death [. . .] She jagged one fang across the inside of her wrist, the pressed it to his lips [. . .] He came alive quickly [and] lapped greedily at the blood she offered him. With a cry, Octavian convulsed like a bolt of lightning had struck him. His body arced between tense and limp as the invisible currents of life and death surged through him.[12]

When Octavian regains consciousness, he displays the beautiful features of a vampire: luscious eyes, shiny hair. His facial lines are 'smoothed'; his slightly 'crooked nose straightened'.[13] Painter does not question the nature of the change, simply depicting it as a quasi-magical fight between life and death that alters the body at both a genetic and biological level.

A similar process is described by D.B. Reynolds in the *Vampires in America* series. The act of turning is only entrained in detail once when the vampire Raphael turns his human comrade, Duncan: 'Raphael turned Duncan's head firmly to one side and held him there [. . .] There was a touch of something hard and pointed, and then a pain as sharp as a knife slicing his neck [. . .] but it didn't feel wrong. It felt . . . wondrous! And then he felt nothing at all'.[14] When Duncan awakes from his slumber, he is a vampire; the details of change itself remain a mystery in the narrative, the drinking of blood acting as the only certainty. An even quicker time is dedicated to the process in Chloe Neill's *Chicagoland Vampires* series, where turning is glossed over in favour of the vampire that comes into being as a result. Here, the vampire approaches a dying human, claiming the he is going to 'saver her'. The narrative then cuts to the newly made vampire waking up, the transformation itself subtly overlooked. All that is recounted of the change is 'deep-seated, dull pain', 'numbing cold', and 'darkness'.[15] On occasions, the process remains so clouded in mystery that is attributed to some obscure magic occurrence, as it is stated in the *Sookie Stackhouse* series; even this idea, however, is not fully explored, and is instead simply presented by stating that the vampires' 'existence itself is rooted in magic'.[16] Turning, it would seem, is often treated as a necessity rather than a feature of interest. It is an obvious occurrence, an accepted process, an understood requirement which is the final part of a journey where the destination is all that matters. The reality is that no one really knows what happens in the 'turning' of a human—or other supernatural creature—into a vampire.

The occurrence that takes place between vampire and human during turning alters the victim's genetic foundation. This is especially true for instances when vampires are portrayed to be dead, therefore not breathing, and without beating hearts that pump blood—which accounts for the majority of contemporary undead vampires, from the examples in Harris' *Sookie Stackhouse* to Painter's *House of Commaré* and Butcher's *The Dresden Files*. Genetically speaking these individuals are very far removed from anything even remotely human. During turning, some parts of the human DNA are 'removed' to make space for the vampiric DNA; the latter will overpower the body and shift its bio-genetic composition, so that it will move differently, look differently, feed differently. The vampire's body is an improved version of the human body, and in a sense, it can be understood as having 'evolved'. Indeed, this is precisely the way in which the process is described in the *Vampire Federation*. After Joel Solomon has been turned into a vampire, humans—who used to know him before he was turned—notice the change in him immediately: something is 'different' about him, even if they 'can't put [their] finger on it. He is still Joel, but an improved version of him, an evolved creature, so physically advanced that old human acquaintances wonder if he has been heavily 'working out'.[17] The focus on having 'evolved' here is revelatory. As a natural process, evolution is known to take a long time, taking centuries, millennia, and often millions of years to accomplish. In the process of turning, however, evolution takes but a matter of minutes. In addition, in natural circumstances, evolution is not usually a controllable progression, and it is influenced by several factors, including environmental ones. In the case of turning, however, 'evolution' takes places at the vampire's whim.

As genetic material prescribes how the individual will be formed and, necessarily, what its pitfalls, strengths, and potential will be, the genetics of the vampire will rule that the new body will 'live' without air, without breathing and, in most cases, without the ingestion of food. This would be, clearly, a genetic impossibility for any human. The altered genetics of the vampire also order the body to grow fangs—which can remain concealed until needed, or be on show all the time—and have the ability for immense strength and agility. The result of this genetic shift will be met biologically as the new vampire form takes place, as the body mutates its appearance and structure to meet the genetic demands of the change. The aversion to sunlight—or different reaction to, as it is in the case of the Meyer's vampires—is also the result of a radical genetic and biological change. The genetics of the vampire rule the new being as unable to withstand the power of the sun, and the biology of the body will ensure that this demand translates into the disintegration of tissue if exposed to sunlight. To put it simply, turning draws attention to a whole system of vampiric physical organisation which does not just exist in the conceptual and cultural understanding of what the vampire means, but inevitably highlights the ontology of what the vampire *is*: a being with a self-standing genetic structure, whose regulations are sustained into existence by a complicated and unavoidably inhuman biological system.

THE VAMPIRE'S EYES

Although, broadly speaking, vampires retain the 'general looks' of humans, the similarities truly end there. The genetic regulation extends to several aspects of the general physical appearance of the body. In contemporary literature, there is a definite emphasis on vampire eyes. These vary in shape and abilities; colour, however, is often the most pivotal and focused part of the description. The colour of the vampire's eyes is seemingly closely connected with the mythology to which the author subscribes, whether traditional or re-invented. In the *Black Dagger Brotherhood*, most vampires have eyes that, seemingly, recall human shades of colour, ranging predominantly from blue to green. However, it is made clear by Ward that even though the shades recall what is human, the vampires' eyes glow in a particular way, that is unavoidably all but human: Rhage's eyes are 'neon, glowing, iridescent. Those had to be contacts. People's eyes just didn't come in that teal colour'.[18] Other vampires in Ward's fictional universe have eyes that completely deviate from the human norm; the twin vampires Phury and Zsadist, for instances, have yellow eyes, which are said to glow 'warm' as 'citrines' and vibrant as 'buttercups'.[19] In similar vein, the vampire Vishous has what is described as 'diamond eyes'; his irises are almost white and circled with a blue rim.[20] A similar instance of deviated colour can also be found in Justin Cronin's *The Passage*, where the mutated vampires have 'orange eyes'.[21] One cannot deny that there are shades of colour that are understood to be as proper to the human species, determined mainly by genomic rather than mitochondrial DNA, which will range from brown and hazel, to tones of blue and green. Other shades such as yellow, red, purple and white are not part of the collective genetic material that defines our species as 'human'. These latter shades are, both genetically and culturally speaking, associated with other animal species, especially those who rely on hunting for survival, such as lions, tigers, and wolves.[22] As yellow, white, and orange are colours unattributable to the human species, the unconventional irises mark the vampires as the fruit of a different genetic branch, whether natural or—as is the case in Cronin's narrative—artificially mutated through experimentation.

In a lot of narratives where vampires are the result of turning, however, the colour of the creatures' eyes takes on a peculiar behavioural characteristic. The communicative nature of vampiric eye colour is indeed a widespread occurrence in post-200 literature. In Reynolds' *Vampires in America* series, the vampires all seem to have colours that are, on the surface, acceptably human. Nonetheless, the shades momentarily change when they are angry or even sexually aroused; in these cases, dark brown— almost black—eyes are known to flash 'silver', and brown eyes are said to burn and glow 'bronze'.[23] The vampires' eyes are also known to flash silver in Susanna Sandlin's *Penton Vampire Legacy* series, an occurrence related to the presence of 'blood hunger', when the vampire becomes 'half a step from losing it'.[24] The 'it' implied here is, of course, control over the vampire's own actions. Even in Ward's *Brotherhood* series, Zsadist's eyes become 'black as obsidian' whenever his anger overtakes him.[25] The relationship between eyes and emotion is extremely noteworthy and continues the cultural allegory of the eyes as 'window to the soul', which finds its foundation in religious symbolism.

Following a peculiar twist in the *Twilight* Saga, vampire eyes change colour according to the vampire's dietary habits; just after they are turned, the vampire's eyes are red, a colour that one might perceive to be the natural, or at least intended, pigmentation: 'Vampires who haven't fed for a few weeks will have solidly black irises. Vampires who have been newly transformed will have bright red irises, regardless of diet'.[26] Natural, however, is a complicated concept in this case. The vampire's eyes will stay red only if he or she feeds on human blood, an act that is portrayed as inherently complicated for the contemporary vampire, both practically and (oddly) ethically. If vampires decide to feed on animal blood instead—therefore avoiding the risks that come with hunting humans—their eyes change colour and turn bright gold. The members of the Cullen family have amber eyes; the amber shade fades to 'butterscotch' when the vampires feed regularly on animal blood and are therefore sated: Edward's 'eyes were open [. . .] Butterscotch today, lighter, warmer, after hunting'.[27] This behavioural quality not only communicates the nature of their feeding habits, but also renders them—in human terms—as a group of 'trustworthy' vampires. If their eyes are amber or butterscotch, then they are not a threat to humans, at least not for feeding purposes. The symbolism of the eyes 'as a window to the soul' finds a new meaning here. The eyes, it would seem, are a window into the vampire's ethical sense.

It is virtually impossible to ignore here not only the blood symbolism that is clearly dominant, but also how the clear shift in genetic composition—from vampire to human, and vice versa—is signalled by something as seemingly simple as eye colour. Red eyes, in particular, are a very difficult, if not impossible occurrence to find in nature. Humans, together with the majority of other creatures on the planet, are unknown to have irises which are naturally red.[28] In the animal kingdom, a rare exception is the *Drosphilia*, a genus of fruit fly that displays red eye colour as the result of a genetic mutation in the X chromosome.[29] Other examples of this rare chromatic incident occur in species of fish, especially the Scorpionfish, where mottled red irises match the mottled red appearance of the fish's head.[30] It would be risky to suggest that the vampires' red irises in the *Twilight* saga bear any affinity to either fruit flies or fishes. Even if, as readers of the series will know, these vampires—captained by the ever-popular Edward Cullen—are known to jump so high they seem to 'fly' and they are, just like the Scorpionfish, predatory in nature. Indeed, it is more likely here that Meyer is recalling, somewhat confusedly, the notion—known and developed in other examples from popular culture, such as films and television shows—that vampires have red eyes. Several examples can be found of this through an extensive list of vampire filmography, with Christopher Lee in the *Horror of Dracula* (1958) cementing the visual impression of the vampire having red eyes in people's mind. Gordon Melton contends that, to a lesser extent than other features such as long fangs and a widow's peak, horror cinemas contributed greatly in establishing 'red eyes' as an unsurprising 'standard aspect of the vampire's appearance'.[31] The particular shade here is meant to recall the colour of blood and communicate the vampire's thirst for it.

For humans, and for most animals on the planet, eye colour is a genetic characteristic, not a behavioural one. Although, speaking in evolutionary terms, behaviour may have had an impact on the way in which chromosomal material developed and was selected for members of the species, the current situation clearly points to eye colour as genetically determined.[32] The representation of vampire eyes, however, is not simply an aesthetic issue. It is not purely a matter of imagining and re-imagining the eye as a beautiful orb, and how it could be attractive or even repulsive to human perception. The presentation of eyes in contemporary narratives calls for the identification of clear genetic shifts in the vampires as a group, whether those shifts are present at birth—when vampires are separate species from humans—or whether they occur through the process of turning, skewing off the human genetic tree to create a new creature. And this is a creature that, of course, does not obey to human physical laws or limitations. If it is true, as Craig Hamilton Parker puts it, that the eyes 'are considered to be a symbol of higher consciousness', then the change in the vampire's eyes—through turning and later on, through emotion and behaviour—is communicative of the importance of the body in discerning the idea of social change.[33] Terror, of course, operates with ocular symbolism in order to construct frameworks of detachment and separation. Feeding into the cultural myth that the eyes tell who one really is, the vampire's eyes communicate the sense of otherness—and to some extent liberation—that is inherent to the Gothic mode.

BLOOD AND GENETICS

One of the biggest differences between the vampire body and the human body is that the vampire—almost exclusively, by definition—must in fact consume blood to live. Blood is an absolute necessity for vampires and still remains, across the narratives, the primary source of nourishment.[34] Even in instances where the vampire has other necessities—including the need for 'psychic energy', drained from symbiotic victims—blood remains an unavoidable part of the vampire's existence and, indeed, an important aspect of the vampire's mystique in the popular imagination.

The emphasis on seeing the vampire's need for blood in terms of hunger has spurred a lot of speculation regarding the metaphorical nature of such a 'hunger', one that goes beyond physical needs. The vampire's hunger for blood has often been equalled to the creature's uncontrollable sexual instincts. Multiple example of scholarship have succeeded in connecting the vampire's hunger to representations of sexual desire and consumerist greed, the latter being a particular feature of both Eighties narratives and criticism. Nina Auerbach has been particularly successful in showing both the sexualised nature of the vampire's feeding—from *Dracula* and 'Carmilla' to Whitley Strieber's *The Hunger*—and its relationship to both contexted intimacy and boundaries of what she calls the 'predatory society'. In the late twentieth century, the vampire's hunger, Auerbach argues, is eroticised through its connections to the 'self-obsessed' glamour of consumerism that 'subordinates history to seductive objects'.[35] In recent years, the vampire's hunger for blood has attracted a lot of attention in terms of the creature's relationships to problematic ethics, from gender politics to medical concerns, as the majority of scholarship on the *Twilight* saga seems to be intent in proving.[36] There is no denying the persuasive nature of these arguments, and their ability to draw attention to the vampire's hunger for blood as a representational presence.

When it comes to discourses of hunger, desire, and accumulation, the vampire is often a creature that is out of control. He does not put limitations to his desires; the vampire's hunger is not a socially domesticated response. Even when social structures are present in the vampire world, blood needs are always indulged, so that the physiological stimuli of hunger actually exceed into the more culturally informed representation of appetite. This point is made manifest in Harris' *Sookie Stackhouse* series. In this narrative, a Japanese company has developed a synthetic blood substitute that has the same chemical properties and provides the same nutrients as real human blood. This allows vampires to live peacefully with humans, without presenting a threat to society (or so it is claimed). However, when the vampire Eric is questioned on his motives for still wanting to drink human blood, his response is disarmingly simple: 'It tastes better'.[37] It is clear here that a split has occurred dividing the concepts of hunger and appetite in the vampire feeding system. 'Hunger' remains an unavoidable concept for the vampire; it is the genetically dictated need, the biological must. The conscious choice to consume one form of 'blood', rather than the other, draws attention to the distinction between need and pleasure, two interconnected and yet separate concepts that become somehow fused in the vampire. Sharman Russell argues that appetite can in fact 'intertwine with hunger', but the former is not just necessity, it is 'desire, born of biology'.[38] The close representational relationship between the vampires' choices in the *Sookie Stackhouse* series, and actual human interaction with sources of nourishment—identified by food biologists and anthropologists alike—opens the possibility of interpreting hunger politics in the fiction as a critique of surplus appetites in contemporary Western societies.[39]

Still, not all vampires are fussy eaters. Some do not indulge in appetite and are driven only by hunger, the biological need. Truly, the most fascinating part of the vampire's hunger for blood in contemporary narratives lies in its ability to signify a shift from human normality, a split in signification that immediately releases the consumer from the constraints of the human world and accordingly, its rules. The immediate need for blood seems to be on the most distinctive results of the genetic and biological changes that the vampire's body goes through during turning. Even when vampires are born as such, the need for blood remains a constant presence, therefore identifying both the individual and the group as a separate species. Blood hunger is one of the clearest vampire signifiers in that it denotes what is different from the human, what exceeds it and—one might venture to say—improves it. The consumption of blood is not simply a nourishment issue; it also releases the vampire from the limitations of the human body in the clearest way. Blood hunger functions both practically and symbolically in highlighting the 'glowingly superior' and 'dominant' nature of the vampire when compared of humanity.[40] As far as contemporary literature is concerned, any interpretation of its meaning must begin from this very starting point: understanding blood hunger as a physiological issue which is necessarily connected to a genetic divide between the human and the vampire. Only then it can accurately be placed within a representational framework, acknowledging its role as a conductive medium for uncovering attitudes, desires and anxieties.

Physiologically speaking, hunger is not such an ungraspable and complicated concept—after all, all living creatures become 'hungry' at one point or another. It seems only fitting that, when the potential undead creatures of the Gothic world are involved, the form that hunger would take will exceed the boundaries of human acceptability. In this sense, vampires emerge as an augmentation of the human, whose 'life and death' are 'linked in a complex rhythm of ingesting, digesting, expelling nourishment'.[41] The defining characteristic of the vampire's hunger is that it cannot be resisted. This point is reiterated in several, if not all examples from contemporary literature, so much that that uncontrollable blood hunger truly re-establishes itself as a universal and long-standing feature of the vampire motif. This constant presence confirms, as Mary Pharr argues, that relentless blood hunger 'remains the linchpin of vampires', and reminds us that, even in the revisionist framework of the twenty-first century', 'vampirism is a metaphor for need', the kind of 'need that can never vanish'.[42] Pharr also refers to the vampire's blood need as 'the red thirst', opting for another physiological function that echoes the liquid nature of blood, and retells the presence of blood as a real necessity; in the human world, hunger and thirst are stimuli that cannot be ignored. Answering to the body's demands is essential as much as it is, culturally speaking, pleasurable.

Nonetheless, if blood consumption is the biological requirement for the genetic being that is a vampire, then the need must be seen as intrinsic. Cross-references between blood and the vampire bring with it preoccupations that touch on something intimately human—physically, physiologically, and psychologically—and question the nature of civilisation, instinct, and routine. These issues emerge as an endemic presence in the genetically and culturally driven representation of the vampire, a thread of both thought and action that questions not only the nature of the blood-drinking creature, but the aspirations of the humans who fear it, love it, or loathe it. The concept of life blood, Nick Fiddes reminds us, is 'evident throughout our culture'.[43] Blood hunger provides an apt metaphor for conceptual mediation: the vampire takes in the blood, the external life force, and thrives on it. In similar fashion, the human being can be said to domesticate the body through what Russell calls 'a circle of messages': the body is a genetic entity, dependant on biology.[44] The embodied self is tied to this connection, a system of communication, feedback, and updates. Hunger is one of the most basic examples of these, and also one of the most unavoidable ones.

Making a vampire the predator and consumer of human blood inevitably draws attention to the inferior state of humans within both the food and genetic chains. This relationship between predator and prey is clearly outlined in David Wellington's *Thirteen Bullets*. Once the vampire feeds on blood, his body grows in strength and becomes impervious to almost all forms of attack: 'Every drop he drank would make [the vampire] stronger. He would be bulletproof in seconds'.[45] The description of a highly evolved, virtually indestructible body becomes an important vehicle for conveying the superiority of the vampire over the human species, and the image of blood and blood-hunger are at the centre of its efficacy. Turning mutates the human being into something different, something genetically remote and detached from its previous incarnation. Of all the physical and physiological changes that affect the vampire during and after the transformation, the most unavoidable and significant one is that they must consume blood in order to live. The vampire's body is able to metabolise blood and turn it into nourishment in ways that the human body never could. The vampire's need for blood is the potent signifier of not only its diversity but also—and perhaps especially—of its manifest superiority.

The motif of blood is, of course, central to the vampire. The association between the two is long-standing, finding its origins in folklore and continuing through an array of narrative incarnations, from literature to television and film. Although questioning the original motives that not only created the vampire, but made it a blood-drinking creature could be difficult to pin down, one cannot deny the importance that blood plays in highlighting vampirism in contemporary literature as a connection that is supported by distinctly human preoccupations. The most distinctive feature of the vampire's association with blood is that, one might argue, in drinking blood the creature 'steals' the elixir of life. The vampire reaches into the most remote depths of the human body to dispossess it of its life force. In this framework, blood proves an apt medium for the discussion of human anxieties regarding the dichotomy of life and death, within the parameters by which humanity itself operates.

In many cultures and religions around the world, blood occupies a sacred position. The connection to Christianity is difficult to ignore, given its profound impact on Western societies and their narratives. In the rituals of Christian Communion, participants drink sacred blood—the blood of Christ—and, forming a bond with God, partake in the Holy Spirit. The interpretation of blood as the source of eternal life is made manifest in Christian tradition. Blood equals the fullness of the body, and it is in this conception that its goriest potential becomes evident. Michael Cox and Desda Crockett comment on the horror of 'spilled blood' by claiming that the very 'concept of blood as the river of life continues to exert a hold' in the contemporary imaginary.[46] Blood, they argue, is 'the very stuff of life', which maintains mythical and psychological associations'.[47] In taking blood, the vampire partakes in these associations, and as the twenty-first century context is thrown into sharp relief, mythology and psychology merge to uncover anxieties of a distinctly historical nature. In contemporary narratives, blood is no longer a mere ritual presence; as the vampire feeds, the nature of that feeding brings an association to socio-scientific modalities that construct the human race for what it is.

For a number of vampires in contemporary narratives, the consumption of blood can take different forms. Some are able to live on chemical substitutes—where the chemical composition is all that matters—while others can live on animal blood, as clearly stated in the *Twilight* Saga and *Nathaniel Cade* series. In the latter, however, it is also made very clear that animal blood will never truly fulfil the vampire's needs, both physically and psychologically. In physical terms, we are told that drinking animal blood will keep the vampire functioning, but will have disastrous consequences. Vampires who drink only animal blood are not as physically strong as others who consume human blood: 'Most vampires of Cade's age would be much stronger, and faster, with a range of abilities Cade does not possess. But unlike other vampires, this subject sustains himself with animal blood'.[48] Vampires like Cade, who do not drink human blood, are 'less resilient, less able to process damage, less efficient'.[49] In addition, vampires who only consume animal blood age rapidly and slowly turn into corpse-like creatures as they reach 'the end of the cycle': 'starved of human blood [. . .] the vampire has parchment skin, crisscrossed with deep lines. His joints frozen with disuse. Tumors swelling his abdomen. And his eyes, screaming with pain, begging for release'.[50] The superiority of human blood here—both chemically and symbolically– is unavoidable.

Overall, the majority of narratives still reinforce the need for vampires to consume human blood as an absolutely unavoidable necessity. It would appear, therefore, that in spite of contemporary efforts to humanise the vampire by making it a creature more akin to our human selves, the most essential point remains: vampires must drink human blood to thrive. It is human blood that is still given the top spot in the vampire's feeding needs. In the contemporary imaginary, 'human' is still interpreted as the highest form of evolved creature, the one who will provide the greatest life force and the one who bestows the greatest strength onto the vampire. As a highly evolved creature, the human is, as Paul and Anne Ehrlich out it, the 'dominant animal', the one who occupies the highest position in view both its genetics and its ability to generate superior cultural organisations.[51] The issue of evolution and hierarchy is indeed an important one, one that is strictly connected to the vampire's blood needs. While human blood is still regarded as the strongest and most efficient source of nourishment, the vampire's consumption of it denies the human being's position as the highest creature in the world's living hierarchy. In demanding human blood, the vampire negates human supremacy over the natural world. The status of the human shifts from historical predator to prey. The role of predator is instead taken on by the vampire, a position reinforced by a high number of texts, including Wellington's *Laura Caxton Vampire* series. In this narrative, Arkley the vampire makes his vampiric superiority over humanity explicit: 'It's the natural order. [We] are predators. You and your kind are prey, that's all. To survive, we must feed on your blood'.[52]

The vampire hunts the human being. Subverting the historical logic of human evolution—which crowned *Homo sapiens* as the technologically superior hunters—the vampire transforms the human into a subjugated species, overpowered by a creature that occupies a superior position on the evolutionary scale. Humans, used to killing other animals and consuming their flesh, are deemed food by the vampire. This shift is significant in highlighting the lesser status of the human, and plays on the subversion of socio-cultural knowledge on the human's part. As Fiddes reminds us, killing and eating other animals' flesh has provided 'the ultimate authentication of human superiority over the rest of nature, with the spilling of their blood a vibrant motif'.[53] Eating other highly evolved animals has functioned as an act communicating a sense of perceived supremacy that has also guaranteed the human ascendance towards world domination and control. In becoming prey, however, humans lose their status. Human dominion is challenged and interrupted. *Vampiro sanguinarius* overtakes the long-standing status of *Homo sapiens* as the ruling creature. The blood is spilled and consumed and, as a result, the human is displaced into the new territory of suppression and defeat. Just like humans historically consumed animals and, in so doing, established their power as the superior species, the vampire also exercises control over the inferior creatures upon which it feeds. The territory of the human being is conquered by the vampire, and the stability of our species is shaken to its very core.

Through the drinking of blood, the vampire channels human fears of not only subjugation, but ultimate extinction. It is the fear of becoming redundant in both the world's power relations and the genetic charts, of being relegated to the status of 'obsolete'. It is the fear of being exposed as inferior by the creature we generated from our own beings—vampires are, after all, a later-stage transformation of the original human body. Through the vampiric blood metaphor, human beings are presented with their own inadequacy, their loss of control and purpose, and the fear that what is commonly known as a fantasy could take on a prophetic quality in predicting the disintegration of the human species by its own doing.

HYBRIDS

As concerns relating to the nature and value of genetic make-up are thrown into sharp relief, hybrids emerge as a common presence in contemporary vampire literature. Although not all narratives give vampire hybrids as an expected occurrence, a number of authors have included the possibility of genetic mixtures between vampires and human—or indeed other creatures—as a feasible outcome of sexual relationships. Unsurprisingly, vampire hybrids have found their most prolific grounds in examples where vampire are in fact 'born' and not 'turned', as the latter does not allow scope for genetic mingling and creation in the way that old-fashioned means of reproduction—through intercourse and pregnancy—purposely does. In view of their intrinsic nature and definition, vampire hybrids are known as different forms of life in the fiction, and are often regulated by differing, yet interconnected principles.

Examples of the concept abound. In the *Black Dagger Brotherhood*, vampire hybrids are a rare occurrence, but are known to manifest; hybrids are commonly referred to as 'half breeds'. Vampires can procreate with various others species including humans, Shadows and *sympaths*—the latter two being two examples of vampire-like creatures who, on the other hand, are seen as genetically separate from the vampires themselves. Incidentally, and rather curiously, *sympaths* recall—in appearance and concept—both the vampires of folklore and the cinematic vision of the creature inspired by early films such as *Nosferatu* (1922). The offspring between a vampire and another species will either go through the transition to become an adult vampire—if, we are told, the vampire blood is 'strong' enough in them—or remain part of the other species, which for humans translates into continuing to lead an 'unremarkable' human life.[54] Ward gives multiple examples of these possibilities: Beth Randall, the hybrid of a human mother and a full vampire father, who goes through her transition and becomes a vampire as expected at the age of twenty-five; Manuel Manello, whose vampire genetic heritage is seemingly not strong enough and remains, in his forties, a full human male; and Xhex, the vampire/*sympath* hybrid who, while displaying the physical structure and outlook of vampires, still retains the enhanced psychic abilities and seemingly evil disposition that is typical of *sympaths*. Ward also makes it clear that, whichever way the hybrid will go, it will remain true to the nature it has embraced genetically and, as a result, culturally.

In L.J. Smith's *Vampire Diaries* hybrids between vampires and werewolves are known to exist—with Klaus being a clear example.[55] These individuals, however, have the mingled strengths and characteristics of both races, including super agility and a venomous bite—inherited from their werewolf parent—and mind compulsion, dream manipulation, and emotional control—abilities held thanks to their vampire heritage. Smith also reiterates the desire for these hybrids to find their own sense of identity, so much that magical rituals, incantations and further genetic mingling is pursued in order to establish the hybrid not as the result of the fusion of two species, but as a separate species in its own right. This overarching question of identity should not come a surprise, especially where hybrids—physically and conceptually—are concerned. Hybrids, as G.E. Coover and S.T. Murphy point out, provide discussions of identity with a process 'definition' and 'redefinition', during which individuals are 'redefined by others as they, in turn, define and redefine themselves'.[56] Vampire hybrids, one might venture to say, are the in-between site for individual and cultural communication.

Although hybrids between vampires and other supernatural creatures are known to occur, it is definitely the combination of human and vampire that receives the most attention in literature. A hybrid is the central character in Richelle Mead's series *Vampire Academy*: Rose Hathaway is a *dhampir*, a vampire hybrid that finds it origins in Romanian folklore. In Mead's narrative, *dhampirs* function as trained bodyguards to the Moroi—living vampires with a finite life span and wide-spread respect for the human race—against the Strigoi, the undead vampires of myth and folklore whose uncontrollable bloodlust makes them (at least accordingly to Mead) inherently evil. The *dhampir* bridges the gap between the two types of vampires, the vampiric nature mediated by the presence of human blood. The eponymous 'vampire academy'—where the *dhampirs* train and come into their own as guardians—is viewed as a protected, coveted, and almost sacred space. The *dhampir*'s job as guardian is also portrayed as a form of identity prescriber for the hybrids; unable to build a coherent conceptual place for themselves, they find their place in the world by building powerful bonds with their vampire charges.

Another famous example of vampire-human hybrid is Renesmee—the hybrid vampire/human daughter of Bella and Edward Cullen—found in the *Twilight* saga. Indeed, the status and nature of Renesmee forms much of the plot and preoccupations of *Breaking Dawn*, the final instalment Meyer's series. The hybrid is viewed with fear and mistrust by vampires and werewolves, both factions feeling threatened by the presence of an individual that, in defying a close sense of definition and boundary, also challenges the construction of binary identities. As a hybrid, Renesmee is neither human nor vampire, and yet she is (paradoxically) both. Genetically speaking, she is a creature of fusion, of mutation, of exchange. Her physical identity is ungraspable in that she does not fit the experience of either group, and cannot therefore be catalogued as a body belonging to a strict social environment. This inability to conciliate the genetic with the social, as Eric M. Eisenberg argues, lies at the heart of the conflict and misunderstanding regarding hybrids of any kind.[57] Her body defies the limitations of the human species; she grows to be a seventeen-year-old teenager at accelerated speed, at which point she stops growing and aging altogether, taking on the more ethereal characteristics of her vampire side. And yet, she is not afflicted by blood lust, her ability to live safely among humans being the gift provided by the genes of her once-human mother. The genetic impact, however, also reaches within the limitations of the cultural realms. As a hybrid, Renesmee does not fully belong to the cultural corollary of either species, while simultaneously incorporating both their concerns and their desires. Renesmee has no identity as either a vampire or a human; her only identity is that of the hybrid, the symbol of mergence, of union, of synthesis. She is both threatening and exciting, holding with her the potential for the development of a new group, genetically and culturally.

This focus on identity formation—and the inevitable boundaries of that identity—is the recurrent, if not formative concept of the vampire hybrid in contemporary literature. To fully grasp this idea, I believe it is necessary to consider the context in which these texts have been produced. The novels belong to the American imagination, and America—one cannot deny—still holds a conflicted and conflating history of simultaneous fusion and resistance. As existence becomes increasingly more globalised, issues of identity inevitably grow increasingly more complex and provide a fruitful site for understanding socio-cultural interactions. Conceptually speaking, 'hybrid' and 'identity' are two terms that seemingly work within the same rubric. Raka Shome and Radha Hedge suggest that identity is an 'expression of transnational change, an era of imminent concern'.[58] Translated into the parameters of the fictional context, the focus on hybridity in vampire literature provides the ground for discussion and evaluation, while the hybrid itself opens the possibilities for understanding, as Amber Zimmerman and Patricia Geist-Martin put it, the relationships between ' individual and collective identities'.[59] The vampire, in this context, can be regarded as the safe component of the identity equation; unaffiliated and unadulterated by racial and cultural accusations, the vampire allows latent critiques of both genetic and cultural fusion to be uncovered without the overstatement of human privilege and favouritism.

Marwan Kraidy defines the hybrid as 'a communicative practice constitutive of, and constituted by . . . socio-political arrangements'.[60] These arrangements are not only creature in virtue of organisational criteria, but also as a result of physical exchanges and perceptions which transform the hybrid into an entity of knowledge and communication. The 'arrangements' that establish the hybrid as such are dependent on cultural structures that dictate the perception of the body as both an individual and communal presence. Hybridity, therefore, is not simply a physical state, but a cultural one two, where the political understandings that decree normality are prescribed onto the body within systems of control. In this light, the hybridisation of vampires in contemporary literature draws attention to how the body is discursively, genetically and culturally situated in relation to dominant structures within the fiction, and—in recalling the hegemonic structures of human societies—exceeds binary structures of normality that proclaim it as alien, different, strange, and ultimately 'other'.

Renesmee's nature in Meyer's narrative inspires fear in others because of what they perceive as her intrinsic otherness, her uncanny sense of existence that lies at the bridge between one species and the other. She looks human, but she is not. She has qualities of the vampire, but is not a vampire at all. She has a beating heart, but she can also 'show people her thoughts by touching their skin', recalling the psychic abilities of many of her vampire kin.[61] She inspires terror because she is unclassifiable according to binary oppositions. In this framework, the notion of Homi Bhabha's hybrid colonial subject proves useful in extricating the American postcolonial context of the novel. The hybrid, Bhabha argues, is 'almost the same' as the mainstream, accepted subject, 'but not quite'.[62] Hybrids, in conceptual, bodily and behavioural terms, prove a sizeable threat to the power established by binary oppositions. In the case of *Twilight*'s Renesmee, the fear of her hybridity comes from her ability to fuse and therefore challenge two sets of cultural regulation. Zimmermann and Geist-Martin argue that hybridity 'is the coming together of two or more cultural identities and, in this process, offers a third or alternative identity' that is often situated outside of linguistic definitions.[63] And yet, the fiction's main narrative stance is to prove that Renesmee is not a creature to be feared, and the concerns surrounding her existence are founded in the ignorance of those who do not understand her status and her nature. The position that hybrids—in whatever shape of form they may come—are not to be feared is emphasised in *Breaking Dawn* when Renesmee herself is found declaring her non-threatening position to others: 'I'm not dangerous at all', she announces, almost metaphysically sending out cultural instructions to the world on how to cope with any form of genetic hybridisation.[64]

Although within the fiction the two 'cultural' identities are identified as those of human and vampire, the contextualisation of this dynamic within the wider American context open the way to interpreting the vampire hybrid as a critique of cultural relations in the United States. Renesmee is not just a hybrid, she is an American hybrid; her heritage is mixed not only genetically, but also culturally. Her mother Bella is an American by birth, while her father Edward is 'alien' in a number of ways: not only is he vampire, but he is also technically a foreigner, a European influence on the American context. In cultural terms, concerns regarding hybrids and their place and function in society are said to belong to particular moments of transition.

In *The Location of Culture*, Bhabha suggests that 'the social articulation of difference [. . .] seeks to authorize cultural hybridities that emerge in moments of historical transformation'.[65] What one can see emerging clearly here is a question regarding the merging of individuals from different factions, nations, and cultures within the American nation, a point of discussion that has been the core of American immigration policies for centuries. The twenty-first century, however, adds its own spin and preoccupations to the mix, as the hybrid condenses not only the fear of inclusion, but also of that separation and fragmentation that might result from incorporating the other into the seemingly stable American context.

Writing about her own experience of hybridity in the United States, Gloria Andaluza views her identity as one that breaks down the 'subject/object' of the flesh, cultivating its own agency by moving away from existing dualisms.[66] This sense of developed agency rings true for Meyer's narrative. What Resnesmee represents is the basic question of American identity: in occupying a separate cultural space from the two factions, she is neither 'alien' nor 'American'. She is, in fact, the 'new American', the new sense of being and experience that can be seen as a consequence of extended commerce and cultural exchange. She is the next stage of identity formation, one which is neither fused or fragmented because it refuses to be catalogued and, in so doing, denies the limitations of binary structures. In her being both fusion and fragmentation—and, simultaneously, denying the hold of both metaphorical engagements—Renesmee refutes both the familiar and the 'other'. In the American postcolonial sense, the vampire hybrid is what Bhabha identifies as 'the third space' of identity definitions, one that moves beyond the known parameters of socio-cultural dualism.[67] In the third space of identity, the hybrid body exceeds 'the frame of the image'; it escapes cataloguing and the imprint of dualistic representation. The hybrid evacuates the self 'as a site of autonomy' and leaves, as Bhabha puts it, a 'sign of resistance' on systems of cultural and social incorporation.[68] This resistance is enacted by defiance and disregard for boundaries. In resisting incorporation into either group, Renesmee finds an autonomy of existence that is rooted in her very own status as a hybrid. 'Hybrid', as a term, is no longer to be understood as an in-between state, a disordered stage of fusion, but becomes a position in itself.

Renesmee's hybrid identity is established not as a complicated and ungraspable mixture of her parents' genetic and institutional heritage, but also as its own ethnic space, where the body exists for itself and formulates an autonomous space of subjective inhabitation. The hybrid opposes the limitations of cultural delineation by remaining fluid, by challenging, as Zimmerman and Geist-Martin suggest, 'the fixity of prescribed identity roles'.[69] Renesmee is the revolutionary incarnation of both social and bodily identities that opens the door for an innovative sense of self-assertiveness in the wider cultural sphere. The vampire hybrid is situated as, to borrow Gust Yep's words, an 'opening and creation of spaces without a map'.[70]

Renesmee transcends her status as a 'mixed' creature; in the narrative, she is proved to be something else, a new entity. She is 'hybrid' in that she is the new beginning of an identity that is not tied by a predetermined goal of identification and classification. With the hybrid state becoming a freedom state rather than a category, Meyers unveil Renesmee as the realisation of individual sovereignty which exists—in the vampire world as well as in the American context—without the constraints of 'suffocating identities and restrictive membership'.[71]

ALIENS

The focus on hybrids—creatures who possess a mixed genetic composition, formed of both human and other traits—also draws attention to other forms of genetic mingling that has become prominent in contemporary vampire fiction. One of the most noteworthy examples of genetic hybridisation in the post-2000 era stems from viewing vampires as an alien form. And by 'alien', what it is meant here is not understanding vampires as a presence or creature far removed from the parameters of human organisation—although that is indeed an important aspect of the vampire experience—but actually envisaging them as extra-terrestrial beings. Two very prominent narratives in which the 'alien-vampire' character is portrayed are Mariani's *Vampire Federation* and Adrian's *Midnight Breed* series. In the former, humanoid vampires were created by an alien species, known as the *Uber-vampires*; these creatures were not humanoid in shape, as their description clearly proves: 'The skull was tapered and bald, the ears long and pointed. Its skin was the colour of a washed-out winter sky, so translucently thin that a thousand dark veins could be seen under its wrinkled surface'.[72] Having arrived on Earth while their planet was decaying, the Uber-vampires bit unsuspecting humans, and through a 'chemical reaction' inspired by elements in their own alien saliva, caused them to turn into a separate type of creature. These creatures were vampires as it is understood in the storytelling sense: blood-thirsty and undead, they act as subservient individuals to the Uber-vampires, the relationship playing testament to the original aliens' perceived sense of both genetic and intellectual superiority. They are also unable to reproduce other than by creating other vampires via turning. In this sense, Mariani's vampires can be understood as alien hybrids: unable to reproduce physically as living creatures, they become an 'other', a 'hybridised form' which is neither human nor alien.[73] While having inherited some of the physical strength of the Uber-vampires, they can also be destroyed, their alleged immortality transformed into an ephemeral concept as a result of their original human nature.

A similar understanding of the genetic triumvirate of alien, human and vampire is presented in Adrian's *Midnight Breed*. In this storyline, vampires—'the Breed'—are the result of the breeding between human females and alien, blood-drinking creatures—known as 'the Ancients'—whose starship crashed on earth thousands of years ago. These vampires can also be understood as hybrids, in that they display some of the characteristics known to both groups: not only do they have the physical strengths passed on by their ancient alien kin, but, being 'human looking' in shape, they also resemble their human mothers. Their mothers—known as breed mates—are not simply human beings, but mutated types whose slightly altered DNA could actually mingle with the alien one: the first vampires 'were conceived unpleasantly and entirely by chance', when the Ancients' violent sexual couplings 'happened to include human females who unique blood properties and DNA were strong enough to sustain a hybrid pregnancy'.[74] The hybrid nature of the newly created vampire offspring is also mirrored in their inability to generate female offspring. Complications in breeding are a known characterise of hybrids, some of which—in the animal world—are even known to be sterile. All Breed specimens are male, that being the only outcome of mating with breed mates. The complication inherent to the alien-vampire, however, ensures a close relationship to special human females. This continues to generate specimens that are neither alien nor human, but are in fact a separate category: 'the Breed'. Echoing the dynamics relating to Renesmee in the *Twilight* saga, Adrian's series factualises the status of the hybrid—both culturally and genetically—as a self-standing category.

The inclusion of the alien as a category in this narrative complicates further the notion of others that is often associated with the concept of 'vampire'. Jenny Wolmark argues that, in itself, the alien is a familiar metaphorical source 'for the notion of otherness'.[75] As a representation for what is different and removed from the human, the alien 'enables difference to be constructed in terms of binary oppositions which reinforce relations of dominance and subordination'.[76] In Adrian's novels, however, the aliens are domesticated—so to speak—through their mingling with human DNA. The Ancients were said to be wild, blood-thirsty and ferocious creatures; only certain aspects of the alien nature are present in specimens of the Breed, their vampire instinct emerging as the result of a genetic transformation which, through hybridisation, retains the 'other' under the yoke of human civilisation. The extra-terrestrial otherness of the alien is exchanged for the seemingly Earth-specific otherness of the vampire, a creature that, in the post-2000 era, has found an unlikely but contented place in the cultural structures of the human race. The conceptual formation of the hybrid—and the specific mixture of alien and vampire mythology within Adrian's storyline—is well suited for allowing the fiction to invest in known metaphors with new meanings which, overall, undermine ostensible straightforward distinctions between human and 'other'.

As cultural and genetic categories are thrown into sharp relief, it becomes virtually impossible to ignore the term 'alien' in its understanding as a non-citizen, an individual not belonging to any nation. What seems to be a latent current in Meyer's *Twilight*, is given a manifest presence in Adrian's and Mariani's narratives. Both series play on issue of inclusion and exclusion throughout; for Adrian, it is the division between 'good vampires' and 'bad vampire's, the latter being the ones who display a behaviour deemed too close to that of their alien ancestors: too violent, too blood-thirsty, too 'savage', and too 'warminded'.[77] For Mariani, on the other hand, the boundaries of inclusion rely on the approach vampires have to humanity, to what is seen as the mainstream existence that does not impose aspects of their own culture, but adapts to the framework in which they have to live. The 'bad' vampires, in this case, are those who maintain a link—both conceptual and behavioural—to their alien ancestors. As it is the case in other literary examples, membership is an important part of the vampire's existence, where genetic composition is but the starting point for categorisation. Nonetheless, the inclusion of the 'alien' term in these narratives complicates the political evaluation of individual and group relationships, and somewhat distances the genetic discourse from simple fears of extinction and overpowering to matters related to social and cultural fragmentation.

Incorporating the perspective of two principally Anglophone contexts— the United States and United Kingdom, respectively—Adrian and Mariani both come from countries who own a history of invasion, appropriation, reconstruction, and, more recently, immigration. Both countries have functioned, at one point or another, as the 'new land' of the immigrant imagination, America being particularly forceful in its appropriation of this new identity for itself and its people. Claiming that 'alien', in this case, could stretch to notions of non-belonging does not seem too much of a stretch. Discussing the sense of detachment that is often associated with the migrant experience, Linda Bosniak suggests that the very term 'alien' decodes the loss of separation and the resistance to incorporation. 'Being alien' is an in-between status, one that, Bosniak argues, does not allow for membership, 'the most desired of conditions'.[78] Although the alien nature of both the Ancients and the Uber-vampires in Adrian and Mariani's narratives is intended to be a genetic issue, the notion also extends to social and, to some extent, cultural representation as well. Here the physical plays both a practical and an illustrative function, as the term 'alien' is re-elaborated from its foundations in the material to its representation in the symbolic.

Proof of this multifaceted interpretation of the word in the text comes from both the physical description of the aliens, and the way they live. The *Midnight Breed's* ancient aliens have refused to accept a peaceful coexistence with humankind, and have therefore been hunted and exterminated by their own kin, the 'mainstreaming vampires' they once created: these warrior vampires are the 'fiercest, most lethal males' of their kind, whose mission is to 'slay the last of the savage Ancients'.[79] Although not hunted for extermination, a similar fate of separation is reserved for Mariani's Uber-vampires: unable to incorporate their existence into the structures they found existing and developing in the human world, the aliens live hidden and separate from human civilisation, excluded from the main forces that populate the 'hostile planet'.[80] The 'alien' status here extends to the political sphere: the old alien creatures refuse membership into the 'country' because they are unable to assimilate. They have no voice, except than of their own rage and sadness; to put it simply, they do not belong.

The newly generated vampire kin, on the other hand, is the one that incorporates the local, the human, the pre-existent. Both Adrian and Mariani communicate a sense of land ownership and membership through constructing the 'new vampires' as the adapted groups, the hybrid formation that, culturally and genetically, has incorporated the strengths of their ancestors and the power of the native group. The fiction here employs the issue of 'alienation'—in the metaphorical, physical, and storytelling sense—to invoke an opposing and much preferred feeling of inclusion and of affiliation. The non-aliens—the cultural citizens, if one may wish to advance an alternative term—emerge as those who do not allow subordination, and refuse the conceptual chains of the dichotomy between known and 'other'. Citizenship may be a complicated and divided concept; nonetheless, through a play on genetic transformation and cultural assimilation, these vampire narrative indulge in a fantasy of unification and nationhood which, far from being distant from notions of conflict and struggle, operates on the hopeful and ubiquitous sense of democratic belonging which is characteristic of Western countries in the post-9/11 era.

THE UNDEAD VIRUS

The specific elements proposed by the fiction—that merge quick genetic changes to the human body to futuristic views of separate genetic branches—make it possible to think of the vampire not simply in terms of evolution, but—more specifically—in terms of genetic engineering. According to Parmalee, genetic engineering often involves 'combining genes of two very different species'.[81] The process differs greatly from other 'natural' processes of genetic intermingling, such as selective breeding, which have been known to take place for a very long time, even in human terms. The experimentation with inter-genetic material that is proper to scientific engineering, however, relies on mixing DNA material not through breeding, but through lab testing. Instead of taking centuries or millennia, genetic engineering 'can insert a gene from one organism into another' in a 'matter of days'.[82]

A noteworthy point about vampirism, and its conceptual connections to lab environments, is that it is often described as a 'virus'. This is directly stated in examples such as Cronin's *The Passage*, or tacitly implied in the *Vampire Federation* and the *Twilight* saga, where the vampire's venom that spread through the human body is claimed to be 'viral' in nature.[83] In the latter, vampirism is seen as taking over the human body, and replacing human cells with itself. Although it is not explicitly stated, the working of vampirism in the *Federation* can be viewed in terms of a permanent infection, changing the genetic material of the carriers and 'turning' them into a different creature. The fact that vampirism is treated as a virus in Mariani's narratives is reiterated even more by the fact that, amazingly, effects of the infection can be monetarily cured by specifically designed pharmaceuticals. The aversion to sunlight—fatal to vampires, as it is in most narratives—can be erased for a few hours by taking 'Solazal', a drug that allows the vampire's body to withstand the rays and be out during the day. It goes without saying here that, if seemingly genetic workings can be momentarily altered with a pharmaceutical drug, then those changes must be reliant on some form of disease, one that can be cured medically, even for just a limited period of time. Even if, and this must be said, viral infections—in medical terms—are rarely treated with antibiotics, as they have no effect on the virus itself. So vampirism in the *Federation* is probably more akin to a bacterial infection, rather than viral. Nonetheless, the reliance on exchange between one cell and the other, one organism and the other, allows it to be conceived more constructively as a virus.

Indeed, the exchange between vampire and victim needed for the turning process holds several similarities to how a virus actually spreads. The biological conformation of a virus makes it conceptually similar to vampires themselves, with a specific reference to those that have been turned. A virus cannot feed and reproduce by itself; it needs a host cell to accomplish both these functions. First, a virus penetrates inside the targeted host cell. Then, it reaches its nucleus, stops working the host's DNA, and starts to produce copies of the viral DNA. Because of the nature of this exchange, a virus is never really seen as being 'alive' until it reaches the healthy cells of the host organism. Viruses, as Stefan Anitei puts it, are 'entities at the limit of living and non-living'.[84] In these terms, a virus can be seen as 'undead', neither alive nor lifeless, constantly in need of another's organism's life force in order to survive. It is this 'undead' quality of the virus that ranks it in a similar conceptual category to the vampire.

To compare vampirism to a virus-like entity is not, in itself, a new concept. Recent studies, such as the ones by Arlene Russo and David J. Skal, have been persuasive in their discussion of how vampirism in late twentieth century fiction and popular culture acted as a metaphorical representation of the fear of diseases such as AIDS, which spread through blood and other bodily fluids. In the Nineties, Russo argues, the extremely prolific publication of fiction centred on 'sanguine vampires', drew attention to how, in a 'paranoia gripped AIDS society', blood exchanges were 'rapidly becoming taboo'.[85] The vampire has been treated as the ideal vector for mirroring the anxiety about the spreading of such a horrible disease; like the disease itself, the vampire worked as unseen by human eyes, and continued to kill people undisturbed. The sexual politics that have been easily associated with vampires for centuries made the connection between the creature and the disease even more solid, as AIDS is usually transmitted through sexual intercourse. Overall, scholarship has been keen on exploring the connection, and has therefore explored it well.

Undoubtedly, the connection between vampirism, viruses, and the spreading of disease in the human world—as it appeared in late twentieth-century fiction—is still visible and identifiable in contemporary examples. Nonetheless, something has changed. While the twentieth century was still keen on maintaining the connection among vampires, viruses, and sexuality, the twenty-first century has 'evolved' into viewing the metaphorical representation of vampirism as a virus into a much more genetically-based issue. What was once a latent connection—both imagistically and linguistically—has now become manifest. Vampires are a genetic issue, and the idea of virus allows this issue to come to the surface. To grasp this, it is important to remember that viruses—unlike other disease-carrying microscopic organism such as bacteria—consists primarily of genetic material (either DNA or RNA), surrounded by a coat of protein. By their very nature, they are able to latch onto a cell and get inside of them. Conceptually speaking, this notion of latching on already brings the vampire to mind, as images of fangs 'latching' onto the victim's body become vivid. The viruses spread by inflicting their own DNA (or RNA) on healthy cells; this is indeed an important element, as the virus, to put it simply, cannot multiply until it alters the genetic material of healthy cells in the host's body, so that the actually host will 'become' the virus. In a way, then it is a possible to suggest that viruses 'engineer' the host's cells by genetically modifying them. Viruses can so be treated as genetic engineers, quickly exchanging one genetic set for the other, and causing a quick, evolutionary mutation.

The notion of seeing the connection between vampires and viruses as connected to issues of genetic engineering is also strengthened by the important knowledge that, when genetically modifying organisms, scientists are known to use viruses to combine the genes of one organism with the genes of another, or even modify a gene. The virus-related practice is known as the 'vector' method.[86] One they have created a strand of DNA in vitro, scientists directly insert it into the host's genome using a virus. As viruses insert their DNA into healthy cells, they also reproduce and carry the mutation, which then becomes systemic to the whole organism. The vector method is considered a quick way of genetically modifying an organism, as it allows the modified genes to take hold of the very genomic reproductive system that allows the organism to exist. The nature of the vector method—relying on a virus to genetically modify an organism—makes it very akin to the way in which vampirism seems to work in contemporary fiction. In *The Passage*, Cronin describes the vampiric virus as 'awakening' a biological 'recollection', an 'instinct, a felling etched over eons into the human DNA': a virulent 'power' that turns the human into a being ravaged by 'blood hunger'.[87] The virus is 'transmitted' through the bite and it quickly spreads throughout the body; as it reaches the genomic cells, the vampiric virus replaces the human DNA with vampiric genetic material, therefore altering the biomorphic structure of the host almost immediately. The liminality of the vampire is transmitted through the own liminality of the virus. As the human cells die, the virus lives. As the human dies, the vampire is resurrected.

The profound genetic-altering nature of both the vector method and vampirism allow the connection between virus and vampire to be seen as a warning in relation to genetic engineering. Culturally speaking, the word 'virus' carries negative connotations; when something it is said to 'spread like a virus', it is implied that it is uncontrollable and often happens without the host's consent. This cultural understanding of virulent distribution casts a shadow over the notion of genetic engineering itself, for which the vampire acts as a ready metaphor. The virus is the medium through which one and the other are connected. As a 'turned' creature, the vampire lingers at the margins between life and death; it is not born, it is engineered to function even though it technically should not. It is 'reborn' not through nature, but through artificial modification. Vampires are indeed often referred to as 'unnatural'. If one considers the genetic connection between vampire, virus and human, that sense of 'unnatural' relates to that which is not born as such, but it is transmitted, recreated, redrafted. It is possible to suggest that, recalling the processes of vector-based genetic modification, the vampire allows any form of genetic engineering to be seeing as an abject form, a liminal practice that defies the boundaries of life, death, and species. The vampirically re-engineered—although admittedly stronger, faster, and virtually eternal—challenges the very concept of life. Whether dead, undead, or technically 'still alive' even after the transformation—as clearly stated in Deborah Harness' *All Souls* series—the vampire is a genetic mutation of the human host. The use of the term virus to refer to vampirism is no longer a latent warning against the spread of disease, but a manifest critique of the nature of engineered organisms, their place in the world, and their relationship to human beings. If genetic material is, biologically speaking, what makes a human as such, then its infectious altering is a paradoxically appealing atrocity against humanity itself.

FRAMEWORKS OF DISEASE

An important element testifying to the genetic, re-engineered superiority of the vampires is that the majority of them—if not all of them—are known to be invulnerable to human diseases, as Ward makes it clear the *Brotherhood*: they cannot 'get HIV or hep C or any STD'; vampires are not 'carriers of those diseases', and 'human viruses don't affect' them.[88] The same series also clearly states that vampires 'don't get cancer', a position shared by several other narratives.[89] The idea that vampirism makes the body impervious to disease in also stated in *The Passage*: 'no cancer, no heart disease, no diabetes, no Alzheimer's'.[90] In spite of small differences in the recounting of the lack of disease from narrative to narrative, the pervasive idea is that, to put it in very simple terms, vampires 'don't get sick'; they are impervious to human illnesses, and their sophisticated, highly evolved bodies do not make them susceptible to developing any form of deadly disease. With this in mind, it is possible to argue that vampirism, in a way, represents the triumph of quick genetic engineering. The exchange of genes, from human to vampire, causes the cells to work more efficiently, and they are made almost invulnerable. There is no denying here that diseases—especially maladies such as cancer—are a deep concern of the contemporary world, and that the dream of defeating them forever is definitely of great appeal. Scientists believe that genetic engineering 'could be used to prolong life and give people superhuman traits'.[91] The fiction answers this desire by providing vampires with strong, 'superhuman' bodies'. The latent similarities between turning and genetic engineering create a connection of possibilities within the storyline that makes the dream attainable. The implications for a lack of disease in vampire narratives are significant. A being that cannot become ill seems to defy any conception of complex organism as we know it; animals, plants, and humans all share a common ground of disease. Sickness, in turn, assumes more than a simple medical value, but steps into the realm of social construction as well.

Indeed, disease is not a strictly physical entity. It is true that in its primary aspects, disease can be construed as a biological event, one not strictly modified by the particular context in which it occurs. Nonetheless, it is important to consider that, in Western cultures, a disease also takes on a social dimension, one that includes lay views of the illness itself, how to react to it, how to treat it—both communally and medically—and what its overall effects are in regard to how the population is organised structurally. Within this socio-biological framework, the understanding of disease in any given culture exceeds its seemingly simple position as a 'less than optimum physiological state'.[92] The body, after all, is also a social entity as much as it is a physical one, so any of its effects, mutations, changes, and embellishments will carry repercussions of an anthropological nature as well. Attitudes towards disease are undoubtedly contextual and are known to change historically. This is not only due to the nature and occurrence of disease itself, but also to the medical advances that allow for treatment of sickness. When we think of disease, therefore, it is important to frame it not only as a biological experience, but also as a social one. Social experience finds its validation, of course, not by simple biological ordinance, but through fellow agreement within the collective opinion.

Disease is a constructed concept; it is a re-elaborated notion which merges both the seemingly un-contextual nature of the organic manifestation with its place in socio-cultural frameworks. Defining the place of disease in any particular organisation is not simply an ontological issue, but also bears connections to discourses of an epistemological and phenomenological nature. As medical thought and practice are rarely divorced from cultural constraints, outlining what a disease 'is' cannot be free of questions regarding how the disease operates, and what effects it has on the populace, both physically and psychologically. Explaining sickness, therefore, is a complex process that is never free of enterprise, and entails considerations over what the sickness represents in its various incarnations. The spread of a disease—or, simultaneously, the lack of a specific illness from both an individual organism and the group in which that organism belongs—relies on 'agreed-upon etiologies' which 'at once incorporate and sanction a society's fundamental ways of organising its world'.[93]

In these terms, disease can be viewed as an important defining characteristic of a society, as it highlights points of focus for the community. Health is not simply a physiological state, but is given meaning in view of interpersonal relationships. In these terms, the relationship between vampires and disease—or lack thereof—cannot be treated simply as a physiological occurrence—that is to say, what physical implications are there for a body that cannot get ill, with longevity and arguable 'immortality' becoming important concerns. Indeed, as disease carries a social dimension as well, one needs to wonder how a society that is disease-free will articulate itself, as the threat of sickness—with its inevitably psychological repercussions—is not a reality to be considered.

A number of scholars have explored the importance of disease as a socio-medical unit, pointing out the varied and various layers of interpretations for illness within a given group. Among the numerous studies, that of Charles E. Rosenberg has uncovered several rhizomatic branchings of disease as an entity, suggesting that the difficulty in tying disease to a single area of life is in keeping with its elusive nature. Specifically, Rosenberg claims that to fully understand disease in its social, medical, historical, and cultural contexts, one needs to understand that the implications of disease are multiple: 'disease is at once a biological event, a generation specific repertoire of verbal constructs reflecting medicine's intellectual and institutional history, an occasions of and potential legitimation of public policy, an aspect of social role and individual—interpsychic—identity,[and] a sanction of cultural values'.[94] One can see here how Rosenberg puts together several aspects of the concept of disease beyond its medical conformation, and views it as an important structuring element for social and societal relations. Rosenberg's identification of the manifold interpretation of the very idea of disease in human societies can be used as a guide to uncover how the absence of disease in vampire narratives takes on an inevitably metaphorical role in providing a critique of interpersonal and institutional relations, accompanied by a multifaceted utopian re-elaboration of corporeal legacies in their cultural contexts.

There is no doubting that, both socially and physically, 'disease concepts imply, constrain, and legitimate individual behaviour'.[95] The behaviour in question here refers not only to the person affected by the disease, but also to how those around the sick will react to them and treat them. Symbolically speaking, disease is a reminder of mortality; it is the proof that the body is not eternal and omnipotent, but a physical entity that could falter at any moment. Unlike cases where death is caused suddenly by accident (for instance), disease often maintain a prolonged chronological presence, and psycho-social relations around the sick need to be re-evaluated to accommodate for the traumatic journey cause by illness. In this, disease creates a developed layer of interpersonal connection; presented with any possibility of finality, humans are known to develop feelings of sympathy. Disease, in a way, can be viewed as a morbid linking agent. The identification of disease—in the majority of Western societies—is the trigger for compassion. One could claim that empathy is indeed a definitive product of the 'social construction of illness'.[96]

If the threat of disease allows individuals to develop an empathetic relation with their fellow man, then the lack of sickness in vampire societies is an important shaping element for the relationships between vampires themselves. Viewed as an intra-psychic entity, the lack of disease in the vampire inevitably causes a shift in psycho-behavioural compounds. Vampires are often described as 'detached' and unable to relate to others, whether human or vampires. This characteristic of the vampiric psyche is clearly stated in examples such as Farnsworth's *Nathaniel Cade* series. Farnsworth clearly describes Cade as naturally lacking social compassion or empathy; the vampire is often portrayed as desperately trying to emotionally relate to his human companions and offer comfort in social situations that seemingly demand, but failing miserably: 'Simple human interaction was often beyond him [. . .] When he became a vampire, he was changed on every level'.[97] Cade's inability to construct a compassionate relationship with others could be connected to his inability to get sick, a state that is marvelled at throughout the series:

> Cade is functionally immortal. That is to say, his cells do not undergo regular cell death, or even aging or degradation [. . .] Cell repairs are nearly perfect—any cells destroyed by an outside force are replaced with indistinguishable copies. [He] can heal from any wound. [. . .] The subject's blood itself is filled with previously unidentified hormones, enzymes and antibodies. The compounds may explain the subject's immunity to our test-panel of diseases.[98]

As disease is a trigger for compassion, the lack of illness in Cade's existence makes him disconnected, emotionally isolated.[99] Rosenberg reminds us that, oncee 'crystallised in the form of a specific entity', disease serves 'as a structuring factor'. In this, disease is a 'social mediator'.[100] In Cade's case, the lack of disease (or even the possibility thereof) does not provide the vampire with any social mediation. For the vampire, functions are not mediated through conceptions of health and disease, and—as a result—neither are interpersonal relationships. In human societies, disease must be articulated and accepted as an entity, in order to become an 'actor' in a 'complex network of social negotiations'.[101] As illness is not a significant 'actor' in Cade's existence, his ability to construct an emotional connection with others is diminished to the point of absence. If it is true that we measure the body and the self not through health, but also through disease, then the inability to become ill removes the vampire from any structure of relationship that relies on bodily functions in their corporeal, cultural, and psychic contexts.

VAMPIRES, OR THE MEDICAL CHIMERA

The changing understanding of disease in contemporary vampire narratives is undoubtedly connected to a shift in attitudes not only towards the concept of illness itself, but also around the very notion of medicine, its uses and its contexts. Nick Fox and Katie Ward have drawn attention to the inescapable connections between health, the body, medicine, and the self, claiming that these must be understood as 'interdependent entities that cannot be separated'.[102]

The social side of medicine is particularly of interest here. In the Western world, medical procedures are employed not just to cure disease, but also to enhance the body and make it more 'acceptable'; cultural parameters act as a key here in deciphering the social value of the body and its appearance. Deborah Lupton points out that, in the post-200 era, it is possible to notice 'an increasing dependence upon medicine to provide the answers to social as well as medical problems'.[103] A vast number of pharmaceutical products are sold—from performance enhancers to diet and even tanning pills—in order to augment the physical presentation of the body and the impact it will have on social relations. The new adage that the twenty-first century is the age of the pharmaceutical comes to mind here, and it undoubtedly rings true when it comes to contemporary vampire narratives. Although it is stressed on a number of occasions that vampires 'do not get sick', they also display a very close relationship with pharmaceuticals and medical research. In the *Black Dagger Brotherhood*, the vampire doctor Havers dedicates much of his time, unsuccessfully, to developing a new medical method that will allow vampire blood to be stored in medical solutions, and transfused intravenously, so that individuals do not have to interact to feed: 'through a donor and storage programme', those 'who chose to forgo the intimacy of drinking could live their lives in peace'.[104] This is aimed at removing the interpersonal connection needed between two vampires (male and female) in order to survive. In the *Midnight Breed*, vampire scientists are committed to finding a drug-based cure to bloodlust, the addictive 'illness' that afflicts the species, so that they can lead a respectable social existence.[105] Considering the lack of real disease in the vampire world, the use of medical research for 'social purposes' emerges as peculiar. Although there is a bio-medical reasoning behind the vampire drugs, their uses seem to be more focused on relationships and notions of an anthropological nature: how the drugs and the medical constructs allow vampires 'to live' in the world with more ease.

This side of the pharmaceutical industry does not emerge more strongly in any other narrative than it does in Mariani's *Vampire Federation*. In this storyline, vampires use specific pharmaceutical drugs to blend with the human population; the medicines are commissioned by the Federation itself and developed in specifically-designed pharmaceutical facilities, run by the vampires themselves. The drugs are distributed by the Federation only to 'registered users': listed vampires on whom the Federation can keep a close eye. Only by registering with the higher power can vampires gain access to the drugs that will make their existence a lot less complicated and socially liveable. This element, it could be argued, already suggests a critique of pharmaceutical companies and medical structures in the Western world, 'controlling and oppressing' patients and 'abusing their medical power'.[106] The drugs supplied by the Federation are indeed quite inventive, and being specifically designed around vampires, they also echo a number of traditional/folkloristic weaknesses and strengths of the vampire. One common drug is known as 'Vambloc', and is used to control the vampire population and protect its existence. Vambloc is injected into humans on occasions when they have been bitten by vampires. The drug allows vampires to feed undisturbed. Vambloc not only causes humans to lose memory of the event—protecting the vampire race from a social exposure that would likely result in fear and persecution—but it also stops the humans 'from turning'.[107] In a way, Vambloc can be perceived as form of vampire contraception, keeping the numbers of the race under control.

Another drug in Mariani's narratives, and an extremely popular one among Federation-registered vampires, is Solazal; true to its name—with *sol* being the Latin term for 'sun'—the drug reduces the vampires' photosensitivity and allows them to circulate during the day, in order to mix with humans more efficiently.[108] Both drugs clearly have a biological function, as well as a social function. Medicine is used to make the vampire more socially acceptable, and able to conform to norms and regulations. Vambloc and Solazal provide the structures for establishing a form of vampiric medical care, where the social and the medical become intertwined. On the one hand, the Federation upholds and echoes the widely-known maxim, at least in most Western societies, that 'access to medical care' is 'a social good and the inalienable right of every person'.[109] Nonetheless, as is often the case in human organisation, only registered vampires are given this 'right'. What are considered to be 'illegal vampires' are not only not given the right to pharmaceuticals, but are also persecuted by the Federation, as the vampire Tommy clearly states in *The Cross*: ' The Feds have got their own way of dealing with illegals'.[110] Unsurprisingly, another Federation-developed drug is employed to carry out the sentence: Nosferol, the most potent pharmaceutical concoction known to vampires, and the only one able to destroy them.[111] The name Nosferol is another linguistic play on the term 'nosferatu', popularised by Murnau's eponymous film and believed to be a calque—borrowed from the Romanian language—of 'undead'.

This message is made so graspable it is almost explicit. Mariani constructs a critique of the medical and pharmaceutical systems of Western societies, which are not only based on control, but are also responsible for seemingly deciding who has access to care—and, to some extent, life—among the population. Drugs are an extension and a symbolic icon of power, a metaphorical incarnation of social, political, and biological control. The Federation exercises hold on its members by asking vampires to register and report on their whereabouts and activities. In turn, it maintains that control by distributing drugs that govern not only the vampire's biological functions but also—necessarily—the individual's social relations. Although 'health' is not seemingly the banner under which the Federation operates, the vampires are controlled by the constant threat of a gruesome, drug-induced death. So, in a way, the healthy and fully operational body remains the centre of the vampires' attention. The focus on the body as the site of control grants the Federation—as a state-power—the power of ritualised scrutiny which enacts a form of social dependency between individuals and their cultural objectifications. The active relationship between health, social control and pharmaceutics within the vampire framework is strongly connected to the practices that, as Mary Douglas identified, construct the body politic through the symbolic medium of the physical body.[112] The healthy and sociable body—encompassing two sides of experience into one—is considered as not simply fashioned by relationships, but as inhabiting the construction of those relationships. The dimensions of the vampire's physicality is simultaneously shaped, unleashed and limited by statutory dogmatic factors. The Federation's monitoring activities over the member's bodies undoubtedly take on a panoptic nuance, and provide a critique of how 'the State'—or any form of monitoring political power in Western societies—undertakes surveillance of its citizens' bodies and their socialities.

The framework in which the relationship between vampires and drug use is developed uncovers questions regarding the way in which embodiment, control health, and disease are experienced and understood in Western societies. The organisation of the vampire's constitutional rights to sociality and pharmaceutical use—as expressed in Mariani's texts—is reminiscent of Bryan Turner's concept of 'somatic society', in which the body—as it is understood in Western contexts—becomes a representation of social organisation and works symbolically with the power structures to maintain order and control.[113] In doing this, the body also shapes into a metaphor for all those social anxieties that are generated by the establishment of a directorial mentality, aided by the extended reach of political and cultural activities. The view on biomedical science and its effects on the body—the fiction seems to suggest—is inevitably generated by larger socio-cultural systems of meaning in ways that often exceed the consciousness of the average individual.

In its medical understandings, the re-engineered body of the vampire becomes an odd mixture of discourse and matter, inseparable from its connections to complex socio-political attributes. Western societies in the early twenty-first century are indeed characterised by a distinct and strong reliance on scientific medicine; that reliance cannot be divorced from its meaning in cultural terms, drawing attention to how an understanding of disease and health—especially when treated as symbolic constructs within biomedical structures –will inevitably be connected to issues of identity. The focus on the medical in contemporary vampire literature, therefore, can be treated as a constituting agent sited at the reciprocally dependent interchange of practice, meaning, and social relations. That site, in turn, allows the metaphorical value of both health and disease to emerge as a representational tool in uncovering the relationship between culture, physicality, and the fantasy of immortality.

Deborah Lupton claims that contemporary societies are obsessed with 'locating the genetic precursor to illnesses, disease and behaviours'.[114] As medicine is now able to cure a large number of diseases, the knowledge that some cannot be treated is cause of extreme vexation for scientists and lay people alike. From the lay people's perspective, there is also an expectation of success. For the populations of Western societies, illness and disease—and indeed the death that results from them—have now been culturally transformed into something 'frightening and unexpected'.[115] With scientific medicine having defeated more fatally infectious diseases in the Western world—and, indeed, using infection in the lab as a way to improve the genetic structure of the human—diseases like cancer are inevitably 'a shock'. In a context of overarching biomedical success, the notion of something being incurable is not only frightening, but also somewhat inconceivable. Contemporary Western societies have developed a high set of expectations surrounding health and the disease-free body prevailing. Genetic research has taken such strides that the notion of being able to identify disease-related genes, or the possibility that they can be mutated and destroyed, is within grasp and very appealing indeed. Often provided with superiorly formed DNA, and a resistance to forms of human disease, the vampire functions as a suitable metaphor for that appeal. The vampire indulges the fantasy that, with appropriate genomic manipulation and biomedical research, disease and illness can be defeated at genetic level.

This specific preoccupation is made evident in Kevin Ashman's novel *Vampire*. In the narrative, the DNA of an ancient Egyptian vampire is identified as the cradle of 'immortality' in genetic terms. The choice of Egypt as the source place for vampires—also referred to as 'nighwalkers'—is particularly significant here, as ancient Egyptians were known to have a cultural and dogmatic preoccupation with immortality that rivals our own contemporary one. The blood of the vampire shows an ability to regenerate and contains specific chromosomic material that, mixed with human DNA, could grant the latter an unprecedented ability to resist disease and, possibly, never age: the body of the vampire, in these terms, is said to 'renew itself', and this is the key to 'true immortality.'[116] Although spiritual belief in 'living forever'—connected to Gods and afterlife—is exchanged for the alleged certainty of scientific research, the focus on the abnormal body as the source of answers remains the same. The shift from religious to scientific in Ashman's narrative is arguably connected to the increasing secularisation of Western societies, which has developed concomitantly with medical research and is a defining characteristic of our time. The increase in average life expectancies and decrease in number of deaths from disease have culturally transformed biomedicine into the ultimate weapon against illness and premature death. The treatment of the vampire body in Ashman's novel mirrors this position.

Unlike other contemporary authors, Ashman does not present the vampire as the product of some magical or supernatural transformation. The original vampire—the human known as 'Sekhmet', who later in the story 'turns' others and claims deity status for herself—has the ability to regenerate and 'live forever.' Her vampiric status is understood as a genetic mutation caused by the serendipitous meeting of two viruses in one organism: 'Two separate infections, both latching onto a blood cell and living long enough to alter the actual structure of the host'.[117] Instead of perishing, the vampire returns 'from the jaws of death', with a hunger for blood that 'envelops every cell 'of her being'.[118] The virulent genetic exchange here is revelatory. Not only does it reinforce the connection between the idea of virus in relation to vampirism and its understanding as a metaphor for genetic manipulation, but it also puts resistance to disease and aging within human grasp. In the narrative, a biomedical research company becomes interested in the vampire's genetic material, seeing it as 'the cure' for our genetic faults. The paradoxical notion of picturing the vampiric 'disease' as a cure is bestowed a level of verisimilitude and authenticity by the knowledge that genetic improvement is indeed carried out by contemporary scientific through virulent diffusion. The vampire here provides not only hope, but also tangibility for the idea of re-engineering the human into a more efficient being.

The vampire, however, is not simply a symbol of hope and the conviction of biomedical science. It is not just a beacon of possibility and potentiality: it is also a reminder. As the list of vampiric super-qualities are listed in the fiction, what steps out of its latency and emerges as truly unavoidable is—in fact—the inadequacy of the human body. This is clearly evident in Ashman's *Vampire*; as the amazing capabilities of vampire organisms are recounted, so are the faults of the human cells. This is of course an overarching quality of contemporary vampire fiction. As descriptions of vampires are indulged in terms such as 'superior', stronger', 'faster' and, on occasions, even 'eternal' and 'immortal', one cannot help but wonder about the light this casts on the second term of comparison, the human.[119] Indeed, as a matter of unavoidability when the comparison is established, humans emerge as 'weak', 'lowly', 'expendable', 'mortal'. Concepts of health and illness in the vampire context are resonant of the social and medical structures that outline the human body as a site of conflict. On the one hand, it is a fluid and changing entity, rather than a static one. Evolutionary and biomedical research assures that that the human body is forever in the process of being made and remade. It is 'an assemblage of relations with other bodies, including non-human phenomena, which is constantly changing'.[120] And it is precisely that possibility of interaction with the 'non-human'— whether actual or representational, as in the case of vampires—that makes the human body open to changes and shifts. On the other hand, however, the fluidity of the human body exposes its fragility, its fleeting nature, its propensity to malfunction, dismantle, and eventually die. Vampires are the medium through which the fragility of the transient human body is conveyed; and this is a body that needs improvement, perfecting, and constant attention in order to survive. The vampire, while providing frameworks for potential evolutionary achievement, is also a sensationalised *memento mori* for the human race. Ultimately the connections between vampires, biomedicine, disease, and genetic futurism are entangled with the paradoxical questions that characterise the human organism in its cultural, social and medical contexts, proving that—even when indulged in fantasies of superhumanity—the treatment of the human body is still surrounded, as Lupton suggest, by 'controversy, conflict, and emotion'.[121]

NEW MONSTERS

Although there are advantages to the human body once it has been 'engineered' into a vampire—from strength and resilience, to virtual immortality and even being able to fly, as in the case of Eric in the *Sookie Stackhouse* series—the opinion on the result of the exchange is often split. Vampires are not all the same, this much is made clear; like humans, they retain the ability to make choices, and how they treat their main food source seems to be one of the most important elements on which they are judged. If one takes 'turning' to be a form of quick genetic engineering, then it is possible to suggest that the moral outlook on vampires—based as it is on evaluations on their bodies—acts as a critique of the issue of genetic engineering itself. In the human world, opinions are divided on the issue. People undoubtedly disagree on whether genetic engineering even does any good, and whether it is moral or immoral.[122] Issues of morality are also prevalent in vampire literature, where some vampires refuse to take advantage of their 'superior' position and drink the blood of humans. This is particularly evident in the *Nathaniel Cade* series, where human blood drinking is the source of extreme moral conflict for Cade himself: 'He refuses to drink the blood of a human, even though human blood is what his vampiric body is designed to mainly consume and metabolize'.[123] This moral struggle already points us in the direction of seeing vampirism as a veiled discussion of the genetic issue, with ethics playing an important part. The moral conflicts experienced by the vampire could be said to mirror those experienced by the general public, and the scientific community alike.

Some scientists, for their part, believe that genetic engineering could be used to cure a number of diseases, or—with time—even to accelerate recovery processes after an injury.[124] This therapeutic function of genetic manipulation undoubtedly holds a strong connection to the contemporary vampire motif. The first thing to consider is, both genetically and culturally, the widespread propensity for vampires to heal at an accelerated speed. This seems indeed to be a universal characteristic of vampires in the contemporary context, present and shared by the narratives. In Kim Harrison's *Hollows* series, we are told that vampires 'have the ability to heal with an unearthly quickness'.[125] Some injuries, however, are said to be too terrible even for vampires to recover from, so even the vampire's body is not completely impervious to damage. Following a time-honoured tradition and folkloristic line, decapitation is the most common way to kill a vampire, with it being the only bodily damage that they will not be able to overcome. In this line of thought, staking comes as a close second in several narratives, yet still maintains the condition that a stake must go through the heart. This is made clear by Fransworth in *Blood Oath*: 'In order to kill [the vampire], it would be necessary to completely destroy his cardiac function—through massive damage to the heart—or sever his head completely from his body'.[126] Overall, however, even gunshot and stab wounds will not propose an immediate threat to the vampire's body. As long as they continue to ingest a healthy supply of human blood—and this seems to be the only true requirements—they will recover quickly, and it will be as if they were never injured in the first place.

'Superhuman' is a provocative term to use here, but it bears important connections to the world of genetic engineering, and strengthens the validity of vampirism as a metaphorical representation of enhanced corporeal improvement. It is exactly this term, however, that points us in the direction of seeing vampirism as a negative outcome, tying contemporary fiction to the tradition of viewing vampires as 'monsters'. There is no denying that this term is still widely used for referring to vampires in contemporary narratives.[127] But the motivations behind the position seem to have changed. This negative outlook could derive from the belief that genetic engineering is in itself 'wrong'. Parmalee reminds us that, in spite of the apparent advantages provided by genetic engineering, there are still those who fear it as an abomination, used to separate classes of people. Theologically speaking, some maintain that the formation of new species should be the act of God, and not of man. We have seen that, in terms of genetics, it is stressed that vampires appear to be at a more developed evolutionary stage than humans, and it often suggested that huamns are, as Ward puts, 'too weak to be of interest' and 'evolutionarily not good enough'.[128] The vampires are efficient in showing the inadequacy of the human. Simultaneously, however, they also show the potential for the human to change, to mutate, to improve. Whether created by turning—a shift from human to beyond-human—or born through (most often than not) interbreeding with humans, vampires are a promise of development, a potential of what could be, an instigation of desire and longing. They are the dream of strength, of perfection, of virtually eternal youth; but that dream is attainable, realisable.

The focus on change, advancement, and improvement on the human here is the key in interpreting the vampire as a new form of twenty-first century monster. They are 'monstrous' in the sense that they occupy the liminal space between 'categories that might just be the future'.[129] They are the monsters of mixing, of experimentation, of new possibilities. They are the face of the new genetic frontier, where the body is a malleable entity that can be manipulated, transformed, improved. To fully grasp this point, one needs to turn to the very etymological links hidden in the very term 'monster'. The word originates from the Latin, and it has links to both the term *monstrum*—meaning portent, omen, and sign—and the term *monere*, which means 'to warn'. With this etymological reading in mind, the 'monster' acts literally as a warning, and is bound to resurface and be reshaped according to the concerns of any given context. In the guise of 'monster', therefore, the vampire takes on a peculiar revelatory and futuristic imperative upon its very representation. As a modified human—in its various biological and aesthetic incarnations—the vampire is monstrous in the sense that it is a potential shape, a virtual form of development awaiting actualisation and, as Pramod Nayar puts it, a configuration of human life awaiting 'corpo-realisation'.[130]

As a genetic re-imagining of what was once humanity, the vampiric monster is a symbol of development, an icon of revolution that inevitably directs the attention to the possibilities of the future. That future is, of course, the home of genetic engineering, of a speeded-up evolutionary system which can be made to happen at will and without delay, just as the genetic shift occurs in the vampire once the changes takes place. Genetic manipulation—veiled in the conceptual folds of the vampire's body—does of course carry a number of cultural, medical, and ethical anxieties, and still has—in the popular imagination—connections to the uncontrollable and the fear of the 'inhuman'. The connection between the vampire and genetic transformations, however, is not necessarily dystopian in human terms, even though—and this is virtually unavoidable when vampires are concerned—it still combines matters of life and death in a clearly ambiguous and uncategorisable way. It is that ambiguity, and that difficulty in recognition—almost human, but not quite so—that adds a layer of uncanny to the vampire's monstrous embodiment; the warning lies in the inability to pinpoint the cause of the difference, just as it is often impossible to maintain control over any form of genetic manipulation in the human world. And it is precisely that impossibility that, however, makes the genetically-controlled vampires into a gruesome, grotesque and yet incredibly appealing artefact, carrying the ghostly outlook of 'something that we can recognise and other elements that we cannot'.[131] The vampire as a monster is a warning not only towards the enticement of possibilities, but also the unease and potential fear that those possibilities might ignite. It draws attention to the breaking of boundaries and the construction of new, and much more flexible ones. In suggesting the potentiality of genetic changes, the vampire fulfils its potential as a monstrous creature in attempting to create a new form of rationality for the species that relies not on borders, but on blended spaces.

In drawing attention to the potentiality of genetic experimentation, and the fluidity of the boundaries between species, vampires inevitably represent—in what Nayar labels 'the true tradition of the monstrous'—widespread cultural anxieties about what the 'human' is and what classifies it as such.[132] The monstrous nature of the vampire truly finds its most effectual *incarnation* in its function as the aesthetic agent of both expansion and extension. In its purpose as a portent of possible things to come, and a simultaneous embodiment of wishes and desires in relation to the body, the vampire raises questions about how to truly identify the human in a context of genetic alteration and biological shifts. Instances where vampires are born out of the interbreeding between humans and 'other' creatures—as is the case in the *Black Dagger Brotherhood* and the *Midnight Breed*—are particularly effective in questioning if it is actually still possible to pinpoint a pure concept of humanity within the structures of the bio-medical and the evolutionary. For if a hybrid of human and vampire is made possible, who is to decide—effectively—where one begins or the other ends. And even in cases when vampires are 'turned', the changes are so radical and yet so subtle, that it is often impossible to tell the two factions apart. That inability to categorise, when presented with the vampire, is the source of unease and confusion. The lack of clear boundary makes the vampire a creature of aesthetic liminality. One might want to recall the contention—already suggested by Geoffrey Galt Harpman in 1982—that classificatory regimes are integral to aesthetic and the identity systems that derive from them, allowing the Gothic and the grotesque to thrive on confusion and the breakdown of category.[133]

The potential dissolution and defiance of borders, or the inability to even identify those borders as existing in the first place, is what marks the body of the vampire as different. That difference, however, is imperceptible because it plays on notions of humanity and challenges its transparency. And if it is true that categories and boundaries are tied to identities, than the very existence of the vampire pushes the frontier of the human self. As the boundaries become permeable, the vampire re-defines limits, and creates visions of newly attainable biomorphic forms. This is truly the core of the anxiety, that genetics are the ideal medium for collapsing categories. And that the monstrous is no longer an entity removed from humanity, but a close relative to it, perhaps even a generation or mis-generation of the human body, something which is no longer conceived only in the realm of the supernatural, but that exists within the dominion of the scientific. Although the vampire in the fiction still retains its pervasively eerie qualities, that strangeness can be read as a metaphorical projection of the anxiety surrounding genetic experimentation.[134] It is an uncanny presence that is not produced by supernatural evil, but born in the laboratory.[135] It is the representational pinnacle of human evolution, the embodiment of physical superiority which guarantees a longer, possibly eternal existence. The vampire indulges vivid human re-imaginings of the world where the physical can be conquered through the ever-improving manipulation of life forms. In so doing, however, the vampire also warns against the ultimate charge that must be paid to science: the price for improving the human—and making sure it overcomes its weaknesses—might in fact be humanity itself.

2   Vampire Bodies

It is without question that contemporary vampires carry the legacy of hundreds of years of folklore and centuries of literary tradition, which have evolved into other incarnations—from film to comics—to cement an idea of the vampire in people's minds. That legacy, of course, comes with the weight of expectation regarding all that is related to the vampire. It would be inconceivable to suggest that, as contemporary thinkers, we are unaffected by the cultural framework—which consolidates ideas of the supernatural—in which we live. Ontological definitions are littered with aesthetic and political augmentations which are virtually impossible to separate from context.

In terms of looks and presentation, the question that seems to be pervasive and at the core of any investigation of the vampire is, in fact, what is a vampire? What is it made of? What are the defining characteristics that form the basis for that very definition? The temptation would be to say that, in the now seemingly established literary sense, vampires are creatures with the white pallor of death, unbearably beautiful in their outlook, with sharp fangs and (possibly) long flowing hair. But even that definition is contaminated, in the contemporary moments, by visions of Anne Rice's vampires, with their ethereal frames and hypnotic eyes. More to the point, contemporary narratives are full of 'vampires' who do fit that description at all, and that range from the unchanging undead to muscular specimens who seem to be the ideal cultural incarnation of strength and power.

Clearly, the ontology of the vampire is not a straightforward one. One may be inclined to give a definition of what the vampire 'is' in relation to not only what the vampire looks like, but what a vampire does. A straightforward answer to any of these questions may be difficult, if not impossible to provide. It is not my intention, therefore, to attempt an overall definition of the vampire, either in relation to the vampire's physicality or the vampire's 'self'. Rather, it proves productive to approach the vampire from a lateral perspective, placing the attention on building a comparative framework for identifying patterns of presentation and behaviour. Those patterns, one can quickly see, operate more efficiently not simply according to the way vampires 'are' in relation to themselves—without falling into questions of an epistemological nature—but also what position they occupy in the structures of human representation, and, to some extent, life.

A TRANSFORMED MORPHOLOGY

Any representation of the vampire body is not just a result of biology. While the genetic side is unavoidable—and, for the most part, a paradoxically undiscussed part of the vampire experience—it is important to remember that ontology is not simply a matter of science. This becomes particularly relevant when the possible sexualisation of any embodied entity takes place, not only in relation to what is attractive and what is not, but also in connection to the structures and outlooks that constitute a clearly identifiable and categorisable individual. Sex, when it comes to bodies—whether they are human or vampire bodies—is not just an element for distinction, but a framework through which the ontological questions regarding the subject can be pursued.

When discussing the 'nature' of the body, Elizabeth Grosz asks an important question: 'Do bodies, all bodies (even nonhuman bodies) have a specifically sexual dimension [. . .] which is physically and culturally inscribed according to its morphology?'[1] While a simple answer to this question may be hard to find, Grosz's enquiry highlights the idea that morphology is but the beginning of categorisation when it comes to highlighting sexual differences between corporeal entities, and that those differences are also reliant on cultural demands regarding physicality. From this, it is possible to derive the preliminary concept that the body—especially the highly conceptual vampire body—is the key to unlocking how physical characteristics are not a fixed idea, but their acceptance and definition is contingent on the historical context and socio-cultural framework in which they are placed. The awareness of this possibility is an essential starting point for any enquiry into the ontology of the vampire, from its physical characteristics to its abstract understanding.

The vampire body is not an inert concept. Although it exists in a fictional framework, its conceptualisation is not that of a universally programmed being who has purely physical characteristics. The vampire body does not function in unchangeable ways. It is a malleable form, one that is never independent of its 'cultural milieu and value'.[2] The differences that one can identify between vampire bodies are symptomatic of specific organisations. Those differences can function on two levels, each bringing attention to the different use of vampire physicality. On the one hand, the physical differences between vampires function inter-narrative; that is, one can identify different types of vampires within the same storyline, each group speaking for a different side of the vampire experience and its uses. Inter-narrative distinctions are also particularly relevant when discussing psychic abilities which, ontologically speaking, complicate the use of definitions. On the other hand, physical differences between vampires can work extra-narrative, and be only thrown into sharp relief when placed into the wider context and compared to other vampire storylines. This way of identifying differences, both morphologically and conceptually, is connected not only to context, but also (and most importantly) to intricate issues of genre and readership. Grosz contends that 'differences between bodies, not only at the level of experience and subjectivity but also at the level of practical and physical capacities, enjoy considerable social and historical variations'.[3] In this framework, an assessment of vampire bodies will be no different in its need to draw attention to how differences—often radical in their conception—speak of different contexts.

It would be unwise to assume that any characteristics of the vampire body are unmutable and collectively consistent, as this would deny the ability of the vampire to mould around its creational setting. Universality is not a notion that can be applied to any question of vampire ontology, as it negates the subject's contextual relevance. When it comes to an analytical assessment of the contemporary vampire's morphology, nothing can be considered, to borrow Grosz's words, as a 'purely fixed' element of 'facticity', or as the result of 'biologically given factors'.[4] Those biological notions exist, unavoidably, within the inter-narrative framework, but their establishment in the extra-narrative world is 'amenable to historical vicissitudes and transformations'.[5]

As a representational projection of the human body, the vampire body is receptive, on a number of levels, to the effects of social organisation. Society impacts on the body, so that its habits, its appearances, its ways of conducting itself—from drinking blood to sex to dressing to killing and fighting—are inevitably shaped by social expectations. Unable to detach itself from the context in which it is placed, the vampire body is, to adapt a human-inspired notion used by Chris Shilling, 'moulded and constrained by the parameters of its social environment'.[6]

The vampire body is not a disconnected entity; it is not separate from the structures of human worlds. It is inscribed with the regulatory trajectories of the human world. Human society reflects on the vampire body and affects its physical understanding, its modalities of operations, its economic relationships, and its intellectual value. As such, the vampire body functions on two levels: not only it gives way into decoding how the supernatural mythology of the blood-drinking creatures has evolved in cultural terms, but an analysis of its workings and representations allows us to decipher the complicated links and connections that form the modus operandi of human society. The vampire body is an apt site for 'the expression of social symbolism', and forms the grounding 'material on which the fixity of forms becomes established'.[7]

Humans are, as Shilling puts it, 'natural beings'. They are creatures who are the result of an evolutionary process, and they are 'possessed of fixed needs which must be met if people are to preserve themselves'.[8] The human body is easily identifiable; it has parameters, of shape and biological organisation, which are inherent to the species and define it at a genetic level. Culturally speaking, humans also possess the capacity 'to add and partly transcend their natural state'.[9] This is evident not only in the contemporary pervasiveness of cosmetic and enhancing surgery, but also in the more mundane examples of anthropological and social organisation, from diet and exercise to beauty additions. Nonetheless, and in spite of the need to transcend the natural, and the several ways in which the human body can 'appear', humans remains recognizable as such. In the vampire world, however, bodily differences between vampires themselves—especially within the same narrative—are of extreme importance; they highlight not only the impact of physical identification in categorising the group, but also the extent to which socio-cultural representation has become essential in discerning the vampire as a distinct creature.

THE YOUTHFUL UN/DEAD

The twentieth century brought a great deal of attention to the immortal side of the vampire, its ability to not only live forever—or, at least, for a very long time—but also have the gift of eternal youth. The idea that vampire bodies remain unchanged for eternity was a very prominent feature of twentieth century vampires, popularised on the grand scale by Anne Rice's novels, which featured hordes of eternally beautiful vampires. Rice, however, also tackled the difficulties of such a concept and the problem that might arise—psychologically-speaking—from the process of never aging. These problems are embodied in the figure of Claudia, the child-vampire who is turned at the age of six and is 'cursed' to inhabit a doll-like body for the rest of her existence.[10] These questions are of course related to the concept of humanity itself, and the 'natural' course of life, which includes aging and eventually dying for all living creatures. It has often been argued that Rice was also tackling disputes over obsessive and excessive focus on youth and beauty, which was particularly prominent in the 1970s and which received criticism from feminist groups of the time. It is an obvious comment, of course, that the preoccupation with aging—or not-aging—operates exclusively as the concern of beings who are destined to grow old and decay, and that the issues emerging from this dichotomy are strongly connected to the human/inhuman shift that occurs during the process of becoming a vampire.

The idea of eternal youth in relation to the vampire has not escaped the attention of academic scholarship, especially in recent years. Literary and cultural critics—from Donna Haraway to Nina Auerbach, Scott Bukatman and David J. Skal, among others—have widely argued for the youthful vampire to be recognised as an apt metaphor able to uncannily evoke the experiences of power desire in relation to capitalist, postmodern cultures. In *Consuming Youth: Vampires, Cyborgs and the Culture of Consumption* (2002), Rob Latham constructs a compelling associations between the vampire motif of twentieth-century literature and popular culture, and the libidinal-political dynamics of the consumerist ethos to young people. The myth of 'forever young' is interpreted as a clear metaphor for capitalist accumulation. The vampire, in turn, is visualised by Latham as a 'literally an insatiable consumer driven by a hunger for perpetual youth'.[11] In these terms, the vampire provides a fruitful model for apprehending the various and varied forms of cultural activity, including those of labour and leisure in contemporary Western economies, that capitalist society has staked out for American youth. While Latham's analysis seems overly focused on outlining the dangerously bleak outcomes of 'being a vampire' in its metaphorical consumerist undertones, the connection between the perpetually young vampire and the constant appeal of 'hungry' capitalism in popular culture forms remains persuasive. Youthful vampires appear in a large number of narratives. They are young enough to be high school students (Edward Cullen and his siblings in the *Twilight* saga), they are trendy enough to look at ease in nightclubs (Eric in the *Sookie Stackhouse* series), they always remain 'healthy looking' even in the face of physical hardship (Thomas in *The Dresden Files*), and they display mesmerising good looks that make them irresistible to the opposite sex (Raphael and his associates in the *Vampires in America* storyline). The dialectical complexity of the relationship between youth and consumerism is of course problematized even further by the presence of blood-drinking, and the vampire's abilities to captivate others—especially humans—and maintain a 'cool' (in all senses of the word) exterior. Contemporary vampires, one might argue, are not only youthful, but also exceptionally wealthy and stylish.[12]

By placing a focus on youthful beauty and perceived immortality, however, the majority of vampire fiction negates the possibility of seeing the vampire as what they are in many other examples: dead creatures which still move around, a charming incarnation of the undead corpse. Contemporary narratives do not indulge much in seeing the vampire as a dead body, a move which would be counterproductive and that would pose a threat to the 'erotic attraction and identification' with the supernatural creature on the reader's part.[13] Bernadette Bosky points out that, in contemporary fiction and popular culture, 'the burden of being dead meat' has 'shifted primarily to zombies', the cannibalistic living dead.[14] This shift became particularly prominent after the release of George A. Romero's *Night of the Living Dead* (1968) and *Dawn of the Dead* (1978), where the zombie ceased to be—in the popular imagination—the soulless revenant of folklore, and transformed into a brain-eating, decaying corpse.

There are of course instances in popular literature where the physical deadness of vampires is alluded to. In Harris' *Sookie Stackhouse* novels, Sookie herself comments on how Eric the vampire is cold and pale. The allusion, however, is never grounds for making Eric unattractive; his charms, good looks, and general vampire mystique are clearly sufficient for convincing potential sex and blood partners into submission. Although deceased (in human terms), vampires are never repulsive; indeed, their ability to 'conquer death' is seen as magical and appealing, and therein lies part of its potent attraction. The coldness of the vampire's skin is treated as a mere consequence of inhabiting a body that does not breathe, and is technically 'dead'.

A good example of seeing the vampire as the corpse, on the other hand, can be found in Jim Butcher's *The Dresden Files*, where vampires from the Black Court are imagined as folkloristic creatures who are not only dead, but also decomposing. As we are told by Butcher, 'the vampires of the Black Court [have] been around since the dawn of human memory'. We are also afforded a clear description of the rotting undead:

> '[The vampire] had been a young man [. . .] Dessication had left its face gaunt [. . .] Death had withered it into an emaciated caricature of a human being. Its eyes were covered with a white, rheumy film and flakes of dead flesh fell from its decay-drawn lips and clung to its yellowed teeth. Hair like brittle dad grass stood out from its head, and there was some kind of moss or mold growing in it'.[15]

The Black court vampires, however, are simply one incarnation—one type, so to speak—of vampire, and are certainly not the one who retain any erotic or charisma for the both characters and readers. The seductive, irresistible vampire is dutifully represented in the vampires from the White Court, beautiful specimens of supernatural creatures who create emotional and sexual bonds with willing humans. Intriguingly, Butcher also provides a third category of vampire belonging to what is known as the Red Court; these vampires are hideous looking because they resemble bat-like monsters. They wear 'skin suits' to masquerade themselves as humans, and they have an insatiable thirst for blood. Butcher's triad seems to dissect and deconstruct the three most famous aspects of the vampire persona, which have become prominent over centuries: the corpse, the lover, and the monster.

INAUTHENTIC FANTASIES

In *Being and Time*—a treatise on the nature of and questions that surround the concept of being—Heidegger proposes an understanding of the subject that is steeped in phenomenological and existentialist accounts of experience. Although, as a work, *Being and Time* presents its difficulties not only for its hermeneutical approach to reality, but also for its complicated—and not uncontested—take on what 'it means' to exist, Heidegger's insights on how to discern the quality and nature of experience in relation to the human being are invaluable. The key discernments of Heidegger's study hover around the relationship between life and death, and how individuals face these two concepts in relation to both psychological and social framework. The principal findings of *Being and Time* are that, firstly, 'death cannot be public and must be faced alone'.[16] Secondly, and most importantly, that 'life without death is existentially meaningless'.[17] While Heidegger's take on matters of life and finality, and their conceptual impact on the individual, have often been accused of being reductive and even bleak, its principles shine an interesting light on the vampire experience, especially for its concerns with death and its relationship to the openly lived-in sphere of human existence.

Heidegger contends that, for all of humanity, the most important realisation is that life ends, and that all living creatures will die. Death is a fulcrum that, paradoxically, puts life into action, and defines it for what it is in terms of experience. Without death, humans could never grasp the totality of existence and the specificity of individual life. Without death, humans would only understand themselves as 'existing forever in a succession of empty moments'.[18] Death is the source of all coordinates of life and provides humanity with a 'temporal arc'.[19] The conceptual finality of death—and its physical consequences—accelerates the sense of experience for individuals, and makes them *alive* in the face of an unavoidable end. Nonetheless, Heidegger contends, humans do not wish to face their mortality, in spite of their knowledge that the end will come. Although we know what we are—beings that will, eventually, age and die—we insist in obfuscating that knowledge with structures that separate our lived existence from the concept of death and provide a buffer for what we recognise—openly or not—as inevitable. Mourning rituals, places of burial and obvious symbols of death—such as gravestones—are part of the distortions and distractions that humans engage in to construct a seemingly permanent 'deception of everyday life'.[20] 'Inauthentic beings', so demarcated, are both things and people who can act to mask and conceal death. Heidegger defines the presence of these structures of deception as 'inauthentic' experience, an imagistic construct for life that is, at heart, a mediated concept. Inauthentic, in these terms, is that which not only obscures the inevitable, but also makes it seem separate from the individual, trying to cloud the knowledge of what we are and what we will become.[21]

In this framework, a vampire can be understood as 'inauthentic experience'. In its position as a separate species that can live for millennia, and even more so in its status as 'undead' who has faced its mortal end and has managed—supernaturally—to overcome it by becoming something else, the vampire can be understood as a tool for separating the human individual from the knowledge of death. The vampire can be interpreted as a counterfeit distraction, a symbol of departure from that which is final, decaying, and impermanent. The vampire is the representation of an inauthentic fantasy for humanity, a being that eludes definition, and evades the final status by clinging on to an in-between state, which, in Heideggerian terms, in uncategorisable as 'existing'. The vampire, however, consumes the obsession of living through the avoidance of death, and is relentless in its experience of concealment and obscuring satisfaction.

Heidegger's insights also suggest that inauthentic beings—the distractions that obscure the finality of human death—are necessarily 'partial and incomplete'.[22] Although this is undoubtedly a clearer condition for vampires who have been 'turned' rather than born—as the latter will, eventually and naturally, experience death as finality just as humans do—one can see how the vampire status emerges as a way of existing blindly into a future that poses no threat and no intimidation. Vampire inauthenticity has no prospect as it only exists in the present; with the aspects of the human being removed from the subject—the aging, the changing, the physical and mental dissolution— the vampire exists only in what Adam Barrows calls, recalling Heidegger, 'an endless succession of present moments'.[23] The vampire is an illusory figure, one that operates on the power of delusion for both itself and the humans around it. The illusion of life for the vampire is visible in its endless need for blood, a representation of that which is living, developing, and final. The inauthentic fantasy of the vampire only finds a way to exist through another inauthentic symbol; the blood here operates as a concealer of that which does not progress and cannot truly exist. For the humans who 'live' around the vampire—and, metaphysically speaking, for the readers and spectators of the vampire phenomenon—the vampire is inauthentic in that it indulges fantasies of the forever, the everlasting—or at least inhumanly long—status of that which is unadulterated by death. The vampire's existence 'gives life to death', and presents the possibility of 'life without end'.[24] In its inauthenticity, the vampire is, essentially, an imitation of life.

BE STILL, MY VAMPIRE HEART

The heart is often at the centre of vampire mythology. In folkloristic terms, the heart played a big part in actually annihilating 'the vampire'. Over the centuries, several ways of bestowing the final death upon the vampire have travelled across Europe and North America, and many, if not all, have included acts to be performed upon the creature's heart. Driving a spiked object through the vampire's heart is definitely one of the most well-known ways to kill it; the objects to be used vary from iron rods to wooden stakes. The latter, however, is the one that has enjoyed the most fame once folkloristic traditions concerning vampires were transported into the literary world. Indeed, the wooden stake has been one of the most popular and recognisable ways to kill a vampire, sensitivity to sunlight notwithstanding. The connection between folklore and literature, and the imaginative impact that one had on the other, is of course nothing new, especially when vampires are involved. Konstatinos reminds us that 'a great many vampire countermeasures from folklore achieved their own immortality in fiction'.[25] The stabbed heart is understood by many to be the calling card of a dead vampire. Undoubtedly, Bram Stoker's *Dracula* has a great part to play in establishing this imagistic mythology. In the book, four vampires are dispatched by having their hearts stabbed and by being promptly decapitated afterwards. *Dracula* indeed does provide, in some ironic fashion, an excellent and very detailed guide towards killing vampires by seemingly traditional methods of stabbing and beheading, with Van Helsing and his associates personally in charge of stabbing vampires with wooden stakes: the stake is placed 'over the heart' and one is to 'strike in god's name' with a hammer, 'so all may be well with the dead'.[26]

The 'wooden stake through the heart' combination seems to be a particularly effective method for killing vampires who have been 'turned', ending their existence as humans who have been 'reanimated into a supernatural existence'.[27] In folkloristic terms, vampirologists contend that the stake or the metal rod used to stab the vampire's heart while it lay in its own coffin 'was meant to do nothing more than hold the vampire in place so it could not rise'.[28] Sources claim that the stabbing was aimed at emptying the heart of the blood that the vampire has taken from its victims, and eliminating the possibility that it might do so again. The heart was understood more as an agent of nourishment, rather than an organ of life. This belief seems to be supported by the idea that, on several occasions, other acts needed to be performed in order to ensure that the vampire was actually dead, such as cutting off its head.

The heart, however, is not just an organ. It has many identities, many shifting incarnations of its very nature and function, so that the perception of the heart goes beyond mere biomedical purpose. In our contemporary Western culture, Thomas Staubli and Silvia Schroer remind us, 'the heart is regarded as the centre of the life force, and also as the seat of conscience, the centre of the self, the seat of the soul and the emotions'.[29] Perceptions of the heart, especially in a popular literary context, can be seen as a highly historical practice, which bears a connection to changing attitudes of the human body, sense of self, and its place in society. In this framework, Albert Howard Carter contends that views of the heart are an 'evolving cultural artefact'.[30]

The heart has been understood as a central part of life for millennia. In a human framework, its very existence and beating character has come to signify existence, presence, continuation, a 'sine qua non for our very lives'.[31] Even in ancient times, our ancestors recognised the importance of a beating heart, a very immediate testimony of the boundary between life and death. A beating heart means life, a still heart means death. This basic biological function has taken on a variety of interpretative meanings, which have interweaved themselves with both the spiritual, cultural, and social fabrics of human organisation. Physiologically speaking, the heart plays a central function for the body, but its place as human metaphor bestows upon it an emotional significance.

The symbolic value of the heart is undoubtedly connected to the fact that this organ is the only one that individuals can actually sense. Although placed internally within the body, the heart speaks to the outside with its beat. Its increased rhythm translates communicatively into physical exertion. With its beating, the hearts speaks of fear, excitement, and extreme joy. The heart is, as Staubli and Schrorer contend, an organ that we constantly 'feel'.[32] Staubli and Schrorer's suggestion is intriguing not only because it draws attention to the physiological working of the heart itself, but also because it opens the way to unravelling how the association between heart and sentiment could have developed. It is not hard to see—without being too speculative—how the changing rhythms of the heartbeat could have cemented the idea that this particular organ was the site where emotions were created in people's minds.

As it beats and establishes its presence—and the presence of the body it governs—into the realm of life, the heart helps to define 'our humanity from within'.[33] It is a sonic flag of existence, a tangible proof of being that, at least in its physiological sense, is testament to the human desire to associate stimuli and responses with a system that is fully working. Nonetheless, the heart's ability to signify a sense of 'being' goes beyond that which is merely biological and medically defined. In Western societies, the heart is a symbolic conduit for that which is pure and unadulterated, the very site of our most inner thoughts and, of course, the emblematic exemplification of love and affection. The heart is a common allegory for romance and, Stephen Gislason contends, entire industries 'depend' on this metaphor.[34] The perpetration of heart symbolism and its connection to love, of course, obscures what is actually going on in the human body: that the brain, and not the heart, is what processes information and causes emotional reactions. Clearly, however, the brain has much less of a cultural appeal, conceptually and imagistically, and does not marry well with 'the whole enterprise of describing feelings and behaviours associated with bonding'.[35] The sound of 'my brain bleeds for you', 'follow your brain', or being 'broken-brained' somehow fails to capitalise on poetic appeal.

As a figurative presence, the heart, in a fictional context, continues to carry its sentimental message, its connection to love metaphors proving, as Carter puts it, 'the symbolic resonance of tradition'.[36] While still not totally divorced from its function as a bodily organ, the heart is an image that communicates in virtue of its non-verbal power, incorporating both its literal and metaphorical meanings of its functions and interpretations. The heart—used as a vector for expression—is an entity that connects individuals through a shared understanding of emotional practice. Used as linguistic device, the heart transmits the essence of any concept that it is related to contextually. The term essence here is used in its most primordial incarnation, as descended form the Latin *esse*, suggesting an ontological definition not only for itself, but also for that which it represents. In a communicative context, the heart—symbolically speaking—stands for a system of internalised cultural reactions to that which is hidden under the façade of sociality. The language of the heart—so to speak—is constructed through a relationship of dependence with its historical, philosophical, and spiritual value. As an illustrative paradigm, the hearts speaks of the imaginative forces which regulate interpersonal relations and their place in political and organisational superstructures.

Carter also contends that in its ability to represent that which is most human, most loved and, simultaneously, most feared, the heart is a 'sort of mirror', or even 'a Rorschach blot' for the human experience. Its various incarnations and interpretations reflect our most fundamental concerns and our most coveted desires. The heart—understood as a cultural entity—gives an entry into human interpretative strategies, an embodied and stylistic guide to unravelling the place of both the body and emotions in a given context. As living animals, humans are creatures permanently driven by a desire to discover and find meaning through interpretation. Visions of the heart are not univocal and certainly not universal in their interpretation. In a Western context, imaginings of the heart are concerned not only with how to deal with it biomedically—especially in association to disease—but also how to integrate it into the illustrative structure of social relation which forms the foundation of human collectivity.

Although, physiologically, it is an organ shared by all humans, the heart is not, as Carter puts it, 'an existential absolute', but it mirrors aspects of consciousness which are intrinsically connected to understandings of what it means to be human.[37] The ontological nature of heart symbolism encompasses two aspects of the identification process, the cultural, on one side, and the biomedical on the other. The cultural heart—so understood—is multiple and numerous in its manifestations, the changing visualisations affected by its presence in different cultures, different moments in history, and, even more aptly to our contemporary twenty-first century context, its different place in 'expressive media'. When something so (apparently) inherently human is concerned, any changes on the themes, or interpretations, of the concept must be viewed with caution, as they are symptomatic of changing attitudes to humanity and that which defined it. Vampires, of course, fall into this conceptual category with ease, both in their psychological and physiological ontologies.

Where the 'vampire heart' is concerned, both aspects construct specific parameters for associative analysis, and become the guiding standards for interoperation. With such a highly mimetic function for human societies, it is virtually impossible not to see the presence of heart discourse in vampire narratives as a projection of human anxiety and expectations about both physical and psychological connections. When it comes to the vampire—which operates as such a highly interpretative metaphor for human existence—one must wonder to what extent the image of the heart is moulded as a representation of vampiric experience and its place in the world. As it is often the case when vampires are concerned, the dichotomy of alive and dead continues to play an important part in determining the status of the vampiric body and its functions, both cultural and biological.

Unsurprisingly, the heart—a signifier which, in its beating state, becomes synonymous with life—is a particularly important presence within contemporary vampire mythology. Numerous narratives dedicate attention to the vampire's heart and how it is perceived. An emphasis on the physical nature of the vampire's heart, however, is inevitably connected to the larger conceptual discourse of identity, the framework for delineating the nature of the individual and its function in the collective reality.

The vampire's heart is portrayed differently in various narratives, its changed status often related to the nature of the vampiric mythology to which it subscribes. That connection, however, is not simply a stylistic choice, but hides careful understandings of what the vampire is relation to existence and, of course, humanity. Examples are, of course, as numerous as they are disparate. In the *Sookie Stackhouse* series, vampires are fully dead, so their hearts do not beat.[38] The vampires in the *Black Dagger Brotherhood* and *Midnight Breed* series are fully alive—being a separate species from the human race—and their hearts beat and pump blood into highly sophisticated and physically impressive bodies. Ward's vampire's hearts are even known to be 'six-chambered', the heightened efficiency of the organ mirroring the overall superiority of the species.[39] In Painter's *House of Comarré* series, vampires' hearts are normally still, but they are given the ability to beat for a few minutes when they consume Comarré blood, which is particularly potent and life-giving:

> 'His heart. [. . .] For the first time in more than five hundred years, it pumped with life. He didn't have time to question how that was possible when the pain kicked in. [. . .] And then, just as quickly as it had flashed through him, the pain left. In its place was a lingering warmth and sense of well-being unlike anything he'd felt since being turned. Strength suffused his body'.[40]

Painter's conception of vampire hearts that 'wait' to be brought back to life is not a common occurrence in contemporary vampire narratives, but it is certainly not alone in its existence. In Kresley Cole's *Immortals After Dark* series, vampires who have been turned initially inhabit a dead body; their hearts, as a consequence, are still. However, this condition is not permanent. One of the most significant moments not only in the narrative, but also in a male's vampire life, is when he meets his predestined woman—referred to as an eternal 'wife', clearly recalling the sanctity of marital union dictated by Judeo-Christian tradition as the basis of Western society. The vampire's wife has a very specific function; aside from potentially providing a long-term companion for the vampire, she also has the ability to turn him back into a 'live' creature. Encounters with his destined wife cause the vampire's body to be restored to life; a clear sign of this process happening is that his heart begins to beat again. Concurrently, his sexual urges—kept dormant since his turning—are also reawakened. The process of returning to life—referred to by Cole as being 'blooded'—is described as both physically painful and emotionally unsettling for the vampire.[41] It is not worthy of note here that the emphasis on blood communicates how the heart 'exists' only if it has a function, if it pumps blood and conveys, in so doing, the presence of some sort of life within a given creature. The physical awareness of his beating heart—coming back to its human beat after, on occasions, hundreds of years—causes the vampire to face the traumatic knowledge of his previous death; as his heart beats and becomes alive once again, his emotions also flow back, and he becomes aware of his own forgotten ability to 'love'.

It would not be too ambitious here to claim that the heart possesses a dual function. Cole's narrative emphasises the Western perception of 'the heart' as the centre for love and emotion; this metaphor has been long-standing in Western cultures, the broken heart or the 'loving heart' acting as a basic allegory for the poetry for courtly love, and its imitators, across centuries.[42] Through the metaphor of love and emotion, and its representational attachment to the heart, one can argue that the process of 'bloodying' also has a lot to do with the vampire's identity. Popular wisdom dictates that 'knowing one's heart' means knowing who one truly is. This seemingly ontological notion, however, has a lot more to do with identifying our needs and desires, fears and anxieties. Knowing one's heart, in the human sense, can be seen as coming into being. Schroer suggests that 'the heart represents the identity of the human being', which individuals desire 'to share fully and utterly with the beloved'.[43] It is possibly to argue that the process through which the vampire's heart begins to beat again in Cole's mythology is a metaphorical transposition of a very human wish for communion and knowledge of self. The vampire's bloodied status, with his beating heart as the flagstone of the process, signifies knowledge of what he truly is: in this case, a vampire who must drink blood to maintain his strength, and who is able to love a woman to its fullest. The sexual impulse is a result of that strength, associating knowledge of self and emotional attachment to a partner through the representational power of intercourse.

Unavoidably, the presentation of the vampire's heart—whether beating, still or, as it would seem, waiting to beat—is illustrative in nature and tells us a lot about very human anxieties about the spheres of Western society concerned with the heart; emotion, love, and empathy, on the one hand, and biomedical function, on the other. Both notions pivot around conceptions of 'health' and bodily boundaries, in both their psychological and physical constructs.

ORIFICES

To say that the vampire is all about an obsession with orifices would not be an outlandish claim. Points of entrance, points of exit, mingling, mergence, and exchange. At the centre of the orifice debate, when it comes to vampires, are two substances: blood and semen. Although this might seem like a redundant claim to make—the figure of the vampire, after all, has always hovered around sexual exchanges, desire, and the eventual drinking of blood—the significance of these substances has mutated over time. The idea that by drinking the blood of a vampire, a human can cheat death is quite widespread in contemporary narratives, with the *Vampires in America* series being but as clear example of this. Reynolds stresses how vampire blood has 'healing properties' for humans in a love relationship with vampires: 'his blood keeps her healthy and young for as long as they are together. This is why most matings are between vampire and human. They sustain each other'.⁴⁴

The mythology of the vampire as undead still maintains, for the most part, that vampires cannot procreate in the traditional sense. This is made very clear by the vampire Matthew in Harkness' *All Souls* series, when he states that, when vampires reproduce, it is a case of 'resurrection, not procreation'.⁴⁵ There is a general acceptance that, once they are turned, their bodies are 'frozen in time'—a phrase prominent in Meyer's *Twilight* saga. As they do not age and do not die, vampires cannot generate life from their own bodies in the traditional sense. This is often cause for disappointment among the human mates who are in relationships with vampires, as is the case for Sookie in Harris' series. It is curious to see how Meyer herself subverts areas of this particular mythology in the *Twilight* saga by claiming that only female vampire bodies' are 'frozen in time', while the sperm produced by male vampires is an active substance that can potentially impregnate a human woman.

A number of contemporary narratives, however, have subverted the notion that vampires cannot procreate by allowing them to be warm-blooded creatures, alive in every sense of the word. In this context, the attention to bodily openings takes on a whole different meaning when the orifice is exposed as a site of socio-political exchange, as well as a physical one. In the *Midnight Breed* series, the mingling of blood and semen is essential for procreating between humans and vampires. The humans in questions are known as 'breed mates', genetically enhanced human females 'gifted with unique blood and DNA properties that complement' those of the vampires.⁴⁶ Blood is passed between the vampire and the breedmate during intercourse and it is a vital part of the act, as it creates the bond that will 'bear the seed of a new vampire generation'.⁴⁷. The transference, however, is not univocal. As the vampire drinks blood from his mate, he also returns the favour by feeding her some of his own: 'there was nothing more intimate than the bond they shared. There was nothing more precious he could offer her than the lifeblood that gave her immortality with him and bound her to him for as long as they both drew breath. And drinking from him would heighten her pleasure like nothing else could'.⁴⁸ As long as the breedmate keeps drinking the blood, she will live for centuries, perhaps even millennia, just as her vampire lover does.

A strong relationship is forged between blood and semen as the substances that fill the cradle of life. Blood and semen operate on similar levels in the construction of not only vampire identity, but also the reproduction of the species. The vampire's human lover in the *Breed* can only become pregnant if, during the sexual act, the vampire ejaculates at the same time as he drinks her blood. The dynamics of the act pivot around a circular exchange: as she gives him life with her blood, he returns that 'life' to her in the form of his semen. Impregnation, however, can only happen on a few nights a month, during a crescent moon, a symbolic use of imagery which not only signifies growth, but also proves to be an effective form of birth control for vampires: 'There was a crescent moon tonight. [. . .] he couldn't stop his hips from moving, couldn't stop his seed from its want to boil over. [. . .] One nick of his fangs against her skin. That's all it would take. She'd be pregnant with his child by the end of the night'.[49] The exchange of blood and semen draws attention to how the vampire is reliant on forms of incorporation that are connected to the regulation psycho-social conduct. The focus on blood in the *Breed* is inherently sexual, but the politics of the act are not kept hidden under the surface, they are openly discussed. The mingling of blood and semen to construct interpersonal and physiological connections highlights the conceptual dimension of a social tool set in 'the continuum of standards'.[50] Sexual intercourse—or, to be more specific, blood intercourse—entails the existence of specific regulations which ensure the power of the exchange between vampire and mate is reinforced and developed. Bodily orifices sit at the centre of those regulatory systems. These are not only 'natural' orifices—such as the mouth and the vagina—but also artificial ones, the points of entry created by the vampire's fangs on the human's body.

The artificial orifices—traditionally to be created on the neck—are actually more openly descriptive of the vampire's need to enter, and apply political domination, on his mate. While biting her body during intercourse and drawing her blood out into his own, the vampire lays claim on his lover's body by creating a site of exchange over which he has complete mastery. Mary Douglas points out that ingestion—understood as taking into one's body—is evocative of 'political absorption'.[51] Bodily orifices, Douglas argues, represents 'points of entry or exit to social units', and the pleasure that derives from the exchange 'can symbolise an ideal theocracy'.[52] 'Douglas's 'theocracy' here can be interpreted, in the vampire sense, as the hegemony of sexual desire, which regulates the exchange in an almost otherworldly way. As the 'orifice' which will let the blood flow did not exist before the bite, one can see how the individuality of the act is reliant on fantasies of incorporation and of superior control which accompany the filling of all orifices, with both blood and semen. A similar exchange happens from the human's perspective, as she draws blood from an opening in the vampire's body which has been created for her only, and the blood she receives cements the bond between lovers. That exchange is political in that it is inevitably reliant on laws of control, of definition, of identity: that which is bitten is rendered 'open' to the other's possession. The symbolic power of the orifice is based on a constant negotiation of fluid exchange between beings whose differences and alterities, as Grosz argues, 'are left intact but with whom' exchange is made possible by 'intentionality'.[53] The strength of the incorporation rituals from vampire and human (and vice versa) lies not only in its mingling of life fluids, but also in its abilities to leave its subjects intact, while creating the framework for political exchange and social reliance.

FANGS

When orifices and points of entry are called into question, the presence and function of the vampire's fangs are impossible to overlook. The animal-like teeth serve, first and foremost a practical purpose. Fangs are used to puncture the skin of the blood host when needed, so that blood can flow freely into the vampire's mouth. In the traditional sense, fangs are pictured as sharp, largely elongated canine teeth, which when bared contribute to an 'intimately brutal way to achieve sustenance'.[54] With the exclusion of very rare and conspicuous examples—including John Marks' *Fangland*, where vampire Ion Torgu fails to display the sharp and pointy teeth often associated with the vampiric—fangs are present in virtually all contemporary narratives, and can therefore be considered as a predominant characteristic of the vampire.[55] Usually kept at a 'normal' length—so that the vampires can speak and drink –they elongate when a feeding opportunity approaches, their appearance signifying the vampire's desire for blood. The descriptions given render fangs as truly enormous when used for biting.[56]

In both functional and imagistic terms, fangs are not an apparatus that features prominently in description of vampires within either folklore or pre-1900 literature. In *Dracula*, for instance, Stoker only describes the Count as having 'peculiarly sharp teeth', that 'protrude over the lips'.[57] In spite of the fact that the literary Dracula is often credited by the contemporary imagination as having shaped the overall vision of the vampire for its contemporary and subsequent audiences, the term 'fangs' is never used within the bounds of Stoker's text. And yet, in contemporary terms, it is difficult to imagine a vampire without fangs. Indeed, we have twentieth-century literature and other examples from popular culture—particularly film—to thank for the establishment of fangs as an inherent vampire characteristic. In similar vein, fangs are also not a prerogative of vampires alone. Within the realms of the supernatural, werewolves are obviously gifted with long and sharp fangs, able to cause considerable damage to their victims. In the *Sookie Stackhouse* universe, elves are often gifted with fangs, as are several types of fairies and fae in the *House of Comarré* series. So the question here revolves around what makes vampire fangs so special and particularly worthy of attention, so much that, one can venture to say, in contemporary popular literature and culture, when one thinks of a creature with fangs, the thought translates immediately into 'vampire'.

To attempt to answer the question of how, if not why, fangs are such a vampiric attribute in the popular imagination, one needs to reach out into the symbolic significance of fangs in relation to what the vampire does, and not on dwell ontological debates over what the vampire is. The presence of fangs within the vampire mythology has certainly also evolved into the conceptual realm. Several examples of scholarship over the years have highlighted the make-up of fangs in vampire narratives as a phallic symbol, with the penetration of the teeth into the skin emulating the sexual act. This view—particularly prominent within Freudian understandings of the vampire—has contributed in maintaining the eroticisation of the vampire's bite as 'sexy' and fuelled by different types of desire.[58] Even culturally, this interpretation finds its ground; the neck, a privileged area for the vampire's bite, is considered an erogenous zone, one that leads to or is often part of intercourse. Karg, Spaite and Sutherland contend that, in symbolic terms, 'the biting of one's neck is a highly erotic act, which is in keeping with the vampire's portrayal as a sexual predator'.[59] The appearance of fangs, their use in biting, and the almost unavoidable presence of the sexual act have been complicit in establishing the mythology of the vampire's fangs as a paradoxically erotic emblem, distancing it somewhat from folkloristic visions of dark creatures ripping into victims with their teeth and tearing their flesh to shreds.

And yet, the use of fangs in contemporary popular narratives has evolved beyond the simple representation of the erotic act. Fangs are part of 'being a vampire' as a fighting unit, a separate bodily entity divorced from human physiological structures. Fangs are not only a sexual or functional issue, but also a genetic one. This aspect of the vampire's experience is reinforced by the multiple descriptions of the vampire's teeth as anything but human. In Wellington's *Laura Caxton* series, the vampire's fangs are an unavoidable sign of its inhumanity. Far from being faintly elongated canine teeth, these recall those of a predatory animal. Indeed, the whole face is not quite human, with the fangs drawing significant attention: 'The eye sockets and cheekbones looked mostly human . . . [but] The jaws were larger than they should have been. They also had more teeth than they should. Far more teeth, and none of them were bicuspids or molars. They were wicked-looking triangular teeth, slightly translucent, like those of a shark'.[60] The fact that the vampire looks 'mostly human' highlights its body as an uncertain re-elaboration of the human physique. By using terms such as 'should have been' in relation to the vampire's body, Wellington also plays with anatomical expectations of the human body, which inevitably hold cultural connotations of normality and acceptance. The choice of 'shark' here, as the predator resembled, is also apt as sharks are known—by truth or mythology—to be able to smell blood from long distances in the water. In this

sense, the shark is a 'bloodthirsty' animal, one that finds a conceptual aptitude with the vampire motif. Visualising the vampire's fangs as shark teeth
aids the removal of the creature from the parameters of human existence,
and places it in another territory, that of the beast, that of the 'other'.

As vampires are made as such through turning willing human beings—
accepting what Wellington calls 'the curse'—one can only assume that the
presence of fangs occurs as part of the transformation. The transformation that alters the genetic material of the human, and makes it the vampire, seems to remove all the most distinctive characteristics of the human
being—whilst still retaining a humanoid shape—such as hair, eyes, and
human teeth. Wellington's vampires are bald and hairless all over their
bodies, have penetrating red eyes and shark-like fangs. They also have multiple layers of fangs, that can grow back when damaged. The fangs, in
particular, become a potent signifier of the vampire's body, the immediate
identification of the creature. As these fangs resemble those of a remote
predator—one which is rarely associated with feelings of cuteness and possibly human connection, even in its infant stage—the vampire is highlighted
as a monster. There is no eroticisation of the vampire in Wellington's narrative, no possibility of an empathetic association. The fangs allow the vampire to tear a human body apart quickly and efficiently, so that blood can be
consumed without wasting a drop of the precious liquid. The fangs are the
symbol of the vampire's manifest difference, of its bio-genetic remoteness
from all that is human, and its ability to show feelings in the human way.

If one accepts the presence of fangs as the most disconnecting part in the
equation linking the human and the vampire body, the concept of 'inhumanity' here becomes important as it points in the direction of exclusion
and inclusion in the humanist sense. In his writings on representation and
humanity, Jean-Francois Lyotard calls into question not only the parameters of the human body, but the humanity associated with it through the
concept of 'inhuman'. The term has two meanings for Lyotard. In the first
instance, it refers to the 'dehumanising' effects of technology and science
in our contemporary Western society.[61] This conception of 'inhumanity'
also gestures towards viewing the vampire body as an aberration in that it
relies on unfamiliar, quasi-mystical technologies. Although the 'curse' of
Wellington's vampire narrative is never fully explained, the changes that
result from the transformation are so genetically radical that it can also be
understood as a scientifically applied procedure. In this way, the vampire's
fangs function as the metaphorical presence of the effects of technology
onto the body. Through shark-like fangs, Wellington's vampires open the
way for a critique of technological dependence in the Western world that
affects both the body and the mind.

Lyotard, however, also proposes a second understanding for the term
inhuman, one that seems very fitting to the vision of the vampire as a
removed and dehumanised predator. According to Lyotard, the inhuman
refers to a number of forces and abilities in the human that are repressed

or excluded, but which inevitably resurface—with disruptive effects—when the circumstances allow it. These forces are what Lyotard describes as the 'first nature' of the human being, the one detached from the learned 'second nature' of institution and culture.[62] In this framework, the vampire's fangs can be understood as inhuman because they point to a non-institutionally attached existence. The vampire's body here signals the creature as a human that has become inhuman because it has abandoned the second nature of culture and regulation, and has pursued the first nature of the predatory, the nature that allows it to thrive and survive by subjugating the inferior species. The vampire's inhumanity is a cautionary tale; it reminds human beings of their unforgettable animal roots, their predatory instincts that remain covered by a layer of civility and propriety. And simultaneously, it warns the human against the detachment from institution and government. The vampire's fangs are an agent of potentiality, of 'what if'. Anarchic and animal-like, the blood-dripping fangs remove the body from the constraints of human civilisation and restore it to the frightening freedom of the inhuman. As part of the vampire's body, the fangs in the *Laura Caxton Vampire* series detach the vampire from systems of human law and recognition: the vampire body is a rogue entity. As soon as the fangs are put on display—with their multiple layers of horror and gore—the vampire is understood for the aberration that it is: the transformed human that has lost all of its humanity, and has been left with the hunger of a predator.

STATES OF TRANSGRESSION

Classification—and the sub-division of experience—of the vampire's body is connected to the evaluation of embodiment in its various contexts, drawing attention to how the body must be interpreted as a 'lived-in' entity, even if the subject of experience is paradoxically and curiously undead. Pasi Falk has argued that the body is 'tied to a network of boundaries'.[63] The boundaries range from linguistic signs to concrete practices, from social hierarchies to classificatory codes. The multiple interactions between vampires and humans is where the net of boundaries and divisions of experience are thrown into sharp relief, and the vampire body—together with the activities in which it engages—functions as a communicating medium for states of exception and transformational practice

Contemporary vampire literature underlines corporeality itself as a form of transgression. This is tied to the experience of 'transgressing' limitations—of the body—and therefore being made distinctly aware of it. When using the term 'transgression', I echo the principle as it is formulated in the writings of Georges Bataille, even if a critical interpretation is at work.[64] Transgression—understood by Bataille as the crossing of borders—gestures towards a set of dynamics in which the everyday world, as we know it, is broken and fragmented. Transgression is a form of transition from the 'normal' to the 'non-normal', the extraordinary, the exceptional. It also points, as Falk has suggested, 'to the breaking down and crossing of borders confining and defining the body'.[65] That confinement is imposed by culture and society. Extraordinary experiences—viewed as such because they exceed the limitations of the cultural everyday—are to be interpreted as transgressive, and these range from the unusual suffering of pain to the most extravagant and hedonistic occurrence of pleasure. As such corporeality becomes a historically defined cultural experience. When it comes to the vampire body—and its existence in the human framework as an agent of extraordinary experience—the transgressive nature of corporeality does not become more evident than when fangs and the act of biting are involved. Several examples from contemporary fiction claim that the vampire's bite is a pleasurable experience. Reynolds' *Vampires in America* series, for instance, states the sensual nature of the vampire's bite and how it evokes sexual involvement: 'having a vampire drink from you', Lucas teases, 'is very enjoyable'.[66]

The experience of the vampire's bite highlights the nature of corporeality as a state relying on solid dimensions and definite boundaries, which transgression throws into sharp relief. Anthropological, sociological, and psychoanalytical scholarship have drawn attention to how, for human beings, a particularly pleasurable bodily state is a shift from a 'normal state' to a 'hyper state'. Falk argues that pleasure itself is 'a shift to an exceptional state above what is normal' and acts, at the same time, as 'the characterisation of the very state'.[67] Although this line of thought can of course be pursued for several activities which involve the vampire's interaction with bodily pleasure—from sex to eating—the focus on fangs unveils the status of the vampiric bite as an extraordinary and abnormal act of transgression. In human terms, being bitten and being fed upon in blood cannot be considered a fully 'normal' experience. Although the concept of 'normality' is a contested one, there is no denying that the act in itself should not be considered as a coveted occurrence. And yet, the convenient pleasure that the vampire is able to bestow upon its victim makes it congenial. The normal state of the human body could be viewed as drawing pleasure from seemingly standard pleasurable activities, such as intercourse.

Sexual experiences, however, are portrayed as almost inadequate without the presence of the vampire's bite. And although the connection between biting and sex remains undeniable in contemporary literature, it is truly the act of biting that draws attention to the limitations and the excesses of human embodiment. Being bitten by the vampire, experiencing the penetration of fangs and feeling the drawing of blood as an activity of pleasure can be interpreted as an 'hyper state' of corporeality. Being bitten qualifies as 'hyper' because it is not a 'natural' occurrence for the human body, one that does not have any uses in the advancement for the species and is—therefore—an activity of indulgence and over-stimulation. The vampire's bite does not seem to belong to any pre-existing social structures. It is not tied by the regulations of culture, and is not limited by political perspectives on human interpersonal relationship. The vampire's fangs are an agent of transgression because they transport the human receiver of the bite from the subtleties of the everyday to the realm of the extreme, the outstanding, the Dionysian—to use a term suggested by Nietzsche in his analysis of duality and cultural dynamics.

The state of being bitten—at least in vampire-human relationships—could be viewed as what Bataille terms the 'continuity of being', a condition in which the regulations of cultural existence are overthrown.[68] Indeed, it is the in-between experience which receives the most attention in fiction, and therefore draws attention to corporeality being identifiable not as a 'state' in itself—static and unchanging—but as a dynamic part of existence. While breaking the boundaries between normal and hyper states, the vampire's bite is unveiled as a manifestation of corporeality, rather than a consequence of it. It is a hyper-reaching praxis that is not directly bound to social forms as understood in human organisation, and operates under different ritualistic parameters of construction. The emphasis of the vampire's bite, therefore, must be shifted from apparent and established conceptions of duality—what scholarship has often strived to delineate, from sacred and profane, to common and celebratory—to the 'dynamics operating between the poles'.[69] The vampire's bite is a transgressive practice that relies on transitional experiences such as pleasure to exceed the limits of the corporeal from the normal to the 'non-normal', a hedonistic state that points to pre-cultural organisation in its most symbiotic state. Bataille points out that the pursuit of any hyper-state of experience is accompanied by 'longing' and over-powering desire, a definitive characteristic of trangressive practices of which the vampire's bite is an undeniable example. 'Longing' is indeed a feeling described in contemporary literature in reference to the existence of the vampire's victims, lovers, and mates. They yearn to be bitten, they long to experience the transgressive hyperstate of corporeality that will give them pleasure. In the *Sookie Stackhouse* series, Harris states multiple times that the vampires' lovers want 'to be intimate with the vampires', and that their longing to be bitten makes them 'extraordinary, and extraordinarily pathetic'.[70] This longing, as Bataille would have it, signals the detachment from cultural impositions and social regulation; it is the embodied desire for a return to a natural state, one that pre-dates conceptions of normality and allows corporeality to be experienced in its liberating transience. In this sense, trangressive corporeality become, as Falk would put it, a form of regression—a return to the 'natural' state preceding human and cultural existence'.[71] The experience of the vampire's bite points in the same 'narcissistic' direction outlined by Freud—in ontogenic terms—as a return to a symbiotic 'natural state'.

In this framework, the vampire's corporeality can be understood as having two dimensions—experience and expression. Although both of these have been identified by scholarship as having a part to play in the construction of the subject, and how that subject maintains a relationship of interdependency to the cultural order, I would like to argue that only one becomes evident in the connection between vampire and 'donor'—a playful alternative to the loaded term 'victim'—especially when biting and drinking blood are concerned. Experience, the first dimension, is what is also often known as 'unmediated coporeality', a set of reactions that are allegedly devoid of cognitive agencies. The physiological responses to taste and smell would fall into this category. As the pleasure gained from the vampire's bite is not only just a physiological response, but has a perceptive dimension to it based on ritualised structures—adorned with longing and desire—the 'experience' side of corporeality seems hardly an adequate explanation for being bitten as a trangressive state. Indeed, one needs to turn to the second dimension of corporeality: expression. The expression of corporeality, Falk argues, takes place in the guise of externalising functions of man's bodily being, such as convulsive laughter or the consequences and signs of sexual stimulation.[72] One can see here how, already, the connection between vampire, stimulation, and pleasure is established through conceptual cycles of cause and effect.

The externalising process, however, must be started quickly by stimuli and acts which throw corporeal existence into sharp relief. These stimuli will—to different degrees—push the body of out of its passivity and limitations, and demand both a physical and cognitive response which relies on definitions of inter- and outer- boundaries. External stimulation—which, in turn, triggers the externalisation of the corporeal effect—is seen as something strange and unfamiliar to the body itself. It is, as Bataille terms it, 'an alien force', which becomes sensualised precisely because it transgresses the boundaries of the body and the borders of expectation. And, placed in the context of modernised contemporary existence, momentarily dissolves the 'boundaries of the self'. The vampire can be understood as the agent of this 'alien force'. The presence of fangs and the bite they inflict on the donor's body flood it with stimuli which are unfamiliar and do not belong to the boundaries of human experience. The vampire is the quick starting effect, the instrument of transgression that allows the body to be not only experienced—in its first dimension—but also expressed.

FACES

In contemporary narratives, a lot of attention seems to be dedicated to the vampire's face and how it often has distinctive capabilities for enhanced movements, shifting or, on several occasions, an eerie capability for no movement at all. Of course, connecting the very idea of the vampire to distinctive and often horrific facial features and shapes is not a new occurrence, and it goes back to nineteenth-century examples of vampire fiction within the English language. Stoker's *Dracula*, for instance, offered a detailed description of the Count's face, paying particular attention to the seemingly strange nature of his features and their arguably uncanny detail:

> Hi face was a strong—very strong—aquiline, with high bridge of the thin nose and peculiarly arched nostrils; with lofty domed forehead, and hair growing scantily round the temples, but profusely elsewhere. His eyebrows were very massive, almost meeting over the nose, and with bushy hair that seemed to curl in its own profusion. The mouth [. . .] under the heavy moustache was fixed and rather cruel-looking [. . .] his ears were pale and at the top extremely pointed; the chin was broad and strong, and the chin firm though thin. The general effect was one of extreme pallor.[73]

Following the notoriety of Dracula into the early twentieth century, popular culture has undoubtedly been complicit in cementing the idea that the vampire's face is, if not ugly and horrific, at least undeniably different from that of the average human being. In the early twentieth century, the iconic representation of the vampire in *Nosferatu* can be seen as responsible—at least partially—for constructing a vision of the undead vampire's face in the popular imagination. The bone structure of the vampire was presented as grotesquely inhuman, mirroring the merciless nature of the creature, which spurred him to seek the blood of human beings.

   In contrast to earlier visualisation of the vampire as a hideous creature, the late twentieth century spurred the fascination with the vampire as an unbearably beautiful creature, owning facial features which were striking, compelling, and often ethereal in their splendour. The publication of Anne Rice's *Vampire Chronicles* arguably had a big part to play in re-imagining the vampire's face as gifted with beautiful features, which often stood—metaphorically speaking—in stark contrast to their cold-hearted behaviour and predatory endeavours. The description Rice gives of Louis' face aptly communicates both the appeal of his beauty and the repulsion of his predatory nature: 'the vampire was utterly white and smooth, as if he were sculpted from bleached bone, and his face was seemingly inanimate as a statue, except for two brilliant green eyes that looked down [. . .] intently like flames in a skull'.[74] The mix of beauty and horror is of course a very distinctive feature of Rice's *Vampire Chronicles*, and started a new trend for conceptualising the vampire as a beautiful, blood-hungry, and yet often conflicted creature. The mesmerising features of the vampire's face—made beautiful by the change and transition into the undead state—acted as one of the principal materialisation of the 'new vampire'. The idea that vampire faces are beautiful and enthralling is a feature that twenty-first century narratives have undoubtedly inherited from the late twentieth century, and have truly transformed into an accepted and conventional characteristic of the vampire itself.[75]

Nonetheless, while Western conceptions of beauty—encapsulating symmetrical features and unblemished complexion—are a common, if not universal feature of the narratives, the focus on the uncanny and eerie nature of the vampire's face continues to have a presence in several examples. Even when the vampires are portrayed as beautiful in human terms, their faces have the ability to unearth and display the seemingly 'other' side of their nature, the undoubtedly unhuman side of the creature which emerges when the opportune conditions are in place. This question of 'slippery beauty'– one that can be moulded and remoulded around conceptions of 'the natural—echoes Gilles Deleuze's consideration of 'the thing of beauty'. Deleuze's considerations draw attention to the different between 'beautiful things' and the 'essence of beauty'. The two are seen as inherently different in that former condenses empirical visualisations of a concept, while the other uncovers a dialectic of amalgamation that are intrinsic to life in the epistemological sense.[76] The essence of beauty, therefore, in ungraspable in itself, but is mediated and mediated by the human mind through incarnations of that which is contextually seen as 'beautiful'. In this framework, the beautiful or unbeautiful nature of the vampire's face—a creature that is, in itself, an operational channel—opens the way for uncovering the boundaries of cultural perceptions and their significations. The face, one might venture to say, speaks of the vampire's literary peculiarities as a symbolic representation of the ungraspable essence of the human.

The focus on the face as the locus of vampiric idiosyncrasy should not be a surprise. As an anatomical area, the human face has received a lot of attention, inspired by tradition, science and even common sense. These three strands of approach converge in agreeing that faces act as an opening 'into emotions'.[77] The connection between facial expression and emotion was the centre of several discourses on human sensibilities within a number of theoretical strands throughout the twentieth century, and still continues to be today. Psychology, sociology, and phenomenology—to name but a few—have explored the place occupied by the face in highlighting emotional responses, so that human expressions could be understood as being directly connected to feelings. Phenomenology, in particular, has been keen to build a connection between emotion and the mechanically driven movement of facial muscles, seeing the connecting process as an essential part of the famous Husserlian notion of 'being in the world'. Maurice Merleau-Ponty links faces and emotions so closely, that the two are seen not as being in a consequential relationship, but as direct phenomena that depend on each other for the understanding of human behaviour: 'anger, shame, hate and love are not psychic facts hidden at the bottom of another's consciousness'. They exist, Merleau-Ponty claims, 'in the face', 'not hidden' behind it.[78] In this framework, the neuromuscular activities of the face, caused by a chain of cause and effect, can be understood as the realisation of 'emotions'.

The face, Thomas Alley reminds us, 'is widely recognised as the most important are of our bodies in influencing and regulating interaction with others'.[79] In contemporary fiction, the presentation and uses of the vampire's face replicate this sociological interpretation of the face in the human world. The vampire's face works on similar grounds as do human faces in that it is the chief bodily part associated with the expression of feelings, and the reading area for emotional responses. It reflects intentions and attitudes, but its way of communicating is not always in human terms. Reaction, it would seem, is a term working on a different framework in the vampire world. It ranges from the intense externalising of emotion—which causes momentary disfigurement and even bone restructuring the vampire—to extreme stillness, leading to the impression that vampire faces are, as Christopher Farnsworth puts it in the *Nathaniel Cade* series, 'like stone'.[80] The fact that vampire faces can remain stone-like regardless of the emotions experienced by the creature introduce the idea that, in some narratives, the face itself betrays the vampire's inherently sociopathic nature to humans. This idea is strongly suggested by the *Nathaniel Cade* series, where the vampire Cade's inability to connect to humans socially and emotionally is exemplified by his almost permanently motionless face. The ability to remain motionless, and not betray any form of intention through expression or outlook is also, of course, a definitive characteristic of predatory animals.

Arresting beauty, animal-like features, and unreadable stillness cannot be taken on a superficial value, and one must enquire what part they play in constructing social relations for the vampire, or even in ensuring the creature's own survival, when sociability ceases to be of importance and predatory instincts become the driving force of the interaction. Alley points out that 'the social importance of facial appearance has made the elaboration of faces a common activity among humans'.[81] This contention, put in vampire terms, suggests that the vampire's ability to control facial features lies at the base of its survival. Beauty inspires trust, it is mesmerising, and enhances the vampire's ability to attract its prey. As the perception of others' faces is an essential component of social perception, the vampire's facial features exert a strong influence on social interaction. Several narratives portray the vampire's features shifting from their human outlook to their actual composition, what is often known as the 'real face' of the vampire, which—carrying with it a succession of metaphorical interpretations—is often kept concealed from the world, and is revealed only when the vampire is extremely angry, hungry, or even sexually aroused. This conceptualisation of the 'real' vampire face was popularised in the later twentieth and early twenty-first century by *Buffy the Vampire Slayer* (1997–2003), where vampires are often depicted as shifting into their unequivocally vampire faces; in these instances, the bone structure of the vampire shifts and grows additional extremities, distancing itself from any notion of human feature, and stepping more convincingly into the presentation of an animal close in its outlook to predators of a feline or wolf-like denomination. In *Buffy*'s case, the shift in the vampire's face had both practical and conceptual usages; it would not allow more space for their fangs to emerge, but would also function as a physical illustration of the predatory and blood-thirsty nature of the vampire, divorced from the concept of humanity both in perception and outlook.

The shifting outlook of the vampire's face—from beautiful to horrifically animal in less than a second—propagated by popular culture examples has been continued and developed in contemporary popular literature. The duality of the facial expressions also seem to bear a connection to the conflict experienced by several vampires, the dual qualities of their faces matching and recalling the dual and often ethically-inspired nature of their 'souls'. An ideal example of this can be found in the *House of Comarré* series. Vampires are said to 'wear' either their human of vampire faces. Ordinarily, vampires display a 'human face'—one that they wear like 'a mask'—with properly human features in terms of both bone structure and colour.[82] However, it is revealed that this is not the 'natural' outlook of the vampire; their bone structure is different from humans, and they have a more animalistic outlook to their features. Wearing a 'human face' requires concentration from the vampire's part, and it is virtually impossible to upkeep when the vampire's emotions—be it anger, sadness or lust—become uncontrollable and overcome them. When vampires are ready for combat, their faces 'shift' into their natural vampire structure.[83]

In this sense, the vampire's face can be understood as emblematic of both their emotions and responses. I employ the term 'emblematic' here recalling the use that David Efron (1941) made of it in relation to the facial display of emotion. An emblem refers to 'symbolic actions' where 'movement has a very specific verbal meaning'.[84] The meaning is connected to the psychological state that is culturally associated with the movement, and is typically employed, whether consciously or unconsciously, 'with the intention of sending a message'.[85] A facial emblem—a movement, a change or a shift in the facial features—has meaning because it is tied to context and, just like words, signifies something precise. The interpretation of that meaning, however, is always dependant on behaviour and situation. Facial features, therefore, are emblematic because they signify a contextualised connotation within a system of non-verbal communication. In the case of the shifting vampire face, the features can be seen as emblematic of its change from seemingly human to something other. The face of humanity is shed in favour of the real nature of the vampire, a creature that is presented as tightly connected to emotion. The physiological foundation of the vampire's body is therefore strictly connected to psychology, as emotion and feeling have the ability to re-mould the structure of the face, so that its outlook becomes—at least in human terms—as separate from the norm and as 'other' as that which is being felt. The malleability of the vampire's features in The *House of Comarré* shows how the face become the 'geometric locus' of the 'inner personality' of the individual, to the degree that the vampire's own responses to outside stimuli—kept otherwise concealed in the mind—are enhanced to a psycho-anatomical degree that is perceptible.[86]

Nonetheless, if it is true that the face is what highlights the individual as unequivocally human, then the propensity for the vampire's face to be different hides the secret of the vampire's own unavoidable otherness. That difference is not necessarily anatomical; while there are instances in which the vampire's 'real face' is structurally divorced from the human outlook, the tendency is to maintain vampire's face looking humanoid, with eyes, nose, mouth, cheeks and so on. The reasons for this are multiple, and they begin, naturally, with practicality. Seemingly human faces allow vampires to mix with humans more seamlessly. Mingling is of course an important part of the hunt and closely connected to the vampire's survival; therefore, the ability to circulate undisturbed transforms the human-like face into an important asset. Indeed, in cases where the vampire's face is unavoidably and unchangeably 'inhuman', efforts are made on the vampire's part to hide it. A powerful example of this can be found in *The Dresden Files*, where the vampires of the Red Court—bat-like creatures of human size—wear 'human suits' with human faces (also known as 'flesh masks') so that they can mix with the crowd and not elicit fear in humans. The masquerade is of course part of a careful plan for vampires, so that they can approach their prey and claim a place of power—often rather political—in the human world.[87] The vampire's face plays a very important role in aesthetic judgements. Scare tactics are seen as counterproductive by the vampires in the Red Court, and hiding their animal features is an essential element in maintaining the stability that allows them to hunt, survive and exert control over humans. As faces have a major influence on social interceptions, vampires are portrayed as capitalising of the pervasive human belief that facial expressions are a window into the emotional structure of an individual.

Indeed, the vampire's face does not simply have seemingly practical reasons. The maintenance of human features also exposes a critique of the concept of humanity itself. The term 'feature' is used here in relation to characteristics and details—such as eyes, nose, and mouth—as they are understood in everyday parlance, and not in the often obscure and elusive ways that are pursued in cognitive psychology.[88] The vampire's face—seemingly human but not quite—is suggestive of a sense of humanity that was either lost (during turning) or overcome (in cases when vampires are seen as a different species, inevitably higher on the evolutionary scale). The vampire's face hints at humanity, but simultaneously eludes it. It is a memory made manifest, the embodiment of otherness, the vector of separation and declassification. In this sense, and especially unavoidably in relation to the dynamics of the human face, the vampire's face is uncanny. It is apparently human enough in its features to be recognised and understood, but it also has an array of manifestations and features which make it unmistakably inhuman. It is known and unknown at once. It is knowledge and confusion. It is familiar, and yet strange. The vampire's face, with all its features, embodies—more than any other bodily part—the vampire's uncanny removal from the human world, and its concomitant insistence in merging with it.

DERMAGLYPHS

As marks of bodily difference are concerned, the vampire's skin emerges as an important part of the creature's perception perception, and representation in both the literary and cultural sense. In contemporary fiction, descriptions of the vampire's skin range from being 'golden' and 'smooth' (*Black Dagger Brotherhood* and *Vampires in America* series), to 'white' and 'pale' (*Fangland, Twilight, Sookie Stackhouse,* and *Nathaniel Cade* storylines). In examples where vampires possess the corpse-like qualities of the undead, their skin is said to be decaying, flaky, and as delicate as parchment. Whether pale or golden, smooth or decaying, the vampire's skin receives a lot of attention and its characteristics act as a powerful signifier of the vampire within the narrative.

And when it comes to the vampire's skin, an example that presents itself as significantly different from the rest can be found in the *Midnight Breed* series. The description of the vampires' skin in Adrian's narrative is worthy of note because it distances itself significantly from other incarnations, adding a communicative function to its bodily representation. The vampires' bodies are covered by what is known as 'dermaglyphs': these are coloured markings that are naturally inscribed within their skin. The glyphs, however, are not simply decorative. Their colour, outline, and numbers are determined by a number of factors. They change according to emotion and experience: 'the glyphs changed hues according to a vampire's emotional state. Dante's were currently deep russet-bronze, indicating satiation from a recent feeding'.[89] Dermaglyphs are genetically determined, and a tell-tale sign of an individual being 'breed'—the categorising term that Adrian uses to identify the vampires.

'Breed', however, implies a genetic quality to the category, and this is indeed confirmed by a number of important elements. The glyphs are, to start with, part of what Susan Bordo describes as the 'natural, biological body'.[90] They exist as a reflection of the genetic material that composes the Breed. As relayed in this volume's Chapter 1, the current Breed members are the descendants of aliens which landed on Earth thousands of years prior to the main and contemporary storyline starting. These aliens—referred to as the 'Ancients'—were humanoid in shape, but notably different from humans in their appearance. Reaching over seven feet in height, their bodies had blue-ish skin, and were completely covered by 'the changeable' and 'camouflaging pigments' of the dermaglyphs.[91] When the Ancients procreated by unions with human women, their offspring inherited their fathers' dermaglyphs. Indeed, the quantity of the dermaglyphs of Breed specimens varies according to how long ago they were conceived and how distant their relation to the Ancients was: 'Glyphs typically were a source of pride for the Breed, a unique indication of lineage and social rank'.[92] The first vampires born of the direct union between humans and Ancients—referred to 'Generation One' and conceived over one thousand years ago—have dermaglyphs on the majority of their bodies, with the exclusion of their faces and hands. The appearance of the dermaglyphs, however, is not as pronounced in further generations; as the Ancient genetic material became weakened by exponential interbreeding, so did the reach and number of dermaglyphs. We are told that the current generation of Breed has very few dermaglyphs showing indeed: 'Not a single visible *dermaglyph* on that young skin. Definitely current generation Breed. Probably not even out of his twenties'.[93] As the appearance of dermaglyphs became diluted by the mingling of Ancient blood with the genetically mutated human DNA of the Breedmates, so did the strength and physical abilities of the vampire Breed.

As the tangible creation of hereditary genetics processes, the Breed's dermaglyphs can be understood as birthmarks. Although, scientifically speaking, birthmarks are not technically viewed as directly hereditary, there is a sense of biological connectivity—that links the genetic material of a parent to that of a child—in which the birthmark finds its place as a skin trait that is transmitted from one generation to the other. Birthmarks—signalled here as any form of skin pigmentation present from birth—are not just visible metaphors for the working of genetics and the biomedical understanding of how any body works. The appearance of the skin—with its natural markings and contours—can be treated as the tangible exemplification of how genetic material is transmitted. Although all aspect of the body are genetically determined, the markings of the skin—especially in instances when they are peculiar, like in the case of birthmarks—profess to the direct connection between parent and child, constructing the threads of generational moulding. In a way that hair or eye colour never could, the skin speaks loudly of one's family connections. As a result, all skin markings, as Steve Connor puts it, 'have the flagrancy of the blatant', as 'they blurt out what the tongue might prefer to keep directly veiled'.[94]

Although these biometric considerations of skin have been developed in relation to the human body, it is possible to suggest that, in their ability to reveal both genetic and anthropological connections between individuals, they also provide a framework for unravelling the complexity of the vampire body and its social function. The Breed's dermaglyphs lend themselves to this interpretation. As a form of birthmark, the dermaglyphs allow us to expand the gaze of genetic discourse into understanding what moves the portrayal of the vampire body in contemporary narratives, and how that portrayal is inevitably connected to issues concerning the place of the human body in an increasingly genetically modifiable society.

Gisli Palsson points out that, in their genetic role, birthmarks stand for embodied nature against the artificiality of nurture'.[95] The Breed's dermaglyphs, one might say, represent a biomarker of racial belonging which identifies the genetic material of a whole group, a whole population. That population is, in this case, vampire, a hybrid creation that is the result of selective breeding between alien creatures and genetically enhanced—or one might say, mutated—human beings. The presence of dermaglyphs on the vampire's body stands for the genetic mixture, the interbreeding and, ultimately, is illustrative of the fact that what we are being presented with is not human. The Breed's humanoid appearance is 'betrayed'—if this term can be used—by the dermaglyphs, a birthmark of difference that catalogues not only the morphology of the body, but also the parameters of behaviour between a specific group. The fact that quantity and effectiveness of the dermaglyphs change with cycles of breeding testifies to the fact that vampire genetics, just like human ones, are inherently tied to both biological interchange and performative organisation. In so doing, however, the Breed's dermaglyphs also attest to how natural skin markings represent the 'hereditary signatures' of the person as a separate entity.[96] The presence of dermaglyphs emerges as a mixture of the genetic material that ties the body to biological structures, and an identification practice that works as a metaphorical barcode for membership. The vampires' skin markings, in the same way birthmarks are known to do, represent 'a direct link to the past, the ancestors, and the identity of the unique individual'.[97]

In spite of their colour-changing abilities, the Breed's dermaglyphs are often taken to be tattoos by human eyes: 'He had a tattoo on his neck—at least, [Gabrielle] thought it was a tattoo. Intricate swirls and geometric-looking symbols rendered in ink just a few shades darker than his skin'.[98] Although not the result of voluntary marking and inscription, the dermaglyphs do indeed share some of the semiotic qualities of tattoos, even if their presence as a genetic imprint positions them in a different conceptual category. In her essay 'Inscriptions and Body-Maps' (1990), Grosz explores the illustrative power of tattoo inscriptions, treating the body as a communicative surface on which messages and meaning can be inscribed. Grosz argues that tattoos construct metaphorical texts for the individual; the inscribing procedure, based as it is (usually) on voluntary choice, constructs 'bodies as networks for social signification, meaningful and functional "subjects" within assemblages composed with others'.[99] Although the critical register of the tattoo varies from that of the vampire's dermaglyphs, the two share the ability to signify, in one way or the other, belonging to a particular group, even if that affiliation is a genetic construct rather than a conscious decision. Dermaglyphs are not inscribed on the body by choice, they are 'natural' inscriptions. In this, they are the result of genetic composition and, as such, they can be understood as a form of genetic mapping. Dermaglyphs stand for 'Breed' and their quantity also speaks of the genomic history of the individual.

Nonetheless, and just like human tattoos, dermaglyphs also have a social function, which goes beyond their hereditary qualities in terms of genetics. In human terms, tattoos can work as symbols of affiliation and preference. In a number of Polynesian communities—especially those based in Tahiti and New Zealand—tattoos operate as the signifier for community and the place that an individual holds within it. In Western societies, tattoos can act as the symbolic representation of group affiliation; in the past, this was mainly understood as symptomatic of criminal activity. In contemporary organisation, however, tattoos have also acquired an aesthetic quality, which enhances and emphasises the ability of inscription practices to site the individual within social, economic, and cultural structures. Living through all its different morphologies, practices, and functions, the tattoo, as Jane Caplan suggests, 'occupies a kind of boundary status on the skin, and this is paralleled by its cultural marker of difference, an index of inclusion and exclusion'.[100]

Resembling the treatment often bestowed upon tattoos in the human world, the dermaglyphs speak—or, at least, they are intended to speak—of the individual vampire's personality. A higher number of dermaglyphs means a closer relationship to the Ancients, a group that has become despised by the Breed in virtue of their known aggression, ruthlessness and cunning. Individuals who resemble the Ancients to a greater extent are also considered to be not only more physically resilient, but also naturally more aggressive. Dermaglyphs, therefore, categorise individuals not only genetically, but also socially in that they are a vehicle for prejudice. The inscription of the natural body, which is seen as proper to the vampire, operates similarly to the inventory of human tattoos. In this sense, the biology of the vampire's body is the instigator for community. Dermaglyphs outline the carrier as the individual member of a faction, not just biologically, but also anthropologically speaking. They are a sign of belonging, of the desire to maintain the presence of the vampire community as a separate entity. As it is the case with bodily instances of inscription and marking, the dermaglyphs also operate publicly in that they construct a social position for the individual within the collective imaginary of the Breed as a cultural group.

The ability of dermaglyphs to speak socially for vampires is founded on a delicate and relational dynamic between the interiority and exteriority of the individual, which finds a point of exchange in the surface of the body. What appears on the skin can be understood and exemplified as part of a process of both genetic and social branding. The latter is essential for categorising the individual as a subject within the community. According to Grosz, inscription allows the individual to be 'named' and 'tagged' on its surface, therefore 'creating a particular kind of "depth-body" [. . .] a psychic layer that the subject identifies as its disembodied core'.[101] What appears physically on the outside is a vehicle for identification, and signals the construction of an interior sense of self, which is mapped on the surface of the body. Grosz is speaking here of voluntary practices which rely on the individual on being 'inscribed' by coercive forces. And while the skin markings on the vampire's bodies in the *Midnight Breed* series are, to some extent, placed forcefully on the surface of the body, they still play a part in the process of subjective internalisation. While clearly the result of genetic definition, and the biological structures that derive from it, the dermaglyphs are also internally lived, in that they allow members of the Breed to have grounds for identification. And while that identification begins with the group, it extends to the individual when he chooses to live as part of that community. The glyphs are an external representation of anthropological structures, the way of life that has allowed the Breed to develop and flourish. The body of the vampire allows the vampire identity to be internalised and experienced. The seemingly shallow surface of the vampire's skin, marked as it is by such a defining presence as the dermaglyphs, is given emotional depth by channelling the association to the concept of 'Breed' in its social and cultural constructs.

THE (SEXY AND POWERFUL) MALE BODY

The late twentieth-century already offered fertile ground for debate and conversation when the vampire form was involved. Rice's *Vampire Chronicles* were instrumental in marking the shift from the corpse-like vampire if folklore to the ethereal creatures of beauty many still associate with vampire today: porcelain white skin, diamond-like eyes, luscious hair and youthful appearance are just some of the characteristics that Rice's vampires were able to flaunt. On the popular culture front, Erotica fiction and B-class movies worked studiously in establishing a portrayal of the vampire (especially male) as shapely and well-endowed, the centre of attention as a sexual object/subject, able to inspire the most erotic fantasies in those poor, unsuspecting humans who had the mis/fortune to lay eyes on him. In the late nineties, the hunky vampires of *Buffy the Vampire Slayer*—Angel and Spike in particular—paved the way for the creation of a horde of physically attractive vampires who would dominate the scene in the twenty-first century. And dominate they do. Contemporary vampires make a virtue of their gorgeous bodies, which they use for different purposes (such as fighting and, of course, sex) whenever the action demands it.

It is not a surprise that the body proves to be such an important part of the definition of what is vampire and that, in so doing, is connected to issues of identification, separation, and subjectification. The male vampire's body has become overly exaggerated with muscle. Ordinarily, vampires who were born as such tend to be over 6 foot four in height; if they were descended from warrior bloodlines—a common occurrence in contemporary fiction, where a fascination with warriors is widespread—they tend to be between 6 foot six and six foot nine in height. The height would be, perhaps, regarded as unbelievable, even grotesque, when humans are involved. But for male vampires, that is the norm. In examples such as the *Black Dagger Brotherhood* or the *Midnight Breed*, the male body lies at the centre of discourses of power, domination, and gender. In Ward's storyline, it is made very clear that the selective breeding resulting in the warrior class has undoubtedly created what is conceived as the ideal specimens of males within the species, who are deemed worthy—oddly more physically than morally—to be initiated into the Brotherhood. As the Brothers' sole occupation is to protect other members of the species from the threat of extinction, physical superiority is seen as an essential characteristic, and one can only be carried by a male body in its perfect working order. The members of the Brotherhood have highly developed bodies. Ward dedicates entire sections within the narrative to describe them in their idealised perfection. The Brothers are all over six foot six in height; Wrath, the only pure-bred vampire left on Earth—and therefore the most flawless incarnation of the male body within the vampires—is said to be six foot and nine inches tall, a towering giant even among his own species. The Brothers' bodies are overall muscular and lean, described as 'colossal'.[102] Their thighs are said to be as wide as an average human woman's waist, with powerful quadriceps; their 'powerful arms' are coupled with 'heavy shoulders'.[103] Their chests are 'wide and well-defined'.[104] The absence of obvious fat layers on the male vampires' bodies testifies to a high metabolism, and the ability to burn calories quickly in order to upkeep their layers of muscle. Every time the Brothers' bodies are described and placed on show, there is no doubt left about their physical superiority; their advanced bodies make them faster, agile, and more efficient in combat.

Nonetheless, the emphasis on muscle, height, and overall size does not just play testament to the Brothers' ability to fight and protect both themselves and others. There is no mistaking the fact that the muscular characteristics of the male vampire warriors are deemed as a clear signalling of their masculinity. The recurrent focus on the developed male bodies is reconciled with a sense of masculinity which is not only physically prescribed, but also socially understood. Kenneth McKinnon points out that, visually and conceptually, 'the male body takes on a crucial role in masculinity'.[105] Since the body is so clearly physical, unavoidable and as McKinnon puts it 'so obviously there', the suggestion often seems to be that if a body is clearly male, then it is also masculine. The treatment of the male, muscular bodies communicates a sense of masculinity which, at least in Ward's conception, is viewed as natural.

This detailed exchange is particularly elucidated when the Brothers' bodies are placed in action; it is in the midst of fighting that their bodies showcase their perceived masculinity. The Brothers are said to be excellent fighters, their movements fluid and precise, their bodies flowing in sync with the action: 'Rhage handled [the enemies] by himself, all animal strength and reflexes. He was ripping some kind of martial-arts hybrid, his trench coat flaring out behind him as he kicked heads and punched torsos. He was deadly beautiful in the moonlight, his face twisted in a snarl, his big body pummelling'.[106] The dynamics of the male vampires' bodies when in action are indeed not casual. The emphasis falls on their muscular superiority and their abilities to use it to their advantage in a number of situations. But muscle does not only translate into superiority in the battlefield;

it also allows the Brothers to construct fighting personas. The body itself is not a marginal presence in the warrior's lives, but the centre of their characterisation.

Fighting, however, is not the only area in which the male vampires' bodies excel at exposing the seemingly inherent masculinity of the Brothers. We are told on a number of occasions that the Brothers are exceptional lovers. This ability is not just learnt, but seems to be a collateral happening of their physicality. The warriors' bodies, Ward makes it clear, are 'made for sex'.[107] The extreme muscularity of the Brothers' bodies is associated with intercourse, carrying the assumption that a developed and powerful male body will find its most masculine rendering in the sexual act. Indeed, Ward stresses the fact that the Brothers' bodies are also equipped with large penises, which are described on a number of occasions as 'huge' and 'enormous'.[108] It is not a surprise that sexual prowess is associated with being masculine, especially when the body takes on such an important role in the dichotomous division of gender and sexuality. Laurence Goldstein points out that 'the sign of the male body is of course the penis', and that such a seemingly unassuming anatomical characteristic carries a wealth of representational power with it.[109] Freudian theory—originating with Freud himself—has explored and studied in detail the symbolic presence of the penis in psychological and social terms, culminating in the emblematic incarnation of 'phallus' as the fulcrum of representation between masculine and feminine identities. It would seem that Ward is subscribing to a traditional interpretation of the penis as symbolic presence in establishing a patriarchal hierarchy of physicality, and in delineating the uses of the vampire body.

Through the presentation of the male body in the *Black Dagger Brotherhood*, it is clear that masculinity is not a static concept. Although the developed body of the male vampire warrior is seen as a defined characteristic of its masculinity, masculinity itself is not simply a physical construct. The body is also, as Michael Messner puts it, 'an object of social practice'.[110] Its creation and perpetration is also a collective matter, as the body is bestowed layers of value within specific parameters of preference and taxonomy. The vision of the tall, muscular male, however, is projected as preferred, and most definitely desirable for the species. Muscular males are clearly more masculine in that they will also possess the other definitive qualities— aggression, agility and extreme territoriality—which are associated with an idealised vision of male vampire perfection. The body, it would seem, is an agent of masculinity not only visually, but in its role as a constructed representation of inclination and ability. The muscular male body is coupled with ancillary social characteristics that are viewed as the epitome of vampire masculinity, and it is in that conception that their representation becomes an agent of authority. Although not the exclusive representation of the male vampire in the *Brotherhood* and the *Midnight Breed*, the type of masculinity exhibited by muscular, heterosexual characters is presented as the favourable manifestation of male identity. The conception of the body gives us an outline of what it means to be 'masculine', a clear definition of the social state of muscle and aggressive behaviour in the vampire world.

The strict differentiation between male and female, masculine and feminine—as closely based on physical parameters—does have a sense of performativity attached to it. In both the *Midnight Breed* and the *Black Dagger Brotherhood* physical appearance also seems to carry implications of a more social nature. In the latter, particularly, sexual difference—naturally conceived as the result of biological difference—implies a pervasively strict division of role within the social group. The term 'social role'—and its more biologically specific 'sex role'—does of course carry a number of allegations with it, that are connected, in both theory and practice, with binary-based categorisations of gender. The sex role can be understood, as R.W. Connell puts it, as the 'cultural elaboration of biological sex difference'.[111] In this line of thought, masculinity can be interpreted as internalised conceptions of the male, the simple product of 'learning and socialisation'.[112] An approach leaning towards sex roles inevitably exaggerates the degree to which an individual's behaviour is prescribed according to their physical formation and biological sex. It assumes that very little exchange takes place between the sexes in collective terms, and that all situations are suited and suitable for specific gender interaction to take place. The strict categorisation that derives from this view insists on reducing gender categories to physical interaction, and linking the biological differentiation of 'male' and 'female' to structures of social relations. Yet, it is precisely this strict categorisation that forms the operational framework for masculinity within the Brotherhood. Males—defined as such as having a penis, large quantities of muscle, and a good dose of testosterone—internalise the masculine role, and are expected to perform acts that are sitting as fitting to their gender category. They fight, they protect, they are aggressive. Females, on the other hand, are expected to conform to their biologically prescribed and socially acceptable role as the 'fairer sex', and engage in activities of a more domestic nature.

Fighters, it is made clear, must be male, and display the appropriate characteristics of their sex. Females are not intended to fight, and their physical inferiority is treated as a testament to this. If female vampires are interested in endeavours that go beyond the domestic, and ventures into the warrior realm, their intentions are met with confusion, suspicion and often ridicule by other members of the species. This is the case of Xhex, the tough security guard and later ally of the Brotherhood, who is said to be an excellent fighter. That fighting ability, however, comes at a price. In order to perform like a male, she also must take on what is seen as the hegemonic characteristics of the masculine. She wears men's clothes and, for all intents and purposes, 'acts' like a male: 'Hair jet-black and cut like a man's [. . .] With the wife beater she had on, she was popping the upper body of an athlete, all muscles, veins, no fat. The vibe she gave off was that she could break bones and enjoy it'.[113] Ward seems to suggest that the sociality of gender also has a performative, if not biological register. For female vampires to take on the masculine role, and perform what is seen as male activities, they must abandon socially and culturally prescribed constructions of the feminine and, as Margery Hourihan puts it, 'behave exactly like the boys'.[114] Among the vampires, it would seem, the warriors and protectors are unequivocally men, so it is possible to suggest that the very concepts of courage and fighting skills are gendered.

As it is often the case when warrior narratives are involved, violence emerges an important feature and occupies an important part in the storyline. Physical combat is unlikely to come without an abundance of blood, injury, pain and death, and Ward and Adrian are no exception is portraying violent enterprise as an essential part of the categorisation of the masculine ideal in the vampire warrior class. In conceptual, social, and cultural terms, the association between violence and masculinity should not come as a surprise. Connell suggests that 'violence becomes important in gender politics among men. [It] can become a way of claiming or asserting masculinity in group struggles'.[115] The Brothers kill their enemies indiscriminately, and very little thought is given to those who are efficiently dispatched in fights: 'In a flash, Zsadist was on top, straddling the [enemy]. He bit the [enemy] in the neck, right through the oesophageal column. The [enemy] hollered in pain, thrashing wildly between his legs. And that was only the beginning. Zsadist tore his prey apart'.[116] It is through violence that the male vampire establishes his dominion over others in combat and, in so doing, also ascertains his powerful sense of masculinity in the eyes of other, comrades, females, and enemies alike. It is worth recalling here that a persistent cultural belief (at least in the West) is that there is an almost unbreakable relationship between masculinity and violence. Glen Lewis and Toby Zoates argue that, 'within certain limits, aggressive male behaviour is accepted as a normal part of everyday life'.[117] In this framework, the body occupies, once again, central stage in these dynamics of power, as it is the physical superiority of the vampire warriors that allows proclaims them victorious in the fights. The constant employment of the body in physical activities—as violent and murderous as they might be—is an essential characteristic of the masculine vampire character. The general sense of accomplishment and male pride that results from the fights confirms Stephen Whitehead and Frank Barrett's claim that 'masculinity' is a process of 'ongoing construction,' a determined 'action' between 'individuals' and systems of 'power'.[118]

Within that system of power, there is no denying that Ward's contemporary depictions of the vampire offer an exaggerated sense of physicality, pushing the boundaries of cultural acceptability, at least in Western terms.[119] The focus of muscular maleness and the pursuit of violent, yet necessary, acts somehow call into question the male warriors' sense of masculinity. Through its presentation as a construct that needs careful and constant interaction between body and sociality, the vampires' status is exposed as 'hypermasculinity', an inflated and hyperbolic representation of the (Western) male ideal. This can be defined as the overly exaggerated display of is seen, culturally, as the defining traits of what it means to be 'a man. As Murray Healey suggests us, 'the more he [the male] resorts to his body as proof of his virility, the more he "unmans" himself, in effect admitting that his only asset is his body'.[120] The vampire warriors are, without resulting to humorous evaluations, slightly too 'macho', constantly trying to complement their virile bodies with actions that are seen as befitting to the masculine ideal. That physical display is, however, conceptually challenged on a number of occasions. Their recurrent introvertedness is a sign of their overreliance on their physical presentation to grasp a sense of self. In presenting the masculine body as exceedingly tall, excessively muscular, and overly prone to acts of aggression, Ward transforms the male vampire ideal into a paradoxically grotesque figure. The sense of masculinity that derives from their physical depiction is, at least in human terms, unbelievable and strangely unattractive.

In overcompensating—and forcibly imposing an excessively 'masculinist' expression of male physical domination—the warriors' hypermasculinity in the *Brotherhood* unveils a pervasive instability in the construction of male vampire identity. This oblique conception of the contested masculine is exposed by Ward through the male vampires' inner conflicts and inability to find psychological stability. That stability will, on a regular basis, be granted to the male vampires only through the engagements with a female companion, who—taken as she is with their amazingly sexual bodies—will also find time to lift the vampires' spirits and transform them into mentally sound individuals. This interaction is indeed a characteristic of Ward's narrative, one that, while answering to the apparent storytelling demands of the paranormal romance, also exposes the fragility of the hypermasculine vampire persona in its most idealised incarnation.

The focus on the hyper-representation of hegemonic masculinity in the *Black Dagger Brotherhood* is emphasized by the fact that that the Brothers, as warriors, adorn their bodies with specific garments and objects that are described on numerous occasions as their fighting attire. The vampires do indeed 'dress for fighting'—as Ward puts it—and accessorise accordingly. Their weapons consist of the eponymous black daggers—carefully held on their chests through a criss-crossing harness and position—and an array of other weapons, including guns, knives, and *hira shirukens*. Their clothing gear includes the famous shitkicker boots and the 'leathers', a full collection of leather garments—ranging from trousers to jackets—that are considered the epitome of the fighting apparel. It is tacitly suggested that this carefully displayed sartorial composition adds to the menace of their warrior bodies and, in so doing, strengthens the existence of their masculine identity. Female vampires are never depicted wearing leather; the sole exception being Xhex, who often replicates the Brothers' fighting style.

Within the narratives, the use of weapons and clothing choice is meant to be practical for the vampires.

Nonetheless, Ward is not oblivious to the fact that the emphasis on wearing 'masculine clothing' for the purpose of fighting may be an ambiguous term of reference. Black leather clothing is, indeed, surrounded by several associations in contemporary Western cultures. These associations are not lost in the narrative. When the vampire Butch is inducted into the Brotherhood, he is presented with a set of leathers, enhancing the representational value of specific clothing as a symbol of male aggression and ability in the field. Butch, however, claims not to be 'feeling' the leathers, and that the whole attire is a bit too reminiscent of the 'Village People'.[121] Here the leathers show the complications of relying on the value of imagistic iconography to evaluate and re-evaluate masculinity. Leather pants are often culturally associated with the gay community, communicating a sense of masculinity which—within patriarchal, heterosexual systems—is seen as inferior. Nonetheless, the Brothers transform leather into a highly heterosexual icon of hegemonic masculinity. The result, however, is once again exaggerated and verges on the comical. In spite of the manifest desire to construct a reliable sense of masculinity, Ward' narratives maintains an unavoidably ambiguous outlook on the possibility of grasping a defined and un questionable sense of masculinity for the vampire.

As a series, The *Black Dagger Brotherhood* often mocks and, at times, even openly ridicules the intent of viewing masculinity—and all that is associated with it—as undisputed and undisputable. Male identity and its symbolic construct of masculinity could be viewed here through Mikhail Bakhtin's interpretation of the carnivalesque. According to Bakhtin's definition, carnival stages reality as a 'syncretic pageantry of a ritualistic sort'.[122] In diligently wearing clothing and accessories that are perceived in the narrative as 'masculine', the Brothers draw attention to the nature of gender as a comical performance of the self. The masculinity of the Brothers emerges as an act of pageantry in that it ritualises the exposure of the male body through objects that intensify its social value. As an act of performance, the visually and conceptually ambiguous dressing for fighting evokes the buffoonery of the carnival, subverting the parameters of definition and exposing the derisive nature of binary delineations of gender. In the Brotherhood, this sense of equivocal masculinity unearths how the biological formation of the body finds its most ceremonial use in the display and flaunting of material characteristics that inevitably define it at a social and cultural level. The vampires' carnivaleque masculinity epitomises the crisis of definition in contemporary Western societies, and the unreliable nature of visual iconography. The abstruse interpretation of ritual buffoonery in the Brotherhood—set as it is in a paradoxically authentic fantasy world—unveils, to borrow Stefan Brandt's words, 'both the absurdity and the sadness of the "real" and the "surreal'" sides' of male experience.[123]

VAMPIRE SYNTHESIS

Elizabeth Grosz argues that the body 'is a pliable entity whose determinate form is provided not simply by biology, but also through the interaction of modes of psychical and physical inscription'.[124] Although Grosz was undoubtedly thinking of the 'human body' when making this claim, her suggestions about pliability and psychic/physical interaction can indeed be fruitful when thinking of the vampire. Biology, it would seem, is a very important part of being a vampire, especially when vampires are portrayed as a separate species, and not as a creature which resulted from 'turning'. The cellular formation of the vampire body is given attention in several series, with the *Black Dagger Brotherhood* and *Midnight Breed* leading the way. In these plotlines, the focus is definitely not only on how the body is formed, but also how it has an impact on the identity of the individual who inhabits it.

The human body, when compared to that of a vampire, fails to satisfy miserably. The history of humanity shows a distinctive desire for improvement and enhancement of the body, with procedures ranging from the ability of performing better in sport, to the 'gift' of beauty and the chimera of eternal youth. The human body exists in a state of perpetual ungraspability in that it changes constantly, whether that change happens 'naturally' (through aging) or through rigorous techniques such as physical training, or even surgery. Biology, for the human race, has proved to be both a definer—of species, sex, race and the likes—but also a limiting factor, a merciless judge of what can and cannot be unaccomplished. The human body, even in its most perfect and sophisticated working form, has limitations which, whilst being disliked by people themselves, comprise a list of definitive characteristics for the species. Grosz points out that 'the body is not open to all the whims, wishes, and hopes of the subject'.[125] In spite of the desire that operates the attempt at change and improvement, the human body has restrictions; there are things that it 'cannot do'. Biology is the ruthless companion of the human race.

But vampires, it is made clear, are not subject to the same bodily limitations that humans must obey. Vampire bodies are not only an improvement, but also a personification of the corporeal perfection that, in human terms, cannot be achieved. The vampire body can 'do' what the human body cannot. It has strength, agility, speed and beauty without training or maintenance. It can heal fast and without consequences, sometimes it can even re-grow or re-attach its own limbs if they are lost in a fight— a curious ability made manifest in the *Sookie Stackhouse* series, when Sookies witnesses the vampire Thalia re-attaching her severed arm: 'Indira squatted beside [Talya], patiently holding the severed limb to its source. As Thalia drank [blood], I noticed that the arm looked more and more natural. The fingers flexed. I was astonished'.[126] A vampire can run faster than a human, can jump higher, and (at times) it can even dematerialise—with dematerialising being the preferred means of transport for all full vampires, male and female alike, in the *Black Dagger Brotherhood* universe. In spite of its aversion to sunlight, the vampire body maintains its strength—and indeed, even the vulnerability to sunlight has been often dispensed with in contemporary literature.

Overall, it is a common misconception to think that, in both traditional and folkloristic terms, vampires lead an existence which is confined to the night time hours. Aversion to daylight is, undoubtedly, a principal characteristic of the vampire motif, but this characteristic in itself owes its origins much more to twentieth century popular culture than it does to nineteenth century literary representations. Examples of vampires which can actually emerge in the daylight are abundant in literary tradition, one should also think of Le Fanu's 'Carmilla'. The vampires' ability to be out in daylight has been conceptually resurrected in recent years by Meyer's *Twilight* Saga. In the storyline, vampires can not only go out during the day, but their 'powers' as such are not diminished by the act. To this mix, Meyer added her own special addition by giving the vampires the ability to 'sparkle' like diamonds when their skin come in contact with sunlight. This characteristic of the daylight vampire has become almost synonymous with conceptions of the Twilight saga, and—as much as being a beloved fact of Meyer's avid fans—has also become the object of much ridicule in global popular culture circles. Several examples of 'viral' spoofs—with the sparkling Edward Cullen as the unwilling protagonist—have emerged and been disseminated through social media portal even since Meyer's vampires reached their high popularity through their cinematic incarnations.

The vampire body can also scatter its molecules and transform into something 'other', from insects to wolves—as they do in the *House of Comarré* series. For the most part, it does not age, and even when it does, it is at such a slow rate that vampires can live up to one thousand years. The vampire body is resilient to the point of immortality, the most definitive quality which puts in on the opposite scale to its human counterpart. The vampire body is the fantasy of human power; it accomplishes what the human body cannot, and what humans—with medical procedures, training, and genetic engineer—can only dream to possess. It is a reflection of the limitations of what is human, biologically and psychologically. The vampire takes for granted what humans covet to own, and know they most likely will not. Ever. The vampire body compensates for human deficiencies. It is the quintessential extension of human limitations, an imagistic crutch to the ever-wanting human psyche and its imperfect carnal counterpart. Grosz points out that the constraints of the human body are 'perceptually' capable of being 'superseded, overcome', even if that process exists only in psychological terms. Grosz terms this need for improvement 'prosthetic synthesis', where additions and changes to the human body are conceived and sought after.[127] And this is exactly what the vampire body does. The vampire body operates as a prosthetic annex to the human form, fulfilling human desires of invincibility and perfection through mergence, development, improvement. The human body is conceptualised as lacking, but wanting, and both its limitations and potential are embodied through a process of what I lie to call 'vampire synthesis'. This concept—and the idea that the vampire body act as a prosthetic addition to the physical restriction of the human body—is even more evident instances when vampires are 'turned', and therefore make a clear transition between what is human and what is not.

Firstly, one needs to remember that in the turning mythology, most vampires are in fact 'dead' (or undead, as it were). Although this not always the case, it is a common occurrence in the process of becoming a vampire. In the *ChicagoLand* series, for instance, vampires do not display the characteristics usually associated with that state. They are not cold to the touch, they breathe and their hearts work perfectly, pumping blood as it is expected.[128] Being a vampire means being 'dead' from the human life, but also being 'reborn' into another. 'Dead vampires', on the other hand, are much more common and the obvious result from the process of turning . . . they have no pulse, no breathing and, most importantly, no pumping hearts. Vampires of this category are the norm in the *Sookie Stackhouse* and *House of Comarré* series. In spite of its several incarnations, the 'turned vampire' still carries with it the complications of going from human to 'other', and their bodies are the quintessential personification of the shift from humanity which took place. Grosz argues that at the moment when we have a visualisation of the 'improved' human body, we can also see that 'through incorporation' it is possible to highlight 'the most blatant cultural anxieties and projections' of 'the natural body'.[129] The 'organic body', as Grosz calls it, exists in a state of nature and is subject to the 'modalities' of its own space'.[130]

It is curious to think of the human body, unadulterated through processes of change, as 'organic'; a functioning space that relies on biological connections and, by definitions, restrictions. In this light, and in human, Western terms, the vampire body is as inorganic as it could be. It is a version of the human body, but it has abandoned the physical fragility and concerns that made it human. It is changed and re-elaborated, its strength and appearance working as a projection of the anxieties of the human race to which, clearly, it must no longer submit. The vampire is an incorporation of all those human anxieties about the non-permanence of the body, which passing through the filter of supernatural transformation, emerge as irrelevant. The limitations of that which is organic can only be surpassed by tapping into the unnatural, by initiating a discourse of 'open materiality' that exposes a 'set of tendencies and potentialities'.[131] The seeming perfection of the vampire bodies finds the affirmation of its state through the trajectory of development, a necessity that of change that the body must go through. The vampire body is a paradox of human potential, and, in a strange twist, human fantasises of excellence only find their justifications in a corporeal space that is not human at all.

3 The Vampire's Influence

Discussing the dynamics of power hierarchies, Mervyn Nicholson points out that power 'takes many forms', from the ability to influence desire through 'empty signifiers', to the capacity to exercise control over 'things' and 'others'. Power, Nicholson suggests, can be summarised in the ability to 'manipulate consciousness', so that the 'mystique of control' is intrinsically connected to the vision of 'value' that 'people at large' hold.[1] This overarching understanding of 'power' finds a correlation to the portrayal of the vampire's influence on others in contemporary popular literature. The vampire's control does not negate any aspect of existence: it acknowledges and exploits the physical, the psychological, the emotional, and the technological. One moment, vampires are all about physical control; the next, they rely on psychic domination. And in the next moment still, the body's presence is forfeited in favour of technological extensions and digital representation. The vampire's influence, it would seem, is not a univocal concept. It relies on the power of contradiction, on the strength of adaptability. Although one side of the vampire's reach appears to contradict the other, the inconsistency that results aids the uncanny mystique that makes the vampire itself a channel for illogical attractions and incongruous responses. The vampire's control is a mixture of signs which, even in their paradoxically contrasting and often conflicting aspects, find logic and sense in the unconstrained limits of manipulation.

FEAR

The connection between the vampire and transformative structures in contemporary popular literature draws attention to the importance of responses—both emotional and physiological—in delineating the boundaries of influence and control. Those boundaries operate not only within the narrative structures of the fiction itself, but also in the metaphysical outreach of the vampire as a literary and cultural figure. As both psychological and physical responses go, fear is indeed an important part of the reaction to vampires, one which—historically—has been connected to the recognition of the vampire as monster, evil, and 'undead'. The abomination that is the vampire warranted repulsion and fear in virtue of its very existence. The association between fear and the vampire seems obvious, almost logical, given that, by its very nature, the vampire has been conceptually connected to cultural anxieties relating to the human being and its place in the world. As Barbara Karg, Arjean Spaite, and Rick Sutherland argue, 'fear is a powerful component within the human psyche', one that 'feeds off' an individual's imagination and 'lays patiently in waiting in the dark corners' of one's minds.[2]

Contemporary fiction, however, has given the concept of fear various, varied, and often contrasting treatments. Vampire categorisation, and its metaphysical connection to literary genre taxonomies, plays a vital role in deciding the levels of 'fear' which the creature will elicit, if any anxious response is to be had at all. This claim is a reminder of Otto Fenichel's long-standing contention that, psychoanalytically speaking, 'every fear', or lack thereof, uncovers 'other unconscious ideas'.[3] Taxonomy and the classification of appearance is a key element in deciphering fear in vampire fiction. On one end of the literary spectrum—and strangely comprising of a large group of contemporary fictional figures—are the vampires who have forfeited their ability to elicit fear. Although this is clearly not a conscious act on the vampires' part, these examples are, to some extent, victims of their own appearance. Attractive and seductive in nature, the beautiful vampires only enjoy the ability to inspire fear for a very short period of time, that is until the human (or even other vampires) with whom they are dealing assess them as potential sexual partners. This is a definitive characteristic of the 'paranormal romance' sub-genre within contemporary popular literature: the idea that vampires are 'scary' persists, but that fear can be overcome by connecting with them in emotional and sexual terms. Indeed, part of accepting the existence of vampires if getting over 'the fear'.

A now famous example of this dynamic can be found in the *Twilight* Saga, where Bella Swan's attraction to Edward Cullen overcomes the fear of dying that would be seen as a 'normal' response to encounters with a predatory creature. Bella goes as far as openly declaring that she is 'not afraid' of Edward, but she does have one fear: the fear of 'losing' him.[4] A similar absence of fear is pervasive to Ward's *Black Dagger Brotherhood* series. Famous instances of 'fear and love' exchange are commonly repeated whenever a human woman becomes aware of her male partner's true nature as a vampire. In *Lover Eternal*, we are explicitly told that Mary, a human, realises she 'should be terrified' of Rhage the vampire, but is instead attracted to him and wishes to be his lover.[5] Although the sight of fangs is rendered as initially terrifying—recalling, not without a touch of ironic humour, fantasies of 'funky choppers' and 'Dracula moments'—the exaggerated beauty of the vampire's body is enough to wipe away all fear, and replace it with sexual fantasies.[6] All other 'vampire characteristics' are treated with similar parameters; the fear generated by witnessing the vampire in action—drinking blood, dematerialising, or killing his enemies—is quickly condoned in the name of friendship or 'love'. Fear is no longer an issue here, and paradoxically, many human characters view the vampire as a creature who is capable of loving them and protecting them. It seems clear that not all vampires are treated equally and that 'depending on the type of vampire' the reaction 'can trigger' various responses.[7]

In spite of the unavoidable impact of love-centred dynamics on the overall conception of vampire literature in our twenty-first-century context, not all instances of paralysing vampiric fear have been erased from fiction, however. While examples within the sub-genres of paranormal romance rely on the portrayal of vampires as potentially caring and loving individuals—an outlook where momentary fear operates as a form of tantalising aphrodisiac—other instances within the broader scope of contemporary literature re-iterate the vampire as a frightening creature. Although often relegated to certain sub-genres of urban fiction and thriller narratives, the corpse-like folkloristic interpretations of vampires still demand a high level of fear from those unlucky enough to encounter them. Rotting, decaying, and violent, the corpse-like vampires obtain a frightened reaction from human and supernatural creatures alike. The Black Court vampires from Butcher's *The Dresden Files* function as an apt example here: the fear of encountering these vampires is connected to the overall terror of death itself, a notion almost unavoidable for any living creature.[8]

In similar terms, one can see how another category of vampires—usually those who have clear disregard for human life and wish to 'drain' them dead—are also granted fear as an acceptable reaction. Detached from humanity and 'crazed' by bloodlust, these vampires bear their fangs and are a clear representation of that which 'will kill you'. Examples from these categories include the Rogues from the *Midnight Breed* series, demented vampires who are not capable of any cognitive processes which do not result in the drinking of human blood, with all its consequences for the victim. The inability to connect on a human or even vampire level with these creatures renders them as something to fear. Indeed, fear is a response that these vampires 'thrive on' and enjoy as part of their existence.[9] In this framework, fear is also what drives human reaction to vampires in Wellington's *Laura Caxton Vampire* series.[10] The fear of the vampire is seen as a 'natural' reaction, as the creature itself—void here of the romanticised qualities forced by romance narratives—represents danger and is envisaged as an agent of death.

Wellington and Adrian, however, are not alone in portraying the vampire as the embodiment of fear, one that—while oddly resembling human features—functions as the iconographed representation of what is not human at all. An apt example of this can be found in another vampire thriller literary universe, Farnsworth's *Nathaniel Cade* series. When Nathaniel Cade—the vampire protagonist of the narrative—is introduced in the narrative, it is made very clearly from the beginning that he has a tremendous presence.

The first encounter with Cade occurs through his meeting with Zach Barrows, the young politician who is assigned the unwanted job of being the vampire's relation into the human world. Zach's first view of Cade leaves the young politician speechless:

> He was taller than Zach, wearing ragged black fatigues. He looked young. And pale. Very, very pale. He stood there, perfectly calm. Too calm, even. Unnaturally still. Almost the kind of stillness you'd only find in a casket. But just standing there.[11]

The reference to Cade's stillness as 'unnatural' immediately communicates that the vampire is something that does not belong to the world—in both scientific and traditional worlds—as humans understand it. Nonetheless, his outlook is clearly that of a human; Zach is able to identify him as 'young', leaving tacit the assumption that he is young in human terms, and therefore could be potentially taken as human. Cade's stillness, however, challenges his presence as a human being. Indeed, he is likened to a corpse, something that still looks human, but has lost any expression of life. The fact that Cade looks arguably dead, but is still standing like a live creature, is cause of unease and eventually fear for Zach. The vampire here embodies two things: the absence of life, and the ability to overcome it. He is at once familiar and unnatural, mysterious and yet known. The mixture of recognition and confusion that Cade elicits on those who look upon him comprises a mixture of curiosity, incomprehension, and dread. Cade is, to put it simply, an uncanny presence. The idea of viewing the vampire as part of an uncanny experience is of course, in itself, not a new one. The mixture of familiarity and unfamiliarity that surrounds vampires—creating feelings of unease in onlookers—was explored in detail by Ken Gelder in his article 'Vampires and the Uncanny', where the vampire Carmilla in Le Fanu's eponymous story is seen as generating uncanny feelings in those who encounter her.[12]

Farnsworth, it would seem, follows in Le Fanu's footsteps by playing with the vampire as an uncanny figure. The eerie nature of Cade, however, goes beyond just challenging notions of familiar and unfamiliar, of *eimlich* and *unhemlich*. By recalling the stillness of the corpse, Cade challenges 'nature'. Nicholas Royle argues that the uncanny is 'a crisis of the natural, touching on everything that one might have thought was "part of nature"'. It defies, as Royle puts it, 'the nature of reality', of human nature and the world.[13] In Cade's case, the vampire is unnatural in a number of ways. It is implied that he looks too pale, as pale as a corpse. His stillness is also that of an inanimate body. His apparent youth—although it is not explicitly stated—is implied to be at odds with the general outlook of his body. Cade is a creature of inbalance, an entity of defiance. He is unnatural because, in spite of the fact that he imitates many features of what is human—his shape, his clothing, his voice—he is in fact an 'unnatural' replica of the human.

The vampire is presented as a creature that, while playing with humanity, is in fact strange and mysterious, and generates doubt. This inability to decipher the vampire's nature is a distinctive feature of the uncanny, which usually involves 'feeling of uncertainty' regarding 'the reality of what is being experienced' in those who encounter it. The inability to decipher Cade's nature—too still to be human, and too seemingly alive to be really dead—results in Zach's conclusion that while unable to pinpoint an exact category for the creature, Cade is undoubtedly 'something inhuman'.[14] Zach's reaction to the vampire is revelatory:

> Zach felt a stirring of instinct honed on humans huddled at the edges of campfires, terrified of the noises in the dark [. . .] There is a reason humans are genetically programmed to fear the dark. Zach was looking at it. Then [he] saw the fangs at the edges of the smile.[15]

The fangs act as the confirmation of Cade's otherworldly nature, a breaking signifier which highlights the split between humanity and otherness. Zach's initial fear and subsequent shock at encountering Cade is reinforced by the announcement that Cade is not just a vampire—almost implying that could have been acceptable, if strange—but that he is in fact 'the president's vampire'. His astonishment at learning that the president—the symbol of power in the United States—has a vampire at his disposal adds to the eerie, uncanny feeling of the encounter. Although able to categorise Cade as a vampire—thanks to his general inhuman look and the unavoidable manifestation of such an iconic presence as fangs—Zach is unable to interrupt the unease that surrounds the creature. Zach has a visceral reaction to Cade and the revelation.

The knowledge that a vampire—understood traditionally to be a 'creature of the night', and at the centre of tales of the supernatural—is in fact openly entangled with the politics of the State, dispenses with latent feelings of strangeness and mystery, making the fear of the unknown manifest. Cade becomes the embodiment of the weird, but that weird is made so not only by his vampiric nature, but also by the uncanny coupling of the public with the private and the secretive. Royle points out that the uncanny is a 'crisis of the proper'; it has to do with 'a sense of secret encounter', the revelation of something 'unhomely' in the 'heart of the home'.[16] Cade breaks the boundaries of the proper because by his very existence and profession—working for the president—he merges the rational with the irrational, the human with the inhuman, the political with the supernatural. The vampire acts uncannily because it exposes the nature of what is secret, the knowledge that something that should have been kept concealed is made apparent. The 'secret' here can be understood not only as the very existence of the vampriric, but also the confirmation that the State engages in act that the citizens are unaware of. In addition, Cade challenges Zach's very understanding of home in its notion of belonging and stability; the vampire recalls what is gruesome and terrible, and in so doing breaks the boundary between safe and dangerous, both physically and conceptually. In this, Cade truly fulfils Freud's understanding of the uncanny experience, embodying that 'class of frightening which leads back to what is known as old and long familiar'.[17]

THE POWER OF SIGHT

The potentially frightening nature of that which is simultaneously familiar and yet alien—the very notion of the uncanny—lies at the basis of the relationship vampires construct with the bounds of human organisation. From the physical to the emotional, from the tangible to the ephemeral, the vampire's influence engages with multiple layers of human perception. In Chapter 2 we surveyed the importance of 'eyes' in constructing the parameters of vampire identity, and how it is perceived through the fiction. What seems to be a simple re-elaboration of anatomy and physiology, however, cannot be divorced from its conceptual functioning within the wider vampiric scope. As a medium for the senses, the vampire's eyes open debates over what is surveyed and what is, to some extent, under control. In this context, the focus on the eyes draws attention, inevitably, to the power and influence of 'sight'.

As one of the senses, sight has occupied a privileged position in both philosophical and religious accounts for millennia. Plato regarded sight as the most noble of all senses, surpassing greatly the two-partite nature of its meagre brothers: touch, taste, hearing, and sense of smell. The sight's nobility, according to Plato, came from its need to operate on a system that involved three parts: the seer, the seen, and the Sun, intended by Plato not only as the medium of light, but also as a metaphorical interpretation of knowledge and consciousness. In similar fashion, Aristotle's *De Anima*, also proclaims 'sight' as the highest ranking of all senses.[18] Although sight occupied a privileged position in Western organisation for centuries—with a number of influential theoretical paradigms being born at the intersection between philosophy and Christianity—it was in the eighteenth century, and as a result of framework surrounding the Industrial Revolution, that the interpretation of sight began to shift from matters spirituality to issues of cultural aesthetics.[19] The growing influence of human industrial architecture—and its impact, both negative and positive—on the human landscape, allowed sight to 'assume precedence' over the other senses, when understandings of beauty began to have an impact on people's everyday choices, supplanting touch and smell from their acknowledged pre-modern cultural positions. In the nineteenth century, the reign of the visible was documented by writer and art theorist John Ruskin: 'The worst of me is that the Desire of my *Eyes* is so much more to me!'.[20] Ruskin undoubtedly drew attention to the lack of ease with visual modernity that was pervasive to the nineteenth century.

By the time the twentieth century arrived, the predominance of sight as a cultural coordinate became the centre of debates over the impact of the image on everyday life, and the subsequent disassociation from 'real' experience that derived from it. As both an artistic and a cultural icon, the vampire was caught up in the debates over the supremacy of the visual, on the one hand, and the Lacanian-inspired belief that all interpretation happens linguistically, as part of discourse, on the other. Twentieth-century scholarship drew attention to the vampire's gaze, usually in concomitance with critiques of patriarchal systems within Gothic literature. For its own part, the twenty-first century has witnessed the 'return of the visual', a re-vindication of the image and the uses of sight. The act of seeing has indeed taken up its rightful place as part of contemporary psychological and cultural scholarship. Undoubtedly inspired by the interdisciplinary intersections with popular culture, the representation of the vampire's visual abilities in post-2000 literature resists 'subsumption under the rubric of discursivity'.[21] While the description of vampire's eyes is still sighted in the realm of language, its imagistic connections to cultural understandings sight still place it, conceptually, in the intersecting visual corollary of the contemporary Gothic. The pervasive fascination with eyes and sight in contemporary vampire narratives draws attention to the shifting importance of the concept of 'seeing', and how this is closely related to notions of a cultural nature. The focal centre of any depictions of vampire eyes is, one might argue, not only what the vampires see with—the physical eyes themselves—but also how they see. Contemporary narratives clearly emphasise an awareness of different modes of seeing. The interest in the vampire's eyes exposes a wide-spread and latent captivation with 'the enigmas of visual experience'.[22]

While the physical parameters of the body seem to have become somewhat commonplace in contemporary scholarship—both in its scientific, cultural, and artistic incarnations—the return to the vampire's eyes unveils the nature of conceptual interpretations of physicality which are both historical and social. A renewed emphasis on the eyes and not only what, but how they see, appears to be, as cultural historian Martin Jay puts it, a newly recovered 'paradigm' in the 'cultural imagination of our age'.[23] The seemingly unarguable universality of human eyes and ways of seeing is challenged through the elaboration of not only vampire eyes, but also the vampire's gaze. The conceptual and practical understanding of what sees and what is seen is inevitably connected to questions and ruminations of a contextual nature. What cannot be achieved by simply dissecting the human parameters of vision will be uncovered by displacing the power of sight onto the preternatural and the supernatural. In drawing attention to the eyes, how they appear, how they change—if and when they do—allows us a clearer view into the vampire's 'scopic regime', to borrow the term used by Jay. For the vampire, sight—one might venture to say—equals power.

Instances of sight operating as an instrument of the vampire's influence, and an overall agent of control, abound in the fiction. In the *Black Dagger*

Brotherhood, powerful vampires gain control over others—especially humans—through 'catching their eyes' and directing their sight: the vampire Phury can will humans to obey his command by 'locking his stare' into theirs.[24] 'Look into my eyes' is a phrase that is theatrically uttered by Ward's vampires on a number of occasions later in the series when overtaking their victim's will, exemplifying the power exercised by sight in the structure of control.[25] A similar instance can be found in Painter's *House of Comarré* series, where Mal the vampire 'hypnotises' his victims and bends their will by looking into their eyes and channelling 'persuasion' into his voice: 'Mal refocused his power [and] got the bartender's attention . . . his [the bartender's] eyes were slightly glazed. Humans were so suggestible'.[26] The vampire's eyes are a tool of manipulation, sight functioning here as the framework for control over both the body and the mind.

Reinforcing the power of sight, however, can be a hazardous move, not only for the representation of the vampire as a cultural icon, but also for the implications that the 'seeing icon' will have for the human as a whole. Peter de Bolla maintains that any investigation of the eyes—in their physical and philosophical meanings—will inevitably grant an 'entry into visuality' which puts any notion of universality at stake.[27] An interest into the realm of visuality will not just initiate conversations and debates about 'modes of looking', but will also expose preoccupations of a more psychological and even generational nature. If the eyes are a metaphor for the entry into knowledge, then that which sees will be tied by the bonds of interpretation. It is in this interpretation that vampire eyes can betray the human onlooker, revealing the illusory nature of that which is seen. After all, de Bolla reminds us, 'the activity of looking says something about the looker'.[28] This claim rings even more true when the system of vampire sight is involved; it opens the way to asking questions about both the desire and fear which find a venue for existence through the gaze. Attention to the vampire's eyes allows us to dissect the contemporary meaning of the vampire motif; it also reveals the voyeuristic fascination of the human audience it captivates. As the vampire looks, its gaze speaks of humanity.

THE OLFACTORY REGISTER

In antiquity, Plato showed a reluctance—perhaps even a certain inability—to distinguish between the senses and emotions, often equalling a sensorial response to the notion of 'feeling'. In one of his famous accounts of the senses, Plato discusses the nature of perception in relation to sight, hearing, and smell; leaving out taste, Plato does not refer namely to what is seemingly the sense of touch, but opts instead for a direct discussion of hot and cold feelings, together with an exploration of the result of tactile experiences, such as desire and discomfort.[29] The study of sensorial experiences and their place in relation to psychological responses has, of course, moved along greatly since Plato's times, and distanced itself from Ancient Greek conceptions of the senses. Nonetheless, an awareness of Plato's understanding of the senses in relation to emotion and experience draws attention to how, even conceptually, there still exists a relationship between sensorial input and the ability to categorise their effects in relation to 'feelings' and psychological stimuli.

Within this frame of thoughts, the idea that vampire's sensorial organs should play an important part in the display or perception of feelings—and be, in various ways, part of the vampire's influence—does not seem so unimaginable after all. There is no dying that, in contemporary narratives, vampires possess a distinctly developed sense of smell. Enhanced olfactory capabilities are often presented as a defining characteristic of the vampire and the uses of smell—so to speak—have a wide range of nuances. In the *All Souls* series, Deborah Harkness writes of how vampires have a highly developed sense of smell which enables them to pick up on such precise olfactory elements that their abilities are portrayed as preternatural. Vampires have smell classification for every creature; the smell perceived by vampires is often connected to the nature and personality of the person they encounter. Demons smell of 'lavender and peppermint', while the 'smell of a witch' is that of honeysuckle.[30] The millennial vampire Matthew Clairmont has such a developed and attuned sense of smell—undoubtedly acquired and trained over centuries—that he can even detect elements in the bouquet of particular wine that will communicate the provenance of the vintage, both chronologically and geographically. After only one sip, the vampire claims to be able to 'smell the fields' where the grapes were grown and 'taste' the year the wine was made.[31] This ability is viewed with amazement by other creatures in Harkness' narrative, human, witch, or demon alike. In similar fashion, Painter's vampires in the *House of Comarré* series possess a sense of smell that is particularly attuned to picking up the scent of human blood, which they often relate to the person that possesses it. The blood of the Comarré, for instance, is said to be sweeter to the taste and carry a particular 'honey' smell to vampires. The smell can be detected by vampires even through the skin, without any need for blood to be spilled. When the blood does flow from the vein, however, the scent proves overpowering: 'the smell of her uncontained blood infected him like a virus. Her scent became his blood, his reason, his brain'.[32] The 'scent' allows the vampire to identify the special source of blood within a vast crowd, and becomes the explicit vector of the vampire's need for possession.[33] One can see here that, in both Harkness' and Painter's narratives, smell, due to its developmental and functional nature, becomes an important part of the vampire's technologies of control.

Harkness and Painter, however, are not alone in subscribing to the notion that the vampire's sense of smell has preternatural qualities. Advanced olfactory capabilities are a trait of vampires in a multitude of examples, including the *Midnight Breed*, *Sookie Stackhouse*, *Hollows*, *Dresden Files*, and *Black Dagger Brotherhood* series. Particularly in the latter, the vampires' sense of smell takes on a completely different function, as it does only detect the presence of other individuals—vampire or human that they might be—but it also assumes a communicative role. Vampires often recognise each other according to their individual smells, which singles them out from the group and renders them as a separate entity. Female vampires are often detected by the males in virtue of their smell, which is different from vampire to vampire; female smells range from 'night blooming roses' and the 'smell of the ocean', to 'cinnamon' and 'lavender'.[34] There is indeed a propensity in Ward's narratives to build a comparison between the odour of the female vampire body and flower-like smells. Female scents are portrayed as what is culturally understood in the West as 'delicate', subdued, and even elegant. The smells of female vampires are understood to be more 'feminine', prescribing to acculturated notions of olfactory perception. Male vampires, on the other hand, are said to carry individual smells which, in their several nuances, are more akin to what is described as 'dark spices'. The smell of male vampires is also subject to cultural identification and is said to carry a 'masculine' characteristic to it. It is clear that Ward is relying on rigid and inevitably Western conceptions of the nature of smell and olfactory stimuli, associating that which is fragrant and delicate with the feminine, and overpowering and 'spicy' with the masculine.

In human organisation, smell occupies an important part for the construction of relationship. The dichotomous construction of 'good' and 'bad' smells plays an important part in the building of interpersonal relationships. The interpretation of smell, of course, is not universally conceived. Constance Classen reminds us that 'olfactory codes' are 'conveyed' differently in 'different cultures'.[35] Smells also take on what Classen, David Howes, and Anthony Synnott go on to describe as 'olfactory symbolism', the categorisation of scent according to situation, class, gender, and, inevitably, what is perceived as either positive or negative in social-cultural organisation.[36] That symbolism is used 'to express themes of identity', and operates as a point of distinction in different cultures. The cataloguing of odours is therefore used to classify people, objects, and situations, with conceptions of 'sexy', 'dirty' and 'exotic' playing a particularly relevant role.

With this olfactory framework in mind, the dichotomous differentiation of vampire smells in Ward's *Brotherhood* ceases to seem to be casual. Delicate smells can be perceived as part of the female vampire's influence on members of her species, and a way of establishing her position of control within wider social structures. Classen, Howes, and Synnott remind us that, in the human world, there are several categories of smell when it comes to conceptions of the feminine, and that 'certain women are not considered fragrant at all in Western traditions'.[37] This category is said to include any woman who defies the rules of male-dominated society, such as prostitutes or even (in a more contemporary light) the conception of an independent, often-single woman. Such women, Classen, Howes, and

Synnott argue, are 'bad odours on the olfactory scale of feminine value', and are often associated with strong and pungent artificial perfumes. At the other end of the culturally-prescribed olfactory scale, one can find the virtuous woman, virginal in thought if not strictly behaviour—in other words, docile and relatively submissive to a male's control—who is usually considered to be naturally fragrant and should smell 'of nothing stronger than the flowers' with which she is associated.[38] In the *Brotherhood* series, Ward pledges a conceptual allegiance to the olfactory delineation of the worthy female as delicate and fragrant, recalling the smell of flowers and all that is culturally considered as 'clean'. The female vampires' flowery smell shows their positioning in a vampire world that is inherently patriarchal. Unsurprisingly, the subtle smell of female vampires is seen as the most appealing fragrance they could imagine and acts as an aphrodisiac to the males, who tend to associate the tantalising nature of the smell with the promise of mating. By having a delicate smell, female vampires gain control over the males, and even though the political power of the vampire structures lies outside of the female's reach, the olfactory influence of her body places her in control of emotional relationships.

The fragrance of the vampires' bodies, however, is rarely referred to as their 'smell'. The term is usually exchanged for the more culturally specific 'scent'; this indicates, by virtue of its social linguistic qualities, that the odour is intended to be a pleasant one and should be interpreted as a welcome occurrence, whether it is presented in its pointedly feminine or masculine varieties. The word scent, however, also has other connotations; once again, the connection to animalistic behaviour is reinforced through the conceptualisation of smell as a scoring category. This understanding of the term is elaborated on even more when male vampires are described as having specific 'bonding scent', an enhanced version of their natural spicy odour which emanates from their bodies when their sexual and territorial urges are set in place. Indeed, the male vampires in the Brotherhood are known to 'mark' their sexual partners through their own smell: '[Wrath] wanted to mark [Beth]. Mark her as his. He wanted that special scent all over her so no other male would come near her. So that they would know who she belonged to'.[39] The male's scent is an agent for ownership, forfeiting the human symbology of possession that is culturally expressed in the West by icons such as rings and jewellery. This emphasis on smell within the exercise of power relations is clearly in opposition to the human conceptualisation of odour in relation to power. Classen argues that, in Western organisation, the power elite 'usually governs from a position of olfactory neutrality'.[40] In the Brotherhood's world, however, the vampire's position of dominance is created and re-created through the establishment of olfactory parameters of authority.

The understanding of the vampire's olfactory power as an agent of control highlights manipulations of the sense of smell as part of regulatory systems. Ward's vampires have a smell for every emotion and response: sadness is said to smell like 'wood smoke'; fear smells like 'lemon'; tears smell of 'rain'.[41] Vampires can even detect when a person is lying, as often intimated on a number of occasions; all they have to do is 'breathe in through their nose' and 'read' a person's 'emotions' through smell.[42] This vampiric ability is bound to make a number of human readers jealous and wishful, as the skill to detect lying and subterfuge would indeed be a coveted possession for many a human. When it comes to the uses of the vampire's sense of smell to detect emotions, that use is, it would seem, allegorical. Smell stands for the ability to contextualise people and emotions beyond the barrier of language.

Emotion is, technically speaking and in human terms, closely related to sensorial responses. Sight is, once again, privileged in this sense, as it allows individuals to pick up on behavioural reactions that communicate an emotional state. Fear, anxiety, sadness, and happiness are usually associated with movements—or other type of physical response—that are picked up more readily by seeing. In the vampire world of the Brotherhood, however, sight is not the most reliable sense, nor is the one on which relationships seem to depend on, as it is often the case in human organisation. Where sight would fail a vampire's evaluation of another creature, smell leaves no doubt. Smell is, in a way, perceived as an unmediated—and unmediatable—sense, directly related to the individual's emotions. It is made clear by Ward that smell cannot be obscured or tampered with; while the eyes may deceive, the vampire's nose picks up on the most ephemeral and yet paradoxically tangible pieces of information. Through smell, the vampires can visualise emotion, giving permanence to an otherwise transient state. One can see a critical conflation here, with what are usually disembodied parts of the living (human) experience being given palpability through the physical responses they elicit. As emotion is not, in human terms, something that can be 'smelled', its vampiric conceptualisation in terms of olfactory responses questions the limits of perception.

Vampires, one might venture to say, 'see' through smell. In this sense, the vampire's engagement with the senses, particularly that of smell, takes on a synesthetic quality in contemporary literature. The term 'synaesthesia' itself is a blend of the Greek words *aesthesis* (sensation) and *syn* (union, or together). The composite translates, loosely, into 'joined sensation', and therefore implies the experience of two or more sensations at the same time.[43] In psychometric terms, the word has been used—at least since the late nineteenth century—to denote the presence of sensory hallucination; in most cases, the experience of the individual is viewed as hallucinatory because it does not match the sensory modality with which it is associated.[44] Practically speaking then, this would be the ability to see music, or taste colours. Phenomenologically, however, the term synaesthesia is wide-reaching and groups together a number of similarly conceived, but profoundly different responses. In an everyday sense—if this appellative can indeed be used—synaesthesia bears a distinct similarity to other cross-activation symptom, which are particularly known to involve smell and visual responses. These are known as 'functional hallucinations' and denote the presence of strong sensorial imaginings—perceived as pseudo-hallucinations—triggered by regular sense perception.[45] These include the Tullio phenomenon—the occurrence of vestibular phenomena triggered by auditory stimuli—and the Proust phenomenon, where overpowering biographical memories are evoked by the experience of taste and smell. Both these examples draw attention to the ability of the senses, even in their regular modality, to merge in creating responses that allow the individual to visualise situations and generate physical, ancillary responses in the midst of sensorial fusion. This ability is known as 'pseudosyneathesia'.

Although human history has tended to honour sight and its seemingly rationalised dependability, the late twentieth century challenged the predominance of visual information as unadulterated. Culturally speaking, digital technologies have shown us how images can be easily manipulated, questioning the nature of the image itself and the consistency of visual parameters to deliver information. By the time the twenty-first century arrived, the tendency for the image to be constructed digitally or 'retouched' through CGI technologies threw into sharp relief the unreliable nature of image as a carrier of information. The image is fickle, mouldable, untrustworthy. Even though, in contemporary popular literature, we see a return to the power of sight, we also notice a desire to re-vindicate the place of other more commonly 'forgotten' senses, and their function in perceptual control.

In the vampire world, it would seem, synaesthesia is part of the experiential workings of the species. Individual vampires are not 'gifted' with the ability to operate on synesthetic or pseudosynesthetic terms; instead, the merging of the vampire senses—from vision to smell and taste—is a distinct characteristic of the group. In this sense, one can see how there is nothing supernatural about their abilities; in their close connections to rare abilities found in the individual, the vampires' heightened senses and capacity to reimagine responses from one modality to the other is preternatural in its understanding. The vampires use abilities that humans can experience only on occasions; the ability to attribute a 'feeling' to a particular smell is synesthetic by its very nature, as it blends the regular modality of smell with psychometric categorisation. We see here that the taxonomy of vampire smell extends beyond odour and delves into the world of not only what is visual, but also what is invisible to the human eye as such. In human terms, the ability to visualise emotions through the sensorial information they emit can be interpreted as hallucinatory in itself, in that it operates on an irregular framework of perception. For the vampire, however, the response does not lie in the realm of hallucination. It is part of the creature's ability, what categorises it as a different sensorial vessel. Within the synesthetic structure, one can see here the delineation of what I like to call the 'vampire phenomenon', a wishful reorganisation of human sensorial abilities that are not tied—both physically and figuratively—to the limitations of human perception.

Narratives such as Ward's, Harkness', and Painter's show a return to smell, a sense that challenges the supremacy of the image and can be seen, arguably, as a reaction against the way in which visual characteristics can be manipulated . Where the image fails, the immediacy of smell leaves very little doubt for estimation. The vampire's developed olfactory system, and the uncontrollable nature of bodily smell, leave very little space for emotional and social subterfuge. One sense is not given priority over the others, but the blended swirl of intertwined stimuli uncovers the vampire as a creature who does not rely on univocal responses, but embraces the blurred nature of the senses as a vector towards identification and control. In the vampire's synaesthetic engagement as the basis for interpersonal relationship, one can see a reclaiming of 'the feeling', a return to the unadulterated. In an era of retouching and reimaging, the vampire's emphasis on synaesthesia unearths Western fears about perceptual manipulation and the cultural desire to find a more unswerving ground for communication and exchange.

MINIONS

The focus on the vampire's powers, techniques of manipulation, and extra-sensorial control draws attention to a particular ancillary figure that has emerged as a common appendix to the vampire's control: minions. These creatures act as the vampire's servants, completely subdued to their master's will, and seemingly eager to satisfy the vampire's every whim. The presence of a minion as such—whose mind appears completely taken over by the vampire's command—is not a new trait of post-2000 literature. Minions have populated vampire narratives for centuries, beginning—at least in the wider popular imagination—with Dracula's Renfield in Stoker's novel. In contemporary narratives, however, minions refuse to be a background, contextual presence, and play an active part in the construction of the vampire's world. Although it is true that not all narratives present creatures whose consciousness has been removed as the vampire's loyalty servant, patterns can be constructed across storylines, so that—when they do appear—minions themselves have taken on characteristics that seem to have a universal reliability in the fiction.

The most common approach to minions is that they are, in fact, humans who have been transformed into 'something else' by a powerful vampire. The initial power over minions is established by the vampire draining the human body of its blood, almost to the point of death; the intended result seems to be that, as the unfortunate victim is subjected to the practice, the human soul leaves the body. The human is then left in not so much a consent, but a conscious state. The de-souled human acts only upon the vampire's command, and the only cognisant desires 'it' possesses are the need to obey the master, and whatever other intent the vampire transmits at any given time. The metamorphosis leaves the human as a shadow of its former self: a minion, a creature devoid of will except for the necessity to serve the vampire who created it. The procedure for transforming humans into minions is echoed in similar terms across several examples of the fiction. In Adrian's *Midnight Breed*, minions are 'humans enslaved by the draining bite of a powerful vampire that rid them of their conscience and free will, leaving only unquestioning obedience in its wake'.[46] In Harris' *Sookie Stackhouse*, a minion is a human who has been 'taken over' by a vampire and has become a 'degraded creature'. In this storyline, the role of the minion is of course that of the servant; however, the price for this is high: we are told that the 'human is lost when the vampire assumes too much control'.[47] In Mariani's *Vampire Federation*, a minion is a loyal servant, 'not quite a vampire, but not quite a human either'.[48] Minions, also referred to as 'ghouls', dwell 'in a shadow world somewhere in between'.[49] In this last storyline, the minions actually over go a physical transformation, as well as psychological one. As they acquire superhuman strength similar to that of the vampire, their appearance also mutates into a grotesque caricature of what humans look like: they lose their hair, their features becomes more angular, and they pale out significantly. Although 'not quite a vampire', a minion—it is intended—has lost its humanity, and its appearance reflects, in a dark humorous twist, the appearance that several narratives (especially early cinematic ones) have established as one of the many looks of the undead, Nosferatu-like vampire.

Although one might be tempted to assume that creating a minion is seen as an expected and expectable feature of the vampire, minions are, in fact, at the centre of an ethical dispute in the vampire world. It is made clear that only 'old-school vampires'—who have no respect for human life, or even a desire to co-exist with humans—will be inclined to create minions. These vampires are deemed as 'bad' in the eyes of their mainstreaming vampire folk, and 'good vampires'—whatever that may be truly mean—regard minions as an abomination. In Harris' *Dead and Gone*, Eric maintains that minions are looked upon with 'disgusting' and 'with distaste', and that the 'best' vampires 'look askance at a vampire that makes servant after servant'.[50] The main abomination, it is made clear, is the fact that the human becomes a soul-less creature, but that concept of soul, I might argue, is more akin to interpretations of mind in the secular sense, rather than a pseudo-religious understanding of the immortal essence. Making a minion is abominable because it deprives individuals of their consciousness, their control, and, ultimately, of their free-will. It is peculiar to see how standards are established for mind control in the vampire world: where the temporary 'glamouring' of humans is allowed as part of a survival strategy for vampire, the complete metamorphoses of the human individuals—body and mind—into puppet-like creatures is met with disgust and disdain, even by members of the vampire community. And just like a puppet, the vampire's minion hovers 'along the line' of re-animated 'madness' and 'intelligence'.[51]

The evaluation of the minion as a soul-less being devoid of will is particularly noteworthy here because it makes the vampire's servant—oddly—more akin to a zombie than any other creature. I use the word 'zombie' here in its folkloristic incarnation, before the impact of twentieth-century cinematic production transformed the understanding of the term into the Romeresque creature of popular culture. A zombie, in its historical and holistic sense, finds its origins—at least for what concerns literature—in its relationship to colonial politics. Originating in African spirituality, and travelling to first Brazil and the Caribbean, and then to the English-speaking world, a zombie was understood as a 'split creature', a result of some magical metamorphoses that caused the severance of the spirit from its bodily vessel. Faced with the Western world, and confronted with imperial preoccupations in the fallout of slavery, the zombie came to signify, as Marina Warner puts it, 'a vehicle to express a new, psychological state of personal alienation, moral incoherence and emptiness'.[52] With the advent of the twentieth century, the uses of the word changed to signify 'a vacant person, a husk, a shell, a living dead'; the zombie is, in this sense, the body living 'without a soul'.[53]

In conceptual, if not rubric terms, the vampire's minion fits the original description of zombie in an apt way. The fact that minions can be understood as zombies is made manifest and reiterated in Lori Handeland's *Shakespeare, Undead*, where vampires are actually seen creating zombies—physically depicted in the Romeresque tradition—who will serve the vampire when instructed, without ever questioning orders: 'they are raised for a reason; they have a mission. Nothing will stop them from completing it'.[54] Although neither technically alive nor dead, the minion is seemingly dead to the world, as its former human individuality was erased in favour of a state of unquestioning servitude. The minion is, to put it simply, an annulled presence. It functions consciously—in that it can act singularly and of its own accord—but without power over its own behaviour. Its consciousness has been, zombie-like, taken over from it and another—the vampire—works his will through it. While the vampire operates as an undead with consciousness, the minion is, on the other hand, a spiritually undead without consciousness. The abomination that the minion generates in the fiction results precisely from this lack of control, of will, of individuality. What made the creature a person has been removed and only the subdued shell remains. The vampire's minion, as a zombie, gives local habitation—at least in the Western context—to the terrifying possibility, as Warner puts it, 'of a person who has been vacated of all the faculties and qualities that make person-hood: of memory, of will, of thought, of sensation'.[55]

In becoming the controlled and will-deprived zombie—who is ready to do the vampire's bidding—the minion also draws attention to a discourse of power and dependency that is reliant on conceptualisations of labour in contemporary Western societies. The politics of consumer-capitalism appear to meet aptly with zombie and vampire folklore to generate a conceptual association between cause and effect, desire and satisfaction. This is indeed a projected relationship that is virtually unavoidable in contemporary popular literature, having developed from a substantial metaphor to a framework for relationships between individuals and factions. The connection to capitalist economies here lies in identifying the minion as the vampire's worker, the controlled servant, the psychic employee. The minion is submissive to the vampire, but its position is not one of desperation: it is one of adoration and longing. One must not forget that, overall, the workings of consumer capitalism—and, particularly, the role of the worker-consumer—rely on a connection among labour, dependence, production, and desire. Vampires and zombies, and the connection between the two, have figured prominently as representational vectors for discussion of capitalism in literature, starting with Karl Marx. Indeed, Marx is known to amply use Gothic terminology to address the relationship workers and capitalist structures. In his understanding of capitalism, Marx famously views the capitalist as a vampire-like creature. The constant need for growth and accumulation in the capitalist economy finds a suitable representation in the vampire's hunger for blood, an unquenchable need that must continue to be fed in order to ensure survival. Marx refers the capitalist as 'dead labour', one that must constantly feed on 'living labour'—the workers—in order to survive.[56] Vampires are, in this context, passive creatures, constantly needing to drain life from others in order to exist. The passivity finds the ideal correlation—or so it would seem—to the capitalist, the one who does not necessarily 'work', but produces and gains wealth through the exploitations of workers' operations.

So far, the argument is nothing new. One might be tempted to state that this imagery also fits the nature of the post-Fordist worker-consumer, in saying that labour within consumer capitalist societies is aimed at an endless cycle of production and consumption, one that—in spite in the inevitable shifts in economy in the post-2000 era, caused by the explosion of digital technologies—still rings true to our context. Latham, among others, constructs a persuasive connection between the post-Fordist regime and the increased consumption of labour systems. He claims that vampires in the Post-Fordism era can be associated easily with the merging culture of postmodernism, which is intrinsically linked to 'spectacle', 'difference', and 'accumulation'.[57] Although a relationship of interdependency is established here, this approach, focusing primarily on 'vampires' and 'victims'—dead labour and living labour—does not fully satisfy the question of 'control' that is so prevalent in contemporary literature. The traditional view of vampire-like consumer relations seemingly has no place for the minion, a controlled creature that is attached to the vampire, but that does necessarily provide nourishment and 'life' for its master.

In order to grasp the full extent of the minion as a psycho-technological creature in the vampire world—one that finds a place in discourse of consumer desire and, potentially, capitalist interest—one needs to return not only to the use of minions in fiction, but also to Marx's full critique of capitalism, where the 'zombie' figures prominently. In contemporary vampire literature, minions work as the vampire's servants; their payment is not monetary, but can be found in a form of returnable gratification from the vampire, a sense of attachment that strengthens the connection between master and slave through layers of psychic control. The power that the vampire exerts on the minion's mind forces the servant to do their master's bidding, to act when instructed, to 'work' when commanded. This dynamic is clearly shown in Wellington's *Thirteen Bullets*, the first book in the *Laura Caxton Vampire* series, where the minions are sent by the vampire to lay siege on the enemy, in the hope that they will also 'herd victims to the master'.[58] The idea that minions 'work' for the vampires—without being able to detach themselves from the yoke of the master's command— is present, it would seem, throughout all fictional examples where undead servants figure prominently.

A similar situation—based on power, labour, and control—is described in *Capital*. In this text, Marx maintains that, in a capitalist context, 'all powers of labour project themselves as powers of capital'.[59] This connection creates not strictly dependency, but rather assimilation. The workers are therefore rendered, as David McNally puts it, as 'appendages of the monster'.[60] In what can be seen as a deviant dialectical transposal, the powers of dead labour that are meant to be reanimated by the living, also have the ability to 'deaden the living', reifying them, 'reducing them on a zombie-state'.[61] In instances where minions appear, a third aspect is added to the living-dead dynamic. The vampire's own power keeps the minion under control; once the minion is claimed by the vampire, it becomes the vampire's possession, an expendable part of the system which does, nonetheless, prove useful and necessary. The minion is, to put it simply, 'free labour' for the vampire.

And in this status, the minions are often disregarded by the vampire, uncared for and left to rot. In *Thirteen Bullets*, Wellington picks up on the conceptual nature of the minion by projecting a view of their 'decaying state' into their physical being: 'They rot pretty quickly. After a week or ten days they can barely hold [their bodies] together [. . .] [their skin] peels off like a cast-aside shroud'.[62] Not quite existing as an incarnation of strength and 'living labour', the minion is the in-between state of capitalist economies: the one that is decaying, and will never rise to the higher level on the power chain—the vampire. The minion becomes the zombie, the controlled creature, the operational tool. And, like any controlled zombie whose consciousness has been removed, the minion 'becomes subservient to and led by an alien will'.[63] It is the uncovered critique of the system, the slave that cannot be detached from the master, the other face of the consumer capitalist context. The vampire's minion has no identity: it is the one who is neither of this world nor of the next, the one that exists only to serve, to provide labour, to strengthen the (capitalist) monster.

VAMPIRE TECHNOLOGIES

Placed within the contexts of both verbal and non-verbal communication, the notion of 'a vampire's control' over the surrounding environment—with its predatory streak—not only includes the easily conquerable boundaries of the human mind, but is also complicated further by the recurrent presence of technology in contemporary vampire fictions. There is indeed no denying that the new vampires show an aptitude for all things computer-related. In the *Black Dagger Brotherhood*, Vishous is said to be a 'genius' with computers.[64] Extremely served in the art of hacking and on-line access, Vishous is 'in charge of communications and security'.[65] A similar situation can be found in the *Midnight Breed*, with Gideon—known as the resident 'computer guru'—being able to operate systems without any effort and relying on the internet for most manners of communication.[66] In *Sookie Stackhouse*, Bill dedicates a lot of attention to databases and computer technologies, and all vampires rely on digital systems to run their business and maintain communication with both kin and customers.[67] Harrison's *Hollows* series, Mariani's *Vampire Federation*, Farnsworth's *Nataniel Cade* and Merz's *Lawson Vampire* series—to name but a few in a long and almost inextinguishable list—all show vampires as computer-savvy and technologically capable. From phone to computers, from blue-tooth to GPS systems, vampires have evolved into digitalised creatures.

This close relationship to sophisticated mediums of connectivity puts vampires on display as living a fully encoded existence, meeting the demands of Western, globalised societies, and simultaneously enjoying its privileges. Vampires are so entangled with the use of technology in contemporary fiction that it is virtually impossible to think of one without the other. Susan Broadhurst and Josephine Machon have poignantly claimed that, within the bounds of our super-high-tech twenty-first-century context, 'the complexities of identities' can be 'uncovered, displayed and demarcated' by 'strategies of empowerment, embodiment, and technicity'.[68] This suggested connection between control, technology, and the body allows the relationship between vampires and technological devices to be viewed in terms of subjective identification. Technology itself can be seen as an extension of the vampire and, through this, becomes a metaphorical representation of the creature's newly-found incarnations. Technological devices—whether digital, electronic, or automotive—have become a surrogate for the vampire's power, and just like the equipment, the vampire takes on instrumental and symbolic functions through the icons that represent it.

The association of vampires and technology is, however, a complicated one. This is mainly due to the nature of technology itself, and the fact that it is profoundly entwined, often indistinguishably, with cultural frameworks. The relationship between technology and culture is one of interdependence. Although it is true that cultures govern what forms of technologies develop, those technologies also shape cultures. Technology, as Pramod Nayar puts it, 'is not merely an effect or cause of culture, but is both'.[69] Culture and technology, as fundamental concepts, cannot be divorced from one another, and it is likely that any conception of each will unearth hopes and anxieties about the other. If one bears this connection between culture and technology in mind, then the correlation between vampires and technologies also takes on implications of a cultural nature. That is to say, that any notion of technological involvement in the narrative needs to be considered in relation to the cultural framework that generates it and, therefore, can act as a medium of critique for the framework itself.

Technologies possess, *in primis*, an instrumental value. They allow for tasks to be completed and communication to take place. This side of the technological framework should be seen as the point of departure in contemporary narratives. Vampires use technologies of communication—such as mobile phones and computers—to keep in touch. They use automotive technologies—such as cars and airplanes—to move around, as they are the most efficient ways to travel. Echoing the development of human usages, the instrumental side of technology is depicted as inseparable from the life of the modern vampire. Efficiency is advocated through the embracing of technology and it is made clear that, in its most utilitarian understanding, technology is viewed as a necessity for the contemporary, civilised vampire to survive in society. This is clearly conveyed in the *Black Dagger Brotherhood* when a group of 'Old World' vampires—who had been used to living in the 'old way', in an almost medieval-like state—realise that the only way to gain an edge in the 'New World' is to embrace the use of technology as part of everyday life: 'This is a new era in a new place. Things are different here [. . .]. We need cell phones'.[70] The contrast between 'Old World' and 'New World' here is not, of course, simply a geographical one, but a reference to a way of life where technology has not only become part of the functional everyday, but an inseparable feature of it.

All technology, of course, needs to be understood as context-bound. Connected as they are to cultural set up, technologies need to be viewed as integral part of the everyday. They are not simply something that is 'out there': 'they become part of our lives'.[71] In contemporary societies, technologies are often the most essential cog in systems of human communication, and have become, as Roger Silverstone and Leslie Haddon have suggested, 'domesticated'.[72] The mutual reliance of technology and culture informs the notion that 'domestication', in this case, entails that technology is not simply developed to improve human relations, but that, in so doing, it informs the way in which we run our lives around them. The deeply incorporated use of technology in vampire fiction, therefore, also takes on notions of an anthropological nature, opening the way to a possible critique not only of technology itself, but the way in which it is inseparable from modern life. Even if, admittedly, the word 'anthropological' should be exchanged for a more apt term. 'Vampyrological' may indeed be a more consistent choice.

The use of technology in vampire fiction, however, transcends functionality. It is true, undoubtedly, that technologies of communication and transportation are included to add verisimilitude to the narrative, to make the vampires seem 'real' and part of the structure of the modern world. Nonetheless, the use of technology also possesses cultural value of prestige, safety, and sociability. One needs to remember that, in contemporary contexts, a mobile phone (for instance) is more than just a phone. It is a 'personal diary, an entertainment device, and a status symbol'.[73] I would like to place the emphasis here on the notion of 'status symbol', conveying the notion that items of technology have ceased to be simply coveted for their instrumental uses, but have stepped into the realm of 'signs', in the Baudrillardian sense. Those signs have cultural significance because in communicating what has become desirable for a culture, they also highlight the structural foundations of the relationship between object and individual within a given context.

New technologies are both, as Nayar puts it, 'efficient and attractive'.[74] They simultaneously encapsulate values of productivity and instrumentality, and symbolic significance. The values attributed to technology are incorporated into 'the thing'—the technological device—through design and in answer to public expectation.[75] The 'thing' is not just an object and it is a more than simply a commodity. It represents aspirations, lifestyle choice, and social values. The great majority of the newly incarnated vampires are both attractive and efficient in their tasks, two important qualities that—just like the technology they use—makes them desirable and aspirational. The vampire is, one could say, a 'thing' of new design, made desirable by the incorporation of culturally sought-after qualities. Vampires are, therefore, highly technological beings themselves, their own 'technologies' encompassing—to follow a Foucaldian trajectory—those of the body, the society, and the self.

PSYCHIC POWERS AND THE DIGITAL UNCANNY

The majority of contemporary narratives show vampires not only as technologically-savvy, but also as psychically gifted. The psychic abilities of the vampire is indeed 'of the most insidious characteristics' of this particular group.[76] From hypnotism to telepathy, vampires have at their disposal an array of techniques for the manipulation of unsuspecting human minds. Their powers are so great that they can bend victims to their will, the aim of the psychic handling usually being sex, followed by the drinking of blood.

Although variations on the theme provide different nuances on the ability, vampires are projected as being able to exert some form of psychic response from humans and other creatures. Some can even communicate with each other telepathically, as it is the case of Reynolds' *Vampires in America*, and Harrison's *Hollows* series. From 'glamour' to 'thrall', vampires have mastered the art of psychic manipulation. They invade the human mind, and they gain information against the individual's will; vampires use and abuse, and then leave undisturbed.

The 'dark gift' of psychic domination elicits horror reactions in that it takes away the ability for humans to regulate, organise and, in short, decide for themselves. So when it comes to contemporary vampires, 'fear', it would seem, has taken on a new guise; it is not only found in the terror of fangs and monstrous bodies, but in the ethereal shivers of mind control. The connection between information gathering, control, and fear should not come as a surprise, considering, as Marita Sturken and Douglas Thomas argue, that any form of unknown and new 'technology' is, culturally speaking, perceived as the 'object of fascination, hyperbole, and concern'.[77] The vampire's gaze is transfixing, and results in the victims surrendering to the creature's will. The ability to manipulate minds is a very distinctive characteristic of the contemporary vampire and, as such, it is source of great anxiety. What is presented as a seemingly animalistic tactic is actually one of the greatest invasions of twenty-first century Western humans, an 'evolved' group who pride themselves in their abilities to control the world around them, through technology and science.

It is in this multiply technological framework that the vampire's control, as well as his body and his presence in the human world, takes on the apt vestiges of the contemporary uncanny. The relationship between the uncanny and the vampire, as we have already seen, has always been one favoured by Gothic scholarship across decades. Contemporary literature maintains the uncanny connection to the vampire by seeing the creature as both alien and familiar at the same, as examples such as Farnsworth's *Nathaniel Cade* attest. In the new millennium, however, uncanny anxieties have also found another relationship to the vampire. They do not only apply to extending connections between class, race, sexuality, and gender, automation, and colonialism, as it did for most part in the nineteenth and twentieth centuries. The notion of the uncanny in the twenty-first century helps us to understand what might be the affective response to the hold that digitality has on lives. As a theory of fear and the ghostly, as Royle suggests, the twenty-first uncanny, is 'much concerned with the question of computers and technology'.[78] The new vampiric uncanny is evident in relation to notions of digital technology and what has often been described as 'programming'.

In contemporary Western societies, there seems to be a 'general acknowledgment that our loves, our experiences, the comings and goings within and all around us are increasingly programmed'.[79] The reliance on technologies of communication, especially in their digital format, has shaped the out-look of twenty-first century existence; 'programming' here can be under-stood as the essence of that prescription, a close-relationship to technology and gadgets that, while seemingly intended to simplify modern life, has actually transformed it into a very precise organisation of methods and systems. This sense of paradoxically detached connectivity is at the heart of globalisation, and perhaps exemplifies it in its most extreme understand-ing. Discussing the distinctly contemporary relationship between technol-ogy and the uncanny, Christopher Johnson points out that people are at once 'animated and agitated by the power of the programme', which seems at once to' violate' and inspire our most intuitive sense of self-determi-nation'.[80] By saying this, what is meant is not that the 'programme'—the metaphor for digital connectivity and reliance of technological systems—is actually a representation for the unconscious, but that, as Johnson puts it, with the 'increasing relief of human motion, memory, calculation and com-munication', it becomes increasingly impossible to locate the programme'.[81] Lives merge into the digital, and in spite of the fact that this type of exis-tence has become almost common-place in the Western world, symptoms of the disease are still visible to some, and become embodied in symbols of that technologically-driven hold.

If it is true that technology and computerised living have become part of a new system of uncanny experience, then the close relationship between computers, digital technologies, psychic control and vampires becomes revelatory. The vampires, with their open connection to the computerised and the digital, act as the metaphor for the uncanny nature of technology, the potential loss of self in a globalised world, and the increasing 'delegation of the vital to the programmatic'.[82] By virtue of being technically dead, or at least conceptually separate from the human world, the vampire provides the perfect set up for exposing the simultaneous technological connectivity and suggestively emotional disconnection of contemporary existence. The uncanny nature of the programme is made manifest through an allegory of comparison that, although it should inspire fear and loathing, is actually accepted as normal and 'everyday'. The vampire's superiority –physical and evidently technological—allows the boundaries between real and digital to fall, and to engulf the human self. This critical focus on the vampire's technological uncanny provides a way of exploring what may be 'one of the most interesting dimensions of the coming decades': the future of human emotion and determinism.

It is in this widespread ability that the vampire constructs its most defined relationship to the uncanny: the vampire is a projection of free will in the digital information age. Like a mysterious form of supernatural internet, the vampire gains information outside of people's control, and in its reliance on both the *heimlich* and *unheimlich* frameworks of tech-nology, it is the embodiment of the digital uncanny. The vampire is the computer, the programme, the communication system. Without being too provocative, it is possible to suggest here that a connection is established in contemporary literature so that the digital world of technology can be understood as a form of vampirism, sucking information from individuals in order to gain some form of control on choices, actions, and ultimately life. The vampire's psychic abilities cater perfectly to the strong anxieties about constant surveillance that are proper to several strands of thought in contemporary society. The power exercised by the vampire—both through the mind and through the digital system—not only constructs the creature as mesmerising and attractive to others, but also makes it easier for vampires to 'move about in society', and generally obtain what they want with minimal effort.[83] The technologically apt vampires, with their reliance on computers and mind control, expose the cultural fear of a programmed existence. Vampires expose 'the ghostliness' of machines, the eeriness of digitality, the disturbing nature of modern systems of communication. In providing a presence that can be erased whenever it is no longer required in the receiver's mind, the vampire is 'spectrally effective' in demanding a rationalisation of relationship, and then falling short of it.[84]

Although the eerie nature of programming technologies—automating human life and making it increasingly more paradoxically disconnected from humanity—is suggestive, it does not fully answer the question of how vampires' relationship technologies acts as a critical signifier for the contemporary uncanny. In order to grasp this, it is necessary to reach out into all systems of vampire communication, and enquire how connectivity in the vampire world takes intriguing, yet problematic forms which link computerised digitality to a possible 'loss of self'. In a highly technological world, the vampire's psychic abilities—which find an effective allegorical parallel in the vampire's constant use of highly-conceived technology—are a projection of a human fear of the all-pervasive power of digitalisation, which allows subjects to be constantly monitored and, to some extent, controlled. It is the fear that our thoughts and our minds do not belong to us anymore, and that humans are but a shadow of their digital selves.

CYBER-CONTROL, ADDICTION, AND THE LOSS OF MIND

In channelling the fear of 'losing one's mind' through technological control, the vampire uncovers, and to some extent embodies, the collapse of the 'digital free will' in the post-information age. Behind the façade of pleasure, excitement or even ease, vampires influence the mind and, in so doing, erase any conception of determinism. Humans cannot trust their minds, themselves, the system; they are not in charge, they are at the mercy of radical systems of communication that, while being presented in an appealing package, are out of their control.

If one keeps the close relationship between the vampire's psychic powers, technology, and control in mind, it is possible to establish a conceptual connection between the way in which vampires are said to enthral human victims and how digital communication systems—such as the internet— have been found to engage users. Studies in sociology and anthropology attest to the impact that digitality has on people in terms of responses and decision-making. Richard Watson argues that, when engaging with screen technologies such as computers, tablets and mobile phones, people 'always appear to be in a hurry' and 'are not fully concentrating, waiting [. . .] for some new bit or byte of information to flash across the screen'.[85] A similar situation is often presented in contemporary vampire fictions when humans encounter vampires. This is made particularly clear by Harris in the *Sookie Stackhouse* series when describing the humorously named 'fangbangers', humans who are so taken with the vampires that they are willing to offer themselves completely, just to be provided with some form of thrill and excitement. Fangbangers love 'vampires so much they want to be around them every minute the vampires were awake'.[86] The humans are described as impatient, desiring, filled with excitement. 'Fangbangers' are also often depicted as seemingly confused, not fully concentrating, completely at the mercy of the vampire's commands. The potential parallel between the users of digital technologies, and the humans who are about to be 'used' by the vampires is virtually impossible to ignore. Except, of course, that the humans engaging with vampires are not waiting for a new 'bit or byte', but craving (as it were) for a 'bite'.

In these contexts of excitement and craving, the vampires are often described not only as exciting, but literally irresistible. Mariani openly describes them as 'mesmerising', hinting at the aura of hypnotic power that surrounds them.[87] This is an idea that several narratives subscribe to, gen- erating the notion that vampires attract their victims (and their lovers) with a commanding promise of pleasure and enjoyment. Harris makes it clear that, for the majority of fangbangers, vampires represent the possibility of new experiences, not just psychically but also physically. In *The Gardella Vampire Chronicles*, Colleen Gleeson also makes it clear that the psychic pull exerted by the vampire draws people to the predator, and makes the call unable to resist: 'With [the vampire's] touch came the strength of her thrall [. . .] [the human male] felt her presence and it seeped into him'.[88] The effects of the internet and other systems of digital information shar- ing has often been described in similar vein. Watson contends that 'there is a growing cohort of people for whom the merest hint of new informa- tion, or the faintest whiff that something new is going on somewhere else is irresistible'.[89] 'Irresistible' here is the key term that, both in concept and in practice, establishes a conceptual link between the power of the infor- mation systems and the thrall of the vampire. Just like digital information finds a perfect distribution platform in the internet, the vampires persuade, mould, influence. In both representational and actual terms, the vampire and the internet are exciting because they promise to offer something new, to improve, to enthuse.

In a conceptual twist, Mariani also describes vampires being 'like a drug', and states that anyone who encounters them continues to 'want more'.[90] The implications that vampires are, like most drugs, 'addictive', is revelatory in reinforcing the conceptual connection between vampires and the internet. Contemporary studies within the discipline of behavioural psychology have found that regular users of digital technologies—aimed at information gathering and sharing—act as if they literally cannot function without them. The internet has been particularly studied as the source of compulsive behaviour in terms of usage. Research conducted on users of Google search, Facebook and Twitter—to mention but a few—have shown that people crave information, and the thrill that digitality gives them in terms of knowledge and attachment to the system. This digitally-based desire to constantly have access to the new, the moving, the exciting is known as 'connectivity addiction'.[91] The parallel between the two types of addition here—the vampire and the digital—suggests that vampires themselves can be read as a metaphorical rendition of the impact of information technologies.

In spite of the constant amount of information that gets processed through the use of the internet and other forms of digital communication, it has become a known fact—both culturally and scientifically—that the use of quick-access technologies can have a negative impact on cognitive functions. This is caused precisely, and somewhat paradoxically, by the excessive amount of data that one needs to handle when presented with the famous digital 'information overload'. This state causes the individual's enquiring abilities to drop, and the validity, or the safety, of the information that is being processed is not questioned as assuredly. Cognitively speaking, therefore, a brain that is over-engaging with digital ways of communication is a 'trusting brain', which makes the individual person an easy target for persuasion. Cordelia Fine points out that, when presented with little or two much information, 'the brain's default setting is to believe'.[92] Watson agrees with this position by claiming that 'when the brain is especially busy', it starts to 'believe things that it would ordinarily question or distrust'.[93]

It is a common contention in sociological research that the impact of digital information sharing on the human brain is so pervasive that users become 'unable to exclude what is irrelevant and retain an objective view' on experience.[94] The inability to distinguish and evaluate information properly puts individuals in danger of being manipulated and exploited. There is no doubting that a similar situation occurs in contemporary vampire fiction, when humans are unaware of the danger that vampires represent once they fall under their control. In the *Sookie Stackhouse* series, the fangbangers are so enthralled with the vampires that they are unaware of the risk they are putting themselves through—with losing their lives being but one of them. They are often described as 'dazed' and 'confused', unable to make decisions for themselves, and unaware of their function as 'props' for the vampires to use at will.[95] In addition, they also seem to lose touch with their fellow humans, seeing them only as threats in the fight for the vampire's attention.

The knowledge of the impact of digital engagement on psychic activities complicates the workings on the vampire's glamour abilities on the human mind. Vampires are said to have such highly developed psychic skills that they can mould and influence human minds easily. This is done, it would seem, by instilling a sense of desire in the human receiver, who wants to experience what the vampire has to offer and is willing to ask for more. In a way, it is possible to argue that, just like a digital platform, the vampire causes an information overload in the human mind. In the *Sookie Stackhouse* series, Sookie herself who—thanks to her own telepathic abilities— is able to resist the vampire's call, describes the feeling of this information overload in detail, as Eric tries to impose his 'glamour' on her: 'I felt power tweaks kind of flow over me and had an uneasy feeling Eric was trying to influence me'.[96] Presented with a large number of psychic activity, human brains are incapable of questioning the information that is being received; this makes people malleable, willing, and easy to manage. Echoing the influence of the digital on cognitive abilities, the vampires take over the human mind through supplying visions and images that are of interest to their targets. The human receivers are shown as unable and unwilling to question or distrust the vampire's call, and they therefore answer to it eagerly. The vampire overpowers the human mind by, paradoxically, making it too excited, too active, too 'enthralled'. Operating in a similar manner to digital communication channels, the vampire makes information difficult to track. Looking into the vampire's eyes, the humans conceptually replicate the function of staring at a screen and receiving information, when 'decision-making abilities are at risk' because they are 'too busy to consider alternatives properly.'[97]

One of the most intriguing elements of the vampire's psychic control is that some of them are able to manipulate the minds of humans, so that they can erase themselves from their memories, maintaining the existence—and often supremacy—of the vampire race hidden from public knowledge. This is clearly shown in the *Black Dagger Brotherhood*: 'Wrath stalked out of the bar. On his way to the door he wiped the memory of himself from every human cerebral cortex in the place. The strong ones would think they had dreamed him. The weak ones wouldn't remember him at all'.[98] Indeed, the vampires in Ward's series can even create 'new memories' for their victims, so to keep them happy and unlikely to pursue and hunt the vampires in any way. This is not only presented by Ward as a self-preservation technique, but also as a way to maintain a hold over unsuspecting human minds, so that they will do the vampire's bidding: Phury 'cleaned up the memories of most if not all of the OR staff [. . .] [he then] stared [the nurse] into a stupor, planting the urgent need in her front lobe to get to staff meeting'.[99] The lack of memory here is an important notion that advances the connection between vampires, control, and technology. Milas Kundera has argued that 'the struggle of man against power is the struggle of memory against forgetting'.[100] The ability to remove information from a mind is clearly a strong agent of control. The fact that the vampires seem to do this, arguably, through a 'wireless', telepathic system introduces the possibility that the vampire functions as the ideal medium for critiquing the way in which the information system maintain a hold over people's interests—and 'minds'—by constantly supplying new information that will 'erase' what was supplied previously.

The pull of the new and the agreeable—which is what the memory-removal activities represent—puts the vampire's psychic manipulation in line with technological frameworks of information dissemination. The vampire's mental abilities unveil anxieties about the influence of the digital on the mind, and the possibility that the quick exchange of information will eventually make the human mind unable to retain information, and suffer a cultural memory loss. The human receivers of the vampire's psychic abilities are often portrayed as 'losing their minds'. This echoes fears regarding the segmentation of the human mind and the widespread inability to act as agents of chance, what Fredric Jameson labels 'culturally induced schizophrenia'.[101] In wiping memories and moulding human minds, the vampires channel the increasingly well-known Western preoccupation that digital technologies 'can create a cerebral whiteout'.[102]

Studies in techno and cybercultures, such as the on conducted by Pramod Nayar, tend to celebrate the virtuality of the digital world for enabling the user to 'transcend the geography of the body'.[103] The use of technologies of communication allows individuals to communicate beyond physical boundaries, establish cybernetic connections that go beyond the boundaries of the body. Within this line of thought, digital technologies of communication can be seen as disembodied, overcoming the body's limitations in favour of a 'purer' form of thinking. The vampire, one could argue, embraces this sense of controlled disembodiment on a number of levels. Firstly, the use of digital technologies—computers, phones, satellite navigators—allows vampires to establish their presence and control even when the limitations of their already highly advanced bodies fail them; even when they are forced indoors by sunlight—as they still are in the majority of narratives—the vampires are able to reach 'the outside' through computerised systems of communication. Connectivity is one of the contemporary vampire's biggest strengths, allowing them to exert control, as clearly shown by examples such as Vishous in the *Brotherhood*, Alex in the *Vampire Federation*, and Gideon in the *Midnight Breed*, who use technologies to literally own the world, from something as seemingly mundane as managing financial accounts, to the running of sophisticated operational structures.

The disembodied control of the vampire is, of course, also to be found in its psychic abilities. Technology, glamouring, and telepathy are joined in the system of bodily transcendence. The body's obvious restrictions are overcome through what Katherine Hayles has termed a 'technological prosthesis'.[104] This is not to say, of course, that the vampire transcends the body. Physicality is, as we have seen, an important part of the vampire experience. What the metaphor of disembodied digitality allows for is the generation of an augmented body, which is able to generate and employ forms of control to be unleashed into the world. In this sense, the vampire's engagement with the disembodied embraces one of the core elements of the concept posthumanity, where subjectivity is 'dispersed' through the connective network of communication.[105] Psychic control represents the ultimate overcoming of the physical, and one of the most definitive characteristics of the contemporary vampire. The incorporation of data—to borrow a very aptly technological term—from the outside and into the vampire's body suggests that cognizance, for the vampire, does not have to be confined to the body. Sophisticated cyber and psychic connections allow for a radical 'extension of consciousness' into spaces other than the individual body.[106] This ephemeral system of communication is given representational grounding through the constant use of technology of communications, where digitality extends the connectivity of the vampire into the world.

In communicating both physically—through digital devices—and mentally, the vampire becomes the pinnacle of disembodied interaction, the allegory of contemporary cyberconnectivity. With their superior physicality and overarching control over that which is disembodied, the vampires achieve control beyond the limits of human consciousness. While technologies for humans provide but a pale vision of incorporeal connectivity, the vampire's domination of the system, in its various forms, supersedes the limitations of that which is human. The question posed by many scholars on whether technology, particular digital, causes emotional detachment and loss of intimacy for human individuals, becomes redundant for the vampire, as its mastery over venues of connectivity opens the discussion to the possibility that, indeed, there are more than one kind of consciousness.

In this way, technological and psychic abilities are reciprocal metaphors in the vampire context; just as technology acts as a surrogate for the transcendence of physicality, so do psychic abilities unveil a critique of contemporary system of cyber communication, where technology allows the disconnection of the bodily and encourages the establishment of disembodied relations. It becomes an unavoidable thought that, in this context of technological advancement, disembodied transcendence and psychic control, notions of life and death, real and unreal, and human and in/trans/posthuman, are soon called into question. The use that vampires make of technological artefacts—such as computers and mobiles phones—and their overarching ability to extend means of communication beyond the body, combines a sense of both awe and unease, and unearths questions about the very nature of digitality in the world.

Vampire technocultures and cybercultures cannot be separated by the larger context in which they emerge; they emerge out of the mergence of a number of factors in the 'human world', such as the hybridisation of cultural forms, dispersed forms of communication and production, and large scale movements of people of both a national and an international scale. Above all, however, one must considered how techno/cybercultures have overall emerged out of what Nayar calls the 'widespread flows of capital', the result of a fast-paced, globalised economies that necessitate the creation and usage of highly sophisticated technologies of production, circulation, and ultimate consumption.[107] The increasing mobility of capital and commodities demand not only greater connectivity but, as Jon Stratton already forewarned in 1997, greater control.[108] It is therefore possible, and indeed necessary, to build a connection between technological advances and the digitalisation of communication and culture, and the growth of a global economy. Matters of capital, commodity, and consumption become entangled with priorities of connectivity.

Scholarship from various disciplines—from communications to cultural and economic studies—has agreed in saying that, in the post-2000 era, we live in what is known as the 'information society'.[109] Globalisation—and within the effects of this phenomenon I include, of course, both globalised cultures and globalised economies—has been enabled by the advent of high-speed communications. Capitalism, Nayar argues, is increasingly becoming 'technocapitalism', because 'the nature of production, marketing and consumption demands technological linkages and synchronous 24/7 communications'.[110] The working of contemporary capitalism—and the foundations of consumer cultures—are therefore intrinsically connected to the concept of technology, with its latest incarnations encouraging digital encounters and trans-geographical communications. Technology, one might argue, is not simply a matter of symbolic value and functionality at micro level, but is linked to systems of economic reproduction that work at the macro level. Technology itself, therefore, is a consumerist issue. And it is this unavoidably contemporary link between technology, consumerism, and culture which complicates the presence of highly-prized technological commodities in contemporary vampire fiction. The appeal of the vampiric 'thing', it would seem, relies on a multifaceted construct.

4   Vampire Rituals and Customs

The emphasis on technology in consumer capitalist economies, and the focus on the vampire's influence in terms of both representational and practical experience, has drawn attention to the way in which vampires have become organised as a socially and economically independent group. This re-location of the vampire subject within operational systems unveils the inevitable presence of culture as an important and deeply re-discovered part of the twenty-first condition. In this framework, it does not come as a surprise to see the presence of distinct rituals and customs in contemporary popular literature. Indeed, vampire groups appear to rely on specific customs and traditions, which exist as separate and autonomous in their own right. This network of practices that highlights vampiric groups not as clusters, but as working societies.

The customs of behaviour are varied, and take several forms within the social contexts of the fiction. In the *Sookie Stackshouse* series, for instance, a strict vampire custom is that vampires 'don't shake hands'.[1] What seems to be one of the most widely acknowledged interpersonal gestures within the Western world is removed from the vampire's world. The effects of the custom on others is unavoidable; on the one hand, it causes great embarrassment to those who do not know and, offering a hand for the vampire to shake, commit an irremediable *faux pax* in vampiric social circles. On the other, the presence of such a different custom highlights the vampire as a creature that, although networked with the human world, does not subscribe to the rules and regulation of the human system of conduct.

The example from Harris' novels, however, is one among many, and instances abound across the fictional storylines. In *Vampires in America*, it is offensive and 'not custom' to ask vampires how old they are. The question results is outrage and causes anger in the vampire, as the human Cynthia quickly discovers when she asks how old one of Raphael's vampires was when he turned her: 'such a question', we are told, 'is an unforgivable breach of etiquette' among his kind.[2] 'Etiquette' surrounding age and the process of turning is also important in Mariani's *Vampire Federation*, where 'you never ask anyone how they turned'.[3] In similar vein, bowing to an individual who occupies a higher position in the vampires' social hierarchy is considered to be 'custom' in the *Black Dagger Brotherhood*. Behavioural rules are important here in stressing that vampires operate as a separate civilisation—a point stressed by Ward on several occasions—and that the sociality of encounters, expressed through custom, highlights their status as a highly organised socio-cultural group. After all, customs are, as Klaus-Peter Köpping, Bernhard Leistle, and Michael Rudolph suggest, a 'symbolic presence', uncovering the 'complex, multi-layered set of relations between individuals, social groups, and their material environment'.[4]

Even more symbolically enhanced, communicative and unavoidable than custom in the fiction is the presence of ritual. This presence, for certain, does not come as a surprise. In *Totem and Taboo*, Freud clearly uncovers the relationship between ritualised existence, socio-religious structures and psychological resonance.[5] 'Ritual', of course, differs from 'custom' ns that it is not simply a matter of practice or habit—whatever the source of that practice might be—but is ceremonial in nature, and relies not only on particular actions in a particular order, but also on pre-ordained assemblies in order to gain its value. In distinguishing 'ritual' from behavioural rules and regulations, I take the term to signify the practical performance of systematic structures of belief and control that outline the vampire's organisational structures—political, religious, economic, and interpersonal—as a separate entity. In taking this approach to the concept, I follow Catherine Bell's suggestion that, unlike custom, ritual is a form of elaborative data through which one can uncover and interpret the nature of religion and civilisation'.[6] And rituals do abound in vampire societies: rituals of marriage, of death, of consumption. These dictate the parameters of the vampire's life and, in their ceremonially calendric functions, offer a dynamic guidance into understanding the relationship between vampiric and human behaviour in relation to belief, value, and a sense of structural permanence.

In an anthropological framework, human beings 'have been involved in ritual activities of some sort since the earliest hunting bands and tribal communities'.[7] Although it has been the claim of a number of scholars that rituals—ranging from their ancient religious incarnation to their more recent worldly representations—have lost their impact in the secularised context of the twenty-first century, ritualised organisation has found a representational site of existence in the literary vampire. Köpping, Leistle and Rudoplh have long maintained that rituals, in their various forms, are part of a socio-cultural system of performance that delineates and materialises issue of identity for a population in any given context.[8] The presence of rituals, in this sense, is inseparable from not only the boundary of the individual, but also the society in which he is placed.

This concept forms the point of departure for unveiling rituals in contemporary vampire literature as a representational critique of identities and affiliations in Western human societies. If the vampire is to be interpreted as a metaphorical agent channelling human anxieties and desires, then the rituals and customs shaping the vampire's social and cultural existence give us an insight into the structures regulating human life in the post-2000 era. Freud, of course, draws attention to the relationship between ritual, belief, and representation, claiming that whenever rituals are involved—most likely to do with any form of supernatural element—what is really being put under scrutiny is the human being.[9] In this framework, the vampire's rituals gain their importance at the intersection between debates of society, culture, and understandings of the 'world' in its broader sense. The vampire's rituals allow discussions regarding the notions of normalcy and normality to come to the surface.[10] Although ceremonial in nature, ritual finds a connection with custom in highlighting the importance of everyday practices, habits, and agents of human recognition, such as family, food, and even death. In this, 'ritual' takes on an important communicative role not only in channelling the dynamics of social organisation in the vampire/human world, but also, and perhaps primarily, in its function as an agent of cultural transference that transmits cognitive categories forming the overall sense of the vampire's reality. And vampires, as Harris states in *Dead Ever After*, have 'a ritual for everything'.[11]

WEDDING RITUALS

A distinctive feature of contemporary literature is that vampires marry. Marriage is now portrayed as an almost expected feature of many vampires' lives in the post-2000 era, and although the conceptual foundations and ritual of the same take different shapes across narratives, weddings remain a newly-established presence impossible to miss. Of course, the idea that vampires can marry—whether in their undead or living existence—is not completely new in itself. Dracula, after all, had brides, an example occasionally followed by a number of vampires even in the pre-2000 era. Contemporary vampires, however, have made a virtue of ritualising marriage as part of the socio-cultural organisation of their societies.

The idea of marriage in vampire narratives is indeed presented in an array of forms and formats, and the nature of spouses if just as varied as is the ritual. Vampires are known to either marry humans, other vampires, or (on occasion) even other supernatural creatures. The rubric of marriage is maintained in several examples, as the terms 'wife', 'husband', and 'married' is reiterated throughout, as one can see in example such as the *Sookie Stackhouse* series, when the human Sookie becomes vampire Eric's 'wife'. A similar use of terminologies is also reinforced in the *Hollows* series and the *Twilight* saga. A noteworthy point here is that Harris' narrative stresses that vampires can acquire either a human or a vampire spouse, but that the vampire spouse would always be of a higher ranking individual in the eyes of vampire society. Sookie confirms this herself in the fiction: 'it's not done, to have a human wife and vampire wife. The vampire wife must be the only one [. . .] In vampire eyes, [a human wife] is ranked as [the] number one designated concubine'.[12] A human wife is perceived as a 'second-class citizen.[13] Hierarchy, it would seem, plays an important part in vampire circles, and there is no doubting the superiority of the supernatural creature when compared to a lowly, mortal human.

In rubric terms, however, the terms 'marriage', 'wife' and 'husband' are not the only terms subscribed to when it comes to the nature and context of vampire unions. 'Mated' is perhaps the most common term used for referring to what is understood as marriage in the narratives; instances of this abound in the fiction, with the *Black Dagger Brotherhood*, *Midnight Breed*, *Vampires in America*, and *House of Comarré* working as prime examples here. As the term 'mated' replaces 'married', the titular identification for the two individuals involved also shifts, as spouses are commonly referred to as 'mate'. Ward's series goes as far as creating new titles for the mated couple, adhering to the distinctive linguistic structures that vampires hold in the narrative. 'Wife' is replaced by the term *shellan*, while 'husband' becomes *hellren*. The important point to remember, however, is that while rubric changes are applied to the identification of marital unions within these narratives, the expectations regarding the union remains the same as those associated with Western understandings of marriage, where love and—above all—monogamy play an important role.

While rubric definitions are diverse and often changes according not only to the actual narrative trajectory, but to the context in which that narrative is developed, the element that appears to stay the same across the fiction is that vampire marriage—very much like a human one—necessitates ritual. Although in the ritual itself vampire unions find simultaneous points of intersection and levels of disparity, the need for a ceremony—whether public or private—remains a constant presence. Across the fictional board, vampire wedding ceremonies are portrayed differently according to the narrative, and it would be virtually impossible to recount the different ways in which vampires are joined with their spouses. Two particular elements, however, emerge as overarching requirements of the vampire marriage ritual across the fiction: the shedding of blood and the ritualistic use of a knife. The former, of course does not come as much of a surprise, as blood has always played an important part in not only constructing vampire relations, but also in building the strength of the vampire mystique. Harris stresses this connection when recounting the development of the vampiric marriage ritual: everyone should know, the protagonist Sookie tells us, that 'a vampire ceremony would include a blood exchange'.[14] The knife, on the other hand, could seem an odd instrument to choose when delineating any form of vampire structure, as the creature's fangs are usually given the most attention as the designated sharp object at hand. Both presences, however, work on similar parameters, providing both practical and metaphorical use for cementing the union. And although they are connected, 'blood' and 'knife' should first be approached separately.

As it has often been stressed in several examples of criticism, blood carries unavoidable symbolism for the representation of both life and death. While being life-giving in its conception, its presence is also significant as a figurative rendition of death; the shedding of blood often symbolises destruction and, potentially, the end of existence. It is in this last point that the vampire holds its strongest connection to blood: the vampire is both representative of life and death, of ending and continuation, and, in this, finds a strong conceptual connection to the various yet interlacing blood symbolisms in existence. The presence of blood in vampire wedding rituals fits into this conceptual structure. A common occurrence is to see the future spouses exchanging blood. In Adrian's *Midnight Breed*, for instance, a vampire wedding, and the union the results, is not complete if the two individuals do not drink each other's blood: '[He] pressed his scarlet lips to her lips . . . Richer than wine, instantly intoxicating, his blood flowed over her tongue like an elixir crafted for the gods. She felt all of Lucan's love pouring into her, all of his power and strength'.[15] A similar exchange is described in the *Sookie Stackhouse* series, where blood from both spouses is collected into a chalice, and then drunk by both: 'Russell took a sip from the chalice, and the handed it to Bart, who drained it dry. Then they kissed'.[16] The exchange of blood here signifies the joining of the two lives into one. As a symbolic representation of life itself, the incorporation of the spouse's blood in vampire wedding rituals also symbolises the strength of union, communicating how the two are now entangled in love and devotion.

Love and permanence, however, are not the only concepts associated with the symbolic presence of blood in the ritual. Shedding blood implies, traditionally and ritualistically, a form of sacrifice. This side of the blood ritual is emphasised in the *Black Dagger Brotherhood*, where the male must offer his blood to his *shellan* and suffer the pain of bleeding in silence. At Beth and Wrath's mating ceremony, the importance of spilling the male's blood is made manifest: ceremonial cuts are made into Wrath's body. As his blood 'trickles' down his back, it is made clear that bleeding is the only way to marry and 'keep his honour in front of his brothers'.[17] The blood of the warrior is then soaked into a pristine white cloth and offered to the female, as the representation of her *hellren*'s love for her and his pledge to keep her safe at all costs: 'Take this cloth to your shellan as a symbol of your strength, so she will know you are worthy of her'.[18] The sacrifice, in this case, takes multiple interpretations. It signifies not only the meaning of the union in the forsaking of others and the commitment of the two spouses to each other, but also reinforces the parameters of patriarchal control onto the ceremony. On the one hand, the virginal white cloth feeds into the cultural representation of the bride as 'pure'; on the other, the colonisation of the white cloth itself by the male's blood also communicates his ownership of his female in body and spirit. As only the male vampire's blood is shed in the ritual, his is the control and the power, and the rule over the union that the female accepts in exchange for his love and his protection. In a way, the wedding ritual in the Brotherhood also subverts traditional views of the marriage union, where the female's virginal blood is shed on the wedding night, functioning not only as the symbolic seal of matrimony, but also as the representation of the ownership the husband holds over his wife. While in the vampire's wedding ceremony the blood which is shed is that of the male, the conceptual and sacrificial nature of the act remains the same. This sense of blood submission is confirmed by Ward when it is made clear that, once the female has mated the male—and, therefore, accepted 'his blood'—he becomes in charge of her, and all her decisions and actions must first obtain his permission: 'What he says goes'.[19]

For blood to flow, however, a cut into the skin must be made, and the instrument of choice in vampire weddings is a knife. This appears in a large number of vampire wedding rituals and takes on a ritual use for the occasion. A knife, for instance, scores the skin of two vampire individuals in the *Sookie Stackhouse* novels, and allows the blood to flow in the ceremonial goblet: the wedding celebrant 'whipp[s] out a knife and cut the two wrists with two movements too quick to separate' and the two spouses 'ble[e]d into the chalice'.[20] A knife is also used in the Harris' narrative to perform the wedding between a vampire and a human. Even though blood is not exchanged between the two on this occasion, the ritual use of the knife remains. In this context, however, the knife is presented to the vampire by the human, therefore signifying union in much the same way as it does in vampire-only rituals. Even when a knife is exchanged for the more ceremonial outlook of a dagger—as it is the case in examples such as the *Black Dagger Brotherhood* and *Midnight Breed*—the uses and, one might argue, the symbolism, remains the same. In Adrian's series, vampires score their lips with a ceremonial dagger and kiss their human brides—with lips 'glossy with dark red blood'—so that blood can flow into her mouth.[21] In the *Black Dagger Brotherhood*, on the other hand, a dagger is used not only to draw the male vampire's blood, but also to seal the union in a contract-like manner. The name of his *shellan* is carved onto the male's back, so to indicate ownership and devotion.

The metaphorical nuances of the knife in vampire wedding rituals take the symbolism of this particular object beyond its utilitarian uses. Freudian scholarship has of course drawn attention to the representational use of the knife as a phallic symbol. Freud's own interpretation of dreams made what is now an commonly-known association between sharp, long objects, and parts of the male anatomy: 'if you dream about a long or penetrating object, such as a knife or a sword, the symbol refers to the penis'.[22] In this context, the use of knives—or knife-like objects—in vampire wedding rituals symbolises the sexual nature of the union itself. As the phallic nature of the knife comes into play, the image of sexual connection becomes more vivid, especially when individuals are said to drink each other's blood to complete the ritual, and seal their marriage contract. Sexual desire is, unsurprisingly, one of the most common results of the wedding ritual in vampire literature. Couples are said to want to consummate their unions immediately and Adrian goes as far as clearly stating that the blood exchange inspires a sense of desire: 'She [the bride] felt desire . . . more intense than it had ever been'.[23]

In this scenario, the ritual of exchange—involving both blood and knife—is equalled in use and effect to sexual wanting. This representational use of knives is also recalled by Barbara Creed in *The Monstrous Feminine*, where she claims that desire is often 'expressed through a symbolic exchange of objects', such as the knife.[24] The wedding opens the way for marriage, a social and well as a psychological state where sexual activity and, potentially, the birth of children will be present. The knife is, after all, a penetrating object in itself, so it is not difficult to connect it to representations of intercourse. The knife, however, can also be interpreted as a symbol of severance. As an object, the knife can cut the skin, and open the way for two lives to symbolically become merged into one married existence. As the skin of vampire spouses is cut, so are their apparent connections to their previous status. The skin is cut, and the blood flows. The two parts of the ritual are representative of the multifaceted aspects of the wedding ceremony: as individual lives are cut by the knife and 'ended', the blood—either actually or symbolically—gives life to the new union, the new existence of the couple in their married state.

The common inclusion of wedding rituals in contemporary vampire fiction draws attention, inevitably, to the role of marriage in the construction of those social, political and—to some extent—aesthetic parameters that construct interpersonal relationships within the narratives. Marriage is, after all, an intrinsically human occurrence; even when the vampire couplings in the fiction are referred to as 'mating' rather than 'marrying', the ritual that allows the two individuals to be joined still carried the prerequisites to be understood as a wedding and, as such, is subject to the same evaluative criteria as any human marriage union. Although, even in the human world, different types of wedding rituals and matrimonial organisations exists, marriage itself can be considered to be a universal human entity, and examples of it can be found in virtually all cultures across the globe. As Jean Elshtain argues, 'no one is left untouched by marriage, including those who never marry'. Marriage, Elshtain goes on to say, 'is a pervasive institution in our society'.[25] There is no denying that both the idea of wedding and marriage are constantly subjected to the scrutiny of any given social group, and the concept itself—it would seem—has taken on a political role rather than simply an emotional one. The universality of marriage, and controversy that the concept is going through in the twenty-first century, highlight the persistent presence of wedding rituals in vampire fiction as a way of initiating conversations regarding the nature and place of this type of union in the human world.

A return to wedding rituals in the fiction could be interpreted as a response to 'marriage' as a disputed entity in the post-2000 era. A number of scholars have associated the twenty-first century with what has become known as the 'marriage crisis'. This perspective puts marriage at the centre of complex and contested areas of discussion, which take the role of unions between human beings into social, cultural, and political discourses. This perspective began to become prominent in the late twentieth century, when divorced rates increased, and the nature and even function of marriage—in both the religious and secular sense—began to be at the centre of social debates. In the twenty-first century, the prognostic outlook for marriage does not seem to have improved. Although divorce rates have levelled off, they have by no means receded. There is now even evidence, as David Shumway suggests, that fewer people are getting married.[26] And yet, wedding rituals have been transformed into a common presence in the fiction. This, however, may be viewed as a feature of sub-genre identification, rather than an overarching re-evaluation of the vampire motif.

Wedding rituals—and the subsequent outlook on marriage that results from them—are prevalent in certain genres of vampire fiction, and conspicuously omitted from others. Vampire rituals of unions are common in examples of what is often identified as the 'paranormal romance'—such as the *Black Dagger Brotherhood*, *Midnight Breed*, Feehan's *Carpathians*, and Cole's *Immortals After Dark* series –where love stories are at the centre of the plotline. A similar inclusion is also present in examples from urban fiction, where 'love' as such—although not at the centre of the narrative organisation—still plays an important part in the plot and character dynamics. Avid readers of this particular vampire sub-genre will recognise the presence of vampire wedding rituals in a number of narratives, of which the *Sookie Stackhouse*, *The Dresden Files*, and Melissa de le Cruz's *Blue Bloods*, series are apt examples. Wedding rituals, however, are noticeably absent from contemporary vampire fiction belonging—at least on the surface—to other sub-genres, such as the vampire thriller, a group of narratives to which the *Nathaniel Cade* and *Laura Caxton Vampire* series clearly belong. A noteworthy point is that wedding rituals seem to be concomitant with the re-imagination of the vampire as a seemingly 'human' creature, able to have feelings of love and devotion which, clearly, are an important part of romance storylines. It is unsurprising, then, that narratives that negate the human side of the vampire—and favour an overall understanding of the concept as a cold, emotionless, blood-thirsty creature—do not show an interest in engaging with any form of ritual that, culturally speaking, has conceptions of love and devotion at its heart.

Nonetheless, if one decided to put the question of genre aside, it would become almost impossible to refute the impact of vampire weddings and marriage in contemporary literature. The narratives, one might argue, encourage a conceptual return of the wedding as an expression of love and romance. The widespread insistence on weddings draws attention to a desire to reinforce the importance of unions in society, an idea underpinned by an inescapable desire for social stability that has often been associated with the married state in Western societies. As Catherine Anne Gildae contends, even though 'the meaning of marriage' has undergone 'seismic shifts' in recent times, the importance of marriage 'as an institution' in the social sense remained untouched.[27] This, however, is but the starting point for unravelling the significance of wedding rituals in contemporary vampire fiction. To uncover its most culturally important interpretation, one must turn to the overall discourse of marriage as a locus of closeness that has becomes prominent is twenty-first century understandings of human unions.

There is no denying that marriage is a contested notion in the post-2000 era, and that the very concept of 'a wedding' initiates ample discussion regarding notions of 'right' and 'wrong' in society. In recent years, discussion over same-sex marriage has had an impact on the way in which marriage is viewed. Although same-sex marriages are still not legal in a number of countries or even areas in the Anglo-American world, the growing acceptance of alternative types of unions—so defined—have opened the way for re-establishing marital rituals as an important topic for conversation. David Shumway reminds us that the most remarkable part of the challenge that advocates of same-sex marriage have presented is their demanding reconsideration 'of the basic terms in which marriage had been understood' in Western contexts.[28] Most of all, the re-evaluation of weddings and marriage in Western societies has somehow re-vindicated the role of the union as an expression of 'love'. And this is indeed the message that appears to underpin the multiple representations of wedding rituals in contemporary vampire fiction. Although the majority of the mainstream fiction still portrays vampire weddings as indications of strictly heterosexual unions—an element that might indeed be connected to genre and readership—the idea of unconditional love connects the two spouses being joined in matrimony, and therefore removes the union from its role as a political and social tool belonging to the community rather than the individual.[29] This is not to say that weddings and marriage were ever removed from the peripheral interest of the individual in terms of 'love'. The essential elements emerging from the focus on wedding in vampire fiction is the re-evaluation of unions in the human world, where closeness and attachment are promoted as the result of balance between the psychological, the passionate, and the anthropological.

Without generalisation, it is possible to say that narratives tend to include weddings at times of high conflict in the vampires' world, where war, struggle, and civil disputes are threatening the safety of groups and individuals. In the *Black Dagger Brotherhood*, Wrath and Beth get mated at the height of political struggles, as he decides to ascend the throne. In the *Midnight Breed*, Lucan and Gabrielle get married as the war between vampire factions intensifies. In the *Sookie Stackhouse* series, Sookie and Eric get married by vampire law when a change happens in the vampire socio-economic and political regime, and the union ensures Sookie's safety.

Love prevails, one might be tempted to say, and weddings—in their most varied forms—continue to occupy their important place in the social structure, fitting into the discourse of closeness and familiarity that claim, as Shumway puts it, that most individuals still value marriage very highly.[30] In the most developed stages of later capitalism—where society encourages growth, but negates intimacy, and is said to cause the fragmentation of the social and interpersonal self—the almost forceful inclusion of wedding rituals and marital existence in vampire fiction provides a refuge against emotional disintegration in a climate of political upheaval.

BLOOD TIES

The idea that vampires like to congregate was already a recurrent feature in late twentieth-century literature and popular culture. From the chilling, wolf-like packs of Rice's *Vampire Chronicles*, to the 'nests' scattered throughout the narrative of *Buffy the Vampire Slayer*, vampire showed a predilection for assembling and constructing relations. Safety, it was made clear, was often found in numbers, and the most distinct characteristic of vampire groups was their ability to hunt together, feed together, and kill together. Assemblies of vampires are also a feature of twenty-first century literature, but something has changed. Undoubtedly, vampires still congregate and operate together, seeking each other's company—often—as a better option to humans or other super/preternatural creatures, as it is the case in Harris' *Sookie Stackhouse* series, where groups of vampires have been known to 'nest' together for long periods of time.[31] And yet, vampire relational dynamics have mutated from simple groups of like-minded and like-bodied creatures. A distinctive trait of contemporary narratives is the emergence and establishment of vampire families. The term family alone distinguishes this type of social organisation from simple congregating, as it implies the presence of highly organised and, to some extent, institutionalised principles that regulate them.

Instances of vampire families abound. The *Twilight* saga presents the Cullen coven as a family, with its members all carrying the same surname— the one given to them by the patriarch and maker, Carlisle Cullen—and referring to each other as father, mother, brother, and sister, accordingly. In Harkness' *All Souls* novels, the vampires reborn into the De Clermont family are all given the surname, and show undying loyalty and love for each other, suffering for the loss of any family member. In the *Black Dagger Brotherhood*, the family is the most important institution for the vampires; this ranges from the strength of biological connections—the family that is connected physically by blood—to metaphorical representations of the group—the figurative familiar connections established through blood rites in the narrative. The 'Brothers', we are told, are not brothers because they 'were born of the same female', but because they were connected by blood oaths and a common goal.[32] Whether biological or figurative, however, blood connections are treated as extremely important, and Ward even goes as far as saying that family is 'everything to vampires'.[33]

These are not, however, solitary occurrences. The importance of the family –whether nuclear or extended—is present in several examples within the fiction, and more instances of a similar nature can be found, with Adrian's *Midnight Breed*, L.J. Smith's *Vampire Diaries*, Richelle Mead's *Vampire Academy*, and Rachel Caine's *Morganville Vampires* providing further proof. These narratives tend to portray vampire families as ancient and long-standing institutions, often connected to folkloristic interpretations of the vampire motif. A particular emphatic example of this is to be found in Painter's *House of Comarré* series, where the noble vampires are organised into 'houses' and see their affiliation to other members in terms of family. Each house issaid to have been founded by one famed vampire individual, and the house names range from St. Germain and Paole, to the infamous Bathory and Tepes: members of House of Tepes, unsurprisingly, are 'directly descended by Lord Vlad Tepes'.[34] Each House member is said to inherit traits and abilities that are typical to the group they are reborn into when they become vampires—such as the ability to transform into insects and scatter, or an aptitude for magic and alchemy—thereby strengthening the familiar nature of the grouping and the importance of vampiric blood connections within the narrative.[35]

Families, it would seem, have become a striking feature of vampire ethology. The decision to organise vampires around the concept of family signals, *in primis*, a desire to humanise them. Anthony Stevens reminds us that, anthropologically speaking, 'family formation is a universal characteristic of mankind'.[36] Different cultures around the world undoubtedly favour different kinds of 'family', ranging from multiple spouses and recognition of children, to monogamous connections which act as the foundation of blood relations. All societies, however, seem to support family ties of one type or another, and use these familial associations as the founding agent for political organisation. This notion immediately draws attention to the newly developed need for vampires to have a family as a possible agent of socio-political concerns. Fiction from the previous century often had the tendency to visualise vampire gatherings in terms of groups or packs, constructing a metaphorical association between the way in which vampires lived and congregated as an expression of their predatory nature. One need only think here of Whitley Strieber's *The Hunger* and how Miriam Blaylock chooses human companions and transforms them into vampires so that they can live and 'hunt' together .[37] Undoubtedly, the idea that vampire families hunt for blood together—as a pack—remains strong, as noticeable in the *Twilight* saga. Nonetheless, the use of the term 'family' implies an institutionalised conception of relations that goes beyond seemingly simple assembling aimed at feeding and safety.

The family, Anthony Stevens argues, 'is an expression of archetypal functioning'.[38] It has not only a sense of universality attached to it, but also a layer of persistence that indicates a particular evaluation of both biological and cultural relations. Historically, humans opted for the protective alliance of the group in order in order to ensure the safe-guarding of adult individuals and their offspring. Needless to say, however, the nature of family—with its apparent emphasis on blood-ties—evolved greatly, in both social and cultural terms, beyond the desire for protection. Family, as both a definition and an institution, implies an expected layer of obligation, if not affection; it demands interest and involvement on the individual's part, so that it can become part of a specific group with its specific dynamics. Unlike other social and political groupings, family implies the existence of a network reliant on kinship, systems of attachment that—usually based on blood relations, both biological and constructed—hold people together within conceptual (and often geographic) bounds.

Family, however, also implies ownership; traditional interpretations place a focus on the power that individuals—the father, in patriarchal organisation, and the mother, in matriarchal structures—have over the other members. With its strong organisation and system of affiliation, the family has been, traditionally, a distinctly human concept. Its extension to the vampire world inevitably has implication of a domesticating nature. It implies, on both tangible and abstract levels, that it is possible to understand vampires on a human level, highlighting a desire to colonise the vampire motif through the bounds of human relation. The distinct affinity between vampire and human social familial organisation transforms the concept of vampire family into an ideal metaphorical incarnation of the human, a perfect vector for the discussion of political and psychological orientation in the anthropological sense.

Vampire families maintain, for the most part, a strong patriarchal organisation. The impact of the father figure in the vampire family is visible through the fiction. Surnames are the first signal of the patriarchal nature of vampire familial, social, and political structures. The vampires' children are still given the family name they inherited from their father. Even when human-like family names are not present—as in the case of Ward's Brotherhood—the name of the father continues to generate affiliation and construct family relations, as the offspring is patronymichally taxonomised as 'daughter of' or 'son of' the father—Rhage, son of Torture; Tohrment, son of Hharm; Phury, son of Ahgony; Wellesdandra, daughter of Relix. Across contemporary storylines, however, the influence of the father is not seen in name alone; indeed, the patriarchal nature of the vampire family extends to envisaging the father as the head of the family, in charge of all its members. When the father dies—whether for the first or final time—the control of the family is passed onto the oldest male child, who then inherits both the powers and the responsibilities of having to care for the entire family. This layer of family succession is heavily subscribed to and clearly signalled on several occasions—as it is in Harkness' A *Discovery of Witches*, the first novel of the *All Souls* trilogy. When a vampire is recognised as 'head of the family', he has the power to make all decisions regarding its members.[39]

In contemporary vampire narratives, the father figure functions as an archetype. In using this profoundly Jungian term, I refer not to an image that is innate to the figure of the vampire as a patriarchal incarnation, but, more specifically, to how the familial interpretation of fatherhood within the vampire motif operates on the psychological dynamic of precedence and social interaction. The father archetype is interpreted here as the symbolic residue of the dynamic between imagination, phylogeny, and artistry in unveiling the impact of universality on the collective unconscious. The vampiric father, whether taking on the role in virtue of biology or metaphor, is part of the symbolic canon that operates at the centre of interpretative systems, the connection between the inner and the outer, the individual and the group, the family and the world. Stevens suggests that, in the great majority of patriarchal and patrilineal societies, the father acts as 'the bridge between family life and the life of society at large'.[40] The father's role is not only representative, but also conductive in its cultural understanding. The emphasis on the father's name suggests the logocentric nature of vampiric organisation, based on communicative parameters and complicit in the establishing and re-establishing of patriarchal structures. It is the father, through his presence and name, who institutes the family as such; the name groups together the members of the nucleus through affiliation, association, and duty. Simultaneously, the father acts as the representative of that emotional and structural triumvirate, his position in relation to his children that of possession and demonstration.

Instances of this paternal interaction are prominent throughout the fiction. In the *All Soul* novels, the influence of the vampire Philippe—head of the de Claremont family—is visible in the lives of all hid children. He rules sovereign within his family. His role, however, is not only a commanding one; his name alone protects his family members and acts as a shield between individual and outer sphere as 'none at all will cross' their father.[41] In similar vein, the *Black Dagger Brotherhood* signifies the impact of the father as the representative symbol by clearly stating that it is the father's role to make the presentation of a newborn to the world, and ask friends and members of the extended family to accept the infant, as Zsadist does in asking for his own blooded brother's acceptance of his daughter: 'Zsadist held up his hand [. . .] Wouldst both thou honor my birthed daughter with the color of thy lineages and the love of thy hearts? [. . .] Z Bowed deeply, offering the bow'.[42] The depiction of the vampiric patriarch—in its expressive and connecting social responsibilities—seems to subscribe to what Talcott Parsons describes as the 'instrumental role' of the father.[43] According to Parsons, the father—as a social entity—possesses a centrifugal orientation, aimed towards society and that which is outside of the family nucleus. This is, Parsons suggests, usually in contrast to the mother's centripetal concerns, which have developed anthropologically to focus on the inner circle of the family. In patriarchal organisation, the father, as Stevens puts it, represents 'society to the family and his family to society'.[44] In the vampiric sense, the father becomes the representation of the blood lineage that created the vampire as a creature, whether that blood connection is generated via biological reproduction, or through the process of turning. As the symbolic representation of the family, the vampiric father takes on the binding and bonding role by facilitating the transition of the child from the home into the world. In its representational role, the father becomes the archetype of knowledge, proprietorship, individuality, and kinship. The vampiric father is a reminder of the potential of blood and its place in socio-political organisation. As a connector between individual and society, the 'transpersonal father'—as Vera Von der Heydt terms it—represents the vampiric family's consciousness as it moves and as it changes within a shifting world.[45] In the vampire world, the father figure is subject to the changing of time, and 'his image changes with the culture he represents'.[46] Carrying with him the weight of name and symbology, the vampiric father is the epitome of the extraverted latency of the vampire motif. The father is the representation of the vampire's autonomy, while his role as a reminder of bloodline constellates for the vampire children the reach and impact of world-family relations. This interpretation of the vampiric father is, naturally, predominantly reliant on attributes of masculine psychology that are, archetypically, identified in human groups and are adapted to the vampire motif to unveil the nature of blood relations within the structures of social actualisation.

In the case where vampire families are constructed by turning, specific politics seem to be at play. There is no natural, human, physical connection between the vampire parent and the newly-born vampire child. The only biological exchange that seems to take place—on some level—is the exchange of blood. In the majority of turning cases, reciprocal blood drinking forms the basis for the transformation. Either way, it seems clear that blood is at the centre of the exchange. The biology of the act makes it clear that, although vampires do not physically give birth to their children—in the mammalian sense—the blood exchange bestows upon the act some of the characteristics that we understand being at the centre of familial connections. Blood is, after all, one of the most well-known metaphors for biologically-connected families, and in the case of vampire its connecting significance remains unchanged: by taking the other person's blood—and, in most cases, returning it with its own—the vampire seals the bond that connects.

The act is both symbolic and peculiarly physiological. The vampire's blood becomes the other's blood, as the former takes the latter to be their own. Simultaneously, by giving their own blood to the other, the vampires bear their children into a new life—just as any mortal mother or father would. The human's body goes through a biological change that marks it as vampire and, in so doing, becomes 'reborn' into a way of being, into a new family. The metaphorical and organic nature of the exchange allows the vampire to take on the role of mother or father, according to gender. As the limits of the family are established, so are the obligations of both loyalty and affection that derive from family connections. The bestowing of the vampire's family name to the child makes the association even stronger. Even in instances when the term 'maker' is preferred to mother or father— as in the case of Harris' *Sookie Stackhouse* series—the connection between birthing and newborn vampire still bears the characteristics of the familial relationship. In Harris' narrative, for instance, Ocella still refers to his own made vampire Eric as his 'son', and announces his other creation Alexei as Eric's 'brother'. The devotion that the two younger vampires are expected to have for Ocella leaves no doubt, culturally and socially speaking, to his quasi-dictatorial position of 'father' in the exchange.

In spite of the symbolic interpretation of family connections that take place in the narratives, one must be alert to the fact that turned vampire families are not fully akin to human understandings of the term. Vampire family connections seem to place themselves somewhere in the middle between the two known ways of establishing in the human world: biological generation or adoption. The latter, of course, takes many nuances and it can range from the legal adoption of children and other family members, to a more symbolic interpretation of the notion, when the term 'family'— for instance—is extended to close friends. In the first instance, the traditional family is presented as a social agent, undoubtedly constricted by the limitations of social and cultural guidelines. In the case of extended adoption, however, the family is afforded a different paradigm, what Heidi Hartmann refers to as a 'social location', a more flexible and inclusive relational model for competing forces and overlapping roles.[47] In the light of this interpretation of human familial connections, vampire families seem to place themselves somewhere in the middle of the two definitions. The blood exchange undoubtedly creates an understood bond between maker and turned, but that bond conceptually remains—in spite of its physiological consequences—firmly sited in the realm of the symbolic. The illustrative nature of the vampire's claim is further explicated by the appropriation of terms such as 'mother', 'father', and 'child'; the extension of familial relations here highlights the adoptive nature of the vampire's claim.

The representational power of blood functions here as the agent through which the vampire reconceptualises the idea of family as an entity of inclusion, which transcends the boundaries of traditional family connections and exposes it as the locus of overlapping identities. In the process of turning, vampires neither physically 'give birth' to their children, nor do they just 'adopt' them. The arbitrations of familial relationship in the vampire world go beyond the limitations of linguistic expression. Although human terminology is commonly used, the terms are negotiated on a different systematic understanding. The vampire does not succumb to the restraints of rubric definition, nor does he submit to what Jes Battis calls the 'normative powers of language'.[48] The vampiric family is founded on an alteration of language, a re-evaluation of term and concept that finds its own social, cultural, and political dimension of inclusion. In claiming positional stances through the linguistic re-ordainment of 'father', 'mother' and 'child', vampires alter the interpretation of the family unit, so that it 'more suitably describes' their own 'visible reality'.[49]

The organisation of the vampire family, as it comes to life through turning', exposes preoccupations with the cultural re-evaluation of the concept of family which is a very prominent feature of Western societies in the twenty-first century. Although it would be simplistic to assume a direct and overarching connection between the newly interpreted vampire families and the emergence—both legal and social—of alternative family units in Western countries, it is virtually impossible to deny the conceptual similarities that seem to exist between the two. Familiar legacies are representative of the vampire's desire to 'maintain normalcy' in a world that calls for horror and abomination.[50] Valerie Lehr points out that, in contemporary societies, one of the principal debates about social organisation is centred on deciphering the nature of single-family units. She argues that the question lingers around families that appear 'virtually normal', and families who disrupt institutionalised patterns by 'queering' the nuclear-family model.[51] The notion of 'normality' is of course a contested one, cultural and contextual in its understanding. Nonetheless, Lehr's suggestion draws attention to the ability of alternative conceptions of the family to destabilise social systems. Lehr is particularly concerned with gay and lesbian families, who she sees as often too centred on performing a notion of normalcy that, in relation to institutional and inevitably patriarchal models of the family, can never be achieved.[52]

It is this understanding of the family as a re-evaluative unit that unveils vampire familial organisation as an evolving and mutable notion. In narratives when vampires are 'made' part of a family—by ritual of blood and linguistic appropriation—the concept of family is complicated by a mixed notion of recognition and rejection of the very concept itself. Vampiric familial groups rely upon the concept of family as a bonding trope, but also depend, as Battis would put it, on 'the disruption of that trope in order to find a living space'.[53] The vampire's family is a reconstituted unit, a paradoxical formation of balance and imbalance that, while still subscribing to model of affiliation that are recognisable in human terms, refuses to surrender its identity to pre-established schematics of the institutional axis. The creation of a new vampire, and the claiming of its existence as part of an established family, exposes a decisive queering of social and biological boundaries. As the identifying terminology extends, so does the reach of the vampire's family, an idiosyncratic entity of transmutation and metamorphosis. In the vampire family—'made' as it is through bonds of recognition and affiliation—one can see the simultaneous prescription to institutional parameters and the challenge of prescribed notions of normality. Vampiric familial connections offer disregard for both control and fear, and uncover how the family, in its various incarnations, acts as a social 'signifier to be enlarged, distended and ultimately exploded'.[54]

FOOD MATTERS

In contemporary narratives, blood has ceased to be the only source of nourishment for vampires. Although not a universal occurrence in all examples from the fiction, numerous instances depict vampires as consuming food as much as blood. Indeed, the two are often placed on the same level on the nutritional scale, one as important and necessary as the other. A clear example of this is given in the *Black Dagger Brotherhood*, when vampires are revealed to consume and enjoy 'human food' as much as humans: blood has 'necessary nutrients in it', but they 'need food, too'.[55] We are told that they have favourite foods—with lamb figuring prominently on the list—and a distinct penchant for alcoholic drinks, such as whiskey, vodka, and wine. Although other examples of a similar nature can be found across numerous storylines within the fiction—with *The Dresden Files*, *All Souls*, and *Hollows* series functioning as prime examples here—Ward's narrative is undoubtedly the most effective at rendering vampires as sharing meals that go beyond blood, with food becoming an importance presence in the story.

The re-current presence of food is curious to find in the vampires' lives, from the necessity to consume it to the symbolic nuances that sharing it with family and friends undertakes. One must question here why contemporary authors—Ward in particular—would be drawn to integrating 'human food' into narratives about vampires, and what that inclusion represents. Although the exact answer to this question may be difficult to provide, one can find a directional clue in the role that food itself plays as a culturally-inscribed bonding agent. Deborah Lupton argues that 'food is instrumental' in strengthening 'group identity'. Sharing the act of eating, she contends, 'brings people into the same community'.[56] One must remember here that, as anthropological scholarship contends, eating can never be interpreted as a historically detached practice; every food communicates a social narrative which contributes towards the formation of a concept of mutual belonging.[57] In *Tasting Food, Tasting Freedom*, social anthropologist Sydney Mintz reminds us that 'food is never simply eaten [. . .] [it] has histories associated with the pasts of those who eat' it.[58] If it is true that human beings do not simply eat, but the practice is embedded with meaning, then one cannot avoid seeing the inclusion of human food in the vampire's diet as much more than a simple nutritional shift. Food will provide a passageway into the vampire's material experience, and will inevitably be connected to important cultural concerns such as family and group belonging, which form the bases for shared practices of consumption.

The attention not only to food, but also to specific practices of consumption in contemporary vampire fiction, unveils a shift in socio-political interest that openly engages with preoccupations of a cultural nature. If one accepts the contention that, as David Bell and Gill Valentine put it, for most inhabitants of (post)modern Western societies: food has long ceased to be merely about sustenance and nutrition', then it is virtually possible not to see the inclusion of consumption rituals and customs in contemporary vampire fiction as a highly representational and significant act.[59] Although food and drinks are often viewed as ordinary and conventional parts in human life—a position that recent food studies scholarship has successfully attempted to discredit—their presence in vampire narratives is peculiar and raises questions. Food occupies an unrivalled centrality in human lives, and this centrality is transported to the vampire's world. With this transference, however, also come the matters generally associated with food, particularly its role as symbol of social bonding. By focusing on an allegedly commonplace set of food customs and culinary practices—from eating to drinking, cooking, and even food shopping—vampire fiction begins a conceptual conversation with a whole set of contemporary social and political issues, such as health, ethics, aesthetics, and even the impact of globalised economies of consumption. While seemingly portrayed as a common occurrence which have no other use rather than adding a paradoxical sense of verisimilitude in the story, consumption practices in the fiction serve to structure lives, and forge relationships. This vision of the culinary—encompassing both human food and drink and, of course, blood—in contemporary vampire literature is reminiscent of Arjun Appadurai's suggestion that all consumption practices can be simultaneously viewed 'as highly condensed social facts' and vectors of 'collective representation'.[60]

The dinner table, in particular, is given a lot of attention in Ward's fiction. The Brothers are often portrayed at the dinner table, all sitting together and sharing meals. Indeed, meal times are taken very seriously in the Brotherhood's household, and all members are expected to attend. When Vishous refuses to regularly join the Brothers and their mates for meals, he is reprimanded by the others as if he was committing a crime: the vampire is clearly told by one of his Brothers that he either 'shows' at the table the next time, or they will 'come' for him, and Vishous will be 'picked up like mail'.[61] Meals do not simply occupy a feeding function, however; they are also important coordinates for the day. They dictate the passing of time in a house that is never given the privilege of sunlight, and provide a focal point for the 'family' to gather.

With its repertoire of culturally inscribed conventions, eating affords a performative arena in which social relations can be created, cemented or destroyed. Bell and Valentine point out that, in sociological research, the dinner table 'has been identified as an important site for the socialisation' of the family.[62] It is not simply a place to consume food, but a social medium through which the integrity of the Brothers' family can remain intact. In virtue of its logistical organisation, the dinner table virtually demands some form of contact and engagement between individuals. For the Brothers, consuming meals together acts as a symbol of group affiliation. As a result, Ward's narrative comes to validate Nicki Charles and Marion Kerr's contention that food 'has a part to play in cementing and reinforcing relations'.[63] In the Brotherhood, meals, one might argue, become synonym with community, and act as the linking medium for individuals to feel part of the collective group. They are viewed as the pinnacles of family life, and therefore given a special place of importance in everyday activities. Consumption—particularly when portrayed as a shared act—is a practice that calls for habituation, and compartmentalises existence as a regular and highly ritualised entity.

The focus on strict consumption practices in the Brotherhood draws attention not only to the social structures that regulate the sharing of food as a cultural presence, but also to how eating in itself can be understood as an activity of order and restraint for both the body and the self. As a technique of the body—to use Foucault's terminology—eating is connected to the 'genealogy of the subject'. This is the genealogy of both morality and desire for individuals, which demonstrates—according to Foucault—how subjectivation is 'internalised' as a reflection concerning one's own body and the experience of corporeality.[64] In its role as a subject-defining activity—an area thoroughly investigated by psychoanalytical, phenomenological, and cultural scholarship—eating can be treated as a technique of the body which highlights the boundaries of the self as individual, and places it in a meaningful relation with the rest of the environment, be it in its social, political, or aesthetic incarnations.

Shared consumption practices—regulated by both time and place—draw attention to the fact that, of all socially regulated activities, those that centre around the body take on the function of providing rhythm and sense on which more complex and 'chaotic' patterns can then be built.[65] In this light, it becomes easy to interpret the Brothers' emphasis on shared consumption as an act of ritualisation that is aimed at not only encouraging individuals into feeling part of a given group, but also at regulating and structuring existence through the settings of culturally-understood temporal measures. Appadurai has written about the role played by food in 'punctuating or periodising all our lives through repetitive "techniques of the body"'.[66] The vampire—a creature that is in itself, through the very disturbance of life and death boundaries, a representation of chaos—is given a ruling structure by the very act of including consumption practices within its existence. Scholars of food studies have long argued that food consumption 'creates time'.[67] As everyday practices, eating and drinking do not simply respond to universal notions of the passage of time, but regulate the organisation of life through culturally understood notions of 'meal time' and 'food occasion'.

It is possible to argue here that food can be interpreted, for vampires, as a normalizing tool, one that naturalises the rhythms of the family and makes social, aesthetic, and seasonal definitions easy to grasp. Eating—even when taken to be an individual and self-centred activity—is never disconnected from systems of control and regulation. Although existing as a technique of the self', it is also reproduced as part of what Foucault terms 'techniques of domination'.[68] It is in this area of thought that eating assumes its most important role for the analysis of the vampire body and vampire relations in the Brotherhood. As a socio-cultural activity for Ward's vampires—which often transcends its seemingly simple uses of nutrition and necessity—eating is a technique of the self that can no longer be reduced to a mere sequence of cause and effect, or even a system of habitual continuation. Indeed, even 'habit' implies the presence of regulatory systems, and the observance of the Brothers' controlled consumption patterns suggests that structural subjugation may in fact be at work.

Although sharing food allows the vampires to construct both individual and collective identities, the focus on strict rules regarding the act of consumption can be interpreted as dominating activity. Operating within the parameters of the body, and extending the domain into the realm of socio-political relations, sharing meals at the Brotherhood's household becomes an activity of control. The vampires' bodies—and, by extension, their sense of self within the group—can be said to be 'disciplined' through the act of eating. According to Pasi Falk, a body 'becomes' a 'human body' only when it is constructed as part of 'an Order' which encompasses both socio-practical structures and cultural meaning structures.[69] In drawing attention to the physicality of the body as being subject to not only representation, but also to divisions of labour and power hierarchies, Falk is undoubtedly gesturing towards a framework of corporeal control that is dependent on Foucault's understandings of corporeal and intellectual power structures. In this context, food and eating act as powerful agents in highlighting the social status and purpose of any corporeal experience within systems of classification and distinction—the group of regulation that scholars have termed 'the Order'. Although centred on the human body, Falk's argument—and its focus on the process of 'becoming'—is reminiscent of the conceptual and corporeal relationships highlighted in the Brotherhood, and draws attention to the interdependency of inclusion, acceptance, and reference that constitute the foundations for vampire identity in contemporary literature.

In *Dark Lover*, the first book of the Brotherhood series, we witness Wrath—not only the head of the household, but also the King of the vampire race—exercising his power by demanding that all the Brothers live and operate together. Ward stresses on a number of occasions that the sharing of meals and living spaces is an activity that Wrath 'insists' upon for all the Brothers, their mates, and their guests.[70] This focus on 'control'—especially when the act of eating is concerned—emphasises the presence of not only bodily, but also intellectual subordination. Wrath is said to be 'everything' to the race; upon his ascension to the throne, he re-establishes customs—including festivals and festivities—for the individual vampires which are seen as reinforcing the 'community spirit' of the vampire race overall. Food is often at the centre of both celebration and daily rituals, and the strict rules over shared meals and serving times are but a reflection of this. As King, Wrath regulates the rhythms of his vampire subjects, starting with the members of his royal household—the Brothers and their families—and continuing into the greater collectivity of his realm. The control of the body in its corporeal needs translates into the political control of the vampire group; one can take Wrath here to be the metaphorical transposition for all those cultural, political, and social rules that regulate the lives of individuals, and draw attention to the hierarchies of power to which the body is subjected to in its corporeal understandings. The bodies of vampires are controlled through the practice of eating, and so are their intellectual allegiances. By transforming them into operating parts of the collective, and building the grounds for a sense of both individual and group identities, shared consumption practices regulate the vampires through cultural authority. The individual self and the social self of the vampires can be viewed, as Falk puts it, not as 'parallel entities', but rather as 'a cyclical succession' of psycho-social 'metamorphoses'.[71] The 'discipline' imposed on the body shows the points of mergence between techniques of the self and techniques of domination. By integrating the presence of food and eating into the usually blood-dependant world of vampire consumption, Ward unveils the structures of control and domination which are inherently connected to corporeal habits and preferences, and how those habits play a role in the construction of identity systems. The social subjectivity of the vampire is embedded and embodied in the living entity of the body, and the parameters of social/cultural/political discipline find a fertile ground in its material functions.

The echo of human consumption practices in the fiction—unavoidable and radical throughout the narrative—takes on a percussive role and allows the vampire's seemingly insignificant daily food habits to be understood an classifying agent in cementing socio-cultural arrangements through culinary repetition and creativity. In an era allegedly dominated by scopophilia, physical manipulation, and transience, the 'return to food' in contemporary vampire literature signals a systematic departure from unregulated practices of the body, drawing attention to a desire for regulation and sensorial accumulation that is inevitably connected to the daily rhythms of family and community. Distancing itself from simulacaral conceptions of consumption and assimilation—undoubtedly visible in examples from the pre-2000 era—the seminally twenty-first approach to food expressed by Ward in the *Black Dagger Brotherhood* merges the vision of food and drinks as 'signs'—symbolic presences in everyday life—with their material function as ritualised consumption practices. Occupying a localised space in the vampire's life that is somewhere in between the procedural and the hedonistic, eating food draws attention to the role that physical activities have, as David Morgan puts it, in forging familial connections and an 'anchorage to the past'.[72] As ephemeral and fleeting experiences threaten to engulf the overly technological lives of the vampires, their existence is kept grounded in the tangibility of relationships through the idiom of food.

THE BLOODY USES OF PLEASURE

As the need for tangible experience emerges as an important concern, food is not alone in cementing corporeal ritualised relationship for vampires. In spite of its important culturally regulating capabilities, human food takes a secondary position when matters of consumption and sexuality are involved. Blood still occupies a prime position in reinforcing the relationship between sex and feeding in contemporary literature, a tropic adage that has long been associated with the vampire. Sex and blood are shown as related entities, and one does not seem to be able to happen without the other. As such, the vampire's desire to feed and desire to have sex 'are impossible to separate'.[73] The emphasis on the relationship between consumption and sexual intercourse is widespread, and a common feature in contemporary narratives. In *Vampires in America*, we are told on several occasions that blood and sex 'go together' for vampires. In *Sookie Stackhouse*, the blood urge is enhanced by the sexual urge: as vampire Bill's virility seems enhanced by the act of sharing blood with his lover Sookie, as waves of 'dark delight' overtake them both at the height of sexual climax.[74] In the *Black Dagger Brotherhood*, blood is seen as a potent aphrodisiac. In the *Vampire Federation*, intercourse makes the need to take blood almost irresistible. After the vampire Alex makes love to her human lover Joel 'for hours', blood hunger overtakes her:

> The familiar tingle came over her. She needed to feed. Glancing back over at Joel's still form under the sheets, for a few intoxicating moments she could sense nothing bu the blood pumping through his veins [. . .] Her heart began to quicken as a force that was stronger threatened to impel her towards the bed. Not to love him this time, but to bite him. Her fangs began to elongate in her mouth.[75]

The examples abound and, in their profusion, they establish the connection between taking blood and having sex almost as a commonplace feature, a matter of expectation when vampires are involved.

It has long been argued that practices of preparing and consuming food are highly sensual and, at times, can even gain a sexual dimension. Deleuze and Guattari's argument about alimentary and sexual practices claims that these two dimensions of experience produce bodies at various states of 'intermingling', creating 'all the attractions and repulsion, sympathies and antipathies, alterations, amalgamations, penetration and expansions that affect bodies of all kinds in their relations to one and another'.[76] In their evaluation, Deleuze and Guattari draw attention to both sex and eating being activities of mergence and fusion, when the boundaries between bodies and objects become indistinguishable—albeit for a short period of time. In a vampire context, the two aspects of the vampire's existence are so connected, that it is almost impossible to separate them, even if 'eating' should be substituted with 'feeding' for the most part.

Conceptually speaking, the links between feeding and sex are plentiful. Like sex, food has the propensity, as Elspeth Probyn argues, for 'hazing frontiers [and] categories'.[77] And like food, sex can capture the contradiction of absolute individuality and complete universality. In truth, feeding is much more of a universal activity than sex. George Simmel does rightfully point out that, 'of everything that people have in common, the most common is that they must eat and drink'.[78] Sex, however, can be seen as an 'essential' activity in that it ensures the continuation of the species, and can therefore be granted a place in the conceptual scale that elevates it –just like food—beyond simple notions of hedonistic pleasure. In joining the two dimensions together, the vampire already suggests an association between the corporeal and conceptual which points us in the direction of boundary-breaking and identity construction, where individuals do not wish to transcend the physicality of the body, but embrace it as a matter of necessity. Both eating and sex possess inherent metonymic qualities, which engage with the peculiarities of the vampire as subject in order to offer a reassessment of the human in its contemporary context.

The association between feeding and sex in vampire literature unveils an evaluation of corporeal involvement as an active and conscious modality of experience. Simply put, re-thinking the vampire through the intermingled dimensions of sex and food is compelling because it shifts and focuses the attention on the interconnectedness of corporeal dimensions. Sex and consumption can be interpreted as vectors that lead into other areas of conceptual experience—the realm of the ritual—showing how the constitution of the ethical subjects in the social context encapsulates the paradox of subjugation and control. Probyn has pointed out that 'what we know of the body' at any one time 'will of necessity result from a recognition of enactments of corporeal practices'.[79] At a basic sensorial level, therefore, one can recognise that a different relationship to the body is established after activities that involve it first-hand. And of all activities, feeding and sex are the ones that draw the most attention to the experience of the body, as they can both be associated with extreme feelings and stimulations, including pleasure and disgust. The focus on the vampire's connection to feeding and sex unveils a re-evaluation of the body in terms of experience. In the arguably corporeally disconnected context of the twenty-first century, the vampire re-appropriates the body as the most primordial site of experience, through two of the most primordial activities known to man. If it is true that, as

Probyn has argued, in both eating and sex 'we experience different parts of our bodies', then it is possible to suggest that the vampire reclaims the body as the origin of all stimuli, the source of all experience.[80]

As the vampire's bite takes place—and the activities that either follow it or precede it—the knowledge of past experiences and the savouring of the present join into one. Through the bite, both the vampire's body and the donor's body become the centre of attention, and both subjects are connected not only on the surface, but also emotionally and conceptually by experiences of hunger, fantasy, and memory. The hunger is that which joins the corporeal to the metaphysical, a term that encapsulates both the tangible and the ephemeral, the actual and the metaphorical. The fantasy is that of the obscure, the indulgence in an activity which is inhuman and yet sensual at the same time—the sensuality derives from the transgressive nature of the act, when boundaries are broken and conceptual fusions established. And the memory is, of course, the return to the corporeal repressed, the re-emergence of the buried and the forgotten, the seizing of the body as the original source of pleasure. By biting and incorporating the metaphorical essence of another's body—the life-giving blood—the vampire builds a relationship of necessity with the host that unveils the body as loosely contained core of experience. That experience is then acted upon with the sexual act, where the corporeal nature of the living being is given concrete existence through the intermingling of bodies, of desires. The alimentary and the sexual can be seen as a regime of tangibility, aimed at redefining, as Foucault would have put it, 'the uses of pleasure'.[81] In the post-2000 era, the vampire is not simply a metaphor for the unspeakable acts of the body, but *is* the body. In the face of physical segmentation and the de-territorialisation of the human in favour of the ephemeral, the vampire's ritualised engagement with feeding restores the seemingly banal and mundane dimension of the body to its seat in the realm of the extraordinary.

DEATH AND COMMEMORATION RITUALS

In contemporary vampire narratives, one can identify the presence of a large number of commemoration rituals. This category is far-reaching and ranges in concept from funeral and mortuary rites, to grieving and remembrance acts, such as festivals for the dead or even monuments. Commemoration practices take several and often disparate nuances in the fiction, and place the attention on specific elements of the rituals which are commonly connected to how vampires perceive death, the dead and—more often than not—the afterlife. In spite of the differences, and before these can be adequately surveyed and contextualised, the point of departure must be to acknowledge that in the twenty-first century vampires do not simply cease to exit, they 'die'. Death, of course, is a highly cultural and political construct, as well as a physical occurrence. Since vampires are now understood as highly social and organised beings, when they die there are warranted practices of remembrance. Although mourning is not a completely new instance on the vampire's part—one should only think here of Louis' almost self-destructive grieving after Claudia's death in Rice's *Interview with the Vampire*—commemoration rituals and mortuary rites add a different dimension to the conceptual understanding of death within the fiction. And, of course, the issues that the death ritual involves.

Commemorative acts in vampire narratives are carried out through traditional and long-standing rituals. It is often tacitly implied that vampires have been disposing of their dead in the same manner for centuries. The death ritual, therefore, operates as a connection to the past and the future, a constructed traditional vector which is aimed at the maintenance of a sense of community and ritualistic validation for the vampire assembly. Human commemorative practices place an emphasis on the merging of tradition and belief, the repetitive nature of both funeral and remembrance acts—and consequent sense of purpose and continuation that derives from it—authenticate the strength of the social group. In spite of the fact that it marks the physical end of individuals, the commemoration ritual adds a sense of continuity to life, and maintains a sense of social and political equilibrium for the wider community.

Indeed, it is virtually impossible to divorce the presence of commemoration rituals in vampire literature from discourses of a cultural nature. Any instances of structural organisation, in the socio-cultural and political sense, hints at the presence of systems of belief which are aimed at the construction of both manifest and latent messages surrounding both group and the individual within it. The fiction provides us with an array of examples where highly-structured commemoration rituals appear, whether these take place straight after death—and can be perhaps better catalogued as 'funeral'—or in years and even centuries after, therefore taking on a distinctly memorable layer. As the presence of commemorative rituals has now become so ingrained in the narratives, it is difficult to present an accurate and fully pervasive list of instances without falling into the repetitive. Funeral ceremonies are usually a presence of narratives that depict vampires as a separate species, which after death will leave a body behind just like any other organic creature. Funeral rites take place in several fashions, but (as a general rule) the body of the vampire is disposed of either by burial or burning—the latter often relying on the incinerating power of the sun as the final marshalling force. The act of disposal is usually accompanied by some form of ceremony that has both religious and secular connotations. In instances when vampires are turned, their bodied normally turn to ash after the death, leaving nothing that needs disposal. In the latter scenario, mourning is the most distinctive feature of the vampire's commemoration ritual; the memory of those who passed is portrayed as being extremely 'alive' for the vampire community, and is experienced as heightened presence in their lives. The grief that results from the loss is depicted as an extremely debilitating force, as clearly shown in examples such as the *House Of Comarré*, where vampires still mourn their dead relatives—human and creature alike—after centuries.[82]

The secular nature of the funeral act is usually presented as the disconnection of the individual vampire from the social fabric of the community. This in particular is the case in the *Midnight Breed*, whre funerals represent the secular occasion for friends and family to symbolically detach from the deceased. The religious side of vampric funeral rites, however, is variable and dependant on what kind of system of belief the narrative portrays. Even in its discordant incarnations, however, the ritual is usually accompanied by the presence of a religious personality for the death ritual, who will represent a connection to the divine and pave the way for the deceased's entrance to the afterlife, as clearly stated in Ward's *Black Dagger Brotherhood* series. Both the religious and secular sides of the commemoration act highlight a connection and emulation of numerous human funeral set ups, opening to the possibility that the portrayal of vampire commemoration rituals can act as a latent critique of the relationship that contemporary human societies have with death. This possibility is ingrained in the nature of funeral and remembrance acts which, as David Simpson reminds us, are 'particularly sensitive occasions for assessing the balance of change and continuity' within the cultural spectrum at large.[83]

In the *Black Dagger Brotherhood* series, vampires take death seriously and have elaborate mourning rituals which hinge on the concept of sacrifice, connected as it is to ritual violence. When his Brother in arms Darius is killed in action by the enemy, Wrath's reaction to his comrade's death is, initially, visceral and steeped in emotion: '[He] let his rage out. The candles exploded and fell to the floor as a whirlwind of viciousness swirled around him, growing tighter, faster, darker until the furniture flipped to the and travelled in a circle around him. He leaned back his head and roared'.[84] His anger, however, is quickly stifled by the awareness of his mourning duties. Mourning, it soon becomes clear, involves not only a psychological adjustment, but most importantly, a physical engagement on the mourner's part. The vampire ritual in which Wrath participates is founded in pain and blood:

> Wrath bowed his head and spoke the words of his mother tongue, [. . .] as he paid tribute to his dead. [. . .] When he finished speaking, he knelt onto the slab, feeling the stones cut into his flesh [. . .] The death ritual required him to pass the day without moving, to bear the pain, to bleed in memory of his friend. [. . .] As his blood turned the marble red, he saw his dead warrior's face and felt the tie they'd shared in life.[85]

The symbolic nature of the ritual is manifest: the blood signifies the kinship Wrath felt with the deceased, and is shed in order to offer a physical and metaphorical representation of the passing. The symbolic meaning of blood as an agent of affinity between individuals here is reminiscent of Judeo-Christian traditions, where blood stands for the relationship of kinship that ties humanity to God. In the Jewish strcture, blood represents the ancient covenant between men and deity, a symbol of the 'alliance between God and humanity and among community members'.[86] In the Christian tradition, this connection is developed even further through the message of the Eucharist, where the blood of Christ is consumed to bind humans to God. The Christian structure, however, also includes the inevitable presence of death as a binding agent, where Christ's life was sacrificed in order to create the metaphor of salvation.

It is in this latter and Christian-based interpretation of blood symbolism in relation to death that one can find the latent meaning of Wrath's mourning ritual. The shedding of the vampire's blood symbolises the ritual death of the individual, intended to honour the memory and passing of the deceased through a form of self-sacrifice. Davies reminds us that sacrificial deaths are a known anthropological presence around the world; ordinarily inspired by a religious belief—whether Christian, or Hindu—sacrificial deaths are aimed at bringing into prominence 'the value of life'. That value, Davies contends, has two different interpretations, which are not, however, mutually exclusive; on the one hand, it is the value 'of the life that is being sacrificed' a physical and metaphorical interpretation of the love and regard that the victim has for the deceased beloved.[87] On the other hand, sacrificial death, especially when part of the mourning ritual, enhances the value of the act as having the ability to 'preserve' the life of the dead in the everlasting underworld, 'if a sacrificial offering is made for it'.[88] It is in this capacity that we see how the blood sacrifice functions for Wrath as a deliberate spiritual act of bereavement.

The most essential element of this ritualistic structure is that the showing of love and devotion is, somehow, expressed through violence. In his book *Violence and the Sacred*, René Girard views violence as an important, even essential part of human relation. Violence is at the heart of human society; indeed, Girard goes as far as suggesting that violence lies at the very core of human nature, therefore establishing an intrinsic connection between behaviour and psychology. Placing violent acts within a ritualised context, Girard suggests that violence itself plays a very important part in the institutional representation of religion. For him, 'violence is the heart and secret soul of the sacred'.[89] Socially speaking, violence can be understood as a polluting presence, destroying life and therefore the social constructions that pivot upon its presence. Ritual, however, has a transformational way of repositioning violence so that it can 'purify' it.[90] This understanding of violence becomes particularly prominent when mourning and death rituals are concerned, where violent acts take on a mimetic function, often through the epithet of 'sacrifice'. Although Wrath does not kill himself, the blood is representative of the loss of life. The shedding of his own blood—a symbol for life itself which, of course, also has several physical implications— can be interpreted as a kind of death. The self-inflicted violence of the act speaks for the sanctity of life that forms the bond between individuals in the vampire community, and which is even more prominent in warrior societies. Self-inflicted violence, and the pain that results from it, honour the dignity of the deceased, in the hope of granting him a safe passage to 'the Fade', the vampire equivalent of heaven. The spilling of blood here counts as what Davies defines as a 'mortuary blood sacrifice', a physical representation of grief and anguish experienced by the living in reference to the dead.[91] Recalling the meaning of Christ's blood, as his life was 'sacrificed' for the salvation of humankind, the spilling of Wrath's blood seals the scared nature of violence within the ritualistic parameters of mourning.

Self-sacrifice, self-inflicted violence, and the pain that results from them also have an emotionally purifying function for vampires. After suffering for hours in a very physical way, and honouring his dead Brother through a blood offering, Wrath seems to rebound from his grief quickly; the acceptance of death is clearly evident, as if the ritual had the ability of tempering the presence of death as inevitable. The pain inflicted on Wrath's body is a physical expression of the vampire's loss, a visceral representation of his sense of attachment and affection for the dead. The blood sacrifice here also works as an illustrative practice, encapsulating the 'transcendence' of mortality, which—intertwined as it is with a solid belief of the afterlife— ensures the absence of fear and anxiety in the face of death. The mourning ritual, for Wrath, takes on a cathartic function, signifying, as Loring Danforth puts it, the 'complete' and 'final' recognition of the 'irreversible nature of death'.[92] The physicality of the blood-shed, and its inherent violence on the mourner's body, have a catalytic effect; the sacrificial pain and blood loss channel a path of emotional transformation, an external expression of internal psychology that, as Davies puts it, 'is an important for coping with the immediate experiences of grief'.[93]

One must be attuned to the idea that vampire commemoration rituals provide a critical function for humanity in terms of its understanding of structure and organisation. Commemoration acts—whether funeral or of later remembrance—undoubtedly maintain a socio-political function, connecting the individual to the larger system of established regulation. Simpson is keen to point out in this context that when it comes to politicising the presence of the individual within society 'nothing is more amenable to manipulation' than commemorative practices.[94] Commemoration rituals undoubtedly expose the forming lines of the fabric of society; the desire to honour and memorialise the dead bears strong affinity with Judeo-Christian beliefs, here interpreted as the forming framework for political, civil, and cultural organisation for several Western countries, including the United States.

It is virtually impossible to avoid the connection between forms of ritual –especially of a commemorative nature—and the conceptualisation of conflict in popular vampire fiction. A concern with war runs through a large number of contemporary narratives, especially those written by American authors. Fighting and conflict are a constant presence and preoccupation for vampires. The types of struggle encountered vary in outlook. We go from the political machinations –which often result in bloody encounters—found in the *Sookie Stackhouse* series, to the magically fuelled confrontations that vampires and other creatures engage with in Butcher's *The Dresden Files*. Fighting, however, is not always just a sub-text in the narratives. In examples such as the *Midnight Breed*, the *Nathaniel Cade*, *Black Dagger Brotherhood*, and *Vampires in America* series, the vampires engage in 'wars' openly defined as such. The conflicts are disparate and take different nuances; the vampires either fight each other for possession of territories and political power, or they wage war with other supernatural/preternatural creatures, who are often set to destroy them. War and all that it entails is commonly treated as one of the greatest worries in vampire societies, the constant threat of annihilation—whether for a sub-group or the entire species—looming over their existence. The vampires are motivated by war, their desire to fight and defend themselves—and their way of life—is the driving force of several plotlines and re-elaborations of the motif. War, however, cannot simply be seen as a convenient storytelling device which is bound to ensure a thrilling mixture of action and emotional involvement. War and conflict, as Mary Ellen O'Connell reminds us, have a socio-dogmatic dimension to them, and 'humanity has sought for millennia to control' their outcome with 'mechanisms of regulation'.[95] Being in a 'state of war', therefore, inevitably questions the conceptual and political development of the vampire as a potential agent of propaganda.

The preoccupation with war is not seen anywhere as prominent as it is in the *Black Dagger Brotherhood* series. As the main male protagonists are portrayed as infallible vampire warriors, the idea that conflict plays an important part in the construction of vampire social, political, and cultural relations is truly unavoidable. It is possible to suggest that a connection exists therein between the war in the Brotherhood and the outlook of American home and foreign politics. The way in which war is portrayed in the novels seems to bear a particular conceptual relationship to the tragedy of 9/11, and the conflicts that followed.

It is imperative to mention here that the connection between American vampire fiction, war, and 9/11 is not to be treated lightly. Nor should it just be assumed that, just because 'American vampires' are at war, they are inevitably acting out political preoccupations on the authors' part. Not everything to do with America and war is a re-evaluation of 9/11, and the horror of 9/11 itself should not be used, as Jeffrey Melnick puts it, as a 'simple cultural bait-and-switch'.[96] It would too simplistic to assume that whenever authors engage with issues of conflict in a vaguely American context they are all filtering a critique of 9/11 and its effect. The aim here is not to argue—insistently—that popular writers are calling for a discussion of 9/11, and the subsequent wars in the Middle East, when they are not. I would be very wary of suggesting that a recalling of 9/11 and the horror of American war acts as an unsophisticated way to solicit interest in readers and way to 'establish authority, seriousness of purpose, and marketability'.[97] All the same, it is virtually impossible to ignore the cultural impact that the 9/11 events had on the popular American imaginary, shaping and reconstructing people's evaluation of international politics between the United States and the rest of the world. In suggesting that the concept of vampire war in contemporary American fiction is connected, conceptually, to the 9/11 tragedy and the 'war on terror', the attention shifts to questioning the cultural significance of war in both its practical and demonstrative incarnations. My intention here is to suggest that the contemporary vampire—entangled as it is with metaphors of blood, persecution and supremacy—can be read as an allegory for the preoccupations with conflict, war, and strife which have become a recurrent presence of political frameworks in the U.S. As an icon, the vampire at war also channels the extents of anger and loss, a new representative symbol for our language of grief and steadfastness.[98]

For this point to crystallise itself, we need to turn to the fiction and see how it engages with war itself. In the Brotherhood, the narrative in Book One introduces the warriors and their endeavours through a very specific event: the warrior Darius—a respected member of the Brotherhood—is killed in a car bomb by the vampires' enemies, the Lessers. The extent of the explosion clearly goes beyond the death of the warrior; his disappearance causes extreme anger, sadness, and grief in the Brothers, who are then shown swearing revenge and thirsting for the blood of their enemies: 'Kill them all no matter how messy it gets'.[99] The death of Darius is treated as a turning point in the war, the evidence that vampires must re-organise and become pro-active in searching for their enemies and destroying them. After the car bomb explosion, the war intensifies and incidents of fighting—as well as casualties—grow in number. The nature of Darius' death—through an explosion—and the conflict-inspiring hatred for the enemy that results from it makes it possible to build a parallel between this significant event in vampire fiction, and the events related to 9/11 and after.[100]

The immediate reaction that the American population—and to some extent the whole Western world—had to the 9/11 attacks was, as Noam Chomsky puts it, a mixture of 'shock, horror, anger, fear, and desire for revenge'.[101] Although claims that the reaction was sensationalised—and fuelled by American newspapers—have emerged in the years after the events, there is no doubting that shock, terror, and grief were emotions experienced by the great majority of Americans at the time. A similar reaction to the killing explosion is shown by the vampires in the Brotherhood. Retaliation seems to be the main preoccupation of the warriors, and their 'eyes' are 'all fired up with vengeance'.[102] In building a conceptual parallel through action and reaction, Ward seemingly evokes the horror of 9/11 to exemplify the impact of Darius' death, and to construct a framework for horror and grief which—much like it did for Americans and their relationship to the Middle East—would support and encourage acts of violence and war.

What is significant about Darius' death is that it does not happen on the field, as it would be expected for a soldier during times of war. The fact that the enemy 'tricks' Darius into death, using explosives, is seen as an extremely cowardly act, unbecoming of warriors and exemplifying the repulsive nature of an enemy who has no respect for the fighting: 'The bastards had no honor anymore. At least their precursors, going back for centuries, had fought like warriors. This new breed were cowards that hid behind technology'.[103] To see the enemies as 'dishonourable', opting for ignominious ways of attack, was also a common stance among the American population in relation to the offensive members of the Al Qaeda group who caused the 9/11 explosions. Islamic groups were seen as inferior and dishonourable, 'too cowardly to face the enemy in open combat'.[104] The cowardly nature of the enemy was placed in stark contrast to the sophisticated methods of the American armies, who had courage to fight and a desire to destroy their enemies via 'proper' methods.

The 9/11 attacks were deemed as terroristic by the American government, in that they caused the loss of human life on American soil, outside of a combat situation. The American legal definition of 'terrorism' draws attention to how terroristic attacks are particularly aimed at intimidating and coercing 'the civilian population' through acts of violence.[105] The events of 9/11 were treated by the American government as the beginning of a new wave of terroristic attacks, when the civilian population was no longer safe, and an immediate conflict was necessary from the American armies in order to restore order and eliminate the threat. In similar fashion, the Brotherhood narrative recalls the terroristic nature of the 9/11 attacks by showing the Lessers attacking vampire civilians 'in their own homes' and 'abducting' them, a decision that acts as further proof of their pusillanimous and morally inferior character.[106] The constant threat of terrorist attacks on the civilian population keeps the vampires on edge, and foments their desire for revenge. That revenge, it is made clear, is intended to mitigate the extreme grief experienced at the loss of so many members of the vampire race, victims that will never be forgotten.

The depiction of the vampires' enemies also bears a conceptual affinity to the ways in which members of Al Qaeda—exemplified in the symbolic figure of Osama Bin Laden—were portrayed after the 9/11 attacks. It is clearly stated that the Lessers do not have any particular belief in any ideal. They fight and aim to annihilate the vampires only to satisfy their thirst for violence and destruction, and 'cherish' the 'chance to kill every time the sun' goes down.[107] They despise the vampires for their financial stability, their strength—which they constantly try to match—and they mock their belief in spirituality, family, and ritual. The Lessers act out of spite; they have no morality and no honour. They are instructed by their master, the evil Omega, to only pursue acts of violence and retaliation. This outlook towards the enemy as an immoral, spiteful entity was encouraged by American propaganda after the new 'war on terror' began in 2001. After the attacks on the Twin Towers, the *New York Times* famously reported that 'the perpetrators acted out of hatred for the values cherished by the West', such as freedom.[108] To picture the enemy as hateful and jealous is undoubtedly comforting, as it immediately gratifies one's position through, as Chomsky puts it, 'the merits of self-adulation'.[109] Just like the members of Al Qaeda in the American popular imaginary, the Lessers in the *Brotherhood* series are voided of motive, divorced from any political, social, or cultural agenda that is not a simple—and seemingly unjustified—enmity towards the vampires. Compared to the loyal and honourable vampire warriors, the Lessers emerge as a 'construction of nothing'.[110] Their vacuous hatred channels emptiness and invites destruction, so that they can be hated in return for any suitable reason, from their dislike for civilisation to their disdain for monetary wealth.

In the contemporary era of the Western nation-states, where the 'war on terror' plays an important role in the popular imagination, commemorative 'soldier rituals' take on a distinctive politicised function that is connected to events of a national significance. In times of war, the commemorative act draws attention to death as part of a designated pursuit, when soldiers die to defend their homelands. The commemoration of deceased individuals that represent the State overall takes on particular implications, as they highlight the importance of 'occasions' on the wider social mentality. In contemporary narratives, this particular cultural and political function of the death ritual becomes no more manifest that when warrior vampires—who dies for their 'country'—are commemorated through a variety of practices. Both the *Midnight Breed* and *Black Dagger Brotherhood* series offer instances of commemorative rituals for warrior vampires, and for several other individuals who were (while not being strictly soldiers) killed by 'the enemy'. In both narratives, the vampires are given grand funerals which are presided over by the highest political and religious authorities, in order to pay homage to the sacrifice that was offered to protect the vampire race against the threat of annihilation. The presence of political authorities—the King for the Brotherhood and the head of the Order for the Breed—allows us to view the commemorative practices for the warriors and the war victims as 'state funerals'. The often ostentatious and violent nature of the funeral ritual in the narratives emphatically proclaims, just like it seems to do in a human context, that the deaths were 'worthwhile', and not to have been in vain.[111] In the Breed, for instance, the vampire warrior Lucan volunteers to take the body of his fallen comrade Conlan to the sun, and withstands the sunlight for as long as possible, in order to honour the dead warrior: 'He bore the light in reverent quiet, training all thought on Conlan and the honor that had marked his long life. [. . .] Lucan dropped his head down, absorbing the pain as Conlan surely would have done for any of the Breed who fought alongside him. Searing heat washed over Lucan as dawn rose, even stronger'.[112] The pain of the exposure, and the longer he can withstand it, is a direct transposition of his desire to commemorate the death and sacrifice of his fellow soldier. The pain, however, also has a semi-cathartic function, as Lucan accepts it in exchange for keeping his life; the exposure to sunlight initiates the grieving process and severs the connection to the dead. This approach to the death ritual recalls Simpson's contention that, when deaths of a national significance take place, 'fellow citizens' are expected to celebrate 'the sacrifices' and observe the soldiers' 'endings with dignity and ceremony'.[113] In vampire narrative arcs, the death of both warrior and war victims is ritually complemented by physical pain for a number of mourners, so to not only make manifest their internal grief, but also to symbolically share the sacrifice of death through the physical dimension of experience.

Sophisticated and carefully developed commemoration rituals in contemporary fiction serve a triple purpose. Firstly, they highlight the importance of death for vampires as a culturally-defined occurrence, which is understood—very much as it is in human—within a delineated civil and spiritual framework. The act draws attention to the desire to conceptualise practices in structural terms, in order to offer a sense of order and direction within the chaos of loss. This is particularly relevant in a context of war, as the shadow of conflict allows a soldier's death to be re-contextualised as sacrifice. Secondly, the commemoration act allows grief to become tangible, unveiling how, even in a seeming context of presumed immortality, separation from a loved one marks an interruption in the socio-cultural make-up of the group. Thirdly, and perhaps most importantly, commemoration rituals, which are connected to war events, function as a highly advanced practice aimed at the politicisation of grief. Simpson argues that wartime rituals of memorialisation—whether they are individual funerals, or collective ceremonies of remembrance—'exist to assimilate' the intense and particular grief of families and friends into the 'received vocabularies' of the nation.[114] The commemoration of death, highly ritualised and often public as it is for soldiers on the home soil, transforms grief into a matter of the State. The suffering of the living is given a quasi-tangible quality through the performance of the ceremony. The ritual itself is symbolic in that it absorbs the death of the individual into the grander plan of the nation. One can see here how the careful articulation of the commemoration ritual—often based as it its own practices of pain, suffering and blood—offers a critique of contemporary human war systems, highlighting how the death of individuals can transcend the localised grief of families and spill into domains of nationalism. Both public and private rituals of memorialisation for warriors, soldiers, and victims of war render pain public and convert the chasm left by death into a mutual linking practice. The routines of commemorative culture highlighted by the fiction are proposed as an agent of mediation to the 'unbearably dissonant agonies of the survivors into a larger picture' that is both metaphysical and dogmatic at once.[115] The vampire 'state funerals' in the *Black Dagger Brotherhood* and the *Midnight Breed* allow the death of the soldiers to go beyond the sphere of the merely personal, and be incorporated into the broader realm of the nationally, culturally, and politically symbolic.

It has often been suggested that war-related commemoration practices rely on the careful balance of acknowledgment of the individual death—and the inevitable grief it caused to individual families—and the place that the death occupies within the larger civic and cultural net. Simpson is keen to remind us that memorialisation rites and death practices in a war context must somehow signify the 'idiosyncrasies of the dead' without allowing those specific qualities to 'disturb or radically qualify the comforting articulation of a common cause and a common fate'.[116] This highly politicised understanding of the individual's soldier's death is often reiterated in contemporary literature. As the vampires commemorate the dead and engage in elaborate funeral practices that honour the fallen soldier, the memory of the greater good and the shared pain experienced by the 'nation' is kept alive by a continuous and radical mention of the 'horrors of the war', of how either the whole vampire race, or the 'good vampires', are under attack. The dichotomy of individual and collective is paradoxically merged through the commemoration of an occurrence that, in itself, is meant to represent separation. In death, however, vampires expose a point of articulation, a fulcrum of mergence which signifies both grief for the loss and hope for the future.

Benedict Anderson meaningfully points out how the tombs of soldiers are part of a system of commemoration practices that are significant of the power of death over the 'imagined community'.[117] Ritualised burial practices and related acts of commemoration function as a linking agent for the community, the group that stand behind and around the death as a framework of civilisation and belief. In joining the public and private, the soldier's funeral contributes to the formation and re-iteration of an imagined sense of collectivity, which validates the death itself as part of a common objective and a common destiny. Vampire commemoration practices stand precisely for that imagined community—the integration of the single entity into the group understood—and act as a mediated form of mourning and separation.

Nonetheless, in spite of the fact that 'state funerals' can be openly identified as part of a grieving process for the families that allows the death to be included in the register of national priorities, later commemoration acts take a slightly different outlook. Western cultures are known to take time to actually engage in open commemoration of a painful war-time event. History teaches that memorials and monuments are often erected decades after the traumatic event, as it is the case with Holocaust and Vietnam war memorials. Dominick LaCapra, among others, has been keen to point out that Western cultures tend to take time to fully articulate memorial practices after funerals have taken place.[118] The chronological separation between death and open commemoration—beyond the funeral ritual—has been identified as part of 'protracted deliberations' which signal a cultural belief and an expectation that the future will allow events from the past 'to be explained and set into context, made part of an intelligible history'.[119] This understanding of commemoration draws attention to a desire to elaborate events through both civic and psychological separation, a system of belief which relies on seeing the future as a hopeful grey area and the past as a construct of hindsight. Psychoanalytically speaking, one could see this desire for both separation and engagement as a state that lies somewhere in between mourning and melancholia, encapsulating both the wish to grieve and the need to 'move on'.[120]

In this framework, the engagement with war, terroristic acts, and death in contemporary vampire fiction—especially of American origin—functions as a system of commemoration for the very near historical past of the United States. If it is true that mourning is a process that relies on both time and separation, and that commemoration acts can fully be carried out only after considerable time has lapsed from the event, then it is possible to suggest—in a rather metaphysical way—that the fiction itself functions as a memorial for the victims of the 9/11 attacks, and the subsequent war in Iraq and Afghanistan that took place. In dealing with a veiled context of war that recalls the experience of the United States in the post-2000 era, these vampire texts can be interpreted as a late memorial for the dead and the victims. The fiction articulates the grief experienced by the survivors and channels the anger at the 'enemy' through commemoration. Simultaneously, however, the vampire—able as it is to express that sense of continuity future through the metaphor of extended and often immortal life—constructs a link to both past and future, while encompassing the strength and conviction of life in the present. Remoulded into the symbolic articulation of grief and warfare, the vampire allows American history to become lucid and commemorated; the fiction itself is the site of the memorial, a representation of the loss and a vector for its enunciation. With its interplay of conflict, life, death, and idealism, vampire fiction gives voice to history and finds a place for acceptance in the American psyche. The chronological separation also validates the memorial function of vampire literature in that it allows the processing of emotions in relation to war-time events and the tragedy of terrorism on American soil, especially for the survivors of the attacks.

Simpson reminds us, of course, that processing history—especially when death and warfare are involved—is not an easy task, for any population. The cultural framework of the West, in particular, calls for a 'sense of guilt' to accompany the assumption of an 'ongoing history with its implicit emphasis on coming to terms with and getting over tragic events'. [121] The events of the 9/11 attacks and the subsequent war in the Middle East are of course 'still raw' in people's memories in the United States, and a conscious desire to work through the grief and move on is attached to feelings of apprehension and discomfort. Forgetting is impossible, and acting out—through more conflict—has been proved as unhelpful in most cases by history itself. Moving forward, therefore, necessitates the presence of symbolic interaction with the events through metaphors of commemoration and ritual. The Gothic screen of the fiction allows for further separation and elaboration of concept without recalling direct feeling of culpability. Forgetting and remembering become entangled in the world of the magical, the preternatural and the supernatural, a seemingly detached structure of historical connection that is not openly threatening to the human consciousness in a context of death and warfare. In keeping with its most well-known tradition, the Gothic element here allows for cultural fears and apprehension to be dealt with through metaphors. The dislocation of Western history is projected onto an imaginary framework, acting as the ideal safeguard for the establishment of commemorative structures uncorrupted by grief. The vampire—conceptually removed from connected assemblies of human guilt—medicates the unease of the experience and allows the critique of post-2000 human warfare to emerge unchallenged by the continuous weight of history.

DUAL NATURES, OR THE REBEL PARADOX

The dual nature of the vampire has become the centre of several narratives within contemporary literature and popular culture. 'Vampire' has ceased to be a straightforward concept not only in physical, but also in social terms. There is indeed an abundance of examples where one can find a distinction between two 'types' of vampire. On the one hand we have the 'good' vampires, creatures who respect human life, and even fight to defend it. These vampires control their need for blood and only take from willing subjects, when the time is right and are averse, as a general rule, to ever taking a human life in the process. The killing—or 'draining'—of a blood source is indeed looked upon in great shame and, at times, even has dire physical and psychological consequences. These good and righteous vampires form the main character pool for series such as the *Midnight Breed*—with its muscular heroes known as the 'Order'—Cole's *Immortals After Dark* series—where the vampire Forbearers do not drink blood from the flesh for fear of killing their human supplier—and Christine Feehan's novels, where the Carpathians—a special brand of blood-drinking creature—refuse to kill their victims when feeding, the price for the slip-up being their consciousness and, it is suggested, their 'soul'.

On the other hand, we have the 'bad' vampires, those who care not for human life and indeed see humans only for what they truly are: a source of blood. These vampire often recall, in physical terms, the creatures of folklore from which they originated. They are deranged and blood-crazy, with eyes often described as 'evil'. Conflict normally ensues between the two types of vampires, as is the central notion on which the plot pivots. The distinction between good and bad vampires is, of course, paradoxical. It is an accepted notion that all vampires must take blood to survive, and even when this necessity is forfeited—as it is in Butcher's *The Dresden Files*—there must be some kind of exchange of 'life source' for the vampire to feed on. Therefore, implying that vampires should 'control' themselves in order to be seen as acceptable creatures within their group implies the application of human logic, laws, and regulation—which punish those who do not obey—and adds a level of active rationality which is part of human expectation, rather than vampire mythology.

The most intriguing part of the division between good and bad vampires is the physical differences that are clear between the two factions, almost implying that the presentation of the body—both aesthetically and biologically—will be a direct effect of an individual's moral conduct. The 'good vampires' are usually perfectly formed specimens; if they are male, as we have seen in Chapter 2, they are muscular, tall, and outrageously handsome. If they are female, they tend to be graceful, and delicate; the *Penton Vampire Legacy*, *Black Dagger Brotherhood*, and *Midnight Breed* come to mind here. The 'bad vampires', on the other hand, are presented differently. In Cole's *Immortals After Dark* series (to give one example among many) the horde vampire—ruthless creatures who drink from the flesh and regularly drain their victims of blood—have read eyes, a reflection of their blood-filled bodies and thoughts. The red eyes are also in indication of their blood lust, which causes them to lose their individuality and sense of self. The Black Court vampires of *The Dresden Files*—also classed as 'bad vampires'—are rotting in more ways than one, their corpse-like appearance acts as a reflection of their despicable nature. The 'bad vampires', needless to say, are often portrayed as engaging in seemingly unacceptable pursuits, such as killing their victims to satisfy their lust for both blood and violence. One can see here how the sense of duality of the vampire nature is perceived both in physical and psychological terms.

The crimes the rogue vampires commit are, technically, of a social nature. By indulging in bloodlust, the vampires break laws and regulations within the vampire world, which dictate there should be respect for the human race and their lives should be preserved. Nonetheless, their social crimes have physical consequences. The changes in their bodies are a representation of the unacceptability of their actions; in losing some of the characteristics shared by the group, they also lose their identities as 'vampires' in social terms. The tension between natural and social here becomes unavoidable. The duality of the vampire is not expressed in terms of body and soul, as it would often be in the human world—with the body being the profane, limiting part, and the sould acting as the transcendental, liberating presence. When the vampire body is concerned, the division pivots on uses of the body, and how they are consonant with social expectations. The possibility of an afterlife is not necessarily the driving force for action: the loss of control over both body and mind is what inspires control over physical impulses. In "The dualism of human nature," Émile Durkheim argues that any instance of duality, when it comes to categorising definitions, suggests the inherent conceptual strain 'between individual and social existence'.[122] From Durkheim's suggestion one can derive the idea that all individuals—whether human or supernatural—possess a body that is constituted by drives, appetites, and sensory impressions. Those drives, in Durkheim's terms, are 'necessarily egotistic', and therefore at odd if any social demands.[123] Nonetheless, individuals also possess the ability to transcend their basic needs, on the basis of 'social categories'.[124] One must wonder how social impressions function in terms of bodily requirements, and whether the social implications of fulfilling needs and impulses have an impact on the perception of the body, by both the individual and the group.

If one were to translate the tension between bodily impulses and social restrictions in vampire terms, it would be possible to read the physiological changes in the rogue vampires as a conceptual breaking between egotistic needs and social representations. The vampire body is instrumental here in showing the limitations that are imposed on the vampire as a social entity. The body is the conduit for expressing patterns of behaviour, which are unable to be kept concealed. Vampires transcend their seemingly untainted corporeal state by 'becoming social beings', who 'fulfil their natural needs' in a 'variety of culturally specific' and acceptable ways.[125] The body speaks loudly of the vampire's intentions, unrestricted by layers of propriety and bodily technologies which affected relationships in the human worlds. One can see here how the dual nature of vampire body is bestowed a representational candour in terms of action and accountability that, unfortunately, the human body does not possess. In this, one can perhaps see a social desire—in social terms—to keep individuals accountable for their actions and the punishment which might derive, an exchange of exploit and consequence that the human legal system is yet to master.

Carol A. Senf has observed that 'vampires in the twentieth century' were perceived as more or less attractive rebel figures, who choose to live outside of society'.[126] On the written front, Anne Rice's rock-star vampire Lestat showed readers what it was like to enjoy the privileges that a rebellious, star-like existence could bestow, associating the vampire in its most glamorous incarnation with the concept of freedom from both legal and moral constrictions. On the wider popular culture front, one should only think of cinematic examples such as *The Lost Boys* (1987), or even Spike in television's *Buffy the Vampire Slayer*, to recognise the characteristics of the recalcitrant, slightly rogue-ish rebel vamp who likes to show fangs and live in the periphery of both human and vampire laws. In the twenty-first century, however, that desire for reprobate adventures and rebellious, outlaw existence is less perceivable once the vampire world is concerned. The strict vampire regulatory structures—put in place by authors of fictional Gothic/ fantasy world—have often transformed the perception of the vampire from a simple outlaw and rebel to a figure who pursues rebellious act in order to maintain order within society.

A clear example of this dynamic can be found in Adrian's *Midnight Breed* series, where the vampire warriors have banded together to defend their civilisation from the growing 'rogue' vampires, who show no regard for both any form of co-habitation law, and kill their human prey indiscriminately. The risk of exposure—and the fear of potential annihilation for the entire vampire race—drives the warriors to hunt and destroy all rogue vampires, and defy the official vampire laws, which call for rogue capture and enforced rehabilitation. In this case, the Warriors' involvement in outlaw activities cannot be perceived as strictly 'rebellious'; although they exist in the margins of society, Adrian's warrior vampirse challenge the traditional conception of dissident individual—who shows completely disregard for maintaining societal integrity. Indeed, their seemingly outlaw hunting is aimed precisely at maintaining order and preserving stability. Without being too contentious, it is possible to suggest that vampire rebelliousness in Adrian's fiction takes on a slightly more political nuance. While maintaining an aura of the rebellious outsider, and still firmly planted in their position as morally right incarnations of an ideal, the *Midnight Breed* warriors function as heroes because they defy the corrupt political systems which seem to show a complete detachment from the vampire citizens they wish to serve. By taking the law 'into their own hands', Adrian's vampires unveil the ability of vampire society in contemporary fiction to function as a potential critique of human organisation. Margaret Carter claims that, because of its rebellious conduct and disregard for the law, the vampire makes a 'fitting hero for late twentieth century popular fiction'.[127] Carter's understanding of the hero here seems at odds with the traditional understanding of the concept. If anything, I would like to suggest that the late-twentieth century vampire functioned as the 'anti-hero', embodying a social desire in the West to defy rules and regulations and, in so doing, glamorising the ability to be 'an outlaw'.

In example such as the *Midnight Breed*, however—and several others, including Ward's *Black Dagger Brotherhood* Series—the vampire's 'heroic' enterprise are often moved by a need for order and structure. Whether personal interests are at work when assuring the existence of vampire laws— like in the case Butcher's *The Dresden Files*, or Harris' *Sookie Stackhouse* series—the idea that vampires act to reinforce order still stands. Indeed, order is often perceived as the only way in which prosperity can be gained, rejecting any conception of anarchy as a feasible presence in the vampire world. Their way of being outlaw is visible only in relation to fraudulent vampire systems or—in an extended way—in connection to the human world, where laws and regulations are in place. Rather than rebellious, Adrian's vampires can be seen as greatly patriotic, pointedly valiant, moved by a yearning for a stable sense of group identity, which is dependent on the clear functioning of vampire social organisations. This re-envisioning the vampire as a 'hero' is as unorthodox as it sounds. Victoria Nelson argues for the vampire as a potentially 'heterodox' creature, in which the categories of 'good' and 'evil' can easily be subsumed within the deeper life principle that expresses itself as a transformation into fullness.[128] With this idea in mind, it is not difficult to see how the vampires' ability to inhabit the margins of lawfulness has evolved into a desirable quality in relation to vampiric organisation and morality, highlighting how 'boundaries' are perceived as no longer a barrier to be breached, but an ideal part of the system which must be enforced in order for society to function. Vampires such as those found in the *Midnight Breed* did not actually step into their role as 'heroes' until the twenty-first century, when their infinite powers to bestow life and death were coupled with an overarching desire to gain and maintain social stability, constructing a clear sense of what can be understood as the 'vampire nation'.

Inevitably, marginalisation still takes places in the vampire world, and it is precisely that sense of lawfulness and social boundary which highlights the differences, in both concept and conduct, within the vampire population. As the heroic vampires struggle to upkeep order and construct solid foundations on which vampires and humans alike can rely, other groups of dissident vampires have emerged within the literature which are still set on defying the rules and regulations. These are the vampires who refuse to obey by any form of official law and, unlike the self-guided warriors of Adrian's series, have no desire to uphold any form of power except their own. Within this specific group of vampires, one can examples such as Marek in the *Breed*, or Xcor in the *Brotherhood*, self-serving individuals who pursue either the breaking of chaos, or the disestablishment of current vampire systems, so that they can crown themselves as the new leader. Within the texts, these vampires are perceived as 'outcasts', the outlaws which are deemed as such in view of their membership to a non-abiding group. Naturally, clear definitions seem to exist about what is considered appropriate vampire laws and 'rightful' vampire structures, mirroring the similar sense of human political morality which often operates in the West. The official vampire laws function as 'the State', and any other—perhaps even revolutionary—strands need to be eradicated as 'enemies' of that State. So the new outlaws function as such not in relation to just human systems, but also within the structure of vampire laws, which are identifiable as a distinct characteristic of twenty-first century popular vampire literature.

5   Vampire Spaces

It is the intention of this book to investigate images and representations in order to uncover the conceptual areas inhabited by the vampire in the contemporary popular context. These 'spaces' should not be understood only in geographical terms, but also as social, political, cultural, and physical loci of knowledge. In this framework, the idea of 'space' has to not only be interpreted as a matter of location, but also has to extend in order to encompass ways of life and ways of being that define the limits of vampyrological claims over society. Nonetheless, if one is to be persuaded that geography, as Jon Anderson argues, 'marks the spot' where any activity 'interconnects with context', then the value of location—in both its micro and macro manifestations—uncovers the importance of both material and ephemeral connections in constructing the figure of the literary vampire as a contextually bound, cultural figure.[1]

VAMPIRES IN THE CITY

There is no denying that, in contemporary fiction, the vampire has moved to the city. Brian Aldiss argues that, in previous centuries, the vampire used to be 'a great country-dweller'.[2] The coupling of the vampire with the wild countryside was meant to provide a conceptual parallel between the desolation of the landscape, and the soul-devoid cruelty of the vampire's nature. This analogy is made very clear in examples such as *Dracula*, where the Count's castle abode is located in a forsaken landscape that acts as a warning for both the readers and the characters who intend to approach it. The late twentieth century, however, made great strides towards changing the conception of the vampire as the inhabitant of deserted geographies. Anne Rice's vampires, for instance, liked to mingle in Paris, New Orleans, and London. Whitley Strieber's vampire Miriam in *The Hunger* owned a glamorous apartment in an upscale New York City building. These examples had such a representational impact that, in the twenty-first century, vampires now live comfortably among the great urban masses of Europe and America. And just like those urban areas, Aldiss claims, the vampire is inclined to take on 'the mantle of civilisation'.[3] Vampires have indeed been unable to resist the call and appeal of the cities which, while presenting a number of shortcomings, have also provided the ideal environment for the vampires to progress into highly sophisticated and technologically-evolved creatures.

There is no doubting that an initial concern that connects vampires to urban living is availability and easy access to technology. The American context provides a wealth of example of this nature; one should only read the *Chicagoland Vampires*, *Black Dagger Brotherhood*, *Midnight Breed*, *Vampires in America* and *Hollows* series to see instances of this. In these narratives, to name but a few in a long list displaying similar cases of urban blending, vampires enjoy the comforts of modern living—such as internet, satellite communications, and commercial services—which are easily granted in the city. New York, Chicago, and Los Angeles are favourite living spots for vampires; even when they opt for smaller centres—such as Caldwell, Boston, and Malibu—the layer of 'urban living' still remains present, with all the facilities of a city remaining firmly in place. On the other side of the Atlantic, a similarly large number of city-living examples exist. London is commonly a favourite location for vampires, not only for their everyday living, but also as a choice location for their political centres. A clear instance of this is presented in the *Vampire Federation*, where the Federation has its main British office in the city. In this storyline, the vampire Alex is known to live in a swanky apartment in London's Canary Wharf, an area she is known to enjoy because of its modern outlook and close-by urban facilities, something she claims she could not live without. Her apartment enjoys the comforts of a contemporary 'open-plan living room'—with its 'plush carpet'– and a upscale 'spiral staircase'. To complete the look, Alex' 'ultra-modern' abode is accessorised with steel glass 'sliding doors' that lead to a 'balcony', where she can enjoy 'the city lights dancing over the river' at night.[4]

The city is not simply a geographical centre. The urban landscape is but the beginning of the city's bounds. The etymological roots of the terms 'city' and urban' might actually provide a useful starting point here in order to understand how large conglomerates of people provide both social and topographical degrees of interaction, and how—in turn—these differing but connecting layers of understanding also function as the ideal ground for vampire mythologies to be perpetrated in contemporary literature. The word 'city' and 'urban' both derive from Latin; urban derives from *urbs*, meaning a large civilised conglomerate. The term was commonly used to refer to the bounds of Rome only, and can therefore be loosely translated as 'city'. The English word city, on the other hand, actually derives from *civis*, meaning 'citizen'.[5] Although the relationship between the two seems almost mundane, the implications arising from the use of terminology are far from obvious. From this analysis, it is possible to suggest that the term city itself does not simply refer to a location and its architecture, but it is specifically connected to civic interaction and, as a result, to concerns of a social and cultural nature. The 'city' must be envisaged as the place where human beings articulate their perspectives regarding what is 'important' and accepted to the fullest degree. The city is not simply an environmental region. It is an area within which, as Joseph Grange argues, 'ideals become enacted, signifiers are elaborated, and categories establish themselves as culturally normative'.[6] In this framework, and when connected to the metaphor of the vampire, the city becomes very fertile ground for discussing the parameters of culture within a given context, and to examine the socioeconomic structures that connect individuals to the wider collective scope. The vampire's relocation to the city, therefore, cannot be interpreted as a simple geographical shift. As the city takes on highly complex nuances as a cultural instrument, the vampire's colonisation of urban spaces inevitably draws attention to how the fiction engages with the deconstruction of values, customs, and habits, as well as political systems of conceptual re-elaboration. The city is not a static entity, but part of a process of becoming and re-becoming in which the vampire features as the fluid mechanism through which preoccupations of a cultural nature can find concrete expression.

In the city, the vampire is not removed from the workings of human society, but is intertwined with it. The city functions as the apogee of human civilisation, not only socially and culturally, but also in technological and perhaps evolutionary terms as well. Traditionally speaking, the city holds the paradoxical appeal of both the hustle and bustle of society, and muted acceptance of actions—whether good or bad—as normal and everyday. The city is both all-seeing and forgetful and, in a way, provides the ideal symbolic transposition for the vampire itself. The city is not simply a location; it is also a metaphorical construct. Although perhaps it does not go as far as being an allegory for vampirism—a rather interesting notion that does deserve attention—the city allows the vampire motif to be made simultaneously known and secret, active and passive, alive and undead. In the city, horror is not kept concealed, and yet it is not related to shock factors either. Cultural conceptions—especially in the West—have traditionally viewed the city as the site of crime, murder, and blood-shed, the pinnacle of human depravity and delinquency. The city is, as Aldiss suggests, the conceptual location where 'blood and horror' are shared by human inhabitants, both fictionally and in actuality.[7] And it is precisely in its figurative relationship with blood and horror that the city collides and merges with the vampire. The vampire—connected as it is to traditional depictions of blood, horror, terror and fear—is allowed full development and open action within the boundaries of the city. As the vampire inhabits the city, and abandons the cultural marginalisation of the countryside, death ceases to be a remote concept, but becomes an almost tangible presence in both fiction and psyche. The city is not simply a vampire playground, it is also an echo of vampiric representation.

As the vampire mingles in the city, death is given a layer of physicality; the vampire becomes the city, and the city embodies the vampire. As the vampire conquers the city—a representational site of life, desire, dread, and eternal gratification—both fear and excitement take on an aura of palpability. In the mingling of humanity and the vampiric, the city allows death to 'strike among strangers'.[8] Death is, in a way, made anonymous. Simultaneously, it becomes normalised, allowing the menace of the vampire to also be regarded as normal, customary if not acceptable. The threat of the Other is no longer hedged in the margins of the poetic and the imagistically detached, but becomes a known entity, a recognisable presence in the known and familiar surroundings of the city. Like the vampire, the city is uncanny, and it is in that mixture of familiarity and terror that it provides fertile ground for a critique of that which is human.

In its role as an uncanny agent, the city facilitates the vampire's ability to mirror very contemporary human anxieties about dispossession and individuality. The ownership boundaries of the city are difficult to pin down. While property can of course be owned in the form of specific buildings in an urban area, 'the city' itself does not belong to individuals. It is a collective term and, as such, belonging to all and yet owned by no one. The city is a fleeting concept; it is fluid, changeable, ungraspable. In metaphorical terms, the city can be seen to be representative of a sense of dissolution and detachment. Echoing the same feelings of separation, fluidity, and boundary-defying terror, the vampire feeds into the human sense of anxiety that accompany the city. The urban nature of contemporary vampires places an emphasis on the difficulty of maintaining borders, and not only on the threat of the horror lashing out, but also of the horror colonising the within. In twenty-first century literature , the city is not simply inhabited by the vampires, as it was the case in late twentieth-century narrative. It is, in fact, merged with the vampiric. By colonising the city and making its own—not only geographically, but conceptually as well—the vampire in contemporary fiction addresses significant issues of identity and subjectivity which are proper to twenty-first-century existence, where the city is not simply a place to live, but an emblematic representation of the human 'life world': how people live, how they interact, how they dis/connect, what they fear, and what they desire. The thematic representation of the city as a vampire site—which feeds the vampire, as much as it is fed by it—recalls the widespread presence of society's 'current anxieties about the dissolution of boundaries between the private and the public, the individual and society'.[9] Through owning the city in a manner that people cannot even dream of, the vampire mirrors the panic of separation and the fear of conceptual, cultural and political amalgamation between a social group and the other, the self and the environment. The vampire's city—as it can be labelled—is illustrative of these in a manner that truly resonates with today's experiences of the individual and the world.

In its cultural connotations, the move to the city also draws attention to a shift in politics within the vampire's world. By definition, the city is a site of events, occurrence and mingling. It serves as an apt metaphor for political, commercial, and intellectual power. This image has not only been created by the actual conformity of cities—holding socio-economic centres which often serve large surrounding areas—but has also been encouraged by decades (if not centuries) of popular culture, depicting the city as a thriving hub whose privileged residents, however, pay the price for success with over-stimulation and anonymity. Sociologists—especially in the Eighties and Nineties—were also keen to reinforce this vision of the soul-less city, insisting—as David Frisby puts it—that the city was the ideal location for 'spontaneous disaggregation'.[10] In view of this, it would seem obvious to claim that the vampire's shift to the city in contemporary literature signals the socio-political conditions of a human society that tends towards disassociation and facelessness, a society that has forgotten the importance of emotional ties while opting for hedonistic, commercial-based satisfactions instead.

While this argument looks persuasive at first, it fails to satisfy. It is, to put it plainly, a little bit dated. Claiming that vampires in the city might have mirrored fears of disengagement and moral decay would have found evidence in the fiction written in the Eighties and Nineties; examples of this are amply provided by (for instance) Strieber's *The Hunger*, where a group of yuppie-like, city-based vampires—who like to hunt in the shadows of New York, undisturbed—provide the ideal metaphor for urban disconnection and greed. In the post-2000 era, however, evidence of this situation has waned in favour of a different set of socio-economic parameters. The contemporary vampires' interest in the city has moved away from the simple gloss of dark corners and silent neighbours. Although it is true that commercial enterprise is often a common presence in the vampire's urban life—see for instance, the several examples of night-businesses run by vampires in the *Sookie Stackhouse* series—vampires seem to have other priorities for preferring the city. Easy access to technology is, clearly, a big factor in the vampires' decision to relocate. Indeed, in keeping with its historical roots, the city provides contemporary vampires with another very important aspect of twenty-first-century vampiric living: the ability to be in the midst of it all. The city is where it all happens, it is active, lively, and involved. The idea that, for vampires to survive and prosper in the twenty-first century, it is essential for them to be where 'life' takes place is reinforced in a number of storylines. In the *Black Dagger Brotherhood* series, for instance, a clear endorsement of this is given when the vampire Xcor—who has been stubbornly dwelling in the countryside, leading a secluded existence—relocates to the city of Caldwell: it is made clear by Ward that even though Xcor 'did not like being in cities '—where 'the musk of smog and sewer' is ever-present and the sounds are all of 'sirens, cars and shouted talk'—he cannot deny the convenience of urban areas, where everything is closely within reach and opportunities of all kind are made available.[11] The city is portrayed as a social site of propinquity and innovation, a view that is undoubtedly shared by a lot of contemporary vampire fiction.

And, above all, the city is presented as a centre of decisional power, a beacon of not necessarily hope—a term that might seem overly-romanticised—but belief in improvement and future-minded existence. This view of the city is one that has been undoubtedly supported both by the wider-society and scholarship in the post-2000 era. Malcolm Miles has described the twenty-first-century city as the site 'where things happen to influence history'.[12] Although the historical importance of the city does ring true for previous centuries, events in the twenty-first century have drawn attention to the city as not only a political centre, but also the ideal location for constructing community ties. Distancing itself from previous incarnation of the city—that saw the city as an emotionally disengaged entity—contemporary fiction shows vampires closing together in urban centres, building communities and constructing ties of friendship—as in the *Black Dagger Brotherhood*, *Midnight Breed* and *ChicagoLand* series—or at least fruitful co-operation, as depicted in the *Sookie Stackhouse*, *Vampire Federation*, and *Lawson Vampire* narratives.

Although it would be somewhat simplistic to claim that, in Western societies, the events of 9/11 changed the public opinion on the view of the city—and that this had a direct impact on the vampires' move to the city in the fiction—it is virtually impossible to deny the newly-shaped portrayal of the city as a social, as well as a political and commercial location. This shift draws attention to how the fiction unveils potential feelings of national and cultural insecurity, which are simultaneously condensed and exorcised through the metaphor of the city. Previously envisaged as either a solitary figure, or as a cruel and emotionally impaired creature who was unable and unwilling to fully connect with large groups of his fellow beings, the vampire functions as the perfect medium to channel a shift in understanding towards urban communities in the twenty-first century. The 'vampire in the city' signals a new desire for community and bonding which, moving away from the dreams of rural idyll which became culturally popular in the late Nineties, re-evaluates the grounds for national and cultural re-affirmation. The coupling of vampire and city, in this context, takes on a conceptually potent function. The vampire is portrayed as a virtually immortal creature, whose strength and resilience are made known to all; whether technically dead or alive, the vampire does not wither, does not decay. The city, for its part, still maintains its image as an allegory for the future, for innovation, for success. Together, the two metaphors provide an image of constant regeneration, of strength, of power. If it is true that, as James Donald claims, the city 'is, above all, representation', then the portrayal of 'vampire cities' delineates the boundaries of metaphorical engagement in relation to concerns of a political, social, and cultural nature within a given national context.[13]

By colonising the city, vampires designate a space for humans that is produced by interaction of both historical and geographical parameters, whilst relying on the development of social relation of production and reproduction. By envisaging urban areas as newly defined centres for vampires to flourish and develop, the fiction adds to 'the city' a layer of diversity and difference. It is precisely within that difference, however, that it finds integrity and coherence.[14] As vampire families, institutions, and political powers thrive in the city, they also unveil a widespread and unavoidable belief in making historical changes and providing the nation—which the city aptly represents—with a new inspiration for development and, possibly re-birth. So while the vampire in institutionalised by the city, the city proffers vampire society with a solid ground for emotional, commercial, and civic support. The humorously metaphorical use of 'vamp and the city' here—especially when humans are involved—is difficult to avoid.

The inclusion of vampire communities in the urban landscape, therefore, is not a single-faceted one. In the majority of literary examples, vampires operates within human parameters either secretively—as in the case of the *Black Dagger Brotherhood*, *Lawson Vampire*, *Nathaniel Cade*, and *Chosen Few* series—under the pretence of human identity—as one can find in the *Midnight Breed*, *Vampire Federation*, the *Twilight Saga*, and the *House of Comarré*—or as a known and accepted group co-existing with humans—as it is the case in *Sookie Stackhouse*, *The Dresden Files* and *Hollows* series. In a way, the amalgamation of vampires into human organisational structures (especially when a known entity), merged with the politics of urban living, could be interpreted as a form of 'immigration' into the human landscape. Given the context of the city as both a geographical and social location, and the place it occupies conceptually as a representation of wealth and intellectual development, the vampire's presence is one that is inevitably connected to—perhaps reliant on—the re-imagination of known and seemingly understood spaces in view of globalising, homogenising and (paradoxically) distinguishing forces. The inevitable focus on technology, commerce, and notions of 'normality' within the fiction draws attention to how the inclusion of the vampire within the urban configuration of human society is a process that has to do with, simultaneously, economic forces and identity formation. After all, 'cultural politics', as Anthony Kings contends, are never too far removed from any debates over the nature and status of the city, especially when issues of migration, immigration and community are involved.[15]

Taken as a both a physical space and an idealised representation, the city must be considered through two lines of thought. The first, in keeping with discourses of political economy, places an emphasis on investment shifts and regeneration, whenever important commercial forces descend upon areas of the city. The second, as Sharon Zukin suggests, 'focuses on representations of social groups and visual means of excluding or including them in public and private spaces'.[16] In this line of thought, the city functions as a symbolic presence which can in turn can help to deconstruct and identify the delineations of any given social group. Although in my analysis of 'urban vampires' I feel more drawn to the second (and inherently representational) understanding of the city, it would be difficult to evaluate the metaphorical impact of vampiric operations in urban landscapes without bearing in mind a knowledge of how those shifts recall issues of an economic nature. After all, economy in itself is rarely separate from culture, and the vampire's relocation—and even appropriation—of the city in the fiction is arguably connected to critiques of the human everyday in its many incarnations, from money to family, from business to emotion.

THAT 'NEW ORLEANS THING'

Of all cities in the world, of all urban and rural areas, none has maintained more of a reputation as a 'vampire city' than New Orleans. In *The House of Comarré* series, we are told that New Orleans has 'such a draw for vampires', that it has become 'synonymous with them'.[17] In similar vein, New Orleans is described as a historical social centre for vampires in Harkness' *All Souls* novels, where the 'boisterous', 'charming' and 'most powerful' vampires are known to reside and thrive.[18] In the *Sookie Stackhouse* series, New Orleans is the centre of the vampires' political power, and functions as a symbolic presence in their society. Harris is particularly attuned to the city's relationship to vampires in Anne Rice's famous novels, and constructs a strong intertextual relation to those texts in building a view of the city for her own vampires: 'New Orleans had been the place to go for vampires and those who wanted to be around them ever since Anne Rice had been proven right about their existence. The city was like Disneyland for vamps'.[19] Naturally, it would be unwise to solely credit Rice as the creator and perpetrator of the connection between New Orleans and vampires. There is no denying, however, that her representationally revolutionary fiction had a significant impact on the place occupies by the city as a 'vampire place' in the collective Western imagination.

Close descriptive parallels are established between fictional and cultural depictions of New Orleans in the popular imagination. As a city, New Orleans is often described—by novelists, poets, philosophers, and historians alike—as being somewhat 'peculiar', existing almost at the edges of human normality and expectation. Simone de Behaviour was known to have remarked that that the city is surrounded by a 'pearl grey' and 'luminous' air.[20] In similar fashion, Oliver Evans claims the city maintains an omnipresent 'fine haze', 'soft and subtle, with opalescent hints'.[21] Although the hazy and luminous outlook is most likely caused by the high levels of humidity in the air, the city has not as much fallen victim to the banality of meteorological considerations as it has acquired a reputation for magic, ethereality and mysticism. To an observing eye, New Orleans seems immersed in an almost otherworldly 'glow', which bestows upon its limits a romantically mysterious quality.

Recalling the radiant and enigmatic qualities of New Orleans, vampires are often described in the fiction using similar adjectives and attributes. Vampires are often said to be surrounded by a 'mysterious air'. In *Sookie Stackhouse*, vampires are indeed said to 'glow'.[22] A similar description can be found in the *Black Dagger Brotherhood*, where vampire bodies are said to bloom with health and shine with the 'golden' glow of a 'summer tan'.[23]. Opalescence and similar qualities are also listed among prevalent vampire characteristics. In the *Twilight* saga, for instance, vampires are portrayed as having an otherworldly 'gloss', as a result of their 'crystalline skin'.[24] In Meyer's storyline, a number of vampires are so pale that their skin often appears 'translucent white', slightly resembling 'the casing of an onion'.[25] Examples of this nature are abundant in contemporary literature. Although the characteristics vary in depiction and degree, it can be suggested that vampires are creature that possess an unnatural glow, adding to their beauty and their role as objects of fascination.

The descriptive similarities that link vampires to the city of New Orleans establish a virtually unmissable conceptual connection between the two. As the elements that comprise physical representation hold such a closeness, it is no surprise that New Orleans is often thought of as a 'vampire city'. Although it would be risky to claim that writers are trying to establish a direct connection between the city and the creatures, it is still possible to suggest that the popularised depiction of New Orleans as an opalescent, mysterious and otherworldly city has contributed greatly in perpetrating its conceptual connection to vampires, beings who are luminescent and ethereal in their own right. The history of the city here could also be an important factor; as the site of extreme immigration and ethnic mingling, New Orleans holds a reputation for magic and mystery. Many spiritual currents throughout Louisiana can be traced back to New Orleans, and the city has often welcomed—either historically or with imagery—the wave of mystifying fantasies that have surrounded it. As both a geographical site and an imaginary construct, New Orleans works on similar ground as other Gothic constructions, with vampires figuring as the most prevalent one.

Indeed, one must wonder why vampires maintain such a hold on New Orleans—or even vice versa. Visual depictions here are but the beginning of the connection, and it is necessary to dig deeper into their conceptual relationship in an attempt to find an answer. I believe a most persuasive response may lie in the popular perception of this particular city as a site not only of mystery, but also of uncanny and appealing dwindling. At its highest point, New Orleans is no more than seventeen feet above sea level, and much of it is at least five feet below sea level.[26] The geography of the city makes it sadly famous for floods and devastation, one example of this being the recent occurrence of hurricane Katrina, which wrecked parts of the city irrevocably. As a result of the floods, New Orleans presents several types of architecture, existing on top of each other, and unable to be given appropriate care in order for their beauty to survive. This is particularly true of older buildings, which are often left to rot and decline in the most historical quarters of the city. The mixture of water damage and social history also makes New Orleans a strange conceptual cousin to Venice, another city which is often plagued by floods which eat away and threaten to destroy—drop-by-drop—the city's historical buildings. It is no surprise that, in Colleen Gleeson's *Gardella Vampire Chronicles*, Venice is hailed the most populous vampire city. While in this particular narrative the excitement of New World conglomerates is exchanged for the romantic historicity of the Old World, New Orleans and Venice maintain a strong connection, pivoting not only on similar visual elements, but also existing as particular conceptual constructs as sites of simultaneous ruin and fascination.

It is indeed in this extremely important element that New Orleans finds the most constructive link to vampires, and the potential source of the connection to the un/dead. There is a tendency to use Gothic terminology to describe New Orleans, even if, in reality, what is being discussed is the city's landscape, landmarks, and weather. Due to its floods, its destructions, its mixtures of architectures, ethnicities, epicurean pleasures, and blissful hedonism, New Orleans has earned a reputation as a city of 'splendid decay'.[27] Louise McKinnon claims that the city—unlike any other in the United States—hinges on perpetual cycles of destruction and regeneration, continuously showing 'the wear and tear of human life.[28] By presenting a mixed architecture and a fusion of beliefs and customs, New Orleans is a city that functions as a metaphor of time. That metaphor, of course, plays an important in building the city reputation as a site of mystery and enchantment. The city is both living and dying, its decaying outlook functioning as a unavoidable sign of how New Orleans continues to absorb, and simultaneously repel, 'the effects of its own history'.[29]

And it is in its existence as a city of both grandeur and decay that New Orleans finds a prolific connection to vampires, one that makes the creature feel truly at home in the city. Recalling popular constructs of New Orleans itself, vampires are creatures of life and death, finality and regeneration, furtiveness and immortality. Vampires hover at the cusp between states of existence. When 'dead', they defy both physics and imagination in continuing to exist; when technically alive, they still grasp life in an irrevocably inhuman way, by living for centuries and exceeding all expectations of human life. By acting as an apt metaphor of both life and decay—especially when compared to the parameters of human existence—vampires are blended creatures, owning an amalgamated space. Just like New Orleans, they can be said to reflect 'the wear and tear of human life', inexorably highlighting—by, paradoxically, not experiencing it—the effects of human history, fears, and fantasies. And, just like New Orleans, vampires are icons of 'psychological and poetic manifestation'.[30] The poetry of expression that exhumes from the city's historical buildings also pervades the layers of reverie in the vampire's mystique.

The relationship between New Orleans and vampires is, however, a multifaceted one. Their connection relies on visions of blending natures and ungraspable underurrents. Any illusion of an overarching definition is something is difficult to pin down for both the city and its vampire residents.

A clear classification of 'nature' escapes both vampires and New Orleans; this muddled state draws the concepts together even in terms of taxonomy. Just as it is difficult—virtually impossible—to provide a definition of the term 'vampire' that applies to all examples of fiction, so it is challenging to offer a vision of New Orleans that satisfies all its facets. As both an urban centre and an imaginary space of existence, New Orleans is a city of contradictions. Rich in history and sites of exchange, it is often argued that the city is unable to reconcile the various cultural currents that have run through it for centuries.

The geographical location of New Orleans makes its historical formation a product of struggle. Peirce Fee Lewis argues that the area is 'a fearsome place, difficult enough for building houses, lunacy for wharves and skyscrapers'.[31] And New Orleans is a city with a conflicted history. It is a site of historical mergence and divergence, with several cultural and sociopolitical influences colliding in the city. New Orleans is a city of blended notions and broken boundaries; or, to be even more specific, of blended boundaries. In this, the city evokes the understanding of vampires which became popular in the very late twentieth century and almost a common place in the twenty-first: vampires stand at intersections, a metaphorical representation that boundaries exist and that they can, in fact, not only be broken, but moulded, pushed, and amalgamated. The vampire is at once heterogeneous and homogenous; a state of being that is clearly visible in contemporary texts. In this, the vampire truly is akin to the city, embodying constantly re-envisioned paths of 'hegemony and disenfranchisement, economy and ecology, socialisation and separation'.[32] And New Orleans, with its own history of assortment and standardisation, provides the most fruitful ground for the analogy.

As ethnicities, customs, and even religious beliefs collide, New Orleans is a city that struggles with its own identity. More so than with other cities in the United States, it is difficult to think of New Orleans as a single entity; the city has many faces and it takes different visual and conceptual incarnations according to the context. One ready example of the city's cultural divergence is provided by the local propensity for its residents to pronounce the name differently; the city's name ranges in pronunciation according to the speaker, its variations of 'New Orleans', 'New Orleens' and 'Nu Orlunz' playing testament to the mixing of (to name but a few) Creole, Cajun, and African influences.[33]

Nonetheless, it is precisely this state of conflict that has transformed New Orleans into a significantly alluring city to visitors from around the world. The tourism industry has capitalised on the city's romantic mixtures and divergences, building a vision of the city which appeals to a number of travellers. Indeed, it is possible to argue that the tourism industry has contributed greatly to the construction of the city's very mystique. Known historically as a blended centre of beliefs and practices, New Orleans is entangled with tourism practices to such an extent that its sense of

uniqueness can be said to derive from the image promoted by the bro-
chures. The tourism industry has undoubtedly made a virtue of the city's
conflicts, conflicts that have become articulated into an image of New
Orleans which—one might suggest—is the one that is predominantly
known around the world. Vivid images of jazz, carnival, voodoo, and spicy
foods jump to mind—fortunately or lamentably—when thinking of the city
itself. This image of the city is lodged into people's minds and—although
publicised and acknowledged both domestically and internationally—has
to be understood as a partial construct of the tourism industry. Indeed, the
fabrication of an 'identity to sell' for the city has been the centre of much
debate and scholarship in recent years. Social historian Kevin Fox Gotham,
for instance, is keen to draw attention to the role of tourism in managing
the cultural undercurrents of New Orleans, for both visitors and residents.
Tourism is both a source of balm and vexation for the city. In a way, New
Orleans is both victimised and benefited by the industry. Gotham argues
that the history and 'sense' of the city cannot be separated from the visual
constructs that accompany it. New Orleans, he suggests, is a 'complex and
constantly mutating city', in which 'meanings of place and community' are
'inexorably intertwined with tourism'.[34]

If this evaluation of New Orleans' tourism industry seems out of place
in a book on vampire literature, then it is essential to remember and point
out that 'tourism' is not a term far removed from the vampire world. To
find evidence of this, one should only to turn to the fiction itself, where
literary incarnations of vampires are part of the tourism and lore of Louisiana. The most manifest example of this can be found in the *Sookie Stackhouse* series. Harris repeatedly mentions how vampires—now a known
and mostly accepted social group—own and operate several businesses
throughout the state. Tourism, we are told, is a big area of trade for the
vampires. They have opened a large number of establishments—usually
bars—that humans can visit. The main attraction for the tourists is, of
course, the vampires themselves. Harris stresses how humans like to visit
the bars to come face to face with a semi-mythical creature and experience the thrill of being close to such a famous Gothic predator, deep in
the 'exotic underworld'.[35] The series mentions that vampires have opened
tourism businesses all over the United States, but Louisiana figures as a
particularly prolific state for the trade. And, unsurprisingly, New Orleans
acts as the vampire tourism hotspot. The city's already known mystique
provides the ideal ground on which the businesses can prosper, the lore of
the vampire becoming entangled with the existing currents of magic and
mysticism which have defined the city on a cultural level.

It is virtually impossible to miss here the suggestion that the vampire
mystique is part of the identity's construction of the city, which has been
fed to people by fictional accounts for decades, if not centuries. In literary
accounts, the vampire tourism trade seems to be experiencing similar issues
which are known to be a problematic point for the tourism industry in the

real-life New Orleans. The problem is, unsurprisingly, that of authenticity. The tourism industry in New Orleans has been critiqued and criticised heavily for its propensity to put forward an inauthentic picture of the city. Gotham argues that the tourism industry draws its selling points by 'transmitting symbols of local culture'.[36] The images of Mardi Gras, jazz players, magic, and sanguinity are portrayed as 'authentic', and have been essential over the years in maintaining the tourists' interest in the location. Meeting the tourists' expectations of New Orleans has historically been an absolute necessity for the successful development of trade, and the tourism industry has undoubtedly been complicit in proliferating symbols and icons associated with the city. Veracity, however, has been the price to pay, so while forcefully trying to idealise the area through its most romanticised images, the tourism industry has been paradoxically responsible for enhancing the cultural conflicts among the city's population.

A similar situation is identifiable in the *Sookie Stackhouse* storyline, where issues of authenticity and veracity surround the vampire business trade. The vampires are portrayed as conforming to the popular images of 'vampires' that have been circulated to the public—especially in the twentieth century—through literature and film. To inspire the tourists to visit the business hotspots, vampires appropriately fictionalised clothing and to adopt a speech that tourists see as befitting a creature of the night. When working at the well-known vampire bar Fangtasia, the vampire Pam is forced to wear a 'filmy, trailing black gown' as her 'work outfit', recalling the dresses worn and popularised by the fictional vampire Elvira in the 1988 film by the same name. This outfit, we are told, is what 'all the tourists that came into the bar seemed to expect from female vampires'.[37] The nod to the wider popular culture scope is unmissable here, and draws attention to the role the media play in constructing images that can be 'fed' to tourists. The outfit is complimented by outlandish linguistic references such as 'son of a misbegotten whore', insults that the vampires like to use when addressing humans in the bar because the tourists—we are told—'like that kind of talk'.[38] Pam, however, is known to despise both the theatrical clothing she has to wear and the speech she has to adopt to keep the tourists' interest alive. It is stressed on several occasions by Harris that, when not on duty at the bar, Pam is a 'pastels-and-twinset kind of woman'.[39]

The issue of authenticity is unmistakable here. Harris seems to be suggesting that vampires have evolved from simple creatures of lore and mystical interest, to 'products' that can be sold to the masses for an agreed price. And in stressing this mystified representation of a popular image, Harris also seems to be drawing a parallel between the tourism trade in New Orleans and the vampire tourism trade. As a native of Louisiana, Harris would have close knowledge of the issues of mis-representation that have forged a constructed identity for the city. Indeed, it could be argued that Harris employs the metaphor of vampire tourism in order to present a critique of the issues of inauthentic representation that are known to be a wide-spread cultural issue in New Orleans. The vampires of Louisiana in the *Sookie Stackhouse* series act as the embodiment of the constructed image of New Orleans as the epitome of the tourist destination. As part of the fictionalised lore of the city, the vampire provides the perfect allegory for drawing attention to the dangers of symbolic construction. The 'inauthentic' vampires of Harris' fiction provide a channelling ground for the issues surrounding the 'inauthentic' state of New Orleans. Both hinge on images of popular representation and desirable symbols. Vampire iconography merges with the commercialised representation of the city in offering a critique of the appropriation of custom and tradition by business and trade.

It has often been argued that tourism, as a global process, encourages layers of 'standardisation and cultural homogenisation that annihilates the unique features' of places.[40] I would like to argue that, instead, if one considers contemporary vampire fiction as part of the tourism trade, standardisation and homogenisation prove to be part of the process of subjective identification for city. There is no denying that New Orleans, as a city, carries a reputation for mysterious experiences and exciting, fun-filled nights. Magic and incantation also come as part of the package and these all add to the construction of what can be labelled the 'New Orleans mythology'. The city itself is undoubtedly invested in perpetrating the idealised vision, so that it can then be promoted to the public. In contemporary literature, vampires engage in similar activities. A conscious knowledge of vampire mythology is present—especially in the *Sookie Stackhouse* series—and is encouraged. The real-life New Orleans, Harris' fictional portrayal of the city, and the vampires in the narrative are all connected—critically and conceptually—by the thread of tourism and enterprise, constructing images that can be sold to paying customers. Great efforts are made to ensure that the portrayal of both city and vampires—and how these are connected within both the fiction and real-life expectations—is perceived as 'authentic' by the tourists. This image—which sociologist Dean MacCannell refers to as 'staged authenticity'—is the basis of the appeal and what continues to bring tourists back, generating profits for vampires and humans alike.[41] Indeed, Harris stresses the fact that humans are happy to help the vampires run their business and attract tourists, as this has an impact on the wealth and general income of New Orleans as a city overall: 'Since vampire tourism now accounted for so much of the city's revenue, even the humans in New Orleans listened to the [vampires'] wants and wishes, in an unofficial way'.[42] It is virtually impossible not to see here how Harris may also be stressing the complicit nature of the business-owners of real-life New Orleans, seemingly happy to encourage images of jazz, carnival, vampires, and voodoo—as believable or as staged as they might be—in order to encourage a steady economic expansion for a city that relies mainly on the tourism trade as its greatest source of income.

And indeed, one cannot avoid the cultural and commercial implications of the vampire-inspired hedonism trade in the fiction—and, to some

extent, in the vision of New Orleans that derives from and is simultaneously inspired by it. For tourism, as Gotham points out, is a 'highly complex set of institutions and social relations that involve capitalist markets'.[43]
Whenever the concept of tourism in involved, one must be prepared for the
fact that the impact of the trade is both monetary and social. On the one
hand, images are generated and encouraged in order to attract the tourists'
attention. Tourism is, after all, part of the business world, and economic
revenue is its main purpose. On the other hand, however, tourism also has
a social aspect, in the sense that at the point when the image becomes an
action—and vice versa—that image also obtains a cultural value, a place
in the everyday fabric of life to which people build an attachment. And
there is no denying that contemporary fiction portrays the vampires of New
Orleans not only as 'normal', but as an accepted presence in the cultural
structure of the city. Kenneth Holditch contends that 'New Orleans is a city
in love with its myths, mysteries and fantasies'.[44] It could be argued here
that, within the iconography of fangs, capes, and magic, the fiction unveils
how New Orleans is a city that not only 'fabricates' appealing images—as
true or false as that might be—but, more specifically, comes to find validation and logic through including vampires into the weaved structures of its
cultural everyday day.

The relationship between New Orleans and vampires is, therefore,
a cyclical and yet mutating one. The history of the city provides fertile
grounds for vampire myths to be circulated. The fiction, in turn, feeds
into this mythology and establishes it as a cultural presence that generates
interest in both readers and residents. And the city, for its part, continues to feed into the vampire mystique, and build cultural associations to
the stories known to the public; vampires, as a result, become a 'normal
presence' when envisioning the city. This process is so culturally cemented
that it would be almost unthinkable—in the twenty-first century—to think
of New Orleans without thinking of vampires. In a way, then, what was
once perhaps only a fictional idea has now become a conventional staged
truth. And it is that staged truth that provides the basis of the success for
the Gothic New Orleans we know today, and the pregnant references that
contemporary vampires fiction makes to it.

THE VAMPIRE'S HOUSE

As the attention to the city highlights concerns about the differentiations
between private and public, the architecture of buildings and constructions—inhabited and commonly used by vampires—also takes on a capti-
vating light. The attention to the vampire's house in contemporary popular
literature is widespread, and almost maniacal in its detail. Descriptions of
vampiric residences abound in the narratives, as the area where the vampire
eats and sleeps takes on a peculiar meaning. More often than not located

within the bounds of the city's urban area, the vampire's place of dwelling ranges in its nature from apartments to colonial houses, country houses, and window-rich apartments in the heart of the city. In Reynolds' *Vampires in America*, Raphael's Malibu house is 'a modern architect's dream, with the sweet, clean lines of the southwest [. . .] the structure was two-storied, with the second floor set far back, leaving a broad, high terrace open to the stars and sea'.[45] In the *Sookie Stackhouse* series, Eric lives in a 'fieldstone house' in 'a gated community with a strict building code'. Inside, Eric's house is extravagant and classy at the same time: the living room has 'sapphire blue' walls and 'gleaming white crown mouldings'. It is filled with furniture that is an 'eclectic collection of pieces', all 'upholstered in jewel tones'.[46] In his *Introductory Lectures*, Freud draws attention to 'the house' as a symbolic representation for 'the genital orifice'.[47] With this idea in mind, one might be tempted to say that, considering the sexualised nature of the vampire—especially male—in several examples from contemporary popular fiction, the emphasis on lavish houses could be interpreted as a metaphorical representation of both sexual desire and social stability, where the house symbolises, simultaneously, the excitement of intercourse and the goal of matrimonial delight to the predominantly female readership.

Stopping at the relationship between image and sex, however, does not fully register the importance of the vampire's house in its wider cultural representation, where matters of 'desire' and 'achievement' transport the relationship between architectonic delights and symbolism to the realm of the socio-political. Culture—understood as what Margaret Rodman labels 'a symbolised system of meaning'—is almost inseparable from any analysis of the contemporary vampire, and this includes the descriptions of house and objects that surround the subject in the fiction.[48] If it is true that visual representations of all objects can be interpreted as a rendition of character for both individuals and social groups, then the continuous negotiation and re-imagination of buildings in contemporary popular literature draws attention to the cultural meanings hidden in the metaphorical cracks of vampic architecture. Thus, the metaphorical meaning of all built forms—from houses to business, from streets to interiors—contributes to the construction of social identities. This approach to buildings and interiors proves productive in itself because it shows a tuned connection to vampire intellectual, aesthetic and political structures which, to borrow Zukin's words, is inherently 'based on interpretations and interpenetrations of culture and power'.[49]

At first glance, buildings in which vampires dwell could appear to be taking on a passive role. One might be tempted to argue that, in the socio-ethnographic sense, they provide the material context and framework in which to analyse, as Rodman puts it, the more valuable interactions of 'household relations and symbolic orders'.[50] I would like to suggest, however, that a focus of the vampire's house—and, consequently, places of business and commercial interaction—can open the way for discussing issues of a cultural nature, moulding what would appear like simple contextual constructions into representational transpositions of the vampire's nature, and its place in frameworks of human relations. In architectonic terms, culture is not (technically) an essential part of a building's construction. The mortar, the bricks, and the allocation of material can be carried out quite easily without considering the custom preferences and traditions of a whole group. The expected 'appeal' of the house, however, is something that transcends the simple technicality of planning and building, and something that not only transforms buildings into a cultural practice, but also draws attention to their function as objects of desire. A composite analysis of the vampire's house in contemporary fiction must begin here, acknowledging the symbolic value of architecture in its cultural understandings, and, as a result, unveiling the concerns and preoccupations of the Western, post-2000 society that these vampiric constructions inevitably mirror.

Luxury is a term that provides a common ground for the vampire's abode across narratives, and whether that luxury is provided by antique furnishings, a sought-after address, or even the presence of highly technological operating systems, one cannot deny that vampires enjoy the quality and experience of an expensive and lavish domicile. Mark Tungate contends that luxury itself is inseparable from notions of 'authenticity' and 'engaging experiences' that, in turn, are intrinsically connected to the 'consumer sensibilities' of our contemporary moment.[51] From a socio-economic perspective, the presence of such lavish vampire houses in the fiction indicates an emphasis on the symbolic nature of possession. The dynamics are work here are reminiscent of Jean Baudrillard's theory of sign value. According to Baudrillard, 'sign value' denotes the value afforded to an object because of the social prestige that it imparts on its possessor, rather than the utilitarian value that would be provided by the primary use of an object.[52] In this framework, the vampire's house provides us with essential grounds for making distinctions between reality and representation, elaborating an understanding of objects that is distinctive of our cultural moment and highlighting preoccupations of desire and intent which (on some level) define the newly-defined twenty-first century.

Unsurprisingly, one can identify several examples from contemporary fiction where super-rich vampires live in super-expensive houses, from the high-tech and high-luxury subterranean compound in Adrian' *Midnight Breed* series, to the swanky and strictly vampire-owned Malibu estates in Reynolds' *Vampires in America* stories. Not to mention, of course, the posh Italianate villas in the *Twilight* saga and the luxurious bachelor pads in Harris' *Sookie Stackhouse* novels. A notable and noteworthy example of the overly lavish vampire house—and a clear representation of, among other things, the vampire's wealth—is to be found in Ward's *Black Dagger Brotherhood* series: 'the mansion' that the Brothers share as their home. The building is interesting on a number of levels. And although a specific example is being used here, its specificity also provides common ground for the analysis of several other examples—from Sandlin's *Penton Legacy* series to Harkness' *All Souls* trilogy—where lavish, mansion-like constructions appear, and similar representational parameters are applied. Outside, the Brothers' mansion is depicted by Ward as a rather intimidating place: 'There was a four-story mansion made of grey stone, the kind of place you'd see in promos for horror films; Gothic, gloomy, oppressive, with more shadows than a person felt safe being around'.[53] The outer look of the building owes a lot to traditional representations of the literary Gothic mansion—perhaps even the vampire castle—a promise of dark and frightening experiences for both the body and the soul. On the inside, however, the mansion has a completely different look:

> The lobby was a rainbow of colour, as unexpected as a garden blooming in a cave. Green malachite columns alternated with one made of claret marble, the lengths rising up from a multi-hued mosaic floor. The walls were brilliant yellow and hung with gold-framed mirrors. The ceiling . . . was a masterpiece of artwork and gold leafing . . . and up ahead, centred among all the grandeur, was a broad staircase that ascended to a balconied second floor.[54]

In spite of its highly decorative value, however, the mansion is not just gold-leafing and mosaics; it is a twenty-first-century technological masterpiece. There are high-tech cameras everywhere, running on the most expensive operating systems. The building even has light-proof shutters that automatically cover the windows during the daylight hours.

In the *Black Dagger Brotherhood*, a nod to the vampire tradition is made through the peculiar mixture of old and new. The openly Gothic, yet dazzling building in which the vampires live exceeds its function as a desirable setting for a desirable creation. It is virtually impossible to miss the metaphorical, almost metaphysical use of the mansion within the literary framework. Ward is using the idea of hidden luxury here to unravel the complex representational shift of the vampire through a special brand of Gothic objectification. The mansion, one might venture to say, functions as an in-text critique of how the vampire persona has evolved in contemporary literature. On the outside, the mansion is the perfect Old-World representation of the Gothic tradition; dark, gloomy, mysterious, and properly scary. But, on the inside, it offers a distinctly modernised brand of palatial luxury. And indeed, this is precisely what Ward's vampires do, they mix Victorian Gothic components, with twenty-first-century visions of the rich underworld. Whilst maintaining an outer façade of traditional vampiric existence, their refined tastes expose them as twenty-first-century, commodified incarnations of the Gothic ideal, a perfected figuration of the vampire as the represented longing that haunts human dreams of possession and virtual fulfilment.

The lavish nature of the vampire's domicile as a 'sign'—in the Baudrillardian sense—draws attention to notions of exhibition and commodified viewing which can be said to characterise Western thought. In their fabulous architecture, sleek interior design, and abundance of expensive decorative objects, the vampire's houses unveil their purpose by being a display of the extents of capitalism. The house, is after all, a commodity in itself, and the emphasis is on its outlook of extravagance and aesthetic indulgence. There is no denying that the vampire's 'house' has transformed over the centuries, going through processes of conversion that have left haunted mansions on cliffs behind, and opted for sleek and contemporary residences. As a recurring motif, the vampire's house of contemporary popular literature allows us to see the vampire as a transformational creature in itself. The shift in the abode's outlook and understanding also signals the transformation of the contemporary vampire's engagement with symbolic preoccupations which cannot be separated from the Western context in which they generate.

The vampire's house, however, is also a place of organised chaos. On the one hand, it familiarises the vampire, by making it—in a way—a more mundane and understandable creature, one that can succumb to the limitations of human aesthetic in the most commonplace of ways. On the other, the vampire's house is also a symbolic, almost ungraspable entity that shifts representational locations, and moulds cultural understandings of what is prized and desirable according to context. Indeed, in reaching levels of aesthetic and technological luxurious living which are often—to use a colloquial expression—'over the top', the vampire's house absorbs one of the peculiarities of the twenty-first century. While the highly decorative house encourages a shameless return to the 'world of goods', it also intimates the conceptual separation of people from the physical world. And it is undoubtedly the figure of the vampire that allows this paradox to ring true, and transforms its existence into a defining characteristic of vampire fiction alone. As an inherently inhuman creature, the vampire occupies a paradoxical place in itself; distanced from the human world by its very nature, it is however connected to it by need, desire and —as it has clearly been the case in recent years—the over-developed appreciation of human commodities. In this, the vampire allows the odd marriage of 'the tangible' and 'the unbelievable' to become identifiable in the metaphor of the house. The seemingly natural distinction between reality and representation is questioned in the context of the vampire's abode. The commodity is not simply an object, but it becomes a representational concept.

The emphasis on recognisable and desirable structures—in human terms—acting as the vampire's home also 'colonises' the vampire for the twenty-first century. Although operating symbolically, the house can still be said to be 'framing' the vampire. The more useful term here is actually 'enframing', a concept introduced by Heidegger and later developed (among others) by Foucault and Timothy Mitchell. According to Mitchell, the reproduction of 'ideal spaces'—or, to put it even more simply, desirable spaces—is a way of imposing order on subjects of culture that need to be 'tamed'. Referring to it as a 'system of magnitude', Mitchell claims that 'enframing' the spatial organisation of desirable areas is the only 'real order' that one can find in society, one that produces and relies on 'a method of dividing up and containing . . . which operates by conjuring up a neutral volume [of] space'.[55] The constant reconstruction of the vampire's space—made visible in the fiction through the house—gives order to the creature and, simultaneously, allows it to be disciplined and controlled for general consumption. By being placed in a space of luxury—an overall common feature of the fiction that is now recognised and almost tediously expected as a founding principle—the vampire is restrained within a familiar space. The once frightening creature becomes embedded into the crystallised house's harmonious system of knowledge.

OUT OF THE GRAVE

As a preference for urban spaces and luxurious houses lodges itself solidly in the vampire cultures of contemporary literature, a clear result of this shift is mirrored in the fact that the vast majority of vampires have long-abandoned their old penchant for sleeping in coffins, graves, or the ground. The use of coffins is one that contemporary authors—together with film-makers and others producers of examples from popular culture—'have modified or even dropped in their vampire sagas'.[56] While Stoker's Dracula was forced to find solace and repose in dirt from his home-land—forcing him to carry around boxes of the matter, and making for undoubtedly inconvenient travel set ups—contemporary vampires opt for more accessible and comfortable sleeping arrangements. And although instances of a Dracula-esque attachment to the home ground can still be occasionally found in contemporary fiction—with John Courtnay Grimwood's *Vampire Assassin* trilogy functioning as a prime example—the use of coffins as a place for resting and renewing their strength was abandoned by many vampires in the late twentieth century. In the late 1970s, Anne Rice's vampires, for instance, left coffins behind, as they were not a necessity, preferring a 'dark sanctuary'—often a crypt—where they could rest for the day.[57]

   In the twenty-first century, coffins have definitely fared badly as a common icon associated with vampires. Examples supporting this claim abound. In the *Black Dagger Brotherhood* and *Midnight Breed* series, vampires rest in luxurious beds, surrounded by expensive covers. Ward indulges in descriptions of 'antique' and expensive beds, adorned by 'satin and velvet', where her vampires feel right at home.[58] In similar vein, Adrian gives her vampires a taste for fashionable colours and accessories, stating that they sleep in 'king-sized bed', surrounded by all kinds of 'luxury'.[59]

These two examples, however, are not an exception in the vampire world and have come to represent the norm rather than an aesthetic undercurrent. Vampires show a predilection for designer-inspired sleeping areas in many other examples from fiction, including Kim Harrison's *Hollows* and Chloe Neill's *Chicagoland* series, where the undead find their dead-like sleep in modern beds conveniently located in historical mansions. In Meyer's *Twilight* saga, vampires do not have any use for any type of sleeping or resting surface, as they have forfeited on their desire for sleep or rest.

Naturally, and as it is often the case with empirically based arguments, exceptions to the rule proliferate. There are still instances where vampires prefer to sleep in coffins, graves, and even the ground. In *Sookie Stackhouse*, vampires like to sleep in coffins during the day, but this choice is a practical one, as it allows them to shield themselves from the sunlight, which would prove fatal to their vampire bodies. Eric, we are told, 'ordinarily' sleeps' in his bed, because 'his room' is 'windowless'.[60] On one occasion, Bill the vampire is seen as sleeping either in a freshly dug grave at the local cemetery, or in the earthly foundations of his ancestral home. It is also made clear by Harris that a vampire's sleeping place is seen as sacred to them, 'a guarded secret', and they of often like to pick a place that 'means' something to them—in the case of Bill, his home soil, or the ground in which his human family were buried for centuries.[61] Another similar occurrence can be found in Christine Feehan's *Carpathians* series, where vampires who are injured 'go to ground' to 'rejuvenate'.[62] The soil, or 'ground', in this case, is connected more to healing and ritual, rather than a vampire's repose, signifying the transference of 'deadly wounds' from that which is immortal (the vampire) to that which is symbolic of mortality and non-permanence (the earth). Feehan provides a very intriguing twist on the old mantra of 'consecrated ground', where vampires cannot tread. The Carpathian vampires, it would seem, can think of nothing better than to find solace in their own version of sacred soil to maintain their strength and super-human abilities.

The shift in vampire sleeping habits holds a string of metaphorical connection to the way in which the creature is perceived and, in the specifics, what sleep itself represents. Sleep, conceptually, is very reminiscent of death; the body lies still and unresponsive, just like it would if it were deceased. Traditionally, once could see why vampires were expected to sleep in coffins or, at least, in some form of grave, whether in the ground or in mausoleums. As the contention was that vampires were, in fact, already dead, it made sense that they would choose graves when the time came for their death-like repose. The deadness of the vampire was something to be feared, a mirroring of its 'dark', sexual, and amoral nature, which bent the laws of physics in its abomination. Michael Rowe reminds us that the associations of the vampire 'with the grave', 'mud', 'dirt and slime' can be understood as a 'metaphor for societal perception' of overtly-sexual behaviour as 'dirty and degrading'.[63] As the 'deadness' of vampires was to be abhorred, the association with objects and locations reminiscent of death—coffins and graves—was aptly chosen, cementing the abject quality of the oddly erotic 'undead' as something which inspired repulsion and disgust.

In contemporary literature, however, the vampire is not given such a repulsive, conceptual association with death; although they are openly not living, that state (for the most part) does not cause revulsion in those who prefer to see that vampire's undead state as a sign of strength and power—in that they have, technically, defeated human death as such. Furthermore, in numerous examples from literature and popular culture vampires are in fact not dead—or undead—at all, but simply a separate species, with living, beating hearts. The association with coffins and graves, in that case, is utterly redundant and unthinkable. With both these ideas in mind—the glamourisation of the undead, on the one hand, and the vampire's new-found state as a living creature, on the other—the replacement of the grave-like repose spot with luxurious beds is easily understood. Beds—or simply dark houses—familiarise the vampire's habits for the audience, transforming their unavailable, sleeping hours into routine, rather than tangible proof of their repulsive nature. Mihaly Csikszentmihalyi and Eugene Rochberg-Halton point out that the bed is one of the 'archetypal symbols of family life'.[64] In the English language, the word itself derives from the Indo-European base of *bhedh*, meaning literally 'to bury' or sleeping hollow in the ground'. So, in a sense, the bed can be seen as both a 'resting place' and a 'foundation' of life as the centre for procreation, love, and regeneration.[65]

On the psychoanalytical front, Freud claims—somewhat unsurprisingly—that, in terms of symbolism, beds often 'stand for marriage'.[66] While the archetypal interpretation seems a lot more persuasive—in its reliance on group psychology and community relations—than the psychoanalytical approach based on repression, denial, and regression, the function of the bed as a symbol of conjugal communion is difficult to contest. The peculiar origin of beds as a site related to burial draws attention to the possibility that, while no longer inhabiting coffins and graves, vampires still function as the subliminal hiding place for anxieties that, although projected through different imagery, still maintain their symbolic potency within the social structure. Through the bed, the vampire is introduced into a system of monogamous—or at least permanent—relationship which is founded in Westernised conceptions of 'good, 'appealing' and, above all, socially acceptable. In response to what can be seen as the pervasive 'crisis' of the family unit, vampires have taken on a stabilising role. The fact that many vampire sleep in sumptuous beds also testifies to the conceptual change in perceiving vampire habits and instincts—including a pervasive eroticisation of the creature—as unthreatening, where beds hold a cultural function as locations of calm and enjoyable family life in a way that coffins never could. The newly-established association between vampires and beds—an almost universal symbol of sexual intercourse—comes to signify the conceptual acceptance of the creature's sexual nature. At the same time, however, the traditional understanding of beds as a location of repose normalises the vampire as an everyday creature, openly proclaiming sex as the ordinary, natural activity which it is. So the old adage of 'getting in bed' with vampires takes on a re-discovered meaning.

THE BRANDED SPACE

As the focus on the vampire's lavish surroundings and sexualised habits draws attention to the commodified nature of the Gothic persona in contemporary popular literature, the notions of 'wealth' and 'possession' becoming increasingly unavoidable. Of course, there is nothing new in claiming that the vampire bears a metaphorical attachment to matters of an economic nature. Indeed, vampires have been interpreted in their connections to money and greed in substantial Gothic scholarship. In Marxist critique, particularly, the joining of vampires with capitalist greed is common. Marx himself used gothic terminology to describe the workings of industrial capitalism: 'capital is dead labour which, vampire-like, lives only sucking living labour, and lives the more, the more labour it sucks'.[67] I intend to argue, however, that the connection has moved beyond mere critical connections within the fiction itself, and has expanded into the cultural realm, building a conceptual relationship between the vampire and the concept of signified commodity. Or, as I argue, the vampire as commodity.

A number of contemporary texts show a predilection for joining the idea of male vampires—often highly sexualised—with infinite wealth and commodities in various forms. Instances of this abound, with the *Black Dagger Brotherhood*, *Midnight Breed*, *Vampires in America*, *Penton Vampire Legacy*, and *Twilight* series acting as prime examples. The vampires have money, and they have lots of it. They are always 'flashing the benjis', to use an expression favoured by J.R. Ward. In the *Black Dagger Brotherhood*, we are told on numerous occasions that the Brothers are of substantial financial means: 'Now that Butch was hanging with the Brotherhood? He had so much green, he couldn't possibly spend it fast enough'.[68] When they go to night clubs, they receive special VIP service: 'Zsadist headed for ZeroSum, the Brotherhood's current downtown hangout. The bouncers let him pass the waiting line, easy access being one of the perks of folks who dropped the kind of cash the Brothers did'.[69] The presence of so much money in the Brotherhood's pockets is somewhat curious. For all intents and purposes, the Brothers have no income and there is no suggestion that their warrior activities come with a fee. A similar situation is put forward in the *Midnight Breed*—another example of the paranormal romance sub-genre—where the warrior vampires have access to great amounts of money, but the source of the wealth itself is never addressed. Even when it is made clear that various openly legal (in the human sense) businesses and enterprises are the sources of the vampires' wealth—as it is made clear by

Eric's Fangtasia bar in *Sookie Stackhouse*, and 'Raphael Enterprises Inc.' in Reynolds' series—it is often tacitly implied that the vampires themselves have other, not-so-human ways of obtaining money. This tacit suggestion is made explicit in Lucas, a late instalment of the *Vampires in America* series, where the ability of gaining money at will is even stated as a distinctive vampire characteristics—stating openly that vampires always 'have plenty of money'—even if the way in which their 'corporate empires' are acquired is accomplished is left hazy.[70] Connections exist between financial affluence and being a vampire, suggesting that, in these representations of vampirism, one almost equals the other.

Although we are rarely told where the money comes from, one thing is for sure: vampires know how to spend it. In Ward's series, the Brothers wear expensive suits, expensive shoes and own impressive bachelor pads in exclusive up-market areas of town. A similar situation is to be found in the *Twilight* saga, where the Cullen family own modern and luxurious houses, drive expensive cars, and wear designer clothing. Deborah Lupton points out that, when it comes to the owning of expensive objects, taste functions as 'the broader understanding of style or fashion related to any commodity'.[71] She also goes on to say that 'the body is the most indisputable materialisation of taste'. This is reminiscent of the Brothers' relation to expensive objects. They surround themselves with the latest gadgets, the latest innovations, and the latest trends, a world of commodities which defines them. Ward stresses on a number of occasions that the vampires in the Brotherhood know how 'to dress', an ability to select beautiful items that runs in their being: when it comes to their wardrobe, the Brothers' sense of 'style and masculine elegance' are 'down to the bone'.[72] In their attachment to fast cars and expensive accessories, these vampires appear to succumb to humanity in the most mundane of ways. What is particularly worthy of note, however, is not that the Brothers show a predilection for luxury items as such, but that they also are unable to function without purchasing their favourite brands. Indeed, Ward's vampire world is a branded world and operates behind symbols of wealth and what they represent socially.

And the brands truly are everywhere in the series, peppering the pages of each novel. When it comes to clothing and accessories, Ward's vampires wear Patek Philippe, Gucci, Valentino, Armani, Hermes, Zegna. When it comes to drink, the Brothers only consume expensive brands such as Lagavulin or Grey Goose Vodka. If they go to the gym, we are told expressively that they carry a Nike bag. Indeed, after they emerge from a workout routine, they are not sweaty from head toe, but from 'head to [their] Nikes'.[73] They don't just tie their shoes: they 'tie their Ferragamos'. They do not just drive cars: they drive Audis, Porsches, BMWs and Bentleys. And they do not even use guns in battle: they 'palm' their Sig Sauers and their Glocks. These examples from Ward's novels also find a resonance in other series such as the *Twilight* saga, *Sookie Stackhouse* and *Vampires in America*, where vampires wear designer clothing and drive expensive cars such as

Corvettes and Mercedes. Perhaps more so than in any other narrative, however, in Ward's series the brands become an extension of the Brothers, not only as a metaphorical representation of their group affiliation—cool vampire warriors who have lots of money—but a physical addition to their being. This is reminiscent of what Grant McCracken calls 'possession rituals'. Material goods—in their relationship to the ephemerality of 'the brand'—do not only function as objects, but also have a broader meaning and significance for social relations.[74] In this context, the use of goods for vampires exemplifies identities; the choice of a commodity creates distinction between sub-groups and expresses membership.

Nonetheless, while the consumerism is evident and the branding unavoidable, the relationship that the Brotherhood and other contemporary vampires have with objects is somewhat different from what we saw in previous vampire novels. There is no denying that previous examples used representations of rampant consumerism to critique the bleak nature of human existence and often politics. The Eighties were particularly good at doing this. One must only think of Strieber's *The Hunger* as an example, in which trendy, elegant and brand-obsessed vampires arguably indict the yuppie consumerism encouraged by American economic politics of the time. In this narrative, the figure of the yuppie vampire emerged, as Latham puts it, 'as an exalted representative of the so-called economic revival that marked the Reaganite 1980s'.[75] Vampire consumerism functioned as an apt metaphor for the way in which our desires for things are stoked by advertising, branding and those alluring displays of shoes, handbags, and overpriced T-shirts. This interpretation of consumerism, however, does not really satisfy when it comes to contemporary narratives, especially if one thinks of the Brothers' relationship with branded objects in Ward's books. I suggest that the connection between brands, luxury, and vampires has moved on from the socio-politics and economic issues that dominated the fiction in the Eighties and Nineties. The warrior vampires do not indulge in brands in terms of escapism; nor are they defined by what they buy in attempt to fill a sense of pervasive emptiness that is brought on by the workings of modern capitalist life. There is definitely a sense of personal definition in the owning of objects, but that sense becomes a culturally acknowledged part of the vampire metaphor in the Brotherhood. Or, at least, of male vampire metaphor.

In the post-2000 era, 'rampant consumerism' is not really the principal concern related to luxurious vampire spaces. Branded objects are a vampire trait. Like many others of their kind through the narratives—particularly those within the paranormal romance and urban fiction genres—the vamps in Ward's series do not crave these objects; they take them for granted. Rather than becoming a symbolic representation for the insatiable hunger of capitalist economies, consumerism in the Brotherhood is just part of what the vampires are, a paradoxically tangible representation of their otherworldly nature. Baudrillard suggests that, in the postmodern era, fashionable brands are part of an 'order of seduction'.[76] Seduction derives pleasure from excess—the sumptuary useless consumption of surplus. And there is no denying that some seduction is at work in the Brotherhood, with the luxury brands working as vector for the cultural romance. The seduction on the reader takes places through glamourising the most consumer-orientated parts of contemporary post-industrial society.

The developed connection between vampires and brands also draws attention to the nature of capital in relation to contemporary literature. Brands, as Adam Ardvidsson argues, are a 'form of capital'.[77] Working as a manifestation of socio-economic knowledge, brands combine aspects of both culture and production systems. They are the fusion of aesthetics and economics, an entity of impression created by the transition away from Fordism.[78] Brands are an important presence in that they occupy a valuable position in what is known as the 'life-world' of consumers. While the brand is incorporeal and intangible, it is not immaterial. Acting simultaneously as visual, experiential, and psychological entities, brands 'subsume and appropriate' what consumers do with the brands in mind. Brands carry the weight of expectations; these transcend the user value of the objects they are associated with, and spill into the domain of sign value. The brand, in this sense, is a source of surplus value and social profit.[79]

The nature of the brand presents an affinity to the way in which vampires are shaped, presented and acknowledged in the fiction. The brand's name, Arvidsson reminds us, 'anticipates future experiences and attachments'.[80] This can also be said, in a way, of the vampire. Although there are multiple and multifaceted incarnations of the concept, an overarching understanding of the term brings expectations and anticipations about what a vampire is and a vampire does. As it was discussed in previous chapters, contemporary notions of these expectations include fangs, blood hunger, and physical strength. These seem to be the calling card of vampires, no matter what the context may be. This, one might venture to say, is the 'vampire brand'. Seema Gupta suggests that the brand 'is a collection of symbols, experiences, and associations', connected to any particular 'entity'.[81] The same can be said for vampires, whose very existence in the cultural world relies on a system of symbols and associations. The term vampire is as intangible and incorporeal as any other brand name, but—just like a brand—the vampire also gains an experiential reality through layers of expectancy and prospect.

Celia Lury contends that the brand works as a 'platform for the patterning of activity', a mode of organising behaviour in time and space'.[82] As a cultural podium, the brand anticipates certain kinds of actions and attachments. The is an agent of conduct; it pre-structures action and responses from the consumer. The brand occupies the in-between space linking consciousness and act. The vampire of popular literature operates in a similar manner. Its pre-determined notions function on a pre-determined frame of action, a particular stage of semiotic levelling that connects what consumers—in this case, the readers—do and what their actions mean to them. The level of expectation surrounding the very concept of 'vampire' in contemporary literature, and its metaphysical association with brands and branding, allows the vampire itself to be viewed as what Rob Shields terms 'virtual goods'.[83] The vampire as brand does not so much stand for products, but rather provides a part of the context in which the product is used.

Perhaps it is possible to suggest that writers such as Ward, Adrian, Meyer, and Reynolds construct the wealthy, attractive, stylish, and highly sexualised male vampire as just another brand to sell, a popular commodity which answers the social and cultural needs of the literary community through a special incarnation of Gothic consumerism. One could see this as a way of selling the fashionable Gothic through the fashionable romance, as it were, to its predominantly female readership. The use of luxury brands is Gothicised here in that it gives us an insight into the characters' essential vampire nature. The objects aid the representation and performance of the 'vampire sense' within the evolved Gothic imagination and their inevitable metaphorical function as objects of desire. So the consumerism that haunts contemporary vampire literature goes beyond the fiction itself; it transforms the novels into the ultimate desirable commodity for the reader. Luxury becomes a vampire 'trademark', both practically and conceptually, as much as the vampire is transformed into the ultimate brand. Stuart and Elizabeth Ewen have long claimed that consumerism 'puts leisure, beauty, and pleasure in the reach of all', so that the logic of consumption is 'embroiled in our intimacies', it is 'the insatiable urge for new things'.[84] And as the Brothers build an intimate relationship with luxury brands in the novels— exemplifying the ideal male for Ward's readership—so does the fiction itself extend into the realm of desire, actually functioning as the coveted commodity. The vampire takes on a cultural value that exposes it, in a rather conjectural way, as a core representation of what is consumable.

It is virtually impossible, therefore, to divorce the vampire as a brand from the tangible products to which it is related. If the purchasable texts are the product itself—the entities with user value—than the sign value of the vampire gains its most potent meaning in the literary context in which it is placed. If it is true that there are expectations related to the concept of vampire as a brand, then those expectations will only find their realisation in the relationship to the brand context. That context is, in this case, the literary sub-genre in which the vampire operates. Although the vampire as a brand is seemingly an overarching concept, its brand nuances are connected to genre. While blood remains a constant presence, the most defining elements of the vampire change accordingly. For instance, the vampires of paranormal romance (especially when male) display characteristics that are seen as proper to the genre: heightened sexual urges, developed muscular bodies, courage in battle, and unavoidable instincts of protection towards their mates. In similar vein, vampire from sub-genres such as the vampire thriller are often portrayed as cold, inhuman, Nosferatu-like creatures, unable to connect to humans—their source of food—on an empathetic level, let alone a sexual one. In this framework, the names of series for vampire literature are an important agent of the branding process: the serial titles—*Black Dagger Brotherhood, Midnight Breed, Nathaniel Cade, Twilight* saga, *The Dresden Files, Sookie Stackhouse*, to mention but a few—do not simply identify texts from a similar storyline for cataloguing purposes. Identification here constructs the brand. The recognisable name of the vampire series tells the readers what to expect, and, in so doing, transforms the vampire from an ephemeral concept into a paradoxically tangible virtual object.

Certain types of vampire, within certain literary contexts, promise to provide certain feelings, whether it is the dreamy fantasy of a fanged lover, or the thrill of an uncanny encounter with a merciless, inhuman creature. Operating within the realm of sign value, the branded vampire series creates not only expectation, but also affiliation and membership. Through this process, the vampire becomes a form of virtual capital. This is the core component of the value that the vampire, as a brand, provides consumers with. Adrvisson summarises the brand as agent through which consumers can 'feel' and 'be' in a particular way.[85] The literary vampire, therefore, is exposed as a frame of action. Just like any other brand, the vampire is not actual—it cannot really be touched as such—but is, in the Baudrillardian sense, 'real'. It exists though knowledge of the consumer, and is given a position in the world of value as a form of simulated presence. It may not have the tangibility of the actual but, through its branded components, finds a way of existing in people's minds—in the anthological sense—that transcends the physical, the composite, and the material. And we see that, while hinting at symbolic and cultural connections that glamorise contemporary post-industrial life, the vampire's consumer space pluralises the political, intellectual and aesthetic colonisation of the Gothic literary genre by media and product. In its branded ephemerality, the vampire 'lives'.

Conclusion

It seems somewhat paradoxical to have a 'conclusion' in a book that openly suggests vampires to be changeable and able to mutate according to context. Having any definitive, conclusive remarks would contravene any analytical and interpretative approach to the literary vampire as an evolutionary figure of interest and meaning. Chapter 1 uncovered the role of the vampire as a metaphor for genetic concerns, medical aspirations, cultural blending, and the possible fear of extinction in contemporary Western society. Developing on the same thread, Chapter 2 focused on the vampire body as an allegory of both unity and disconnection, once again pivoting around the fundamental concept of humanity, and how visions of the vampire's physicality are intrinsically connected to the boundaries and limitations of our human selves, and the inevitably eroticisation of what is perceived as superior and powerful. Chapter 3 unearthed the vampire as channelling preoccupations with social and technological control, and the 'loss of mind' in an increasingly more digitalised Western society. Developing on the concept of habits and customs, Chapter 4 offered an analysis of the ritualised nature of the vampire's existence in contemporary popular literature in connection to social regulation, cultural affiliation, and historical memory. In similar vein, Chapter 5 continued the analysis of vampiric territorialisation by considering both the geographical and conceptual spaces occupied by the vampire in its literary and popular frameworks, highlighting preoccupations related to the commodification of existence in its various forms, especially in terms of genre, expectation, and readership. In its evaluations of the literary vampire as it appears in the contemporary moment, this book has not functioned as a comprehensive and definitive study, but rather as a point of departure, a map for navigating the evolution and changes that the vampire is promising to go through in future years. As such, these findings also have prognostic value.

In these terms, it seems only fitting to conclude with an evaluation of what has become most salient about the portrayal of the vampire itself, and how it interacts with important issues of a social and cultural nature, as this relationship has functioned as one of the principal preoccupations of this study. Joan Gordon and Veronica Hollinger point out that, in the late twentieth century, the vampire inhabited 'the postmodern milieu', representing the effects of 'dissolving borders' and the 'breaking down of cultural' boundaries.[1] This idea seems to suggest that vampires were well-matched predominantly with fluid and undefined groups, moving from circle to circle and defying the reliance on any given sense of organisation, especially those connected to socio-cultural regulation. While this persuasive view might have rung true of pre-2000 incarnations, vampires in the new century have definitely organised. Structures have appeared, one might argue, in response to that sense of cultural and social desegregation that was seen as proper to the postmodern moment in the 1980s and 1990s.

The concept of structure and social organisation has altered in contemporary vampire fiction. In the post-2000 era, one can see a definite shift in the way in which vampire groups are perceived, moving away from single or small gatherings of supernatural creatures, and establishing ritualised structures that are governed by individuals and official organisations in a socio-political way. While vampires in the nineteenth and twentieth centuries seemed to prefer solitude or, on occasions, the company of specifically selected individuals—whether human or not—to spend their immortal days with, twenty-first-century incarnations show a predilection for solid civilisations, entire cities inhabited by vampires both under and above ground.

Indeed, while an intended social and cultural differentiation may have been abhorred and shunned by the fluid postmodern vampires of the pre-2000 era, vampires now make a stand in underpinning their difference, gathering in groups which are organised by laws and strict regulations. These regulations are not only what maintains vampire societies, but also what differentiates them from other groups, whether human or supernatural. Cornelius Castoriadis has long argued that all societies are 'dependent' upon the creation of 'webs of meaning' that are carried by society's institutions and individuals.[2] Society, in these terms, is a self-creation that depends upon values and norms that help to give it a sense of unity. It is not uncommon to find strict political structures regulating the vampire's world in the fiction. In seeking organisation, vampire now show a desire for micro and macro structures, hailing the importance of family (on several occasions) and obeying the rules of their supernatural world. Prevalence is often given to feudal systems, with vampire 'lords' operating at the top of the power pyramid, as proposed in Reynolds' *Vampires in America* novels. Monarchy is also a favourite form of government in the vampire world, with the *Sookie Stackhouse* and *Black Dagger Brotherhood* series providing apt examples here. In the latter, the importance of ruling and having a guide to 'lead' the vampire populations is of paramount importance. Ward's statement that all vampire 'must follow' the king, and the he is 'the beating heart' of vampire society, leaves no doubt on the importance placed on control, regulation, legality and social boundary.[3] So the vampire no longer stands for metaphors of dissolution and social disintegration, but reflects a Western desire for congregation and establishment. One might venture to say that, far from shunning cultural certainty, the vampire has established a culture in its own right, rejecting that overall sense of fluidity which was symptomatic of the late twentieth century.

In a sense, the shifts in vampire persona and habits have been instrumental in creating vampire societies, which are highly organised and relying on boundaries. Gordon and Hollinger also claim that, in the late twentieth century, the vampire reflected 'border anxieties', and the dissolution of boundaries. This idea comes from an analysis of the very nature of the vampire, challenging boundaries between 'life and death', 'love and fear', and 'power and persecution'.[4] Gordon and Hollinger's perspective was strictly reliant on a particular understanding of the vampire itself. Firstly, their idea seems to be based on the certainty that vampires are 'dead', or, more precisely, that they used to be human and, through some form of turning, they have become the famous 'undead'. Secondly, the fascination with the vampire from a human perspective is also reliant on some form of emotional attachment on both parts. Finally, Gordon and Hollinger draw attention to vampires as a persecuted, hunted group, who shun any public contact with humans or other supernatural creatures, in spite of their own great power to take life. While one could see how this interpretation of the vampire might encourage the concept of 'breaking boundaries' (in a human sense), it is also essential to consider that, in post-2000 embodiments of the vampire motif, the concept itself may have become obsolete. If boundaries to be broken still exist, they are those of humanity itself, and how the vampire channels the limitations of the human being, particularly in its genetic understanding.

In these terms, one of the most noteworthy characteristic of contemporary popular literature is that, in a number of examples, vampires are not 'undead', nor were they ever turned from humans. Similarly, vampires do not exist in as persecuted group; they do not fear humans and, even when they are hunted—as in the case of Laurell K. Hamilton's *Anita Blake* and Faith Hunter's *Jane Yellowrock* narrative universes—they still manage to maintain separation and control on most occasions. If there is persecution, it exists strictly in the vampire world, reinforcing the interdependence of cultural difference and social groupingh—even in their supernatural incarnations. Indeed, on most occasions, vampires are not supernatural at all, but exist in concomitance with other species, earthly and grounded just like humans are. Secrecy is maintained for protection and to prevent 'mixing and mingling' with humans, who are often seen as an inferior and useless group. This is particularly true of the world created by J.R. Ward, where vampires do not even need to make contact with humans, as they do not feed on human blood.

Even in those instances where they appear as physically decaying, the vampires are far from being dispersed and disenfranchised, and even with the transformational barrier of life and death firmly in place—and I do mean this in vampire-human terms—the vampires seek organisation and regulation. Indeed, it is their quality as a separate entity which makes them pursue the existence of a cultural grouping in its own right. If it is true that the vampire 'penetrates boundaries' by its very nature,[5] then it must be understood that those boundaries—when they do exist—are constructed by the vampires as much as they are felt by those around them. Therefore, boundaries—in their broader sense—are still a very strong presence in post-2000 literature, but their function and outlook have undeniably changed. Although the distinction between life and death, human and non-human still exists, it has become a symptom of the desire for stability and recognition which, far from being abhorred by the vampiric world, speaks volumes about a very human desire for social permanence. It is precisely that sense of boundary and separation that highlights the vampire as a metaphor for simultaneous and paradoxical distinction and homogeneity, a figure of 'otherness' in which, through a distinctly twenty-first century need for group affirmation in the human world, 'we find a version of' ourselves'.[6]

It would seem that, even in the twenty-first century, a decisive and all-encompassing definition of the vampire escapes us. Although there are common grounds and mythologies that find mileage in a number of storylines, the answer to the ontological question of what a 'vampire 'is' is still virtually impossible to find. The difficulties with definitions are what make the vampires an adaptable creation, one that can mutate in concept and context. The vampire is able to evolve. What is certain, even if the delineations of motives are obscured, is that the vampire functions as an apt mirror for human society's anxieties and desires. Nina Auerbach has long suggested that our Westerns societies 'live in a continuing crisis', and the vampire, in this context, allows cultural worries to 'take shape'.[7] This, I believe, is an important point that has emerged from my study: the changes that the vampire has undergone—as minimal or as great as they may be—are a reflection of the context in which it has developed. Indeed, one might venture to say that the vampire itself does not in fact 'change', at least not in the conventional sense, with in its Gothic framework. What does change is, of course, the context, the technologies, the preoccupations, and the aspired solutions of a given society at a given time. The vampire mediates these concerns and allows their latent nature to become manifest through notions of the monstrous, the desirable, and the uncanny. The mutations that we perceive as pertaining to the vampire are in fact the changes of the cultural context in which the creature is placed.

In terms of mutations and literary connections, further scholarship may need to address the place of the vampire metaphor within the wider Gothic context, evaluating how it functions in relation to the framework of terror in its various manifestations. A comparative study of the vampire in relation to other 'Gothic creatures'—such as werewolves, ghosts, and doppelgangers—might reveal the power of representation in terms of reflexive aesthetics and relational construction in the global cultural framework. A developing area of interest that this book has suggested is how the impact of the contemporary literary vampire extends beyond the literature itself. This comment is not formed only in relation to television and film adaptations—which, in the contemporary context, most certainly abound—but to the outreach of literary structures into more arguably unexplored areas of production, such as the digital media. A number of scholars have already identified the internet as an important communicative centre for the Goth sub-culture. Paul Hodkinson has, among others, conceptualised the idea of 'goth websites' and 'goth discussion groups' as an important part of the exchanges that aid the construction of identity for individuals participants within the sub-culture.[8] A similar analysis could be pursued through the specificity of the literary vampire as both subject and object, as the internet is, undoubtedly, an influential source where 'the vampire' finds multiple incarnations. And while the number of web sites that focus on vampires as such are truly unaccountable, a specific type of role-play based web site maintains a strong relationship to the literary world. Numerous forums and discussion boards have been created where members interact not only with each other, but with digitalised versions of their favourite literary characters. This type of message board and forum area, where vampires are both the focus of discussion and engaged actors, removes the vampires themselves from the 'virtual'—in the Deleuzian sense—context of the internet, and allows them to take shape as an almost tangible force of the modern, twenty-first-century context.

The vampire forum is not only proof of the 'sociological impact' of the internet—as Alison Cavanagh put it—but also opens the way for re-valuating the place of the Gothic in interpersonal and well as literary structures.[9] A widely-known example of this is the message board for the ever-popular *Black Dagger Brotherhood*, where avid fans interact with the vampires of the series, who answer questions and discuss—in a rather surreal twist— their favourites foods, movies, and pastimes. In these recent incarnations of 'cyber-fangs', the popular representation of the vampire breaks the literary fourth-wall and is transported into the fictional hyper-reality of the web site. A point worth noting is that this type of forum interaction—centred on the conceptual blending between the ephemeral and the material—finds its greatest popularity in relation to literary characters belonging to the paranormal romance genres, to which most volumes of the *Black Dagger Brotherhood* series clearly belong. It is not difficult to imagine the appeal of such a form of communication, where the fantasy of the sexualised male vampire extends from the fictional series into what is seemingly understood as 'real life'.

While hinting at symbolic and cultural connections that glamorise the paranormal romance, the metaphysical vampires of the literary-inspired web sites pluralise the political, intellectual, and aesthetic colonisation of the Gothic literary genre by digital enterprise. The impact is undoubtedly monumental not only in terms of the commodification of the vampire character itself, but also in relation to marketing and socio-economic frameworks. The literary vampire's dedicated web sites—among others—complicate the idea of Gothic fiction, as vampiric characters take shape in an uncanny manner. Outreaching into the digital world, the 'real life' vampires of the forums and message boards act as improbable Gothic celebrities, highlighting the social, cultural and economic corollary of the vampire effect in the wider cultural scope. The future of the vampire, one might even be tempted to say, lies in the connection between contemporary popular fictions and their respective fan-based web sites, as the interlinked and interlaced conceptual dependency between the two provides further insights into the popularisation and domestication of the Gothic as part of an accessible and easily manipulated everyday framework.

Notes

NOTES TO THE INTRODUCTION

1. Jean Baudrillard, *Fatal Strategies* (Los Angeles: Semiotext(e), 2008), 71.
2. Justin Edwards and Aignieszka Monnet, "Introduction: From Goth/ic to Pop Goth," in *The Gothic in Contemporary Literature and Popular Culture: Pop Goth*, ed. Justin Edwards and Aignieszka Monnet (London: Routledge, 2012), 8.
3. Joan Gordon and Veronica Hollinger, "Introduction: The Shape of Vampires," in *Blood Read: The Vampire as Metaphor in Contemporary Culture*, ed. Joan Gordon and Veronica Hollinger (Philadelphia: University of Pennsylvania Press, 1997), 1.
4. Fred Botting, *Gothic Romanced: Consumption, Gender and Technology in Contemporary Fictions* (Abingdon: Routledge, 2008), 96.
5. Fred Botting, "Hypocrite Vampire." *Gothic Studies* 9, No. 1 (2007): 31.
6. Nina Auerbach, *Our Vampires, Ourselves* (Chicago: University of Chicago Press, 1995), 3.
7. Ibid., 194.
8. Milly Williamson, *The Lure of the Vampire: Gender, Fiction and Fandom from Bram Stoker to Buffy* (London: Wallflower Press), 2.
9. Jules Zanger, "Metaphor into Metonymy: The *Vampire* Next Door" in in *Blood Read; The Vampire as Metaphor in Contemporary Culture*, ed. Joan Gordon and Veronica Hollinger (Philadelphia: University of Pennsylvania Press, 1997), 19.
10. Rebecca Housel and J. Jeremy Wisnewski, 'Introduction: Undead Wisdom', in *Twilight and Philosophy: Vampires, Vegetarians, and the Pursuit of Immortality*, ed. Rebecca Housel and J. Jeremy Wisnewski (Hoboken, NJ: Wiley), 1.
11. Fred Botting, "Aftergothic," in *The Cambridge Companion to Gothic Fiction*, ed. Jerrold Hogle (Cambridge, UK: Cambridge University Press, 2002), 287.
12. Williamson, *The Lure of the Vampire*, 2.
13. As far as sex and vampires are concerned, my critical starting point is the realisation that there has been a shift in conceptualisation, and that sex itself is no longer the cultural taboo under scrutiny. While in previous centuries sex occupied the latent position when the vampire's sucking was concerned, it has now become –if still present in the narrative—the manifest pretext through which other concerns can be uncovered, such as genetics, the role of the family, and the place of digital technologies in everyday life.
14. S.T. Joshi, "Foreward," in *21st Century Gothic: Great Gothic Novels Since 2000*, ed. Daniel Olson (Lanham, MD: Scarecrow Press, 2011), xi.

15. Ibid., xvii.
16. Danel Olson, "Introduction," in *21ˢᵗ Century Gothic: Great Gothic Novels Since 2000*, ed. Daniel Olson (Lanham, MD: Scarecrow Press, 2011), xxviii.
17. Joshi, "Foreward," xi.
18. Botting, "Aftergothic," 287.
19. Olson, "Introduction," xxviii.
20. Judyth McLeod, *Vampires: A Bite-sized History* (St. Leonards: Pier 9, 2011), 10.
21. Ibid., 11.
22. Ibid., 7.
23. Tim Kane, *The Changing Vampire of Film and Television: A Critical Study of the Growth of a Genre* (Jefferson, NC: McFarland, 2006), 3.
24. Joshi, "Foreward," xvii.
25. John Frow, *Genre* (Abingdon: Routledge, 2005), 1.
26. Ibid., 2.
27. Amy J. Devitt, *Writing Genres* (Carbondale, IL: Southern Illinois University Board of Trustees, 2008), 166.
28. Botting, *Gothic Romanced*, 2.
29. Gail Weiss, *Refiguring the Ordinary* (Bloomington: Indiana University Press, 2008), 6.
30. Frow, *Genre*, 4.
31. Gilles Deleuze and Félix Guattari, *A Thousand Plateaus* (London: Continuum, 1987), 360.
32. Nick Fox and Katie Ward, "What Are Health Identities and How May We Study Them?" *Sociology of Health & Illness* 30, no. 7 (2008): 1007–1021.

NOTES TO CHAPTER 1

1. Thomas Parmalee, *Genetic Engineering* (Edina, MN: ABDO, 2008), p. 19.
2. Jon F. Merz, *The Fixer* (Seattle, WA: Digital Books, 2002), 20.
3. J.R. Ward, *Lover Eternal* (London: Piatkus, 2006), 163.
4. J.R. Ward, *Dark Lover* (London: Piatkus, 2005), 70.
5. J.R. Ward, *Lover Unbound* (London: Piatkus, 2007), 117.
6. Inge Wise, "Introduction," in *Adolescence*, ed. Inge Weiss (London: Karnac, 2005), 1. Pp. 1–6
7. The peculiar shift 'into' being a vampire—and yet not through any form of genetic change from the human being—is also entertained in Christine Feehan's *Carpathians* series and Harrison's *Hollows* saga. In the former, the Carpathians are a separate race that survives by drinking the blood of humans. In this, however, they are not 'vampires' as such, in that they do not kill their prey when feeding. Vampires do exist, but they are a later stage (and avoidable) stage of the Carpathian existence; vampires are transformed creatures that are completely consumed by bloodlust, and void of consciousness and 'morality'. The idea of vampiric transition is still present in Feehan's storyline, but its occurrence is somewhat peculiar. Carpathians only succumb to becoming 'vampires' if they cannot find their destined mate, who will save them from their murderous futures as the vampires of horror and folklore. In Harrison's *Hollows*, all vampires are born as mortal creatures. Although not gifted with unlimited strength and power, they can withstand sunlight and can control their need for blood when needed. Born vampires do not come into their 'true self' until they die; at this stage, they become brutal, soulless creatures who are dependent on large amounts of blood to

live. Harrison maintains a clear division—corporeal, psychological, and political—between 'alive' and 'dead' vampires, stressing the greater powers that the latter possess: 'Dead vamps were utterly without conscience, ruthless instinct incarnate [. . .] They needed blood daily to keep sane. [. . .] And they were powerful, having incredible strength and endurance [. . .] In exchange for their soul, they had a chance for immortality'. *Dead Witch Walking* (2004; London; Voyager, 2006), 10.

8. Barb Karg, Arjean Spaite, and Rick Sutherland, *The Everything Vampire Book* (Avon, MA: Adams Media, 2009), 76.

9. Scott Mariani, *Uprising* (New York: Avon, 2010), 468.

10. Charlaine Harris, *Definitely Dead* (2006; London: Gollancz, 2007), 175.

11. Karg, Spaite, and Sutherland, *The Everything Vampire Book* (76).

12. Kristen Painter, *Flesh and Blood* (London: Orbit, 2011), 273.

13. Ibid.

14. D.B. Reynolds, *Duncan* (Canon City, CO: ImagJinn Books, 2011), 88.

15. Chloe Neill, *Some Girls Bite* (2009; London: Gollancz, 2010), 2.

16. Charlaine Harris, *Dead to the World* (2004; London; Gollancz, 2005), 45.

17. Scott Mariani, *The Cross* (New York; Avon, 2011), 199.

18. Ward, *Lover Eternal*, 94.

19. J.R. Ward, *Lover Enshrined* (London: Piatkus, 2008).

20. J.R. Ward *Lover Revealed* (London: Piatkus, 2007), 105.

21. Justin Cronin, *The Passage* (London; Orion, 2010) , 88.

22. Vampire folklore leaves no doubt about the nature of the association between roaming creatures of the night and animals. The ability to transform, command or even associate—psychologically, rather than physically—with animals is seen as a negative trait. Wolves, bats, and insects have been at the centre of the association for centuries, and the exchange has definitely been detrimental to the cultural perception of these animals in Western societies. On the literary front, *Dracula* had undoubtedly a big part to play in cementing the relationship between vampire and animal transformations, also strengthening the connection between the animalistic (and therefore 'not human') qualities of the vampire and what is seen as evil. The sexual aspect of the exchange was definitely one that received particular attention. Animal responses in *Dracula* are connected to the undead's vitality and virility, his associations with the beasts a reflection of his uncontrollable urges—for both blood and otherwise—which, Bosky suggests, in being literally 'animal', are perceived 'repulsive' (Bosky, 221). The Twentieth century, however, changed things, and the association between vampires and 'animal instincts' was greatly re-evaluated in several contexts. While a connection between virility and animal instincts remains, the vision has been remoulded around notions of love, romance and coveted sexual possession. Especially towards the end of the Twentieth century, and consequently, in the twenty-first century, examples of fiction from vampire erotica and paranormal romance transformed animal or beast-like impulses on the vampire's part into a positive and coveted occurrence. In twenty-first century fiction, this association has always been particularly evident when male vampires are involved, the animalistic and particularly territorial responses to their mates understood as a definitive characteristic of the characters themselves. The vampires 'growl' and 'sniff' to ascertain their surroundings. They are able to recognise individuals according to their smells—imperceptible to humans— just like an animal would.

23. D.B. Reynolds, *Raphael* (Canon City,CO: ImaJinn Books, 2009), 92; *Duncan*, 74.

24. Susannah Sandlin, *Redemption* (Seattle, WA: Montlake, 2012), 21.

25. Ward, *Lover Eternal*, 277.
26. Stephenie Meyer, *The Twilight Saga: The Official Illustrated Guide* (London: Atom, 2011), 69.
27. Stephenie Meyer, *Twilight* (2005: London: Atom, 2011), 229.
28. A note here must be included about humans affected by albinism; on the surface, these individuals could be claimed to have red or pink eyes. However, the specific coloration is caused not by chromatic shades in the iris, but from their absence, which renders the iris itself clear and 'see through'. The red coloration results from the refraction of the blood vessels underneath, giving the illusion that the iris is actually red, when it is not.
29. L.D. Vijendra Das, *Genetics and Plant Breeding* (New Delhi; New Age Publishing, 2006), 13.
30. Gene Helfman and Bruce Collette, *Fishes: The Animal Answer Guide* (Baltimore, MD: John Hopkins University Press, 2011), 32.
31. Gordon Melton, *The Vampire Book: The Encyclopaedia of the Undead* (Canton, MI: visible Print Press, 2011), 22.
32. In human terms, eye colour is not even the result of one gene or its selection. There are many genes involved in the decision and determination of colour. The process for eye colour delineation in human genomic formation is intricate; suffice it to say, for our purposes, that eye colour—once determined by the genetic material that is present at birth—cannot naturally change through conduct or habit.
33. Craig Hamilton Parker, *The Hidden Meaning of Dreams* (New York: Sterling, 1999), 45.
34. A number of examples exist where new incarnations of the vampire do not in fact need to consume blood at all. A prominent example here is the White Court in Butcher's *The Dresden Files*, vampires who actually survive by 'draining' psychic energy from victims. Even if blood is not what is exchanged, the principle of exchanging a symbolic life force remains.
35. Nina Auerbach, *Our Vampires, Ourselves* (Chicago: University of Chicago Press, 1995), 57.
36. Rebecca Housel and J. Jeremy Wisnewski, eds., *Twilight and Philosophy: Vampires, Vegetarians, and the Pursuit of Immortality* (Hoboken, NJ: Wiley); E. David Klonsky and Alexis Black, eds., *The Psychology of Twilight* (Dallas, TX: Smart Pop, 2011); and Melissa A. Click, Jennifer Stevens Aubrey and Elizabeth Behn-Morawitz, eds., *Bitten by Twilight: Youth Culture, Media & the Vampire Franchise* (New York: Peter Lang, 2010).
37. Charlaine Harris, *Deadlocked* (London: Gollancz, 2012), 86.
38. Sharman Russell, *Hunger: An Unnatural History* (New York: Basic Books, 2008), 15.
39. Elspeath Probyn, *Carnal Appetites: FoodSexIdentities* (London: Routledge, 2000).
40. Auerbach, *Our Vampires, Ourselves*, 57.
41. George Slusser, "Introduction: Of Foods, Gods, and Men: The Theory and Practice of Science Fictional Eating," in *Food of the Gods; Eating and the Eaten in Fantasy and Science Fiction*, ed. Gary Westfahl, George Slusser and Eric Rabkin (Athens, GA: University of Georgia Press, 1996), 3.
42. Mary Pharr, 'Vampiric Appetite in *I Am Legend*, *Salem's Lot* and *The Hunger*', in *The Blood is the Life: Vampires in Literature*, ed. Leonard G. Heldreth and Mary Pharr (Bowling Green, OH: Bowling Green State University Popular Press), 93.
43. Nick Fiddes, *Meat: A Natural Symbol* (Lond: Routledge, 1991), 69.
44. Russell, *Hunger: An Unnatural History*, 1.

45. David Wellington, *Thirteen Bullets* (St. Leonards: Allen and Unwin, 2007), 290.
46. Michael Crockett and Desda Cox, *The Subversive Vegetarian: Tactics, Information and Recipes for the Conversion of Meat Eaters* (Wellingborough: Thorsons, 1979), 18.
47. Ibid., 19.
48. Christopher Farnsworth, *Blood Oath* (London: Hodder and Stoughton, 2010), 147.
49. Ibid., 153.
50. Ibid.
51. Paul and Anne Ehrlich, *The Dominant Animal: Human Evolution and the Environment* (Washington, DC: First Island Press, 2008), 68.
52. David Wellington, *Vampire Zero* (St. Leonards: Allen and Unwin, 2008), 310.
53. Fiddes, *Meat: A Natural Symbol*, 65.
54. Ward, *Dark Lover.*
55. L.J. Smith, *The Vampires Diaries series* (New York: Harper Collins, 1991–2001).
56. G.E. Coover and S.T. Murphy, "The Communicated Self: Exploring the Interaction between Self and Social Context," *Human Communication Research* 26 (2000): 125. Pp. 125—147.
57. Eric M. Eisenberg, "Building a Mystery: Towards a New Theory of Communication and Identity," *Journal of Communication* 51 (2001) 534—552.
58. Raka Shome and Radha Hedge, "Postcolonial Approaches to Communication: Charting Terrain, Engaging the Intersections," *Communication Theory*, 12.3 (2002): 266.
59. Amber Zimmerman and Patricia Geist-Martin, "The Hybrid Identities of Genderqueer: Claiming neither/nor, both/and." *Intercultural Communication: A Reader*, ed. Larry A. Samovar, Richard Porter, Edwin McDaniel (Boston, MA: Wadsworth, 2006): 88.
60. Marwan M. Kraidy, "Hybridity in Cultural Globalization," *Communication Theory* 12.3 (2002) 317.
61. Meyer, *The Twilight Saga: The Official Illustrated Guide*, 146.
62. Homi Bhabha, *The Location of Culture* (London and New York: Routledge, 2004), 122.
63. Zimmerman and Geist-Martin, "The Hybrid Identities of Genderqueer: Claiming neither/nor, both/and.", 89.
64. Stephenie Meyer, *Breaking Dawn* (London: Atom, 2009).
65. Bhabha, *The Location of Culture*, 3.
66. Gloria Andaluza, *Borderlands/La Frontera* (San Francisco: Aunt Lute, 1999).
67. Bhabha, *The Location of Culture*, 3.
68. Ibid., 49.
69. Ibid., 89.
70. Gust A. Yep, "The Violence of Heteronormativity in Communication Studies," *Journal of Homosexuality* 45.3 (2003): 35. Yep is discussing the 'state of queer' here, rather than strictly hybrid. However, the conceptual correlations between the two make it possible to translate this understanding of queer identity into the hybrid framework. The two, one might argue, are known to function in much the same way within and across cultures.
71. Ibid.
72. Mariani, *The Cross*, 93.
73. Ibid., 398.

74. Lara Adrian, *Kiss of Midnight* (Constable & Robinson, 2009), 233.
75. Jenny Wolmark, *Aliens and Others: Science Fiction, Feminism, Postmodernism* (Iowa City, IA: University of Iowa Press, 1994), 2.
76. Ibid.
77. Adrian, *Kiss of Midnight*, 202.
78. Linda Bosniak, *The Citizen and the Alien: Dilemmas of Contemporary Membership* (Princeton, NJ: Princeton University Press, 2006), 1.
79. Adrian, *Kiss of Midnight*, 94.
80. Mariani, *The Cross*, 398.
81. Parmalee, *Genetic Engineering*, 21.
82. Ibid.
83. See *The Passage, Twilight*, and *Uprising*. Cronin's explicit definition of vampirism as a 'virus' in *The Passage* also extends to outlining how the virus itself ravages the host's body, while paradoxically making it stronger: 'Their immune systems had gone into overdrive. A hugely accelerated rate of cellular regeneration'. 52.
84. "How do We Fight against a Virus Attack?" http://news.softpedia.com/news/How-Do-Our-Bodies-FIght-Against-Viruses-039-Attack-52395.shtml.
85. Arlene Russo, *Vampire Nation* (Woodbury, MN: Llewellyn, 2005), 85.
86. Parmalee, *Genetic Engineering*, 23. There are other two methods known to be used: plasmid and biolistic. The latter is mainly used for the genetic modification of plants. The plasmid method is most often used on mammals and birds; scientists remove a section of DNA from one organism and replace it with the DNA of another.
87. Cronin, *The Passage*, 111.
88. Ward, *Lover Eternal*, 224.
89. Ward, *Lover Unbound*, 179.
90. Cronin, *The Passage*, 52.
91. Parmalee, *Genetic Engineering*, 8.
92. Charles E. Rosenberg, "Introduction: Framing Disease," in *Framing Disease: Studies in Cultural History*, ed. Charles E. Rosenberg and Lynne Golden (New Brunswick, NJ: Rutgers University Press, 1992), xiii.
93. Ibid., xvii.
94. Ibid., xiii.
95. Ibid., xiv.
96. Ibid.
97. Christopher Farnsworth, *The President's Vampire* (London: Hodder and Stoughton, 2011), 52–53.
98. Farnsworth, *Blood Oath*, 36 and 133.
99. That isolation is only viewable as such in 'human terms'. The vampire as such does not feel isolated because he does not operate through the same empathic system.
100. Rosenberg, "Introduction: Framing Disease," xviii.
101. Ibid.
102. Nick Fox and Katie Ward, "What Are Health Identities and How May We Study Them?" *Sociology of Health & Illness* 30.7 (2008): 1007–1021.
103. Deborah Lupton, *Medicine as Culture: Illness, Disease and the Body* (Thousand Oaks, CA: SAGE, 2012), vii.
104. Ward, *Dark Lover*, 87.
105. Lara Adrian, *Kiss of Crimson* (London: Constable & Robinson, 2009).
106. Lupton, *Medicine as Culture: Illness, Disease and the Body*, vii.
107. Mariani, *The Cross*, 160.

108. Mariani, *Uprising*, 34.
109. Lupton, *Medicine As Culture: Illness, Disease and the Body*, vii.
110. Mariani, *The Cross*, 160.
111. Mariani, *Uprising*, 14.
112. Mary Douglas, Mary Douglas, *Purity and Danger An Analysis of Pollution and Taboo* (New York: Routledge, 2002), 128.
113. Bryan S. Turner, *Regulating Bodies: Essays in Medical Sociology* (London and New York: Routledge, 1992).
114. Lupton, *Medicine as Culture: Illness, Disease and the Body*, vii.
115. Ibid.
116. Kevin Ashman, *Vampire* (Abiquiu, NM: Silverback, 2012), 195 and 166.
117. Ibid., 272.
118. Ibid., 146.
119. As well as describing the vampire's body as superior, Ashman also stresses the weakness of the human form by describing how some humans are desperate to improve their fragile bodies through medical intervention: 'there are people in this world who will pay an absolute fortune for even the possibility of a few extra years'. *Vampire*, 218.
120. Lupton, *Medicine as Culture: Illness, Disease and the Body*, 22.
121. Ibid., viii.
122. Parmalee, *Genetic Engineering*, 8
123. Farnsworth, *Blood Oath*, 147
124. Parmalee, Genetic Engineering, 8.
125. Harrison, *Dead Witch Walking*, 10.
126. Farnsworth, Blood Oath, 79.
127. Mariani, *The Cross*, 28; Farnsworth, *Blood Oath*, 255; Painter, *Blood Rights*, 286. These instances function here only as evocative examples of vampires being called 'monsters' in the fiction, a widespread occurrence that prescribes their status as not only different, but as 'other'.
128. Ward, *Lover Unbound*, 178.
129. Pramod K. Nayar, *An Introduction to Media and Cybercultures* (Oxford: Wiley-Blackwell, 2010), 56.
130. Ibid., 57.
131. Ibid.
132. Ibid.
133. Geoffrey Galt Harpman, *On the Grotesque: Strategies of Contradiction in Art and Literature* (1982; Pasadena, CA: Davies, 2006).
134. Suzanne Anker and Dorothy Nelkin. *The Molecular Gaze: Art in the Genetic Age* (New York: Cold Spring Harbor Laboratory Press, 2004), 109.
135. Of course, other historical instances of the 'laboratory uncanny' exist in Gothic literature across the centuries, with Mary Shelley's *Frankenstein* (1818) and Robert Louis Stevenson's *The Strange Case of Dr Jekyll and Mr Hyde* (1886) functioning as prime examples here.

NOTES TO CHAPTER 2

1. Elizabeth Grosz, *Volatile Bodies* (Bloomington: Indiana University Press, 1994), 190.
2. Ibid.
3. Ibid., 191.
4. Ibid.
5. Ibid.

6. Chris Shilling, *The Body in Culture, Technology and Society* (London: SAGE, 2005), 31. Shilling is referring to the human body here, but his consideration on the impacts of social organisation on corporeal experience can be applied and are also relevant to the vampire.

7. Ibid.

8. Ibid., 41.

9. Ibid.

10. See Anne Rice, *Interview with the Vampire* (1976; London: Warner Books, 1999).

11. Rob Latham, *Consuming Youth: Vampires, Cyborgs, and the Culture of Consumption* (Chicago: Chicago University, 2002), 1.

12. Clearly, however, youth is not a necessary gift in the vampire world, and it is especially absent if the mythology of being 'frozen' in the state in which one is transformed is maintained. A particular example of this can be found in the *Sookie Stackhouse* series, where the Ancient Pythoness—a vampire who is 'ancient' in terms of years, but also in appearance—looks like an old woman. The Pythoness was turned into a vampire too late in her life, and even the power of vampiric transformation could not cure old age and confer upon the body the splendour of passed youth. Youth, it would seem, is a gift that vampirism only bestows on the young, a concrete irony which is hard to miss. See: Charlaine Harris, *All Together Dead* (2007; London: Gollancz, 2008).

13. Bernadette Lynn Bosky, "Making the Implicit, Explicit: Vampire Erotica and Pornography," in *The Blood is the Life: Vampires in Literature*, ed. Leonard G. Heldreth and Mary Pharr (Bowling Green, Oh: Bowling Green State University Popular Press), 218.

14. Ibid.

15. Jim Butcher, *Blood Rites* (2004; London: Orbit, 2005), 24.

16. Adam Barrows, "Heidegger the Vampire Slayer: The Undead and Fundamental Ontology," in *Zombies, Vampires, and Philosophy: New Life for the Undead*, ed. Richard Greene and K. Silem Mohammad (Chicago, IL: Open Court Publishing, 2010), 72.

17. Ibid.

18. Ibid.

19. Ibid., 72

20. Ibid., 73.

21. It is clear here that Heidegger is applying a Western perspective not only to the concept of death, but the ideological structures that surrounding it, such as funeral and ritual officiates. While the starting point for the formulating is inevitably flawed, the insights are extremely useful when considering the figure of the vampire in an Anglo-American context.

22. Barrows, "Heidegger the Vampire Slayer: The Undead and Fundamental Ontology," 74.

23. Ibid.

24. Ibid.

25. Kostantinos, *Vampires: The Occult Truth* (St.Paul, MN: Lllewellyn, 2004).

26. Bram Stoker, *Dracula* (Oxford: Oxford University Press, 1996), 216. Curiously, however, the main vampire of the novel is not killed by the famous wooden stake; Dracula is stabbed by a knife and subsequently turns to ashes, a somewhat anti-climactic end for such an intimidating and magnetic creature.

27. Kostantinos, *Vampires: The Occult Truth*, 99.

28. Ibid.

29. Thomas Staubli and Silvia Schroer, *Body Symbolism in the Bible* (Collegeville, MN: The Liturgical Press, 2001), 41.

30. Albert Howard Carter, *Our Human Hearts: A Medical and Cultural Journey* (Kent, OH: Kent State University Press, 2006), 192.
31. Ibid.
32. Staubli and Schroer, *Body Symbolism in the Bible*, 41.
33. Carter, *Our Human Hearts: A Medical and Cultural Journey*, 192.
34. Stephen Gislason, *Language and Thinking* (Sechelt: Persona Books, 2011), 150.
35. Ibid.
36. Carter, *Our Human Hearts: A Medical and Cultural Journey*, 158.
37. Ibid., 193.
38. Charlaine Harris, *Dead Until Dark*, (2001; London: Gollancz, 2004).
39. J.R. Ward, *Lover Unbound* (London: Piatkus, 2007), 84.
40. Kristen Painter, *Blood Rights* (London: Orbit, 2011), 200.
41. Kresley Cole, *The Warlord Wants Forever* (New York: Pocket Books, 2011), 95.
42. Staubli and Schroer, *Body Symbolism in the Bible*, 52.
43. Ibid., 52.
44. D.B. Reynolds, *Sophia* (Canon City, CO: ImaJinn Books, 2011), 151.
45. Deborah Harkness, *Shadow of Night* (London: Headline Publishing, 2012), 167.
46. Lara Adrian, *Kiss of Midnight* (Constable & Robinson, 2009), 44.
47. Ibid.
48. Lara Adrian, *Darker After Midnight* (Constable & Robinson, 2012), 110.
49. Ibid., 111.
50. Michael Wiederman, "Sociosexuality," in *Sex and Society, Vol. 3* (Tarrytown, NY: Marshall Cavendish, 2010), 666.
51. Mary Douglas, *Purity and Danger An Analysis of Pollution and Taboo* (New York: Routledge, 2002), 193.
52. Ibid.
53. Grosz, *Volatile Bodies*, 192.
54. Barb Karg, Arjean Spaite, and Rick Sutherland, *The Everything Vampire Book* (Avon, MA: Adams Media, 2009), 89.
55. See John Marks, *Fangland* (London, Vintage: 2007).
56. Numerous and uncountable examples of fangs 'elongating' can be found throughout contemporary popular fiction, from Ward's *Black Dagger Brotherhood* to Adrian's *Midnight Breed* and Mariani's *Vampire Federation* (to name but a few).
57. Stoker, *Dracula*, 18.
58. The fangs can be said to be reminiscent of snakes and therefore are representative of sexual intercourse, as the bite of 'the serpent' is an invasive act of possession which cases its victim to subdue. In his *Interpretation of Dreams*, Freud envisages the snake is the animal which is 'the most important symbol of the male member'. *The Interpretation of Dreams* (Ware: Wordsworth Classics, 1997), 198.
59. Karg, Spaite, and Sutherland, *The Everything Vampire Book*, 89.
60. David Wellington, *99 Coffins* (St. Leonards: Allen and Unwin, 2007), 12 and 40.
61. Jean-François Lyotard, *The Inhuman* (Cambridge, Polity, 1993), 2.
62. Ibid., 3.
63. Pasi Falk, *The Consuming Body* (London: SAGE, 1994), 55.
64. Georges Bataille, *Eroticism: Death and Sexuality* (New York: Walker and Company, 1986). Bataille refers particularly to the distinction experienced by the body when in presented to the distinction between everyday life and festive. Although his discussion does not include any mention of vampires

(unsurprisingly), Bataille's focus on the conceptualisation of normal and non-normal states in relation to corporeality become useful in unravelling the dynamics linking the vampire body to the human framework in terms of extraordinary experience.

65. Falk, *The Consuming Body*, 59.
66. D.B. Reynolds, *Lucas* (Canon City, CO: ImaJinn Books, 2012), 43.
67. Falk, *The Consuming Body*, 58.
68. Bataille, *Eroticism: Death and Sexuality*.
69. Falk, *The Consuming Body*, 59.
70. Harris, *Dead Until Dark*, 118 and 115.
71. Falk, *The Consuming Body*, 59. Of course, Freud's concept of regression is well-known and has been the centre of much scholarship and debate.
72. Ibid., 64.
73. Stoker, *Dracula*, 18—19.
74. Rice, *Interview with the Vampire*, 6.
75. The 'beautiful face' is not simply a characteristics of undead vampires, and not always portrayed a s gift bestowed during turning. Indeed, 'beautiful vampires' a strong presence even in examples where vampires are born, not turned. One such examples if Ward's *Black Dagger Brotherhood*, where physical beauty is the result of the purest and strongest genetic material within the species.
76. Giles Deleuze, *Nietzsche and Philosophy* (London: Continuum, 2005), 71.
77. James A Russell and José Miguel Fernandez-Dols, "What Does a facial Expression Mean?" in *The Psychology of Social Expression*, ed. James A Russell and José Miguel Fernandez-Dols (Cambridge: Cambridge University Press, 1997), 3.
78. Maurice Merleau-Ponty, *Sense and Non-sense* (Evanston, IL: Northwestern University Press, 1964), 52–53.
79. Thomas R. Alley, "Social and Applied Aspects of Face Perception: An Introduction," in *Social and Applied Aspects of Perceiving Faces*, ed. Thomas R. Alley (Hillsdale, NJ: Lawrence Erlbaum, 1988), 1.
80. Christopher Farnsworth, *Blood Oath* (London: Hodder and Stoughton, 2010); *The President's Vampire* (London: Hodder and Stoughton, 2011).
81. Alley, "Social and Applied Aspects of Face Perception: An Introduction," 2.
82. Painter, *Blood Rights*, 286.
83. Ibid., 48.
84. David Efron, *Gesture and Environment* (1941), cited in Georg Simmel "The Aesthetic Significance of the Face," in *The Body: Critical Concepts in Sociology*, ed. Andrew Blaikie (London: Routledge, 2004), 11.
85. Ibid., 11.
86. The fact that vampires 'wear' a human face also suggests an element of display, ornament, and performance, in the Barthesian sense. See: Roland Barthes, *Mythologies* (London: Grant & Cutler, 1994).
87. Jim Butcher, *Storm Front* (2000; London: Orbit, 2005).
88. Alley, "Social and Applied Aspects of Face Perception: An Introduction," 2
89. Adrian, *Kiss of Midnight*, 69.
90. Susan Bordo, *Unbearable Weight: Feminism, Western Culture, and the Body* (Berkeley, CA: University of California Press, 2003), 33.
91. Adrian, *Kiss of Midnight*, 69.
92. Ibid.
93. Lara Adrian, *Kiss of Crimson* (London: Constable & Robinson, 2009), 4.
94. Steve Connor, *The Book of Skin* (London: Reaktion, 2004), 96.
95. Gisli Palsson, *Anthropology and the New Genetics* (Cambridge: Cambridge University Press, 2007), 30.

96. Ibid., 33.
97. Ibid., 29.
98. Adrian, *Kiss of Midnight*, 36.
99. Elizabeth Grosz, "Inscriptions and Body-Maps: Representation and the Corporeal," in *Feminine, Masculine, and Representation*, ed. Terry Threadgold and Anne Cranny-Francis (Sydney: Allen & Unwin, 1990), 63.
100. Jane Caplan, *Written on the Body: The Tattoo in European and American History* (London: Reaktion, 2000), xiv.
101. Grosz, "Inscriptions and Body-Maps: Representation and the Corporeal," 65.
102. J.R. Ward, *Dark Lover* (London: Piatkus, 2005), 73.
103. J.R. Ward Lover Eternal (London: Piatkus, 2006), 183.
104. Ibid., 109.
105. Kenneth MacKinnon, *Representing Men: Maleness and Masculinity in the Media* (London: Arnold, 2003), 5.
106. Ward, *Lover Eternal*, 39.
107. Ibid., 73.
108. J.R. Ward, *Lover Awakened* (London: Piatkus, 2006), 39 and 245.
109. Laurence Goldstein, "Introduction," in *The Male Body: Features, Destinies, Exposures*, ed. Laurence Goldstein (Ann Arbor, Mi: University of Michigan Press, 1995), x.
110. Michael Messner, "When Bodies Are Weapons: Masculinity and Violence in Sport," *International Review for the Sociology of Sport* 25 (1990): 214.
111. R.W. Connell, *Masculinities* (Cambridge: Polity, 1995), 22.
112. Ibid.
113. J.R. Ward, *Lover Revealed* (London: Piatkus, 2007), 6.
114. Margery Hourihan, *Deconstructing the Hero: Literary Theory and Children's Literature* (New York: Routledge, 2007), 68.
115. R.W. Connell, "The Social Organisation of Masculinity," in *The Masculinities Reader*, ed. Stephen Whitehead and Frank Barrett (Cambridge: Polity, 2001), 44.
116. Ward, *Lover Awakened*, 198.
117. Glen Lewis and Toby Zoates, *Real Men Like Violence: Australian Men, Media and Violence* (Kenthurst: Kangaroo Press, 1983), 11.
118. Stephen Whitehead and Frank Barrett, "The Sociology of Masculinity," in *The Masculinities Reader*, ed. Stephen Whitehead and Frank Barrett (Cambridge: Polity, 2001), 17.
119. Readers' expectations here could also play an important role. Although it would be risky to speculate over the dreams and desires of the readership, one can see how the representation of the male vampire ideal bears a connection to standardised and traditional visions of masculinity in Western organisation, where the emphasis still falls on muscular outlooks and heroic enterprise. The physically developed and extreme active male vampire could be seen as a reaction to the increasingly more sedentary nature of Western life.
120. Murray Healey, "The Mark of a Man: Masculine Identities and the Art of Macho Drag," *Critical Quarterly* 36 (1994): 88.
121. J.R. Ward, *Lover Unbound* (London: Piatkus, 2007), 11.
122. Mikhail Bakhtin, *Problems of Dostoyevsky's Poetics* (Minneapolis, MN: University of Minnesota Press, 1984), 22.
123. Stefan Brandt, "American Culture X: Identity, Sexuality and the Search for a New American Hero," in *Subverting Masculinity: Hegemonic and Alternative Versions of Masculinity in Contemporary Culture*, ed. Russell West and Frank Lay (Atlanta: Rodopi, 2000), 69.

124. Grosz, *Volatile Bodies*, 187.
125. Ibid.
126. Charlaine Harris, *Dead Reckoning* (London: Gollancz, 2011), 300.
127. See Grosz, *Volatile Bodies*.
128. Chloe Neill, *Some Girls Bite* (2009; London: Gollancz, 2010).
129. Grosz, *Volatile Bodies*, 188.
130. Ibid.
131. Ibid., 191.

NOTES TO CHAPTER 3

1. Mervyn Nicholson, *Male Envy: The Logic of Malice in Literature and Culture* (Lanham, MD: Lexington, 1999), 206.
2. Barb Karg, Arjean Spaite, and Rick Sutherland, *The Everything Vampire Book* (Avon, MA: Adams Media, 2009), 77.
3. Otto Fenichel, *The Psychoanalytic Theory of Neurosis* (New York: WW Norton, 1945), 209.
4. Stephenie Meyer, *Twilight* (2005; London: Atom, 2011).
5. J.R. Ward, *Lover Eternal* (London: Piatkus, 2006), 171.
6. Ibid., 170.
7. Karg, Spaite, and Sutherland, *The Everything Vampire Book*, 77.
8. Jim Butcher, *The Dresden Files*, Vols. 1–14 (London: Orbit, 2000–2012).
9. Karg, Spaite, and Sutherland, *The Everything Vampire Book*, 77.
10. David Wellington, *Laura Caxton Vampire Series* (St. Leonards: Allen and Unwin, 2007–2012).
11. Christopher Farnsworth, *Blood Oath* (London: Hodder and Stoughton, 2010), 23.
12. Ken Gelder, *Reading the Vampire* (London: Routledge, 1994).
13. Nicholas Royle, *The Uncanny* (Manchester: Manchester University Press, 2003), 1.
14. Farnsworth, Blood Oath, 24.
15. Ibid.
16. Royle, *The Uncanny*, 1—2.
17. Sigmund Freud, "The Uncanny," The Pelican Freud Library: Art and Literature, Vol. 14 (Harmondsworth: Penguin, 1987), 340.
18. Cited in Carolyn Korsmeyer, *Making Sense of Taste: Food and Philosophy* (Ithaca: Cornell University Press, 2002), 21.
19. Robert Jütte, *A History of the Senses: From Antiquity to Cyberspace* (Cambridge: Polity, 2005), 186.
20. Ibid., 187.
21. Martin Jay, "Vision in Context; Reflection and Refractions", in *Vision in Context: Historical and Contemporary Perspectives on Sight*, ed. Teresa Brennan and Martin Jay (New York: Routledge, 1996), 3.
22. Ibid.
23. Ibid.
24. J.R. Ward, *Lover Unbound* (London: Piatkus, 2007), 110.
25. J.R. Ward, *Lover Unleashed* (London: Piatkus, 2011).
26. Kristen Painter, *Blood Rights* (London, Orbit, 2011), 12.
27. Peter de Bolla, "The Visibility of Visuality," in *Vision in Context: Historical and Contemporary Perspectives on Sight*, ed. Teresa Brennan and Martin Jay (New York: Routledge, 1996), 70.
28. Ibid.

29. Cited in Constance Classen, *World of Sense: Exploring the Senses in History and across Cultures* (London: Routlegde, 1993), 2.
30. Deborah Harkness, A Discovery of Witches (London; Headline Publishing, 2011), 207.
31. Ibid., 171.
32. Painter, *Blood Rights*, 109.
33. 'Every inch of his flesh hummed with the drive to protect. Possess'. Ibid., 109.
34. J.R. Ward, *Dark Lover* (London: Piatkus, 2005); *Lover Eternal*; *Lover Mine* (London: Piatkus, 2010); *Lover Reborn* (London: Piatkus, 2012).
35. Classen, *World of Sense*, 79.
36. Constance Classen, David Howes and Anthony Synnott, *Aroma: The Cultural History of Smell* (London; Routledge, 1994), 123.
37. Ibid., 162.
38. Ibid.
39. J.R. Ward, *Dark Lover*, 176.
40. Classen, Howes and Synnott, *Aroma: The Cultural History of Smell*, 161.
41. J.R. Ward, *Lover Avenged* (London: Piatkus, 2009), 269.
42. Ibid., 469.
43. John Harrison, *Synaesthesia: The Strangest* Thing (Oxford: Oxford University Press, 2001), 3.
44. Jan Dirk Blom, A *Dictionary of Hallucinations* (London: Springer, 2010), 493.
45. Ibid., 495.
46. Lara Adrian, *Kiss of Midnight* (Constable & Robinson, 2009), 129.
47. Charlaine Harris, *Dead and Gone* (London: Gollancz, 2009), 179.
48. Scott Mariani, *Uprising* (New York: Avon. 2010), 233.
49. Ibid.
50. Harris, *Dead and Gone*, 179.
51. Kenneth Gross, *Puppet: An Essay on Uncanny Life* (Chicago: University of Chicago Press, 2011), 1.
52. Marina Warner, *Fantastic Metamorphoses, Other Worlds* (Oxford: Oxford University press, 2002), 120.
53. Ibid., 121.
54. Lori Handeland, *Shakespeare, Undead* (New York: St. Martin's Press, 2010), 1.
55. Warner, *Fantastic Metamorphoses, Other Worlds*, 122.
56. Karl Marx, *Capital, Vol. 1* (Harmondsworth; Penguin, 1990), 357.
57. Rob Latham, *Consuming Youth: Vampires, Cyborgs, and the Culture of Consumption* (Chicago: Chicago University, 2002), 18. See also: David Harvey, *The Condition of Postmodernity: An Enquiry into the Origins of Cultural Change* (Malden, MA: Blackwell, 1991), 156.
58. David Wellington, *Thirteen Bullets* (St. Leonards: Allen and Unwin, 2007), 47.
59. Marx, *Capital*, 756.
60. David McNally, *Monsters of the Market: Vampires, Zombies, and Global Capitalism* (Leiden: Martinus Nijhoff, 2011), 141.
61. Ibid.
62. Wellington, *Thirteen Bullets*, 100 and 19.
63. McNally, *Monsters of the Market: Vampires, Zombies, and Global Capitalism*, 141.
64. J.R. Ward, *Lover Awakened* (London: Piatkus, 2006), 44.
65. Ibid.

66. Adrian, *Kiss of Midnight*, 68.
67. Charlaine Harris, *Club Dead* (2003; London: Gollancz, 2010), 3.
68. Susan Broadhusrt and Josephine Machon, "Introduction," in *Identity, Performance, and Technology: Practices of Empowerment, Embodiment, and Technicity*, (New York; Palgrave Macmillan, 2012), 4.
69. Pramod K. Nayar, *An Introduction to Media and Cybercultures* (Oxford: Wiley-Blackwell, 2010), 4.
70. Ward, *Lover Reborn*, 24.
71. Nayar, *An Introduction to Media and Cybercultures*, 4.
72. Roger Silverstone and Leslie Haddon, "Design and the domestication of ICTs: technical change and everyday life," in *Communication by Design: The Politics of Information and Communication Technologies*, ed. Robin Mansell (Oxford: Oxford University Press, 1996), 44—74.
73. Nayar, *An Introduction to Media and Cybercultures*, 4.
74. Ibid.
75. Ibid.
76. Karg, Spaite, and Sutherland, *The Everything Vampire Book*, 83.
77. Marita Sturken and Douglas Thomas, "Introduction: Technological Visions and the Rhetoric of New," in *Technological Visions; the Hopes and Fears that Shape New Technologies*, ed. Marita Sturken, Douglas Thomas and Sandra J. Ball-Rokeach (Philadelphia: Temple University Press, 2004), 1.
78. Royle, *The Uncanny*, 24.
79. Ibid., 23.
80. Christopher Johnson, "Ambient Technologies, Uncanny Signs," *Oxford Literary Review* 21 (1999): 131.
81. Ibid., 132.
82. Ibid.
83. Karg, Spaite, and Sutherland, *The Everything Vampire Book*, 83.
84. Royle, *The Uncanny*, 24.
85. Richard Watson, *Future Minds: How the Digital Age is Changing our Minds, Why This Matters and What We Can Do about It* (London: Nicholas Brealey, 2010), 33.
86. Charlaine Harris, *From Dead to Worse* (London: Gollancz, 2008), 180.
87. Mariani, *Uprising*, 67.
88. Colleen Gleeson, *The Bleeding Dusk* (London: Allison & Busby, 2008), 17.
89. Watson, *Future Minds: How the Digital Age is Changing our Minds, Why This Matters and What We Can Do about It*, 43.
90. Mariani, *Uprising*, 83.
91. Watson, *Future Minds: How the Digital Age is Changing our Minds, Why This Matters and What We Can Do about It*, 33.
92. Cordelia Fine, *A Mind of Its Own: How Your Brain Distorts and Deceives* (London: icon Books, 2005), 87.
93. Watson, *Future Minds: How the Digital Age is Changing our Minds, Why This Matters and What We Can Do about It*, 43.
94. Ibid.
95. Charlaine Harris, *Dead Reckoning* (London: Gollancz, 2011), 77.
96. Charlaine Harris, *Dead Until Dark* (2001; London: Gollancz, 2004), 123.
97. Watson, *Future Minds: How the Digital Age is Changing our Minds, Why This Matters and What We Can Do about It*, 43.
98. Ward, *Dark Lover*, 17.
99. Ward, *Lover Unbound*, 108 and 110.
100. Quoted in Watson, *Future Minds: How the Digital Age is Changing our Minds, Why This Matters and What We Can Do about It*, 43.

101. Fredric Jameson, *Postmodernism, Or, The Cultural Logic of Late Capitalism* (Durham, NC: Duke University Press, 1991).
102. Watson, *Future Minds: How the Digital Age is Changing our Minds, Why This Matters and What We Can Do about It*, 48.
103. Nayar, *An Introduction to Media and Cybercultures*, 8.
104. Katherine Hayles, *How We Became Posthuman: Virtual Bodies in Cybernetics, Literature, and Informatics* (Chicago: University of Chicago Press, 1999), 27.
105. Ibid.
106. Nayar, *An Introduction to Media and Cybercultures*, 8.
107. Ibid., 5.
108. Jon Stratton, "Cyberspace and the Globalization of Culture," in *Internet Culture*, ed. David Porter (London: Routledge, 1997), 259.
109. Frank Webster, *Theories of the Information Society* (Abingdon: Routledge, 2006).
110. Nayar, An Introduction to Media and Cybercultures, 7.

NOTES TO CHAPTER 4

1. Charlaine Harris, *Dead Until Dark* (2001; London: Gollancz, 2004), 120.
2. D.B. Reynolds, *Raphael* (Canon City, CO: ImaJinn Books, 2009). 61.
3. Scott Mariani, *Uprising* (New York: Avon, 2010) 44.
4. Klaus-Peter Köpping, Bernhard Leistle and Michael Rudolph, "Introduction," in *Ritual and Identity: Performative Practices as Effective Transformation of Social Reality*, ed. Klaus-Peter Köpping, Bernhard Leistle and Michael Rudolph (Berlin: Verlag, 2006), 2.
5. Sigmund Fred, *Totem and Taboo* (Abingdon: Routledge, 2004).
6. Catherine Bell, *Ritual: Perspectives and Dimensions* (Oxford: Oxford University Press, 1997), 1.
7. Ibid.
8. Köpping, Leistle and Rudolph, "Introduction," 19.
9. Freud, *Totem and Taboo*, 90. In formulating this idea, Freud is connecting ritual mainly to animistic religions and the use of 'magic' and 'sorcery'. The idea that all forms of ritual, religious or secular, are formed by the human beings' desire to represent the world through the human imagination had of course been already introduced by David Hume: 'There is a universal tendency among mankind to conceive all beings like themselves, and to transfer to every object those qualities with which they are familiarly acquainted, and of which they are intimately conscious.' (Quoted in *Totem and Taboo*, 90).
10. Bell, *Ritual: Perspectives and Dimensions* 2.
11. Charliane Harris, *Dead Ever After* (London: Gollancz, 2013), 123.
12. Charlaine Harris, *Dead Reckoning* (London: Gollancz, 2011), 252 and 94.
13. Ibid. 94.
14. Charlaine Harris, *All Together Dead* (2007; London: Gollancz, 2008), 166.
15. Lara Adrian, *Kiss of Midnight* (London: Constable & Robinson, 2009), 358
16. Ibid., 167.
17. J.R. Ward, *Dark Lover* (London: Piatkus, 2005), 388.
18. Ibid., 389.
19. J.R. Ward, *Lover Reborn* (London: Piatkus, 2012), 95.
20. Harris, *All Together Dead*, 166.
21. Adrian, *Kiss of Midnight*, 258.

22. Pamela Thurschwell, *Sigmund Freud* (London: Routledge, 2000), 36.
23. Adrian, *Kiss of Midnight*, 358.
24. Barbara Creed, *The Monstrous-Feminine: Film, Feminism, Psychoanalysis* (Abingdon: Routledge, 1993), 104.
25. Jean Bethke Elshtain, "Foreword" in *The Meaning of Marriage: Family, State, Market & Morals*, ed. Robert George and Jean Bethke Elshtain (New York: Scepter, 2010), x.
26. David Shumway, *Modern Love: Romance, Intimacy, and the Marriage Crisis* (New York: New York University Press, 2003), 36.
27. Catherine Anne Gildae, "Good, Old-fashioned, Traditional Family Values?" (PhD Thesis Northwestern University, 2008), 41.
28. Shumway, *Modern Love: Romance, Intimacy, and the Marriage Crisis*, 26.
29. There are, of course, instances where same-sex weddings are openly allowed and re-enforced for vampires, with examples such as the *Sookie Stackhouse* and *Black Dagger Brotherhood* series providing evidence here.
30. Shumway, *Modern Love: Romance, Intimacy, and the Marriage Crisis*, 26.
31. Harris, *Dead Until Dark*, 81.
32. J.R. Ward, *Lover Eternal* (London: Piatkus, 2006), 135.
33. J.R. Ward, *Lover Unleashed* (London: Pitakus, 2011), 46.
34. Kristen Painter, *Blood Rights* (London: Orbit, 2011), 42.
35. Ibid.
36. Anthony Stevens, *Archetype: A Natural History of the Self* (London: Routledge, 1982), 81.
37. Whitley Strieber, *The Hunger* (New York: Pocket Books, 1981), 22.
38. Stevens, *Archetype: A Natural History of the Self*, 81.
39. Deborah Harkness, A Discovery of Witches (London: Headline Publishing, 2011), 450.
40. Stevens, *Archetype: A Natural History of the Self*, 106.
41. Deborah Harkness, *Shadow of Night* (London: Headline Publishing, 2012), 85.
42. J.R. Ward, *Lover Enshrined* (London: Piatkus, 2008), 532.
43. Sandro Segre, *Talcott Parsons: An Introduction* (Lanham, MD: University Press of America, 2012), 19. See also Talcott Parsons, *Family Socialization and Interaction Process* (London: Routledge, 2002).
44. Stevens, *Archetype: A Natural History of the Self*, 107.
45. Vera Von Der Heydt, "On the Father in Psychotherapy," in *Fathers and Mothers: Five Papers on the Archetypal Background of Archetypal Psychology*, ed. Augusto Vitale, Rich Neumann, Murray Stein, James Hillman, and Vera Von der Heydt (Zurich: Spring Publications, 1973), 133.
46. Ibid.
47. Heidi Hartmann, "The Family as the Locus of Gender, Class, and Political Struggle," *Signs* 6 (1981).
48. Jes Battis, *Blood Relations: Chosen Families in Buffy the Vampires Slayer and Angel* (Jefferson, NC: McFarland, 2005), 21.
49. Ibid.
50. Ibid., 16.
51. Valerie Lehr, *Queer Family Values* (Philadelphia: Temple University Press, 1999), 176.
52. This idea, of course, does not only concern gay and lesbian units, but it does point to the idea of 'queering' in its understanding as an differentiated, unbalanced, and reconstituted entity in a different framework.
53. Battis, Blood Relations: *Chosen Families in Buffy the Vampires Slayer and Angel*, 21.

54. Ibid.
55. Ward, *Dark Lover*, 192.
56. Deborah Lupton, *Food, the Body and the Self* (London: SAGE, 1996), 25.
57. Lorna Piatti-Farnell, *Food and Culture in Contemporary American Fiction* (New York: Routledge, 2011).
58. Sydney Mintz, *Tasting Food, Tasting Freedom: Excursions into Eating, Culture, and the Past* (Boston: Beacon Press, 1996), 7.
59. David Bell and Gill Valentine, *Consuming Geographies: We Are Where We Eat* (London: Routledge, 1997), 3.
60. Arjun Appadurai, "Gastro-Politics in Hindu South Asia," *American Ethnologist* 8 (1981): 494.
61. J.R Ward, *Lover Revealed* (London: Piatkus, 2007), 175.
62. David Bell and Gill Valentine, *Consuming Geographies: We Are Where We Eat*, 63 and 64.
63. Nickie Charles and Marion Kerr, *Women, Food and Families* (Manchester: Manchester University Press, 1988), 2.
64. Quoted in Pasi Falk, *The Consuming Body* (London: SAGE, 1994), 47.
65. Arjun Appadurai, 'Consumption, Duration and History', *Stanford Literary Review*, 10 (1993), 12.
66. Ibid.
67. Ibid., 15.
68. See Falk, *The Consuming Body*, 47.
69. Ibid., 45.
70. Ward, *Dark Lover*, 455.
71. Falk, *The Consuming Body*, 46.
72. David Morgan, *Family Connections: An Introduction to Family Studies* (Cambridge: Polity, 1996), 66.
73. Susannah Clemens, *The Vampire Defanged: How the Embodiment of Evil Became a Romantic Hero* (Grand Rapids, MI: Brazos Press, 2011), 90.
74. Harris, *Dear Until Dark*, 197.
75. Scott Mariani, *Uprising* (New York: Avon, 2010), 314.
76. Gilles Deleuze and Félix Guattari, *A Thousand Plateaus* (London: Continuum, 1987), 90.
77. Elspeth Probyn, *Carnal Appetites: FoodSexIdentities* (London: Routledge, 2000), 62.
78. Georg Simmel, "The Sociology of the Meal," in *Simmel on Culture*, ed. David Frisby and Mike Featherstone (London: SAGE, 2000), 346.
79. Probyn, *Carnal Appetites: FoodSexIdentities*, 60.
80. Ibid.
81. Michel Foucault, *The Use of Pleasure: The History of Sexuality, Vol. 2* (New York: Vintage), 97.
82. See Painter, *Blood Rights*.
83. David Simpson, *9/11: The Culture of Commemoration* (Chicago; University of Chicago Press, 2006), 1.
84. Ward, *Dark Lover*, 29.
85. Ibid., 47–48.
86. Douglas Davies, *Death, Ritual, and Belief: The Rhetoric of Funeral Rites* (New York; Continuum, 2002), 67.
87. Ibid., 72.
88. Ibid.
89. René Girard, *Violence and the Sacred* (London: John Hopkins University Press, 1977), 31.
90. Ibid., 36.

91. Davies, *Death, Ritual, and Belief: The Rhetoric of Funeral Rites*, 82.
92. Loring Danforth, *The Death Rituals of Rural Greece* (Princeton, NJ: Princeton University Press, 1982), 44.
93. Davies, *Death, Ritual, and Belief: The Rhetoric of Funeral Rites*, 50.
94. Simpson, *9/11: The Culture of Commemoration*, 1.
95. Mary Ellen O'Connell, 'Introduction: Defining Armed Conflict in the Decade After 9/11," in *What is War? An Investigation in the Wake of 9/11*, ed. Mary Ellen O'Connell (Leiden: Martinus Nijhoff, 2012), 3.
96. Jeffrey Melnick, *9/11 Culture* (Oxford: Wiley-Blackwell, 2009), 7.
97. Ibid., 7.
98. Ibid., 7.
99. Ward, *Dark Lover*, 36.
100. Car bombs were also known to be a common way of attacking US convoys during the war in Iraq.
101. Noam Chomsky, *9/11* (Stockholm: Aftonbladet, 2002), 20.
102. Ward, *Dark Lover*, 32.
103. Ibid., 28.
104. Simpson, *9/11: The Culture of Commemoration*, 5.
105. Chomsky, *9/11*, 16.
106. Ward, *Lover Eternal*, 151.
107. Ward, *Dark Lover*, 58.
108. *New York Times*, 16 September 2011, quoted in Chomsky, *9/11*, 31.
109. Chomsky, *9/11*, 31.
110. Simpson, *9/11: The Culture of Commemoration*, 4.
111. Ibid., 2.
112. Adrian, *Kiss of Midnight*, 148.
113. Simpson, *9/11: The Culture of Commemoration*, 2.
114. Ibid.
115. Ibid.
116. Ibid.
117. Benedict Anderson, *Imagined Communities: Reflections on the Origins and Spread of Nationalism* (London; Verso, 2006).
118. Dominick LaCapra, *Representing the Holocaust; History, Theory, Trauma* (Ithaca, NY: Cornell University Press, 1994).
119. Simpson, *9/11: The Culture of Commemoration*, 3.
120. Sigmund Freud, "Mourning and Melancholia," in *The Standard Edition of the Complete Psychological Works of Sigmund Freud, Vol. XIV* (London: Hogarth Press, 1974), 243–258.
121. Simpson, *9/11: The Culture of Commemoration*, 3.
122. Émile Durkheim, "The dualism of human nature and its social conditions," in *Emile Durkheim on Morality and Society*, ed. R.N. Bellah (London: Routledge, 1974), 151.
123. Émile Durkheim, *The Elementary Forms of Religious Life* (New York: Free Press, 1995), 151.
124. Chris Shilling, *The Body in Culture, Technology and Society* (London: SAGE, 2005), 41.
125. Ibid.
126. Carol A. Senf, "Blood, Eroticism, and the Vampire in Twentieth-Century Popular Literature," in *The Gothic World of Stephen King: Landscape of Nightmare*, ed. Gary Hoppenstand and Ray B. Browne (Bowling Green, OH: Bowling Green University Popular Press, 1987), 150.
127. Margaret Carter, *Dracula: The Vampire and the Critics* (Ann Arbor: Umi Research Press, 1997), 29.

128. Victoria Nelson, *Gothicka: Vampire Heroes, Human Gods, and the New Supernatural* (Cambridge, MA: Harvard University Press, 2012), 114.

NOTES TO CHAPTER 5

1. Jon Anderson, *Understanding Cultural Geography: Places and Traces* (Abingdon: Routledge, 2010), 3.
2. Brian Aldiss, "Foreword: Vampires—The Ancient Fear," in *Blood Read: The Vampire as Metaphor in Contemporary Culture*, ed. Joan Gordon and Veronica Hollinger (Philadelphia: University of Pennsylvania Press, 1997), ix.
3. Aldiss, "Foreword," ix.
4. Scott Mariani, *Uprising* (New York: Avon, 2010), 103.
5. Malcolm Miles, *Cities and Cultures* (Abingdon: Routledge, 2007), 9.
6. Joseph Grange, *The City: An Urban Cosmology* (Albany, NY: State University of New York Press, 1999), xv.
7. Aldiss, "Foreword," ix.
8. Ibid.
9. Joan Gordon and Veronica Hollinger, "Introduction: The Shape of Vampires," in *Blood Read: The Vampire as Metaphor in Contemporary Culture*, ed. Joan Gordon and Veronica Hollinger (Philadelphia: University of Pennsylvania Press, 1997), 7.
10. David Frisby, *Fragments of Modernity: Social Theories of Modernity in the Works of Georg Simmel, Siegfried Kracauer and Walter Benjamin* (Cambridge,MA: Mit Press, *1985)*, 46.
11. J. R Ward, *Lover Unleashed* (London: Piatkus, 2011), 205–206.
12. Miles, *Cities and Cultures*, 9.
13. James Donald, 'Metropolis', in *Social and Cultural forms of Modernity*, ed. Robert Bocock and Kenneth Thompson (Cambridge: Polity, 1992), 427.
14. Ibid.
15. Anthony King, "Introduction: Cities, Texts, and Paradigms," in *Re-Presenting the City: Ethnicity, Capital and Culture in the 21st Century Metropolis*, ed. Anthony King (New York: New York University Press, 1996), 15.
16. Sharon Zukin, "Space and Symbols in an Age of Decline," in *Re-Presenting the City: Ethnicity, Capital and Culture in the 21st Century Metropolis*, ed. Anthony King (New York: New York University Press, 1996), 43.
17. Kristen Painter, *Bad Blood* (London: Orbit, 2011), 168.
18. Deborah Harkness, *A Discovery of Witches* (London: Headline Publishing, 2011), 244—245.
19. Charlaine Harris, *All Together Dead* (2007; London: Gollancz, 2008), 9. These examples function here only as selected written testimonies; the function of New Orleans as a 'vampire city' is pervasive and well-established across a large number of individual novels and series.
20. Louise McKinney, *New Orleans: A Cultural History* (Oxford: Oxford University Press, 2006), 1.
21. Ibid.
22. Charlaine Harris, *Dead Until Dark* (2001; London: Gollancz, 2004), 2.
23. J.R. Ward, *Lover Unbound* (London: Piatkus, 2007), 152.
24. Stephenie Meyer, *The Twilight Saga: The Official Illustrated Guide* (London: Atom, 2011), 68.
25. Ibid., 154.
26. McKinney, *New Orleans: A Cultural History*, 5.

27. Ibid.
28. Ibid., 6.
29. Ibid., 6.
30. Clarence Laughlin, *Lost Louisiana*, quoted in McKinney, *New Orleans: A Cultural History*, 7.
31. Peirce Fee Lewis , *New Orleans: The Making of an Urban Landscape* (Chicago: Centre for American Places, 2003), 15.
32. Gordon and Hollinger, "Introduction," 7.
33. Kevin Fox Gotham, *Authentic New Orleans: Tourism, Culture, and Race in the Big Easy* (New York: New York University Press).
34. Ibid., 5.
35. Harris, *Dead Until Dark*, 115.
36. Gotham, *Authentic New Orleans: Tourism, Culture, and Race in the Big Easy*, 5.
37. Harris, *All Together Dead*, 2.
38. Charlaine Harris, *Dead as a Doornail* (2005; London: Gollancz, 2007), 212.
39. Harris, *All Together Dead*, 2.
40. Gotham, *Authentic New Orleans: Tourism, Culture, and Race in the Big Easy*, 6.
41. Dean MacCannell, "Staged Authenticity: Arrangements of Social Space in Tourist Settings." *American Journal of Sociology* 79, no.3 (1973): 589—603.
42. Charlaine Harris, "One Word Answer," in *A Touch of Dead* (London: Gollancz, 2009), 88.
43. Gotham, *Authentic New Orleans: Tourism, Culture, and Race in the Big Easy*, 5.
44. Kenneth Holditch, quoted in McKinney, *New Orleans: A Cultural History*, 8.
45. D.B. Reynolds, *Raphael* (Canon City, CO: ImaJinn Books, 2009), 40–41.
46. Charlaine Harris, *Dead in the Family* (London: Gollancz, 2010), 73–74.
47. Sigmund Freud, *The Complete Introductory Lectures on Psychoanalysis*, Vol. 1 (London: Allen and Unwin, 1971), 189.
48. Margaret Rodman, "Beyond Built Form and Culture in the Anthropological Study of Community Spaces," in *The Cultural Meaning of Urban Space*, ed. Robert Rotenberg and Gary McDonogh (Westport, CT: Bergin & Garvey, 1993), 124.
49. Zukin, "Space and Symbols in an Age of Decline," 43.
50. Rodman, "Beyond Built Form and Culture in the Anthropological Study of Community Spaces," 124. This line of thought has proved generally popular within both cultural and literary scholarship, with Gothic scholarship making gestures towards a comprehensive analysis of houses and mansions, but overall displaying a general lack of in interest on the interactive relationship between vampires and buildings.
51. Mark Tungate, *Luxury Goods: The Past, Present, and Future of Luxury Brands* (London, Kogan Page, 2009), 26.
52. Jean Baudrillard, *For a Critique of the Political Economy of the Sign* (Prestatyn: Telos, 1981).
53. J.R Ward, *Lover Eternal* (London: Piatkus, 2006), 199.
54. Ibid., 120.
55. Timothy Mitchell, *Colonising Egypt* (Cambridge: Polity, 1988), 44. See also: Michel Foucault, Discipline and Punish: *The Birth of the Prison* (London: Penguin, 1977). Both Mitchell and Foucault refer to 'enframing' in relation to the reconstruction of ideal villages in colonial locations, such as Egypt. Although the context of discussion is inevitably difference, the notion of the

'perfect house' as socially and culturally containing space remains useful and can be transported to the contemporary Western context of the vampire.

56. Barb Karg, Arjean Spaite, and Rick Sutherland, *The Everything Vampire Book* (Avon, MA: Adams Media, 2009), 92.
57. Ibid.
58. Ward, *Lover Eternal*, 207.
59. Lara Adrian, *Kiss of Midnight* (London: Constable & Robinson, 2009), 242.
60. Harris, *Dead in the Family*, 181.
61. Harris, *Dead Until Dark*, 62.
62. Christine Feehan, *Dark Possession* (London: Piatkus, 2007), 92.
63. Quoted in Bernadette Lynn Bosky, "Making the Implicit, Explicit: Vampire Erotica and Pornography," in *The Blood is the Life: Vampires in Literature*, ed. Leonard G. Heldreth and Mary Pharr (Bowling Green, Oh: Bowling Green State University Popular Press), 218.
64. Mihaly Csikszentmihalyi and Eugene Rochberg-Halton, *The Meaning of Things: Domestic Symbols and the Self* (Cambridge: Cambridge University Press, 1981), 214.
65. Ibid.
66. Freud, *The Complete Introductory Lectures on Psychoanalysis*, 262.
67. Karl Marx, *Capital, Vol. 1* (Harmondsworth; Penguin, 1990), 342.
68. Ward, *Lover Eternal*, 3.
69. J.R. Ward, *Lover Awakened* (London: Piatkus, 2006), 16.
70. D.B. Reynolds, *Lucas* (Canon City, CO: ImaJinn Books, 2012).
71. Deborah Lupton, *Food, the Body and the Self* (London: SAGE, 1996), 94
72. Ward, *Lover Eternal*, 53.
73. Ward, *Lover Awakened*, 190.
74. Grant McCracken, *Culture and Consumption: New Approaches to the Symbolic Character of Consumer Goods and Activities* (Bloomington: Indiana University Press, 1991).
75. Rob Latham, *Consuming Youth: Vampires, Cyborgs, and the Culture of Consumption* (Chicago: University of Chicago Press, 2002), 80.
76. Jean Baudrillard, *Seduction* (London: St. Martin's Press, 1991).
77. Adam Arvidsson, *Brands: Meaning and Value in Media Culture* (Abingdon: Routledge, 2006), 7.
78. Fredric Jameson, *Postmodernism, Or, The Cultural Logic of Late Capitalism* (Durham, NC: Duke University Press, 1991); David Harvey, *The Condition of Postmodernity: An Enquiry into the Origins of Cultural Change* (Malden, MA: Blackwell, 1991).
79. Arvidsson, *Brands: Meaning and Value in Media Culture*, 7.
80. Ibid.
81. Seema Gupta, *Branding and Advertising* (New Delhi: Global India Publications, 2009), 1.
82. Celia Lury, *Brands: The Logos of Global Economy* (Abingdon: Routledge, 2004), 1.
83. Rob Shields, *The Virtual* (London: Routledge, 2003), 177.
84. Stuart and Elizabeth Ewen, *Channels of Desire: Mass Images and the Shaping of American Consciousness* (New York: McGraw-Hill, 1982), 75.
85. Arvidsson, *Brands: Meaning and Value in Media Culture*, 8.

NOTES TO THE CONCLUSION

1. Joan Gordon and Veronica Hollinger, "Introduction: The Shape of Vampires," in *Blood Read: The Vampire as Metaphor in Contemporary Culture*,

ed. Joan Gordon and Veronica Hollinger (Philadelphia: University of Pennsylvania Press, 1997), 8.

2. Cornelius Castoriadis, *World in Fragments: Writings on Politics, Society, Psychoanalysis and the Imagination.* Stanford, CA: Stanford University Press, 1997.

3. J. R. Ward, *Lover Avenged* (London: Piatkus), 61.

4. Gordon and Hollinger, "Introduction," 7.

5. Ibid.

6. Milly Williamson, *The Lure of the Vampire: Gender, Fiction and Fandom from Bram Stoker to Buffy* (London: Wallflower Press), 1.

7. Nina Auerbach, *Our Vampires, Ourselves* (Chicago: University of Chicago Press, 1995), 17.

8. Paul Hodkinson, "Communicating Goth", in *The Subcultures Reader*, Second Edition, ed. Ken Gelder (Abingdon: Routledge, 2005), 567.

9. Alison Cavanagh, *Sociology in the Age of the Internet* (Maidenhead: Open University Press, 2007), 2.

Bibliography

Adrian, Lara. *Darker After Midnight*. Constable & Robinson, 2012.
———. *Kiss of Crimson*. London: Constable & Robinson, 2009.
———. *Kiss of Midnight*. London: Constable & Robinson, 2009.
Aldiss, Brian, "Foreword: Vampires—The Ancient Fear." In *Blood Read: The Vampire as Metaphor in Contemporary Culture*, ed. Joan Gordon and Veronica Hollinger, ix-xi. Philadelphia: University of Pennsylvania Press, 1997.
Alley, Thomas R. "Social and Applied Aspects of Face Perception: An Introduction." In *Social and Applied Aspects of Perceiving Faces*, edited by Thomas R. Alley, 1–9. Hillsdale, NJ: Lawrence Erlbaum, 1988.
Andaluza, Gloria. *Borderlands/La Frontera*. San Francisco, CA: Aunt Lute, 1999.
Anderson, Benedict. *Imagined Communities: Reflections on the Origins and Spread of Nationalism*. London: Verso, 2006.
Anderson, Jon. *Understanding Cultural Geography: Places and Traces*. Abingdon: Routledge, 2010.
Appadurai, Arjun. "Consumption, Duration and History." *Stanford Literary Review* 10 (1993): 11–23.
———. "Gastro-Politics in Hindu South Asia." *American Ethnologist* 8 (1981): 494—511.
Arvidsson, Adam. *Brands: Meaning and Value in Media Culture*. Abingdon: Routledge, 2006.
Ashman, Kevin. *Vampire*. Abiquiu, NM: Silverback, 2012.
Auerbach, Nina. *Our Vampires, Ourselves*. Chicago: University of Chicago Press, 1995.
Bakhtin, Mikhail. *Problems of Dostoyevsky's Poetics*. Minneapolis, MN: University of Minnesota Press, 1984.
Barber, Paul. *Vampires, Burial and Death: Folklore and Reality*. New Haven, CT: Yale University Press, 1988.
Barrows, Adam. "Heidegger the Vampire Slayer: The Undead and Fundamental Ontology." In *Zombies, Vampires, and Philosophy: New Life for the Undead*, edited by Richard Greene and K. Silem Mohammad, 69–79. Chicago, IL: Open Court Publishing, 2010.
Bataille, Georges. *Eroticism: Death and Sexuality*. New York: Walker and Company, 1986.
Battis, Jes. *Blood Relations: Chosen Families in Buffy the Vampires Slayer and Angel*. Jefferson, NC: McFarland, 2005.
Baudrillard, Jean. *Fatal Strategies*. Los Angeles: Semiotext(e), 2008.
———. *For a Critique of the Political Economy of the Sign*. Prestatyn: Telos, 1981.
———. *Seduction*. London: St. Martin Press, 1991.
Barthes, Roland. *Mythologies*. London: Grant & Cutler, 1994.

Bell, Catherine. *Ritual: Perspectives and Dimensions*. Oxford: Oxford University Press, 1997.
Bell, David, and Gill Valentine. *Consuming Geographies: We Are Where We Eat*. London: Routledge, 1997.
Beresford, Matthew. *From Demons to Dracula: The Creation of the Modern Vampire Myth*. London; Reaktion, 2008.
Bhabha, Homi. *The Location of Culture*. London and New York: Routledge, 2004.
Blom, Jan Dirk. *A Dictionary of Hallucinations*. London: Springer, 2010.
Bordo, Susan. *Unbearable Weight: Feminism, Western Culture, and the Body*. Berkeley, CA: University of California Press, 2003.
Bosky, Bernadette Lynn. "Making the Implicit, Explicit: Vampire Erotica and Pornography." In *The Blood is the Life: Vampires in Literature*, ed. Leonard G. Heldreth and Mary Pharr, 217–234. Bowling Green, OH: Bowling Green State University Popular Press.
Bosniak, Linda. *The Citizen and the Alien: Dilemmas of Contemporary Membership*. Princeton, NJ: Princeton University Press, 2006.
Botting, Fred. "Aftergothic." In *The Cambridge Companion to Gothic Fiction*, edited by Jerrold Hogle, 277–299. Cambridge, UK: Cambridge University Press, 2002.
———. *Gothic*. London: Routledge, 1995.
———. *Gothic Romanced: Consumption, Gender and Technology in Contemporary Fictions*. Abingdon: Routledge, 2008.
———. "Hypocrite Vampire." *Gothic Studies* 9.1 (2007): 16–49.
Brandt, Stefan. "American Culture X: Identity, Sexuality and the Search for a New American Hero." In *Subverting Masculinity: Hegemonic and Alternative Versions of Masculinity in Contemporary Culture*, edited Russell West and Frank Lay, 69–93. Atlanta: Rodopi, 2000.
Broadhusrt, Susan, and Josephine Machon. "Introduction." In *Identity, Performance, and Technology: Practices of Empowerment, Embodiment, and Technicity*, edited by Susan Broadhusrt and Josephine Machon, 1–6. New York: Palgrave Macmillan, 2012.
Butcher, Jim. *Blood Rites*. 2004. London: Orbit, 2005.
———. *Storm Front*. 2000. London: Orbit, 2005.
———. *The Dresden Files* series. London: Orbit, 2000–2012.
Butler, Erik. *The Rise of the Vampire*. London: Reaktion, 2012.
Butler, Judith. *Bodies That Matter: On the Discursive Limits of "Sex"*. New York: Routledge, 1993.
Caplan, Jane. *Written on the Body: The Tattoo in European and American History*. London: Reaktion, 2000.
Carter, Albert Howard. *Our Human Hearts: A Medical and Cultural Journey*. Kent, OH: Kent State University Press, 2006.
Carter, Margaret. *Dracula: The Vampire and the Critics*. Ann Arbor, MI: Umi Research Press, 1997.
Castoriadis, Cornelius. *World in Fragments: Writings on Politics, Society, Psychoanalysis and the Imagination*. Stanford, CA: Stanford University Press, 1997.
Cavanagh, Alison. *Sociology in the Age of the Internet*. Maidenhead: Open University Press, 2007.
Connell, R.W. *Masculinities*. Cambridge: Polity, 1995.
———. "The Social Organisation of Masculinity." In *The Masculinities Reader*, edited by Stephen Whitehead and Frank Barrett, 30–50. Cambridge: Polity, 2001.
Connor, Steve. *The Book of Skin*. London: Reaktion, 2004.

Charles, Nickie, and Marion Kerr. *Women, Food and Families.* Manchester: Manchester University Press, 1988.
Creed, Barbara. *The Monstrous-Feminine: Film, Feminism, Psychoanalysis.* Abingdon: Routledge, 1993.
Chomsky, Noam. *9/11.* Stockholm: Aftonbladet, 2002.
Classen, Constance. *World of Sense: Exploring the Senses in History and Across Cultures.* London: Routledge, 1993.
Classen, Constance, David Howes and Anthony Synnott. *Aroma: The Cultural History of Smell.* London: Routledge, 1994.
Clemens, Susannah. *The Vampire Defanged: How the Embodiment of Evil Became a Romantic Hero.* Grand Rapids, MI: Brazos Press, 2011.
Click, Melissa A., Jennifer Stevens Aubrey, and Elizabeth Behn-Morawitz, eds. *Bitten by Twilight: Youth Culture, Media & the Vampire Franchise.* New York: Peter Lang, 2010.
Csikszentmihalyi, Mihaly, and Eugene Rochberg-Halton, *The Meaning of Things: Domestic Symbols and the Self.* Cambridge: Cambridge University Press, 1981.
Cole, Kresley. *Immortals after Dark* series. New York: Pocket Books, 2006–2013.
———. *The Warlord Wants Forever.* New York: Pocket Books, 2011.
Coover, GE, and ST Murphy. "The Communicated Self: Exploring the Interaction between Self and Social Context." *Human Communication Research* 26 (2000): 125–147.
Crockett, Michael, and Desda Cox. *The Subversive Vegetarian: Tactics, Information and Recipes for the Conversion of Meat Eaters.* Wellingborough: Thorsons, 1979.
Cronin, Justin. *The Passage.* London: Orion, 2010.
Danforth, Loring. *The Death Rituals of Rural Greece.* Princeton, NJ: Princeton University Press, 1982.
Das, L.D. Vijendra. *Genetics and Plant Breeding.* New Delhi; New Age Publishing, 2006.
Davies, Douglas. *Death, Ritual, and Belief: The Rhetoric of Funeral Rites.* New York: Continuum, 2002.
de Bolla, Peter. "The Visibility of Visuality." In *Vision in Context: Historical and Contemporary Perspectives on Sight,* edited by Teresa Brennan and Martin Jay, 63–82. New York: Routledge, 1996.
Deleuze, Gilles, and Félix Guattari. *A Thousand Plateaus.* London: Continuum, 1987.
Deleuze, Giles. *Nietzsche and Philosophy.* London: Continuum, 2005.
Devitt, Amy J. *Writing Genres.* Carbondale, IL: Southern Illinois University Board of Trustees, 2008.
Donald, James. "Metropolis." In *Social and Cultural Forms of Modernity,* edited by Robert Bocock and Kenneth Thompson, 417–461. Cambridge: Polity, 1992.
Douglas, Mary. *Purity and Danger: An Analysis of Pollution and Taboo.* New York: Routledge, 2002.
Durkheim, Émile. "The Dualism of Human Nature and its Social Conditions." In *Emile Durkheim on Morality and Society,* edited by R.N. Bellah. London: Routledge, 1974.
———. *The Elementary Forms of Religious Life.* New York: Free Press, 1995.
Edwards, Justin, and Aignieszka Monnet. "Introduction: From Goth/ic to Pop Goth." In *The Gothic in Contemporary Literature and Popular Culture: Pop Goth,* edited by Justin Edwards and Aignieszka Monnet, 1–18. London: Routledge, 2012.

Ehrlich, Paul and Anne Ehrlich. *The Dominant Animal: Human Evolution and the Environment*. Washington, DC: First Island Press, 2008.

Eisenberg, Eric M. "Building a Mystery: Towards a New Theory of Communication and Identity." *Journal of Communication* 51 (2001): 534–552.

Elshtain, Jean Bethke. "Foreword." In *The Meaning of Marriage: Family, State, Market & Morals*, edited by Robert George and Jean Bethke Elshtain, ix-xviii. New York: Scepter, 2010.

Falk, Pasi. *The Consuming Body*. London: SAGE, 1994.

Farnsworth, Christopher. *Blood Oath*. London: Hodder and Stoughton, 2010.

———. *The President's Vampire*. London: Hodder and Stoughton, 2011.

Feehan, Christine. *Carpathians* series. London: Piatkus, 1999–2012.

———. *Dark Possession*. London: Piatkus, 2007.

Fenichel, Otto. *The Psychoanalytic Theory of Neurosis*. New York: WW Norton, 1945.

Fiddes, Nick. *Meat: A Natural Symbol*. London: Routledge, 1991.

Fine, Cordelia. *A Mind of Its Own: How Your Brain Distorts and Deceives*. London: Icon Books, 2005.

Fox, Nick, and Katie Ward. "What Are Health Identities and How May We Study Them?" *Sociology of Health & Illness* 30.7 (2008): 1007–1021.

Foucault, Michel. *Discipline and Punish: The Birth of the Prison*. London: Penguin, 1977.

———. *The Use of Pleasure: The History of Sexuality, Vol. 2*. New York: Vintage.

Frayling, Christopher. *Vampyres: Lord Byron to Count Dracula*. London: Faber and Faber, 1992.

Freud, Sigmund. "Mourning and Melancholia." In *The Standard Edition of the Complete Psychological Works of Sigmund Freud, Vol. XIV*, 243–258. London: Hogarth Press, 1974.

———. *The Complete Introductory Lectures on Psychoanalysis, Vol. 1*. London: Allen and Unwin, 1971.

———. *The Interpretation of Dreams*. Ware: Wordsworth Classics, 1997.

———. *Totem and Taboo*. Abingdon: Routledge, 2004.

Frisby, David. *Fragments of Modernity: Social Theories of Modernity in the Works of Georg Simmel, Siegfried Kracauer and Walter Benjamin*. Cambridge, MA: MIT Press, 1985.

Frow, John. *Genre*. Abingdon: Routledge, 2005.

Gelder, Ken. *Reading the Vampire*. London: Routledge, 1994.

Gildae, Catherine Anne. "Good, Old-fashioned, Traditional Family Values?" PhD Thesis, Northwestern University, 2008.

Gislason, Stephen. *Language and Thinking*. Sechelt: Persona Books, 2011.

Gleeson, Colleen. The *Gardella Vampire Chronicles* series. London: Allison & Busby, 2009–2013.

———. *The Bleeding Dusk*. London: Allison & Busby, 2008.

Glen, Lewis and Toby Zoates. *Real Men Like Violence: Australian Men, Media and Violence*. Kenthurst: Kangaroo Press, 1983.

Girard, René. *Violence and the Sacred*. London: Johns Hopkins University Press, 1977.

Goldstein, Laurence. "Introduction." In *The Male Body: Features, Destinies, Exposures*, edited by Laurence Goldtein, iii-xiv. Ann Arbor, MI University of Michigan Press, 1995.

Gordon, Joan, and Veronica Hollinger, "Introduction: The Shape of Vampires." In *Blood Read; The Vampire as Metaphor in Contemporary Culture*, edited by Joan Gordon and Veronica Hollinger, 1–7. Philadelphia: University of Pennsylvania Press, 1997.

Gotham, Kevin Fox. *Authentic New Orleans: Tourism, Culture, and Race in the Big Easy*. New York: New York University Press.

Grange, Joseph. *The City: An Urban Cosmology*. Albany, NY: State University of New York Press, 1999.

Grimwood, John Courtnay. *Vampire Assassin* trilogy. London: Orbit, 2011–2012.

Gross, Kenneth. *Puppet: An Essay on Uncanny Life*. Chicago: University of Chicago Press, 2011.

Grosz, Elizabeth. "Inscriptions and Body-Maps: Representation and the Corporeal." In *Feminine, Masculine, and Representation*, edited by Terry Threadgold and Anne Cranny-Francis, 62–74. Sydney: Allen & Unwin, 1990.

———. *Volatile Bodies*. Bloomington: Indiana University Press, 1994.

Gupta, Seema. *Branding and Advertising*. New Delhi: Global India Publications, 2009.

Guttman, Burton, Anthony Griffiths, David Suzuki, and Tara Cullis. *Genetics: The Code of Life*. New York, Rosen, 2011.

Handeland, Lori. *Shakespeare, Undead*. New York: St. Martin's Press, 2010.

Hanson, Ellis. "Undead." In *AIDS: Cultural Analysis/Cultural Activism*, edited by Douglas Crimp, 324–340. Cambridge, MA: MIT Press, 1988.

Harkness, Deborah. *A Discovery of Witches*. London: Headline Publishing, 2011.

———. *Shadow of Night*. London: Headline Publishing, 2012.

Harpman, Geoffrey Galt. *On the Grotesque: Strategies of Contradiction in Art and Literature*. Princeton, NJ: Princeton University Press, 1982.

Harris, Charlaine. *All Together Dead*. 2007. London: Gollanz, 2008.

———. *Club Dead*. 2003; London: Gollancz, 2010.

———. *Dead and Gone*. London: Gollancz, 2009.

———. *Dead in the Family*. London: Gollancz, 2010

———. *Deadlocked*. London: Gollancz, 2012.

———. *Dead to the World*. 2004. London: Gollancz, 2005.

———. *Dead Until Dark*. 2001. London: Gollancz, 2004.

———. *Dead Reckoning*. London: Gollancz, 2011.

———. *From Dead to Worse*. London: Gollancz, 2008.

———. "One Word Answer." In *A Touch of Dead*, 77–112. London: Gollancz, 2009.

———. *Sookie Stackhouse: The Southern Vampire Mysteries*. London: Gollancz, 2001–2013.

Harrison, John. *Synaesthesia: The Strangest* Thing. Oxford: Oxford University Press, 2001.

Harrison, Kim. *Dead Witch Walking*. 2004; London: Voyager, 2006.

———. *Hollows* series. London: Voyager, 2004–2013.

Hartmann, Heidi. "The Family As the Locus of Gender, Class, and Political Struggle." *Signs* 6.3 (1981): 366–394.

Harvey, David. *The Condition of Postmodernity: An Enquiry into the Origins of Cultural Change*. Malden, MA: Blackwell, 1991.

Hayles, Katherine. *How We Became Posthuman: Virtual Bodies in Cybernetics, Literature, and Informatics*. Chicago: University of Chicago Press, 1999.

Healey, Murray. "The Mark of a Man: Masculine Identities and the Art of Macho Drag." *Critical Quarterly* 36 (1994): 86–93,

Helfman, Gene, and Bruce Collette. *Fishes: The Animal Answer Guide*. Baltimore, MD: Johns Hopkins University Press, 2011.

Hodkinson, Paul. "Communicating Goth." In *The Subcultures Reader*, edited by Ken Gelder, 564–574. Abingdon: Routledge, 2005.

Hourihan, Margery. *Deconstructing the Hero: Literary Theory and Children's Literature*. New York: Routledge, 2007.

Housel, Rebecca, and J. Jeremy Wisnewski, "Introduction: Undead Wisdom." In *Twilight and Philosophy: Vampires, Vegetarians, and the Pursuit of Immortality*, edited by Rebecca Housel and J. Jeremy Wisnewski, 1–3. Hoboken, NJ: Wiley.

Inoue, Yoshitaka. "Contemporary Consciousness as Reflected in Images of the Vampire." *Jung Journal* (2011): 83–99.

Jameson, Fredric. *Postmodernism, Or, The Cultural Logic of Late Capitalism*. Durham, NC: Duke University Press, 1991.

Jay, Martin. "Vision in Context" In *Vision in Context: Historical and Contemporary Perspectives on Sight*, edited by Teresa Brennan and Martin Jay, 1–12. New York: Routledge, 1996.

Johnson, Christopher. "Ambient Technologies, Uncanny Signs." *Oxford Literary Review* 21 (1999): 117–134.

Joshi, S.T. "Foreword." In *21ˢᵗ Century Gothic: Great Gothic Novels Since 2000*, edited by Daniel Olson, v–xvii. Plymouth: Scarecrow Press, 2011.

Jütte, Robert. *A History of the Senses: From Antiquity to Cyberspace*. Cambridge: Polity, 2005.

Kane, Tim. *The Changing Vampire of Film and Television: A Critical Study of the Growth of a Genre*. Jefferson, NC: McFarland, 2006.

Karg, Barb, Arjean Spaite, and Rick Sutherland, *The Everything Vampire Book*. Avon, MA: Adams Media, 2009.

Khair, Tabish, and Johan Höglund, eds. *Transnational and Postcolonial Vampires: Dark Blood*. London: Palgrave Macmillan, 2013.

King, Anthony. "Introduction: Cities, Texts, and Paradigms." In *Re-Presenting the City: Ethnicity, Capital and Culture in the 21ˢᵗ Century Metropolis*, edited by Anthony King, 1–19. New York: New York University Press, 1996.

Klonsky, E. David, and Alexis Black, eds. *The Psychology of Twilight*. Dallas, TX: Smart Pop, 2011.

Kostantinos, *Vampires: The Occult Truth*. St.Paul, MN: Llewellyn, 2004.

Köpping, Klaus-Peter, Bernhard Leistle and Michael Rudolph. "Introduction." In *Ritual and Identity: Performative Practices as Effective Transformation of Social Reality*, edited by Klaus-Peter Köpping, Bernhard Leistle and Michael Rudolph, 9–30. Berlin: Verlag, 2006.

Korsmeyer, Carolyn. *Making Sense of Taste: Food and Philosophy*. Ithaca: Cornell University Press, 2002.

Kraidy, Marwan M. "Hybridity in Cultural Globalization." *Communication Theory* 12.3 (2002): 316–339.

Latham, Rob. *Consuming Youth: Vampires, Cyborgs, and the Culture of Consumption*. Chicago: Chicago University, 2002.

Lee, Martyn J. *Consumer Culture Reborn: The Cultural Politics of Consumption*. New York: Routledge, 1993.

LeFanu, Sheridan. "Carmilla". 1872. In *Vampires: Two Centuries of Great Vampire Stories*, edited by Alan Ryan, 71–137. Garden City, NY: Doubleday, 1987.

Lehr, Valerie. *Queer Family Values*. Philadelphia: Temple University Press, 1999.

Lewis , Peirce Fee. *New Orleans: The Making of an Urban Landscape*. Chicago: Centre for American Places, 2003.

Lupton, Deborah. *Food, the Body and the Self*. London: SAGE, 1996.

———. *Medicine as Culture: Illness, Disease and the Body*. Thousand Oaks, CA: SAGE, 2012.

Lury, Celia. *Brands: The Logos of Global Economy*. Abingdon: Routledge, 2004.

Lyotard, Jean-François. *The Inhuman*. Cambridge, Polity, 1993.

MacCannell, Dean. "Staged Authenticity: Arrangements of Social Space in Tourist Settings." *American Journal of Sociology* 79.3 (1973): 589–603.

MacKinnon, Kenneth. *Representing Men: Maleness and Masculinity in the Media.* London: Arnold, 2003.

Mariani, Scott. *Uprising.* New York: Avon, 2010.

———. *The Cross.* New York: Avon, 2011.

Marks, John. *Fangland.* London: Vintage, 2007.

Marx, Karl. *Capital, Vol. 1.* Harmondsworth: Penguin, 1990.

McCracken, Grant. *Culture and Consumption: New Approaches to the Symbolic Character of Consumer Goods and Activities.* Bloomington: Indiana University Press, 1991.

McLeod, Judyth. *Vampires: A Bite-sized History.* St. Leonards: Pier 9, 2011.

McKinney, Louise. *New Orleans: A Cultural History.* Oxford: Oxford University Press, 2006.

McNally, David. *Monsters of the Market: Vampires, Zombies, and Global Capitalism.* Leiden: Martinus Nijhoff, 2011.

Melnick, Jeffrey. *9/11 Culture.* Oxford: Wiley-Blackwell, 2009.

Melton, Gordon. *The Vampire Book: The Encyclopaedia of the Undead.* Canton, MI: Visible Print Press, 2011.

Merleau-Ponty, Maurice. *Sense and Non-sense.* Evanston, IL: Northwestern University Press, 1964.

Merz, Jon F. *The Fixer.* Seattle, WA: Digital Books, 2002.

Messner, Michael. "When Bodies Are Weapons: Masculinity and Violence in Sport." *International Review for the Sociology of Sport* 25 (1990): 203–220.

Meyer, Stephenie. *The Twilight Saga: The Official Illustrated Guide.* London: Atom, 2011.

———. *Twilight.* 2005. London: Atom, 2011.

Miles, Malcolm. *Cities and Cultures.* Abingdon: Routledge, 2007.

Mintz, Sydney. *Tasting Food, Tasting Freedom: Excursions into Eating, Culture, and the Past.* Boston, Mass.: Beacon Press, 1996.

Mitchell, Timothy. *Colonising Egypt.* Cambridge: Polity, 1988.

Montague, Charlotte. *Vampires: From Dracula to Twilight.* London: Sphere, 2010.

Morgan, David. *Family Connections: An Introduction to Family Studies.* Cambridge: Polity, 1996.

Mutch, Deborah, ed. *The Modern Vampire and Human Identity.* New York: Palgrave Macmillan, 2012.

Nayar, Pramod K. *An Introduction to Media and Cybercultures.* Oxford: Wiley-Blackwell, 2010.

Neill, Chloe. *Chicagoland Vampires* series. London: Gollancz, 2009–2013.

———. *Some Girls Bite.* 2009. London: Gollancz, 2010.

Nelson, Victoria. *Gothicka: Vampire Heroes, Human Gods, and the New Supernatural.* Cambridge, MA: Harvard University Press, 2012.

Nicholson, Mervyn. *Male Envy: The Logic of Malice in Literature and Culture.* Lanham, MD: Lexington, 1999.

O'Connell, Mary Ellen. "Introduction: Defining Armed Conflict in the Decade After 9/11." In *What Is War? An Investigation in the Wake of 9/11*, ed. Mary Ellen O'Connell, 3–12. Leiden: Martinus Nijhoff, 2012.

Olson, Danel. "Introduction." In *21ˢᵗ Century Gothic: Great Gothic Novels Since 2000*, ed. Daniel Olson, xxii–xxxii. Lanham, MD: Scarecrow Press, 2011.

Painter, Kristen. *Bad Blood.* London: Orbit, 2011.

———. *Blood Rights.* London: Orbit, 2011.

———. *Flesh and Blood.* London: Orbit, 2011.

———. *The House of Comarré* series. London: Orbit, 2011–2013.

Palsson, Gisli. *Anthropology and the New Genetics.* Cambridge: Cambridge University Press, 2007.

Parker, Craig Hamilton. *The Hidden Meaning of Dreams.* New York: Sterling, 1999.

Parmalee, Thomas. *Genetic Engineering.* Edina, MN: ABDO, 2008.

Parsons, Talcott. *Family Socialization and Interaction Process.* London: Routledge, 2002.

Pharr, Mary. "Vampiric Appetite in *I Am Legend, Salem's Lot* and *The Hunger.*" In *The Blood is the Life: Vampires in Literature,* edited by Leonard G. Heldreth and Mary Pharr, 93–104. Bowling Green, OH: Bowling Green State University Popular Press.

Piatti-Farnell, Lorna. *Food and Culture in Contemporary American Fiction.* New York: Routledge, 2011

Probyn, Elspeth. *Carnal Appetites: FoodSexIdentities.* London: Routledge, 2000.

Punter, David, and Glennis Byron. *The Gothic.* Oxford: Wiley-Blackwell, 2004.

Reagin, Nancy. *Twilight and History.* Hoboken, NJ; Wiley, 2010.

Reynolds, D.B. *Lucas.* Canon City, CO: ImaJinn Books, 2012.

Reynolds, D.B. *Duncan.* Canon City, CO: ImagJinn Books, 2011.

———. *Raphael .* Canon City, CO: ImaJinn Books, 2009.

———. *Sophia.* Canon City, CO: ImaJinn Books, 2011.

———. *Vampires in America* series. Canon City: ImaJinn Books, 2009–2013.

Rice, Anne. *Interview with the Vampire.* 1976. London: Warner Books, 1999.

Rodman, Margaret. "Beyond Built Form and Culture in the Anthropological Study of Community Spaces." In *The Cultural Meaning of Urban Space,* ed. Robert Rotenberg and Gary McDonogh, 123–138. Westport, CT: Bergin & Garvey, 1993.

Rosenberg, Charles E. "Introduction: Framing Disease." In *Framing Disease: Studies in Cultural History,* edited by Charles E. Rosenberg and Lynne Golden, viii–xxvi. New Brunswick, NJ: Rutgers University Press, 1992.

Royle, Nicholas. *The Uncanny.* Manchester: Manchester University Press, 2003.

Russell, James A., and José Miguel Fernández-Dols. "What Does a Facial Expression Mean?" In *The Psychology of Social Expression,* edited by James A. Russell and José Miguel Fernández-Dols), 3–29. Cambridge: Cambridge University Press, 1997.

Russell, Sharman. *Hunger: An Unnatural History.* New York: Basic Books, 2008.

Russo, Arlene. *Vampire Nation.* Woodbury, MN: Llewellyn, 2005.

Sandlin, Susannah. *Penton Vampire Legacy* series. Seattle, WA: Montlake, 2012–2013.

———. *Redemption.* Seattle, WA: Montlake, 2012.

Segre, Sandro. *Talcott Parsons: An Introduction.* Lanham, MD: University Press of America, 2012.

Senf, Carol A. "Blood, Eroticism, and the Vampire in Twentieth-Century Popular Literature." In *The Gothic World of Stephen King: Landscape of Nightmare,* edited by Gary Hoppenstand and Ray B. Browne, 20–30. Bowling Green, OH: Bowling Green University Popular Press, 1987.

———. *The Vampire In Nineteenth-Century English Literature.* Bowling Green, OH: Bowling Green State University Popular Press, 1988.

Shilling, Chris. *The Body in Culture, Technology and Society.* London: SAGE, 2005.

Shumway, David. *Modern Love: Romance, Intimacy, and the Marriage Crisis.* New York: New York University Press, 2003.

Shome, Raka, and Radha Hedge. "Postcolonial Approaches to Communication: Charting Terrain, Engaging the Intersections." *Communication Theory,* 12.3 (2002): 249–286.

Silverstone, Roger, and Leslie Haddon. "Design and the Domestication of ICTs: Technical Change and Everyday Life." In *Communication by Design: The Politics of Information and Communication Technology*, edited by Robin Mansell, 44–74. Oxford: Oxford University Press, 1996.

Simmel, Georg. "The Aesthetic Significance of the Face." In *The Body: Critical Concepts in Sociology*, edited by Andrew Blaikie, 5–9. London: Routledge, 2004.

———. "The Sociology of the Meal." In *Simmel on Culture*, edited by David Frisby and Mike Featherstone, 130–136. London: SAGE, 2000.

Simpson, David. *9/11: The Culture of Commemoration*. Chicago: University of Chicago Press, 2006.

Skal, David J. *Vampires: Encounters With The Undead*. London: Black Dog & Leventhal, 2006.

Slusser, George. "Introduction: Of Foods, Gods, and Men: The Theory and Practice of Science Fictional Eating." In *Food of the Gods; Eating and the Eaten in Fantasy and Science Fiction*, ed. Gary Westfahl, George Slusser and Eric Rabkin, 1–18. Athens, GA: University of Georgia Press, 1996).

Smith, L.J. *The Vampire Diaries* series. New York: Harper Collins, 1991–2001.

Spooner, Catherine, and Emma McEvoy. *The Routledge Companion to Contemporary Gothic*. London: Routledge, 2007.

Staubli, Thomas and Silvia Schroer. *Body Symbolism in the Bible*. Collegeville, MN: The Liturgical Press, 2001.

Stevens, Anthony. *Archetype: A Natural History of the Self*. London: Routledge, 1982.

Stoker, Bram. *Dracula*. Oxford: Oxford University Press, 1996.

Stratton, Jon. "Cyberspace and the Globalization of Culture." In *Internet Culture*, edited by David Porter, 253–276. London: Routledge, 1997.

Strieber, Whitley. *The Hunger*. New York: Pocket Books, 1981.

Sturken, Marita, and Douglas Thomas, "Introduction: Technological Visions and the Rhetoric of New." In *Technological Visions; the Hopes and Fears that Shape New Technologies*, edited by Marita Sturken, Douglas Thomas and Sandra J. Ball-Rokeach, 1–18. Philadelphia: Temple University Press, 2004.

Summers, Montague. *Vampires and Vampirism*. New York: Dover, 2005.

Thurschwell, Pamela. *Sigmund Freud*. London: Routledge, 2000.

Tungate, Mark. *Luxury Goods: The Past, Present, and Future of Luxury Brands*. London, Kogan Page, 2009.

Turner, Bryan S. *Regulating Bodies: Essays in Medical Sociology*. London: Routledge, 1992.

Twitchehll, James B. *The Living Dead: A Study of the Vampire in Romantic Literature*. Durham, NC: Duke University Press, 1981.

Von der Heydt, Vera. "On the Father in Psychotherapy." In *Fathers and Mothers: Five Papers on the Archetypal Background of Archetypal Psychology*, edited by Augusto Vitale, Rich Neumann, Murray Stein, James Hillman, and Vera Von der Heydt, 128–142. Zurich: Spring Publications, 1973.

Waltje, Jörg. *Blood Obsession: Vampires, Serial murder, and the Popular Imagination*. New York: Peter Lang, 2005.

Warner, Marina. *Fantastic Metamorphoses, Other Worlds*. Oxford: Oxford University Press, 2002.

Ward, J.R. *Lover Avenged*. London: Piatkus, 2009.

———. *Lover Awakened*. London: Piatkus, 2006.

———. *Dark Lover*. London: Piatkus, 2005.

———. *Lover Enshrined*. London: Piatkus, 2008.

———. *Lover Eternal*. London: Piatkus, 2006.

———. *Lover Mine*. London: Piatkus, 2010.

———. *Lover Reborn*. London: Piatkus, 2012.

———. *Lover Revealed*. London: Piatkus, 2007.

———. *Lover Unleashed*. London: Piatkus, 2011.

———. *Lover Unbound*. London: Piatkus, 2007.

———. *The Black Dagger Brotherhood* series. London: Piatkus, 2005–2013.

Watson, Richard. *Future Minds: How the Digital Age Is Changing Our Minds, Why This Matters and What We Can Do About It*. London: Nicholas Brealey, 2010.

Webster, Frank. *Theories of the Information Society*. Abingdon: Routledge, 2006.

Weiss, Gail. *Refiguring the Ordinary*. Bloomington: Indiana University Press, 2008.

Wellington, David. *Laura Caxton Vampire* series. St. Leonards: Allen and Unwin, 2007–2012.

———. *Thirteen Bullets*. St. Leonards: Allen and Unwin, 2007.

———. *99 Coffins*. St. Leonards: Allen and Unwin, 2007.

Whitehead, Stephen, and Frank Barrett, "The Sociology of Masculinity." In *The Masculinities Reader*, edited by Stephen Whitehead and Frank Barrett, 1–26. Cambridge: Polity, 2001.

Wiederman, Michael . "Sociosexuality." in *Sex and Society, Vol. 3*, 666.Tarrytown, NY: Marshall Cavendish, 2010.

Williamson, Milly. *The Lure of the Vampire: Gender, Fiction and Fandom from Bram Stoker to Buffy*. London: Wallflower Press.

Wise, Inge. "Introduction." In *Adolescence*, edited by Inge Weiss, 1–6. London: Karnac, 2005.

Wolmark, Jenny. *Aliens and Others: Science Fiction, Feminism, Postmodernism*. Iowa City, IA: University of Iowa Press, 1994.

Yep, Gust A. "The Violence of Heteronormativity in Communication Studies." *Journal of Homosexuality* 45.3 (2003): 11–39.

Zimmerman, Amber, and Patricia Geist-Martin. "The Hybrid Identities of Genderqueer: Claiming neither/nor, both/and." In *Intercultural Communication: A Reader*, edited by Larry A. Samovar, Richard Porter and Edwin McDaniel, 87–92. Boston, MA: Wadsworth, 2006.

Zukin, Sharon. "Space and Symbols in an Age of Decline." In *Re-Presenting the City: Ethnicity, Capital and Culture in the 21ˢᵗ Century Metropolis*, ed. Anthony King, 43–59. New York: New York University Press, 1996.

Index

A

Adrian, Lara. *See* Midnight Breed
aliens, 34–37
All Souls (series), 67, 103, 108, 134, 137–138, 172, 182
Anderson, Benedict, 158
America, 5, 7, 10, 31–34, 36, 58, 61, 99, 133, 152, 153–156, 159, 165–166, 174–176, 189
Appadurai, Arjun, 142, 143
Ashman, Kevin: *Vampire*, 47–48
Auerbach, Nina, 3, 6, 8, 24, 57, 196

B

Barthes, Roland, 208
Bataille, Georges, 72, 74–75
Baudrillard, Jean, 1, 115, 181, 183, 189, 192
beauty, 4, 18–19, 54, 57–58, 59, 76–78, 85, 92, 96, 100, 173, 188, 191
bed, 184–187
Black Dagger Brotherhood (series), 11, 15, 16–17, 21, 29–30, 44,52, 65, 81, 86–91, 92–93, 86–97, 101–102, 113–114, 121–122, 126, 128, 129–130, 133–134, 137, 141, 142–146, 150–156, 158, 161, 163, 166, 169, 170, 173, 181–182, 182, 187–192, 194, 197
blood, 23–29, 34, 36, 38, 43, 48–50, 58–59, 61–62, 66–69, 70–72, 73, 76, 79, 89, 92, 97, 103, 108, 111, 115, 128–141, 142, 145, 146, 148, 150–152, 154, 157, 160–161, 167, 190–191
body, 4, 14–17, 20–21, 23, 25–27, 29, 31–33, 37–38, 40–44, 46–50, 52, 53, 54–94, 96, 98, 101, 102, 104–105, 110, 113, 115, 122–123, 129, 138, 143–145, 147–148, 152, 156, 161–162, 188, 193
Botting, Fred, 2, 3, 7, 9, 12
brands/branding, 5, 7, 84, 187–192
Buffy, the Vampire Slayer (tv series), 78, 85, 134, 162,
Butcher, Jim. *See* The Dresden Files

C

capitalism, 57–58, 63, 111–113, 124, 125, 134, 175, 179, 183, 187, 189
'Carmilla'. *See* Joseph Sheridan Le Fanu
Carpathians (series), 15, 132, 160, 185
Chicagoland Vampires (series), 19, 94, 166, 170, 185
Chomsky, Noam, 154, 156
city, 5, 165–179, 180
coffins, 184
Cole, Kresley. *See* Immortals After Dark
consumerism, 1, 2, 5, 7, 24, 57–58, 111–113, 124, 125, 181, 189–192
Cronin, Justin: *The Passage*, 21, 37, 39, 40
culture, 1–14, 15, 20, 22, 23, 27–28, 30–33, 35–37, 40–43, 46–49, 51–52, 54, 56–58, 62–64, 70, 72–75, 84, 88–90, 96, 100–102, 104–105, 111, 114–115, 122–124, 126, 127, 129, 135–138, 140, 143–145, 152, 153–154, 157–160, 166–168, 170–171, 172, 175–179, 180–181, 184, 189–192, 194–198

corpse, 9, 27, 58–59, 81, 85, 97, 98, 161
custom, 5, 125–127, 142, 145, 167,
    174–175, 178, 181, 193

D

death, 3, 5, 6, 18–19, 25, 27, 40, 43,
    46–48, 51, 54, 58–61, 62, 67,
    89, 97, 108, 123, 127, 129,
    143, 148–152, 154, 156–160,
    167–168, 174, 185–186, 195
Deleuze, Gilles, 77; and Félix Guattari,
    13, 146–147
desire, 1, 7, 8, 24, 25, 36, 51, 52, 63,
    66, 68, 69–70, 74, 92–93, 102,
    109, 111–112, 121, 130–132,
    146, 148, 154, 162, 167, 168,
    180–181, 183, 189, 191
digitality, 115–124
disease 40–44
DNA, 20, 21, 35, 37, 38–40, 47–48,
    67, 82
Dracula. See Bram Stoker
dual nature (of vampires), 160–164

E

eyes, 16, 19, 21–23, 27, 38, 54, 59, 71, 76,
    80, 85, 100–102, 106, 121, 161

F

face, 59, 70, 75–80
family, 5, 82, 127, 134–141, 142–145,
    150, 155, 157, 158, 171, 185,
    186, 194
fangs, 16, 19, 20, 23, 39, 54, 68,
    69–74, 78, 96, 99, 116, 128,
    146, 162, 179, 190, 197
Farnsworth, Christopher. *See* Nathan-
    iel Cade
fear, 8, 9, 26, 28, 30, 32, 36, 38, 50,
    51–52, 80, 95–100, 102, 106, 108,
    116–118, 122, 141, 152, 154, 160,
    167–168, 169, 174, 185, 195
Feehan, Christine. *See* Carpathians
femininity, 87–89, 104–105
Foucault, Michel, 143–144, 148, 184
Freud, Sigmund, 70, 74, 87, 100, 126,
    127, 130, 180, 186
food, 16, 20, 24, 28, 49, 127, 141–147,
    176, 193, 197

G

Gelder, Ken, 6, 8, 98
genetic engineering, 15, 37, 39–41, 48,
    49–51

genetics, 2, 4, 7, 15–53, 55–56, 67,
    70–71, 81–84, 93
genre 2, 4, 7, 10–13, 55, 96, 97,
    132–133, 187, 189, 191–192,
    193, 197
Girard, René, 151
graves, 60, 184–186
Grosz, Elizabeth, 55–56, 69, 83–84,
    92–94
Guattari, Félix: and Gilles Deleuze, 13,
    146–147

H

Harkness, Deborah. *See* All Souls
Harris, Charlaine. *See* Sookie Stack-
    house: The Southern Vampire
    Mysteries
Harrison, Kim. *See* Hollows
health 42–44, 46–47, 49–50, 58, 66,
    142, 173
heart (organ), 20, 32, 50, 60–66, 94,
    146, 186
Heidegger, Martin, 59–61
houses, 179–184
House of Comarré (series), 18, 65,
    69, 79, 93–94, 102, 103, 128,
    135, 150, 171–172
Hollows (series), 50, 103, 113, 116,
    127, 141, 166, 171, 185, 200
human/humanity, 4, 5, 11, 12–14,
    15–29, 30–32, 34–53, 54–72,
    73–80, 92–94, 96–99, 102, 108–
    109, 114, 115–124, 126–127,
    133–134, 147–148, 154–160,
    165, 170, 174, 178, 190–192
hunger, 18, 22, 24–26, 48, 72, 111,
    146, 148, 189, 190
hybrids, 29–34

I

inhuman, the, 71–72
internet, 113, 117, 119–120, 166, 197
Immortals After Dark (series), 65–66,
    132, 160, 161

J

Jameson, Fredric, 122, 190

K

knife (ceremonial), 128–131

L

Laura Caxton Vampire (series), 11, 13,
    26, 28, 70–71, 97, 112

laws, 194–196
Lawson Vampire (series), 16, 113
Le Fanu, Joseph Sheridan: 'Carmilla',
 2, 6, 24, 93, 98
luxury, 184, 188–189, 190–191
Lyotard, Jean-François, 71–72

M
magic, 19, 30, 48, 58, 110, 135, 153,
 160, 172, 173, 176, 177, 178,
 179
Mariani, Scott. *See* Vampire Federation
Marks, John: *Fangland*, 69, 81
marriage, 126, 127–134. *See also*
 weddings
Marx, Karl, 111–112, 187
masculinity, 86–91, 104–105, 138,
 188
medicine 44–49
Merz, John F. *See* Lawson Vampire
Meyer, Stephenie. *See* Twilight
Midnight Breed (series), 13, 16, 34–36,
 44, 52, 65, 67–68, 81–84, 85,
 87–88, 92, 97, 103, 109, 113,
 122, 128, 129, 130, 132–133,
 135, 150, 153, 156, 158, 160,
 161, 163–164, 166, 170–171,
 180, 184, 187, 192
mind, 4, 115–124, 162, 193
minions, 108–113
monsters, 1, 2, 9, 49–53, 59, 71, 96,
 112, 113
mourning, 60, 149–152, 157, 159
muscles, 17, 77, 85, 86, 88

N
Nathaniel Cade (series), 27, 43, 50, 78,
 81, 97–100, 116, 132, 153, 171,
 192
Neill, Chloe. *See* Chicagoland
 Vampires
neo-Gothic, 8–10
New Orleans, 165, 172–179
New Testament, 18
Nietzsche, Friedrich, 74
9/11 (terroristic attacks), 2, 5, 37,
 153–155, 159, 170

O
olfactory responses. *See* smell
orifices, 66–69

P
Painter, Kristen. *See* House of Comarré

paranormal romance (genre), 2, 10,
 11–13, 90, 96, 97, 132, 187,
 189, 191, 197
Penton Vampire Legacy (series), 21,
 161, 182, 187
pharmaceutics, 45–46
physicality. *See* body
pleasure, 1, 24–25, 67–68, 73–75, 119,
 146–148, 174, 190–191
popular culture, 1, 6–7, 10, 12, 13, 23,
 38, 57–58, 69–70, 76, 79, 85,
 93, 101, 110, 134, 160, 162,169,
 177, 184, 186
psychic powers, 32, 55, 95, 112,
 115–118, 121–123

R
rebels, 160–164
resurrection: Christian, 18; vampiric,
 67
Reynolds, D.B. *See* Vampires in
 America
Rice, Anne, 54, 57, 76, 85, 134, 149,
 160, 162, 165, 172, 184
ritual, 5, 18, 27, 30, 125–165

S
semen, 67–68
sex/sexual, 1, 4, 8, 10, 12, 13, 16–17,
 21, 24, 38–39, 55–56, 58,
 65–68, 70, 73, 75, 85, 87–88,
 90, 96, 105, 115, 130–131,
 133, 146–148, 180, 185–187,
 191, 197
sight (senses), 100–102, 106, 107
Simmel, Georg, 147
skin, 27, 32, 34, 58, 59, 70, 81–85, 93,
 102, 112, 130–131, 173
smell (senses), 70, 75, 100, 102–108
soil (earth), 185
*Sookie Stackhouse: The Southern
 Vampire Mysteries* (series),
 12, 15, 18, 19, 20, 24–25, 49,
 58–59,65, 67, 69, 74, 81, 92, 94,
 103, 109, 113, 119–121, 125,
 127–129, 130, 132–133, 134,
 139, 146, 153, 163, 169170,
 172–173, 176–179, 180, 185,
 188, 192, 194
Stoker, Bram: *Dracula*, 2, 6, 8, 23,
 61–62, 69, 75, 76, 96, 108, 127,
 165, 184
Strieber, Whitley: *The Hunger*, 24,
 135, 165, 169, 189

sunlight, 16, 17, 20, 38, 61, 93, 122, 142, 156, 157, 185
synaesthesia, 106–108
synthesis (of the vampire body), 31, 92–94

T
technology, 2, 5, 7, 14, 71, 113–124, 166, 169, 171
telepathy, 4, 115, 122
terror, 8, 9, 23, 32, 97, 116, 167–168, 196
terrorism, 154–159. *See also* 9/11
The Dresden Files (series), 12, 20, 58, 59, 80, 97, 104, 132, 141, 153, 161, 163, 171, 192
The Horror of Dracula (film), 23
The Lost Boys (film), 162
The Vampire Chronicles. See Anne Rice
tourism, 175–179
transgression, 72–75
transition, the, 16–17, 29
turning, 17–20, 21, 23, 25–26, 34, 38, 41, 45, 49, 51, 65, 71, 80, 92, 94, 125, 138, 139, 140, 154, 195
Twilight (series), 3, 6, 7, 18, 22–24, 27, 30–34, 36, 58, 67, 81, 93, 96, 127, 134–135, 171, 173, 181, 185, 187–188

U
uncanny, 5, 32, 51, 53, 76–77, 80, 95, 98–100, 115–118, 168, 173, 192, 196, 198
United States. *See* America
urban. *See* city
urban fantasy (genre), 2, 10, 11–12

V
Vampire: and the body, 54–94; and branding, 187–192; and the city, 165–172; and commemoration rituals, 148–164; and disease, 40–44; and the family, 134–141; and fear, 95–100; and food, 141–146; and genetics, 15–43; and genre, 10–14; as inauthentic fantasy, 59–61; and masculinity, 85–91; and medicine, 44–49; and minions, 108–113; morphology of, 55–57, 61–66, 69–72, 75–80; as 'neo-Gothic', 8–10; as 'new monsters', 49–53; and New Orleans, 172–179; and psychic control, 115–123; and sex, 146–148; and the senses, 100–108; and synthesis, 92–94; and technology, 113–124; as transgression, 72–75; as virus, 37–40; and wedding rituals, 127–134; as youthful un/dead, 57–59
Vampire Federation (series), 18, 20, 34, 37, 45, 109, 113, 122, 125, 146, 166, 170, 171
Vampires in America (series), 15, 19, 21, 58, 67, 73, 81, 116, 125, 128, 146, 153, 166, 180, 181, 187–188, 194
vampire studies (as academic subject) 5–8
vampire territories, 13–14
Venice, 173, 174
violence, 9, 36, 39, 97, 150–153, 155–156, 161
virus, 37–40

W
war, 153–156
web sites, 197–198
weddings, 127–134. *See also* marriage
Wellington, David. *See* Laura Caxton Vampire
werewolf, 30, 69, 196

Z
zombie, 58, 110–112